The Research Process

What's your next step? Use this guide to help you along the way.

09-ABH-344

The Bedford
RESEARCHER

Mike Palmquist
Colorado State University

 macmillan
learning

Boston | New York

For Bedford/St. Martin's

Vice President, Editorial, Macmillan Learning Humanities: Edwin Hill
Senior Program Director for English: Leasa Burton
Program Manager: Molly Parke
Marketing Manager: Vivian Garcia
Director of Content Development: Jane Knetzger
Developmental Editor: Sherry Mooney
Senior Content Project Manager: Ryan Sullivan
Senior Content Workflow Manager: Jennifer Wetzel
Production Assistant: Brianna Lester
Media Project Manager: Melissa Skepko-Masi
Editorial Services: Lumina Datamatics, Inc.
Composition: Lumina Datamatics, Inc.
Photo Editor: Angela Boehler
Photo Researcher: Sheri Blaney
Permissions Manager: Kalina Ingham
Senior Art Director: Anna Palchik
Text Design: Claire Seng-Niemoeller
Cover Design and Illustration: William Boardman
Printing and Binding: RR Donnelley

Printed in China.
2   1   0   9   8   7
f   e   d   c   b   a

For information, write: Bedford/St. Martin's, 75 Arlington Street, Boston, MA 02116

ISBN 978-1-319-05848-7

Acknowledgments

Art acknowledgments and copyrights appear on the same page as the art selections they cover.

Preface for Instructors

Alternative facts. Fake news. Political bubbles.

The presidential election of 2016 called attention in an unprecedented way to the credibility and reliability of information sources. But the concerns brought into focus by the election are far from new. In fact, they've been with us for more than two decades. The rapid growth of social networks and the proliferation of news and media providers that adopt particular — and often radically different — stances on important issues have made it all too easy to surround ourselves with people and ideas that reaffirm rather than challenge our understanding of important social, cultural, and political issues.

For this reason alone, it has never been more important to learn how to locate relevant, credible sources, to evaluate competing ideas and arguments, and to share our thoughts with others in a compelling, well-supported manner. Knowing how to work with sources has become critical not only to us as individuals but to our society as a whole.

Research writing, as a result, has become central not only to our individual academic and professional goals, but also to the long-term success of our society. And while that may sound like an exaggeration to many of us (and certainly to many of our students), it is clear that understanding how to work with information, share ideas effectively, and argue for a particular purpose will only grow more and more important over the coming decades.

This edition of *The Bedford Researcher*, like those that have come before it, was written with the goal of helping writers strengthen their ability to understand, assess, and contribute to ongoing conversations about important issues. As past editions have done, it addresses the vast amount of information available to writers, the expanding variety of media and genres used by writers to share their work, the critical importance of evaluating sources that — at first glance — appear to be "just like" the sources in a library, and the demands of managing information effectively and efficiently.

This edition also responds to continuing changes in how writers participate in a complex and rapidly evolving information ecology. It recognizes the variety of ways through which writers connect with readers, the role of social media, and the blurred lines between public and private discourse.

Yet it also recognizes that many important aspects of source-based writing remain unchanged. As was the case in the mid-twentieth century — and, for that matter, in the centuries that preceded it — writers must still consider their purpose and the needs and interests of their readers; they must still make choices about genres and design; they are still shaped by the social, cultural, and historical contexts in which they work; and they must still grapple with limitations and take advantage of opportunities they encounter as they work on their research writing projects.

Meeting these new challenges while maintaining a focus on the fundamental relationships among writers, readers, sources, genres, and contexts can tax even the most experienced writers. Our students, then, face a doubly difficult task: learning the core principles of research writing and mastering the technological context that has vastly complicated the rhetorical situations in which they find themselves. As I've reflected on the challenges facing our students, I've become convinced that students can be most successful if we help them understand research writing both conceptually and practically, combining a rhetorical framework with the accessible guidance students need to help them navigate the world of academic research writing.

In this edition, I've continued my efforts to improve *The Bedford Researcher*, both as a classroom text and a resource for student researchers. I've focused once again on the notion that academic research is an act of "joining a conversation." I've deepened my treatment of researching in various disciplinary contexts, and I've added new coverage of writers' roles. I've also created a new chapter that focuses on genres—including bibliographies, summaries, responses, syntheses and reviews, and research proposals—that can play important roles both as ends in themselves and as intermediate steps toward a wide range of research writing genres.

Features

The Bedford Researcher is based on the premise that the decisions good research writers make are shaped primarily by rhetorical concerns—the writer's purposes and interests; the readers' needs, interests, values, and beliefs; the setting in which a document is written and read; and the requirements and limitations associated with an assignment. To illustrate this premise, the book presents research writing as a process of choosing, learning about, and contributing to a conversation among readers and writers.

Complete Coverage of the Research Writing Process   As in the previous editions, the text is divided into five parts. The first four parts correspond to the stages of an idealized research writing process, although the book stresses the recursive nature of research writing. The fifth part focuses on documentation systems. Part 1, Joining the Conversation, introduces the concept of research writing as a social act. It helps students understand that research writing involves exploring conversations among writers and readers, narrowing their focus to a single conversation, and developing a research question to guide their inquiry within that conversation. Part 2, Working with Sources, establishes the importance of reading critically, evaluating sources, taking notes, engaging with information and ideas, managing information, and avoiding plagiarism. Part 3, Collecting Information, helps students search for information using digital resources, print resources, and field research methods. Part 4, Creating Your Document, guides students as they develop their thesis, organize their information and ideas, frame their argument, develop an outline, draft their document, integrate source material, design their document, revise and edit their drafts, and present their work. Finally, Part 5, Documenting Sources, provides comprehensive and up-to-date chapters on MLA, APA, *Chicago*, and CSE styles.

Engaging and Useful Apparatus   The book is designed so that students can find information easily and work competently through each stage of their projects. Each chapter is structured around a set of Key Questions that enables students to find information quickly and ends with Quick Reference boxes to stress the chapter's main points. Throughout the book, My Research Project activities, in-depth tutorials, and numerous illustrations and tables teach students how to keep their projects on track.

The design employs clear and accessible illustrations, annotations, checklists, activities, and documentation guidelines — the parts of the text students will return to as they write.

A Conversational, Student-Friendly Tone   I've written *The Bedford Researcher* in an accessible, easy-to-follow style that treats students with respect. I want students to gain confidence in their ability to write well, conduct research effectively, and think critically. Clear, relevant examples address students' questions about research writing by concretely illustrating writing, research, and critical reading strategies.

Detailed Case Studies of Real Student Researchers   The work of seven real students, who undertook a variety of research writing projects in a variety of disciplinary contexts (including traditional essays in the humanities, sciences, and social sciences; a multimodal essay on marine biology; and a website about hydraulic fracturing), is featured in the text. Their work provides accessible models for your students as they conduct their own research and draft their own documents.

Help with Analyzing and Developing Arguments   Extensive coverage of argument, both as a writing strategy and as a framework for reading sources critically and actively, is included in Part 4, Creating Your Document. Here students will learn how to establish a position on an issue, how to develop a line of argument, and how to support an argument with reasons and evidence. They will also learn to identify logical fallacies and avoid them in their own writing.

Extensive and Up-to-Date Coverage of Digital Sources and Tools   The text offers relevant, hands-on advice for searching for and evaluating audio, video, and other digital sources; searching for e-books; saving and organizing sources with personal and social bookmarking sites and Web capture tools; integrating images, audio, and video into multimodal documents and multimedia presentations; and revising and editing with digital tools.

New to This Edition

This edition of *The Bedford Researcher* features the following updates.

A Stronger Focus on Academic Writing   A new chapter 7—Engaging with Information, Ideas, and Arguments—opens with an extended discussion of academic writing. The chapter provides a clear discussion of academic genres and academic argument. It extends this discussion to include detailed treatments of the key genres that play an intermediate role in many research writing projects: working and annotated bibliographies, various types of summaries and responses, documents that serve a synthesizing function across groups of sources (including both the review of literature and informal forms of writing), and research proposals.

Unified Coverage of Search Processes   Chapter 10, Searching for Information, provides a comprehensive approach to searching with digital and print sources, diminishing the distinction among databases, Web search tools, and print-based resources. Each set of resources is considered in terms of its distinctive contributions to a writer's search for relevant and credible sources.

Additional Discussion of Collaboration in Field Research   A new section in Chapter 11 provides guidance on collaboration on research gathered through interviews, observation, and correspondence.

Updated Coverage of Documentation Systems   Chapter 20, Using MLA Style, has been updated to reflect the significant changes introduced to the MLA documentation system. These changes have resulted in major changes not only in the MLA chapter but also in the chapters on APA, *Chicago*, and CSE styles. Documentation models include more of a focus on the genre itself and less on the medium in which it is distributed. Each genre section (for example, books, articles, and reference works) includes citation models for sources available in print, digital, and other forms, making it easier for students to locate relevant models and simplifying the presentation of the citation models.

With Bedford/St. Martin's, You Get More

At Bedford/St. Martin's, providing support to teachers and their students who use our books and digital tools is our top priority. The Bedford/St. Martin's English Community is now our home for professional resources, including Bedford *Bits*, our popular blog with new ideas for the composition classroom. Join us to connect with our authors and your colleagues at **community.macmillan.com**, where you can download titles from our professional resource series, review projects in the pipeline, sign up for webinars, or start a discussion. In addition to this dynamic online community and book-specific instructor resources, we offer digital tools, custom solutions, and value packages to support both you and your students. We are committed to delivering the quality and value that you've come to expect from Bedford/St. Martin's, supported as always by the power of

Macmillan Learning. To learn more about or to order any of the following products, contact your Bedford/St. Martin's sales representative or visit the website at **macmillanlearning.com**.

LaunchPad Solo for Research and Reference: Where Students Learn

LaunchPad Solo for Research and Reference provides engaging content and new ways to get the most out of your book. Get assessment tools in a fully customizable course space; then assign and mix our resources with yours.

- **Practice for researchers**—including practice using sources, annotating a bibliography, incorporating sources in context, and documenting—is easy to adapt and assign by adding your own materials and mixing them with our high-quality multimedia content and ready-made assessment options, such as **LearningCurve** adaptive quizzing.
- LaunchPad Solo also provides access to **a Gradebook** that offers a clear window on the performance of your whole class, individual students, and even results of individual assignments.
- Use LaunchPad Solo on its own or **integrate it** with your school's learning management system so that your class is always on the same page.

LaunchPad Solo for Research and Reference can be purchased on its own or packaged with the print book at a significant discount. An activation code is required. To order *LaunchPad Solo for Research and Reference* with the print book, use ISBN 978-1-319-14481-4. For more information, go to **launchpadworks.com**.

Choose from Alternative Formats of *The Bedford Researcher*, Sixth Edition

Bedford/St. Martin's offers a range of affordable formats, allowing students to choose the one that works best for them.

- **Spiral-Bound** To order the spiral-bound edition, use ISBN 978-1-319-05848-7.
- **Popular e-Book Formats** For details on our e-book partners, visit **macmillanlearning.com/ebooks**.

Select Value Packages

Add value to your text by packaging one of the following resources with *The Bedford Researcher*, Sixth Edition. To learn more about package options for any of the following products, contact your Bedford/St. Martin's sales representative or visit **macmillanlearning.com**.

Writer's Help 2.0 is a powerful online writing resource that helps students find answers, whether they are searching for writing advice on their own or as part of an assignment.

- **Smart search** Built on research with more than 1,600 student writers, the smart search in *Writer's Help 2.0* provides reliable results even when students use novice terms, such as *flow* and *unstuck*.

- **Trusted content from our best-selling handbooks** Choose *Writer's Help 2.0, Hacker Version*, or *Writer's Help 2.0, Lunsford Version*, and ensure that students have clear advice and examples for all of their writing questions.

- **Diagnostics that help establish a baseline for instruction** Assign diagnostics to identify areas of strength and areas for improvement on topics related to grammar and reading and to help students plan a course of study. Use visual reports to track performance by topic, class, and student as well as comparison reports that track improvement over time.

- **Adaptive exercises that engage students** *Writer's Help 2.0* includes LearningCurve, game-like online quizzing that adapts to what students already know and helps them focus on what they need to learn.

Student access is packaged with *The Bedford Researcher* at a significant discount. Order ISBN 978-1-319-13521-8 for *Writer's Help 2.0, Hacker Version*, or ISBN 978-1-319-13522-5 for *Writer's Help 2.0, Lunsford Version*, to ensure your students have easy access to online writing support. Students who rent or buy a used book can purchase access and instructors may request free access at **macmillanlearning .com/writershelp2**.

Macmillan Learning Curriculum Solutions

Curriculum Solutions brings together the quality of Bedford/St. Martin's content with Hayden-McNeil's expertise in publishing original custom print and digital products. Developed especially for writing courses, our ForeWords for English program contains a library of the most popular, requested content in easy-to-use modules to help you build the best possible text. Whether you are considering creating a custom version of *The Bedford Researcher* or incorporating our content with your own, we can adapt and combine the resources that work best for your course or program. Some enrollment minimums apply. Contact your sales representative for more information.

Instructor Resources

You have a lot to do in your course. Bedford/St. Martin's wants to make it easy for you to find the support you need—and to get it quickly.

Teaching with The Bedford Researcher is available as a PDF that can be downloaded from **macmillanlearning.com**. Visit the Instructor Resources tab for *The Bedford Researcher*, Sixth Edition. In addition to chapter overviews and teaching tips, the instructor's manual includes correlations to the Council of Writing Program Administrators' Outcomes Statement and classroom activities.

Acknowledgments

With each edition of *The Bedford Researcher*, I have offered my thanks to my family—my wife, Jessica; my daughter, Ellen; and my son, Reid. I do so again, knowing how much easier it has been to write with their support, their patience, and their willingness to share their reactions to my ideas. I remain deeply grateful for the guidance and support I received from David Kaufer, Chris Neuwirth, and Richard Young, who helped me, in graduate school and in the many years since, to think critically and carefully about the relationships among rhetoric, pedagogy, and technology. I offer thanks as well to my colleagues Sue Doe, Will Hochman, Lynda Haas, and Nick Carbone for their willingness to share ideas and offer support as I worked on this book. I am also grateful to Hannah Cabellero, for her thoughtful, thorough revision of the instructor's manual.

I have benefited immensely from the thoughtful advice and suggestions for improvement from the many colleagues who took the time to review this book: Mary Anderson, West Shore High School; Andrea Bewick, Napa Valley College; Mary Paniccia Carden, Edinboro University of Pennsylvania; James Crane, the College of St. Scholastica; Kathryn Crowther, Georgia State University–Perimeter College; Aaron DiFranco, Napa Valley College; Deborah Eckberg, Metropolitan State University; Jeanie Griffin, West Shore High School; Elizabeth Kent, Auburn University at Montgomery; Todd McCann, Bay de Noc Community College; Cathy McCarron, Middlesex Community College; Ilona Missakian, Fullerton College; Kathleen Mollick, Tarleton State University; Rebecca Owens, Boise Bible College; Ruthe Thompson, Southwest Minnesota State University; and two anonymous reviewers. Their reactions, observations, and good ideas led to many of the improvements in this edition.

I have once again been fortunate to work with a dedicated and professional group of editors at Bedford/St. Martin's. My development editor, Sherry Mooney, has offered steady and useful feedback during the planning and drafting of this edition and served as a brilliant organizer as we worked through copyedits and page proof. I offer my thanks to Deb Baker and Ryan Sullivan, who directed the production of the book, and Mary Lou Wilshaw-Watts, who copyedited the manuscript. I am grateful, once again, for the extraordinary design work of Claire Seng-Niemoeller. I am indebted as well to Karen Henry for her good advice and able leadership of the editorial team. And I am grateful for the hard work and good ideas of associate editor Jennifer Prince. I am grateful as well to Edwin Hill, Leasa Burton, and Molly Parke for their support of *The Bedford Researcher* and for their thoughtful suggestions about the directions this new edition might take.

Finally, I offer my thanks to the seven student writers who shared their work, their time, and their insights into their research writing processes with the readers of this book: Alexis Alvarez, Nicholas Brothers, Elizabeth Leontiev, Lauren Mack, Cori Schmidtbauer, Brandon Tate, and Josh Woelfle. As I worked on this edition, their work served as a constant reminder that research writing is a process of continuous discovery and reflection.

Mike Palmquist
Colorado State University

Introduction for Writers

You live in the information age. You surf the Web, text your friends, download music and videos, use e-mail, send instant messages, carry a mobile phone, watch television, read magazines and newspapers, listen to podcasts, view advertisements, attend public events, and meet and talk with others. Understanding how to work with information is among the most important writing skills you can have. In fact, most of the writing that you'll do in your lifetime—in college courses or for a career or community project—requires this skill. Take as examples the following types of documents—all of which require a writer to use information from sources:

- college research essays
- informative websites
- feature articles in a newspaper or magazine
- product brochures or promotional literature
- market research analysis to help start a new business or launch a new product
- proposals to a school board or community group
- PowerPoint presentations for business meetings
- letters of complaint about a product or service
- restaurant reviews or travel guides

Because such a wide range of documents relies heavily on a writer's ability to work with information, *The Bedford Researcher* is not so much about research papers as about research writing. What I hope you'll take from this text is a way of thinking about how to conduct research and write a document based on the sources of information you find.

The primary goals of *The Bedford Researcher* are to help you learn how to:

- choose and learn about a topic
- read critically, evaluate, and take notes
- develop a research question, thesis statement, and line of argument
- collect and manage information
- develop, write, revise, and design an effective document
- document sources of information

Meeting these goals requires thinking about research writing in a new way. Research writing is more than simply searching for and reporting information; it is a process of inquiry—of asking and responding to key questions. Instead of thinking of research writing as an isolated activity, think of it as a social act — a conversation in which writers and readers exchange information and ideas about a topic.

The research writing process you'll follow in this book consists of five main activities, which correspond to the five parts of this book:

Part 1: Joining the Conversation ❯ Chapters 1, 2, and 3 focus on getting started, exploring and narrowing your topic, and developing your research question and proposal.

Part 2: Working with Sources ❯ Chapters 4 through 9 address reading critically, evaluating sources, taking notes, engaging with information and ideas, managing information, and avoiding plagiarism.

Part 3: Collecting Information ❯ Chapters 10 and 11 discuss searching for information with digital resources, print resources, and field research methods.

Part 4: Creating Your Document ❯ Chapters 12 through 18 focus on developing your thesis statement and line of argument; organizing and drafting your document; integrating sources; writing with style; and revising, editing, and designing your document.

Part 5: Documenting Sources ❯ Chapters 19 through 23 discuss the reasons for documenting sources and provide detailed guidance on four of the most commonly used documentation systems — MLA, APA, *Chicago*, and CSE.

As you read about these activities and carry them out in your own research project, keep in mind that they reflect a typical writing process — not a step-by-step recipe. Also keep in mind that the writing process seldom follows a straight line from choosing a topic to producing a polished document; most writers move back and forth among writing processes, rethinking their steps and revising their ideas as they work on their writing projects. Whatever your process turns out to be, remember that the order you follow is far less important than adapting these processes to the needs of your particular project.

Support Throughout Your Research Writing Process

The Bedford Researcher offers a wealth of support—in the book and on *LaunchPad Solo for Research and Reference*—to help you complete a research project.

In the Text

The textbook you are holding provides step-by-step guidance for writing research documents. It includes clear descriptions of research writing strategies, examples, activities, documentation guidelines, and model citations.

Color-coded tabs help you find information quickly.

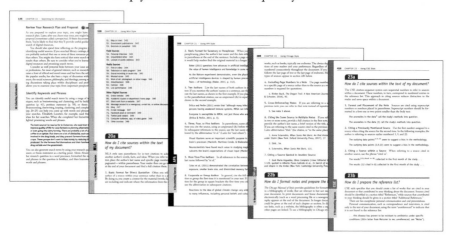

Key Questions begin each chapter and enable you to match your research writing needs to the material in the chapter.

Checklists offer at-a-glance views of a specific research or writing process. They can help you make sure that you've completed the process thoroughly and thoughtfully.

What's My Purpose? sections help you consider—and reconsider—your purpose at every stage of the research writing process. Whether you are writing to inform or trying to persuade your readers to take action on an issue, the questions and guidance in the What's My Purpose? boxes help keep your project focused and manageable.

Framing My Argument sections help you construct your argument one step at a time and use evidence skillfully. They show how your argument is developed over the course of the entire research writing process, not just at the moment you compose your thesis statement.

Information Literacy sections offer suggestions and identify opportunities as you find, evaluate, and integrate information from print, digital, and field sources. They address important, but lesser-known, facts about research and provide tips for using advanced resources.

Annotated examples make it easier for you to learn from the many illustrations and screen shots throughout the text. Annotations point out the features and processes at work in a document or tool to help you get the most out of the resources at hand.

My Research Project activities connect what's in the text with your own research writing. They show you how to put the text's practical advice to work and learn more about your own writing process.

Tutorials in the book provide you with extra help for important research writing issues, such as developing a research question, evaluating websites, and integrating quotations. They break each process down into steps and use examples to demonstrate a research writer's approach.

Quick Reference boxes at the end of every chapter give you a brief overview of steps to take before you move on.

Cross-references to *LaunchPad Solo for Research and Reference* help you extend your knowledge online. Visit **launchpadworks.com** for more information.

Contents

PART I

Joining the Conversation

1 **Getting Started** 3

2 **Exploring and Focusing** 28

3 **Developing Your Research Question** 41

Working on a research writing project is similar to joining a conversation. Before you contribute to the conversation, listen carefully to what others are saying. By reading widely, talking with knowledgeable people, and making firsthand observations, you can gain the knowledge you need to add your voice to the discussion.

In Part I, you'll read about how to get started, how to choose an appropriate topic, how to explore and refine your topic, and how to develop a clearly stated research question.

1

Getting Started

Getting started can be the hardest part of a research writing project. You'll likely find yourself staring at a blank computer screen or twirling a pen in your fingers as you ask, "Is this project really necessary?" or "What in the world should I write about?"

This chapter helps you get started. It explains how you can use your experiences in spoken and online conversations to gain confidence as a writer. It provides an overview of research writing processes and project management strategies. And it discusses how to select, reflect on, and take a position on an appropriate topic.

1a

How can I research and write with confidence?

Even writers who are new to research writing can approach it confidently. That confidence is founded on the recognition that research writing is similar to something you already do well: engage in conversations with people who share your interests in a subject. Your confidence will increase as you learn about the processes involved in research writing and the situations in which it takes place. It will grow as you gain an understanding of the role technology plays in writing of all kinds. And it will become even stronger as you take ownership of your research writing projects.

Think of Writing as a Form of Conversation

Throughout this book, writing is treated as an activity similar to engaging in conversation. As a writer, the conversations you might join will vary widely, from discussions of popular and political issues to conversations about your profession or discipline to exchanges about historical and cultural issues. As you engage in these conversations, you'll create documents that move a conversation forward, using designs that reflect your purposes and those of your readers. By thinking of writing as conversation, you'll be able to use your already extensive understanding of how conversations work to become a confident, effective writer.

Reflect on Your Experience in Conversations   Think about the last time you were at a party, reception, or some other public gathering. When you arrived, you probably walked around, said hello to friends, and listened in on several conversations. Before long, you likely joined a group that was talking about something you found interesting.

If you're like most people, you didn't jump right into the conversation. Instead, you listened for a few minutes and thought about what was being said. Perhaps you learned something new. Eventually, you added your voice to the conversation, other members of the group picked up on what you said, and the conversation moved along.

By thinking of writing as a conversation, you'll realize that good writing involves more than simply stating what you know. You'll see writing, instead, as a process of joining, reflecting on, and contributing to a conversation about a topic or an issue.

Thinking of writing as a form of conversation allows you to build on skills you already possess. In addition, because written conversations take place over much longer periods of time than spoken conversations do, you can use your conversational skills to far greater advantage. You can thoroughly consider your purposes and analyze your readers' needs, interests, knowledge, experiences, values, and beliefs. And you can explore the contexts—physical, social, and cultural—that will shape how your document is written and read.

Use Your Understanding of Conversations to Write Confidently   Much like a spoken conversation, a written conversation involves an exchange of information, ideas, and arguments among readers and writers. Instead of spoken words, however, the people engaged in the conversation communicate through written documents. Just as most people listen to what's being said before contributing to a conversation, most writers begin the process of writing about a topic by reading.

After they've read about a topic, most writers reflect on what they've learned and search for something new to offer to the other members of the conversation. Then they contribute to the conversation by writing their own document. In turn, that document will be read by other participants in the conversation. If these participants are interested, concerned, or even offended by what another

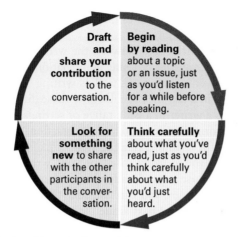

FIGURE 1.1 Thinking of Writing as a Form of Conversation

writer has added to the conversation, they might write their own documents in response. In this sense, a conversation among writers and readers becomes a circular process in which the information, ideas, and arguments shared through documents lead to the creation of new documents.

My Research Project
Create a Research Log

Create your research log now so you'll be prepared to face the challenges of planning and carrying out your project. A research log can take many forms:

- a notebook
- a word processing file or a folder on a laptop or desktop computer
- a folder or binder
- a set of note cards
- notes taken on a smartphone or a tablet
- a voice recorder

Although it might seem like extra work now, creating a research log as you begin your project will save time in the long run. You can also use Web resources to make progress on your research writing project, keep track of sources, and decide how to use sources to develop and present your argument.

Use Your Experiences with Technology to Improve Your Writing   Interestingly, if you ask people who spend significant amounts of time online whether they do much writing, they'll often say they don't. They don't think of creating text messages, e-mail messages, or status updates as writing. Yet it is. And the writing you've done in these settings can help prepare you for the writing you'll be asked to do in class or at a job.

Of course, there are differences between the writing you do online and the writing you do in an academic essay. Using abbreviations such as OMG or LOL in an essay might go over just about as well as writing "In summary, the available evidence suggests" in a text message. Despite these differences, you can build on your experiences as a writer in a wide range of settings. Just as you will adapt your tone or level of formality in a spoken conversation to the people involved in the conversation—for example, treating new acquaintances differently than you treat old friends—you're likely to adapt your writing to the situation in which you find yourself. Just as you'll tailor your comments to friends when you write on their Facebook pages, you can consider the interests and experiences of the people who will read your next academic essay. And just as you've learned to be critical—even suspicious—of what you read online, you can apply the same caution to your reading of the sources you encounter as you work on assignments.

My Research Project

Find a Written Conversation

We're surrounded by written conversations. Some focus on politics, others on sports, and still others on issues in an academic discipline. You'll find contributions to conversations on the front page of newspapers, on websites such as **CNN.com** and **Foxnews.com**, in academic and professional journals, and in the blogs at Tumblr or **Blogger.com**. Spend some time locating a conversation about a topic that interests you. Use the following prompts to find the conversation.

1. **List a topic that interests you.** Because you'll be searching for sources, jot down a list of search terms, or keywords (p. 146), that you can use to locate sources on the topic.

2. **Choose a newspaper or magazine or search for sources.** Browse a newspaper or magazine or search for sources on a Web search site (p. 33), a library database (p. 33), or a library catalog (p. 32) using the keywords you jotted down about your topic.

3. **Identify sources that seem to address the topic.** Skim each source (p. 61) to get a sense of how it addresses your topic.

4. **Decide whether the sources are engaged in the same conversation.** Ask whether the sources are addressing the same topic. If they are, list the ways in which they are "talking" to one another about the topic. Identify any agreements, disagreements, or differences in their approach to the topic.

5. **Reflect on the conversation.** Ask whether the sources you've identified tell you enough to understand the conversation. Consider whether you might need to locate more sources to give you a fuller picture of the conversation.

Understand the Rhetorical Nature of Writing Situations   ? WHAT'S MY PURPOSE?

Your confidence as a writer will grow as you gain an understanding of the situations in which writing takes place. A writing situation is another name for *rhetorical situation*, a concept that has been studied for thousands of years. The ancient Greeks, and in particular Plato, Socrates, and Aristotle, contributed in important ways to our understanding of rhetorical situation. So did rhetoricians in China, Japan, India, Africa, Rome, and the Arab world, to name only a few. Viewing writing as a rhetorical act helps us understand how writers or speakers pursue their purposes, consider the needs and interests of their audiences, adapt to the conditions in which they address their audiences, and present, organize, or design their documents or speeches.

This book is based strongly on a rhetorical approach to writing. Throughout the book, you'll find discussions of how you might pursue your purposes and take on various roles; how readers' reactions are affected by their needs, interests, knowledge, experience, values, and beliefs; and how contexts shape how documents are written and read. You'll also find discussions of other important factors, including the sources you use, the type of document you decide to write, opportunities you can take advantage of, and limitations that will reduce your choices about how to craft your document.

As you read this book, look for What's My Purpose? sections like this one. They will help you consider and reconsider your purpose throughout your research writing process.

Writers Have Purposes, Roles, and Biases   As is the case with spoken conversations, writers join written conversations for particular **purposes**: to inform, to analyze, to convince or persuade, to solve a problem, and so on. In many cases, writers have more than one purpose, such as learning something about a subject while earning a good grade or a promotion.

To accomplish their purposes, writers adopt **roles** within a conversation. A writer might explain something to someone else, in a sense becoming a guide through the conversation. Another writer might advance an argument, taking on the role of an advocate for a particular approach to an issue. As in spoken conversations, these roles are not mutually exclusive. For example, a writer might create a website to inform readers about the potential benefits of geothermal power. In addition to providing information, that writer might also argue for increased reliance on this form of power.

Your purposes will be informed by a set of interests, experiences, knowledge, attitudes, values, and beliefs that shape your understanding of the conversation. Sometimes characterized as biases, these factors are better understood as the reasonable influence of knowledge and experience on your reactions to the information, ideas, and arguments you encounter. As you consider your purposes and roles, reflect on the interests, experiences, and background you bring to your writing project.

TABLE 1.1 WRITING PURPOSES AND ROLES

Purpose	Role	Actions
To share reflections on an individual, event, object, idea, or issue	Observer	Consider a topic by sharing what is learned through the process of reflecting on it
To help readers become aware of the facts and ideas central to a written conversation	Reporter	Present information on an issue without adopting an argumentative or evaluative position
To analyze and explain the origins, qualities, significance, or potential impact of an idea, event, or issue	Interpreter	Apply an interpretive framework (p. 70) to a subject and seek answers to an analytical question
To help readers reach an informed, well-reasoned understanding of a subject's worth or effectiveness	Evaluator	Make judgments about an individual, event, object, or idea
To make progress on understanding and developing a solution to a problem	Problem solver	Identify and define a problem; discuss the effects of a problem; assess potential solutions; offer a solution
To convince, persuade, or mediate a dispute among readers	Advocate	*Convincing* involves gaining readers' agreement that a position on an issue is reasonable and well founded. *Persuading* involves getting them to take action. *Mediating* involves bringing readers into agreement on how to address an issue.
To share new knowledge with readers	Inquirer	Conduct research and other forms of inquiry; report results
To amuse readers in an engaging manner	Entertainer	Although seldom a primary goal of academic or professional writing, writers often write articles in an entertaining way in an attempt to maintain their readers' interest.

Readers Have Purposes and Biases   Just as writers have purposes and biases, so do readers. Among other purposes, readers often want to learn about a subject, assess or evaluate ideas and arguments, or understand opposing perspectives. And like writers, readers are strongly affected by their own needs, interests, knowledge, experiences, values, and beliefs.

As you craft your contribution to a written conversation, ask who your readers are likely to be. Then reflect on their values and beliefs, determine what they probably know about your subject, and take into account their likely experiences — if any — with the subject. Ask what your readers need to know about a subject and what they might be interested in knowing. Most important, ask why readers might want to read your document — and what might cause them to stop reading. In short, attempt to understand and connect with your readers.

Writing Builds on the Work of Others   One of the most important ways in which writing situations resemble spoken conversations is their reliance on taking turns. In spoken conversations — at least in those that are productive — people take turns sharing their ideas. To move the conversation forward, speakers build on what has been said, often referring to specific ideas or arguments and identifying the speakers who raised them. Comments such as "As Ellen said . . ." and "Reid made a good point earlier when he pointed out that . . ." are frequently made in spoken conversations. They show respect for the contributions made by others and help speakers align themselves with or distance themselves from other members of the conversation.

Written conversations also build on earlier contributions. Writers refer to the work of other authors to support their arguments, provide a context for their own contributions, or differentiate their ideas from those advanced by other authors. For example, a blogger concerned with new developments in the health care industry might conduct research on trends and use what she learns to inform readers about their implications. When writers use sources in this way, they provide citations to indicate that the information is provided by other authors and to help readers locate the sources should they wish to review them.

Contexts Shape Writing Situations   Writing is affected by shared social experiences, shared knowledge and history, work within particular disciplines and professions, and the physical and technological contexts in which documents are written and read.

Social contexts shape the relationships between writers and readers. Are they friends? Strangers? Supervisor and employee? Instructor and student? Whatever the social dynamic, social context will influence how writers and readers approach the writing situation.

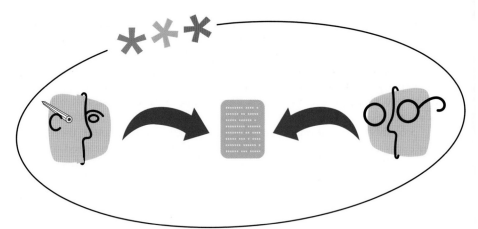

FIGURE 1.2 The Writing Situation

Cultural and historical contexts are a larger set of similarities and differences among writers and readers. The attack on the World Trade Center on September 11, 2001, is one example of a historical event that has strongly affected the people of the United States, influencing much of what has been written in the popular press, in professional journals, and on the Web. Similarly, widely shared cultural values— such as a belief in the importance of personal freedom—can shape writers' and readers' willingness to accept arguments that run counter to those values.

Disciplinary and professional contexts are the shared experiences of members of particular disciplines, such as chemistry or sociology. As disciplines develop over time, members of a discipline develop consensus about the kinds of documents, such as journal articles or grant proposals, that are best used to share information, ideas, and arguments. Agreements also develop about how to document sources of information (see pp. 100–101), how to report new findings, and how to offer criticism of previous work in the field.

Physical and technological contexts include physical and temporal factors shaping the writing and reading of a document. Will your readers have time to read your document carefully? Will they read it in a quiet room, on a train, or in a coffee shop? Will they read it in print, on a tablet or smartphone, or on a large computer screen? The answers to these questions will affect both the kind of document you choose to write and the design of your document.

Writing Situations Influence Genre Choices and Design Decisions Writers make choices about the genre—or type of document—and the design of their documents largely in response to physical, social, and disciplinary contexts. They recognize that they are more likely to accomplish their purposes if they create documents that meet their readers' expectations, that are designed to help readers understand ideas and information, and that present their arguments clearly and effectively.

Genres are general categories of documents. Opinion columns, academic essays, and blogs are all genres. So are scholarly articles and posts on social networking sites. Typically, genres develop to help writers accomplish a general purpose. Informative essays, for example, help writers demonstrate their knowledge to an instructor, while informative articles in newspapers, magazines, and newsletters help writers share information and ideas with their readers.

In most cases, genres are social inventions, shaped by the social, cultural, and disciplinary contexts from which they emerge. When writers and readers form a community — such as an academic discipline, a professional association, or a group that shares an interest in a particular topic or activity — they begin to develop characteristic ways of communicating with one another. As the needs and interests of a community change, genres evolve to reflect those needs and interests. Academic essays, for example, might begin to make greater use of color and illustrations. In other cases, a single genre, such as websites, might evolve into several more specialized genres, such as blogs, social networking sites, and news sites.

Design — or more specifically, document design — is the use of visual elements such as fonts, colors, page layout, and illustrations to enhance the effectiveness of written documents. A well-designed chart, for example, can be far more effective at conveying complex information to a reader than even the most clearly written paragraph can. Similarly, the emotional impact of a well-chosen illustration, such as a photograph of a starving child or a video clip of aid workers rushing to help victims of a natural disaster, can do far more than words alone to persuade a reader to take action. Throughout this book, you'll find design treated as a central writing strategy, and you'll find numerous examples of the design characteristics of the genres discussed in each chapter. You'll also find in-depth discussions of design in Chapters 16 and 18.

Writing Situations Present Limitations and Opportunities   Each writing situation presents a writer with limitations and opportunities. You might be required to use a particular documentation system or expected to produce a document of a specific length. You might also find yourself presented with opportunities, such as access to useful databases or experts on your topic. Recognizing the limitations and opportunities associated with your writing situation can help you work more effectively, efficiently, and confidently.

Understand and Manage Your Research Writing Processes

Research writing involves learning about a topic, taking a position on that topic, and sharing your position with your readers. Understanding how to carry out and manage the processes involved in research writing will help you write with confidence.

WORKING TOGETHER

Analyze a Writing Situation

Work together with your classmates to analyze a writing situation. Generate a list of documents that members of the group have written recently. Then choose one and analyze its writing situation. To conduct your analysis, respond to the following prompts.

1 **What was written?** Describe the document in enough detail to allow other members of the class to understand its main point. Identify the genre and describe its design features.

2 **What were the writer's purposes?** List the purpose or purposes that drove the writer's work on the document. Why did he or she write it? What did he or she hope to gain by writing it? How was the writer's purpose shaped by his or her needs, interests, knowledge, experiences, values, and beliefs?

3 **Who were the intended readers?** Describe the people who might have been expected to read the document, and list their purpose or purposes for reading it. How would their reading of the document have been shaped by their needs, interests, knowledge, experiences, values, and beliefs?

4 **What sources were used in the document?** Identify the sources of information, ideas, and arguments used in the document. Indicate how the sources were used (for example, to support a point or to differentiate the writer's ideas from those of another author).

5 **What contexts shaped the writing and reading of the document?** Identify the physical, technological, social, cultural, and disciplinary contexts that shaped the writer's work on the document and the readers' reading of it.

6 **What limitations and opportunities affected the writing of this document?** Reflect on the potential requirements the writer might have faced. Think about the likely limitations and opportunities that might have shaped the writer's decisions.

View Research Writing Processes as Flexible and Overlapping   Writing processes are best understood as a set of related activities that writers engage in over the course of a writing project. It is rare to see writers carrying out these activities in precisely the same way. In fact, few writers use exactly the same process each time they work on a project. Instead, they assess their writing situation and adapt their writing and research processes to fit that situation.

The discussions of "the research writing process" in this book, as a result, are not intended to provide a one-size-fits-all recipe for success. As a writer, you'll be the best judge of which processes are most appropriate for a given writing project. To make that judgment, however, requires a thorough understanding of your options. Figure 1.3 illustrates the processes that writers typically engage in as they work on research writing projects.

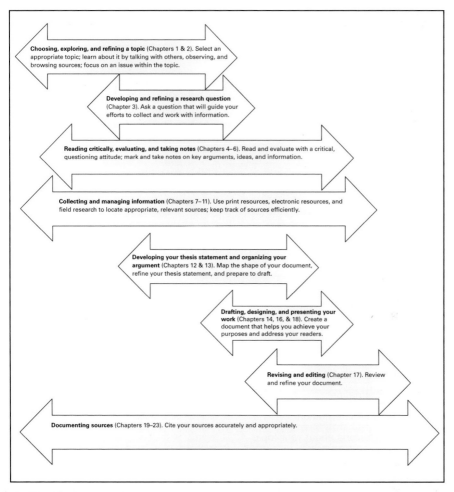

FIGURE 1.3 Research Writing Processes *As you learn about your topic and reflect on your progress, you'll move back and forth among these processes.*

Understand How to Manage Your Research Writing Project   Understanding how to manage a research writing project can also help you write with confidence. Project management strategies include setting aside time to work on the project, deciding when and in which order you should carry out various research writing processes, deciding how to manage the information you collect (see Chapter 8), and monitoring your progress on the project.

Time management is particularly important to the success of a project. If you don't schedule your time well, for example, you might spend far too much time collecting information and far too little working with it. As you begin thinking about your research writing project, consider creating a project timeline. A timeline can help you identify important milestones in your project and determine when you need to reach them.

My Research Project

Create a Project Timeline

In your research log, start a project timeline like the one shown here. The steps in your process might be different, of course, but many research writing projects follow this general process. As you create your timeline, keep in mind any specific requirements of your assignment, such as handing in a first draft, revised drafts, and so on.

PROJECT TIMELINE		
Activity	Start Date	Completion Date
Select your topic		
Explore your topic		
Refine your topic		
Develop your research question		
Read and evaluate information		
Begin to take a position		
Take notes		
Plan your search for information		
Collect information		
Organize your information		
Draw conclusions about your topic		
Develop your thesis statement		
Identify reasons and evidence		
Organize your document		
Write the first draft of your document		
Review and revise your first draft		
Write and revise additional drafts		
Edit your draft		
Design your document		
Finalize in-text and end-of-text citations		
Publish and submit your document		

Be Aware of New Technological Opportunities   ℹ **INFORMATION LITERACY**   Experienced writers know that the tools we use to write affect not only how we write, but also how we access information, reach our readers, and design our documents. It's become a cliché to say "there's an app for that." For research writers, however, it's a factual statement. The number of apps, software programs, devices, and services that are relevant to research writing grows at a steady pace, offering new ways of accessing information, composing documents, and designing and distributing our work. These new writing resources are likely to have an effect on how and what you write. Throughout this book, you'll find discussions of how new resources might help you accomplish your goals as a writer — and where you might turn to find the newest developments in writing technologies. You can identify them by the Information Literacy icon. ▪

Take Ownership of Your Project   Confident research writers have a strong personal investment in their research writing project. Sometimes this investment comes naturally. You might be interested in your topic, committed to achieving your purposes as a writer, intrigued by the demands of writing for a particular audience, or looking forward to the challenges of writing a new type of document, such as a website or a magazine article. At times, however, you need to create a sense of personal investment by looking for connections between your interests and your writing project. This can be a challenge, particularly when you've been assigned a project that wouldn't normally interest you.

The key to investing yourself in a project you wouldn't normally care about is taking ownership of the project. To take ownership, ask yourself how your project might help you pursue your personal, professional, or academic interests. Think about how the project might help you meet new people or learn new writing or research strategies. Or look for unique challenges associated with a project, such as learning how to develop arguments or use document design techniques more effectively. Your goal is to feel that you have a stake in your research writing project by finding something that appeals to your interests and helps you grow as a researcher and writer.

1b

How can I approach an assignment?

Research writers in academic and professional settings often work in response to an assignment. You might be given general guidelines, such as "choose a topic in your major"; you might be asked to choose a topic within a general subject area, such as gender identity; or you might be given complete freedom in your choice of topic. To get started on an assignment, consider your writing situation, generate ideas about potential topics, and choose the most promising topic.

FEATURED WRITERS

Discussions throughout this book are illustrated by seven featured writers—real students who crafted a variety of research projects, including traditional essays, a multimodal essay, and a website. You can learn from these real-life examples as you plan and conduct your own research and draft and revise your own document.

Alexis Alvarez · Writing about the Impact of Competitive Sports on Adolescent Girls
Alexis wrote an informative research essay about the effects competitive sports can have on adolescent girls. She explored the general topic of competitive sports and women before refining her topic to the use of steroids by female teenaged athletes. You can read her essay on p. 375.

Nicholas Brothers · Writing about Private Military Corporations and the War on Terror
Nicholas wrote a research essay that analyzed and argued against the growing importance of private military corporations in U.S. wars. He supported his analysis and argument with published sources and interviews. You can read his essay on p. 404.

Elizabeth Leontiev · Writing about the Impact of the U.S. War on Drugs on Coca Farmers in South America
Elizabeth wrote an argumentative research essay for her composition course. She explored the general topic of the war on drugs and then joined a conversation about the effects of U.S. efforts to eradicate coca farming in South America. You can read her research essay on p. 350.

Lauren Mack · Writing a Multimodal Essay about Saving Coral Reefs
Lauren wrote a multimodal essay—an essay created in PowerPoint that used text, images, audio, and video to convey an argument—about the importance of saving coral reefs. You can see slides from her essay on pp. 279–80.

Cori Schmidtbauer · Writing about Portia's Unconventional Role in *The Merchant of Venice*
Cori wrote an analytic research essay that addressed whether Portia fits the ideal of the Renaissance woman. She used sources from literary theorists to debate whether Shakespeare's play was ahead of its time. You can read her essay in the Palmquist LaunchPad Solo.

Brandon Tate · Creating a Website about Hydraulic Fracturing
Brandon created a website about hydraulic fracturing, a process used during drilling for gas or oil to release hydrocarbons from rock formations. Widely known as fracking, its use had become an important topic of discussion in his community. You can view his website in the Palmquist LaunchPad Solo.

Josh Woelfle · Writing a Scientific Essay about Cancer Research
Josh, who was enrolled in a life-sciences seminar, wrote an informative essay exploring promising new treatments for cancer. You can read his essay on p. 428.

Consider Your Writing Situation

Your assignment will provide important clues about what your instructor and your other readers will expect. To uncover those clues, ask yourself the following questions about your research writing situation.

Who are my readers and why would they read my document?   Your assignment might identify your readers, or audience, for you. If you are writing a research project for a class, one of your most important readers will be your instructor. You are also likely to have additional readers, such as your classmates, people who have a professional or personal interest in your topic, or if your project will be published in print or online, the readers of a particular newspaper, magazine, or website. If you are writing in a business or professional setting, your readers might include supervisors, customers, or other people associated with the organization. In some cases, you might be asked to define your own audience. As you consider possible topics, ask yourself which subjects these readers would be most interested in learning about. Featured writer Cori Schmidtbauer, for example, would probably not have written about the work of William Shakespeare if her target audience had been the readers of a magazine such as *PC World* or *Street Rod*.

What will influence me and what will influence my readers?   Research writers aren't mindless robots who churn through sources and create documents without emotion or conviction — or at least they shouldn't be. Your topic should interest you. An appropriate topic will keep you motivated as you carry out the work needed to complete your research project successfully. Your project should also be your own, even if it's been assigned to you. One of the most important things you can do as a research writer is to make a personal connection with the topic. To make that connection, look for topics that can help you pursue your personal, professional, and academic interests.

Readers are influenced by their interest in a particular topic, their knowledge of the topic, and their values and beliefs. If your readers have no interest in your topic, know little about it, or are offended by it, you aren't likely to meet with much success.

What type of document am I writing?   Assignments often specify the type of document — or genre — you will be writing. You might be asked to write essays, reports, websites, articles, letters to the editor, multimedia presentations, or any of a number of other genres. The genre that is assigned will have an impact on the kinds of topics you choose. For example, consider the differences among the topics addressed in articles in newsmagazines such as *Time,* the topics addressed in scholarly journals in biology, and the topics addressed on websites published by the U.S. Department of Education. Genre will also affect your decisions about the design of your document. To better understand the relationships among genre, design, and topic, review the research essay written by featured writer Alexis Alvarez, the website developed by featured writer Brandon Tate, and the multimodal essay written by featured writer Lauren Mack. As you reflect on potential topics for your research writing project, keep in mind the type of document specified in your assignment.

What contexts will affect my work on the document?   Assignments often give important clues about the contexts — or settings — in which a document will be read. Contexts range from the immediate shared experiences of readers and writers to shared cultures, histories, and disciplines to the physical settings in which documents are written and read (p. 9).

For students, one of the most important social and cultural contexts shaping their written work is academic life itself, that complex mix of instructors, fellow students, classes, tests, labs, and writing assignments that you negotiate on a daily basis. As you analyze an assignment, ask whether it will require you to consider particular disciplinary contexts, whether you'll be asked to consider your class as a community, whether you'll be asked to address readers outside of your class setting, and what physical settings might be involved in the writing and reading of your document.

What role will I adopt toward my readers?   A role is a way of relating to your readers. The roles you take on will reflect your purpose, your understanding of your readers, and the type of document you plan to write. As you consider which topics might interest you, think about how you plan to relate to your readers. Some topics will be more appropriate for an assignment that asks you to interpret an object, an event, or a process for your readers, while others will be more appropriate for assignments that ask you to inform or persuade or solve problems. For a list and explanation of the roles you might adopt, see Table 1.1 on p. 8.

What will affect my ability to work on this project?   The requirements of your assignment, the limitations you face as you work, and the opportunities you can capitalize on will affect your ability to work on your research project.

Requirements and Limitations   If you are writing your research project for a class, examine the requirements of your assignment:

- type of document
- required length
- due date
- number and type of sources (digital, print, and field)
- suggested or required resources, such as a library catalog or database
- requirements about the organization and structure of your document (title page, introduction, body, conclusion, works cited list, and so on)
- documentation system (such as MLA, APA, *Chicago*, or CSE)

TUTORIAL

How do I analyze the audience for a research writing assignment?

Learn about your readers by looking for clues about their needs, interests, and expectations.

COMP 150: College Composition Portfolio 3: Engaging in a Public Issue
Due Date: May 2nd at the beginning of class

1 Analyze the assignment's purpose for clues about your audience.

2 Look for terms such as *reader* and *audience*. Then examine the text near those terms for clues about your readers' expectations.

3 Identify clues about the assignment's genre; look for terms such as *essay*, *report*, *argument*, *article*, or *website*.

In this essay, you will write a public response—an article or essay directed to a specific publication—for readers who are interested in the issue you analyzed in your last portfolio. To accomplish this goal, you will: (a) assess the writing situation surrounding the issue; (b) collect information from a variety of sources, including written texts, personal experience, and, if appropriate, field research; (c) evaluate your sources to choose those that best support your argument; and (d) make a sufficiently narrow argumentative claim and support that claim with sound reasoning and evidence.

You should address your article or essay to readers of a publication that has published work about your issue. You will need to analyze the publication, its readers (specifically, their needs, interests, knowledge, experiences, values, and beliefs), and the writing situation that has shaped discourse about this issue. In general, your audience is likely to expect you to thoroughly explain the points you are making and to support your argument using appropriate forms of evidence. In addition, it is likely that your audience will expect you to use a reasonable tone, to respect your readers and sources, and to avoid slang. Your readers are also likely to expect you to acknowledge and cite your sources in a manner consistent with other sources published by your target publication.

- intermediate reports or activities (such as thesis statements, notes, outlines, and rough drafts)

You might also face limitations, such as lack of access to information or lack of time to work.

Determining your requirements and limitations will help you weigh the potential drawbacks of a topic. You might find that you need to narrow the scope of your topic significantly given your time and page limit.

Opportunities   Sometimes writers get so wrapped up in the requirements and limitations of the assignment that they overlook their opportunities. As you think about your topic, ask yourself whether you can take advantage of opportunities such as:

- access to a specialized or particularly good library
- personal experience with and knowledge about a topic
- access to people who are experts on a topic

For example, Alexis Alvarez thought about her personal experiences and those of her friends before deciding to focus on the impact of competitive sports programs on adolescent girls.

Generate Ideas about Potential Topics

You can use prewriting activities such as brainstorming, freewriting, looping, clustering, and sentence starters (writing prompts in which you fill in the blanks) to generate ideas about potential topics.

Brainstorm   Brainstorming involves listing ideas as they occur to you. This list should not consist of complete sentences; in fact, brainstorming is most successful when you avoid censoring yourself. Although you'll end up using only a few of the ideas you generate during brainstorming, don't worry until later about weeding out the useful ideas from the less promising ones.

Brainstorming sessions are usually conducted in response to a specific question. Featured writer Lauren Mack generated the following list in response to the question, "What interests me personally about this project?"

> I already know a lot about marine biology from my courses, and I learned a lot about the fragility of sea life from my dive trip to the Florida Keys last spring.
> I'd like to do more research and learn about ways marine life can be protected.
> Some of my connections from my internship at the New England Aquarium would be great resources for my research.
> The documentary film about the ocean that I worked on last summer also sparked my interest in the topic and would also provide good background information.

My Research Project

Generate Ideas by Brainstorming

In your research log, brainstorm responses to the following questions.

- What do I want to accomplish with this project?
- What interests me personally about this project?
- What interests me academically about this project?
- Who are my readers?
- What topics do my readers need to read about?
- What topics would my readers like to read about?

Freewrite   Freewriting involves writing full sentences quickly, without stopping and—most important—without editing what you write. You might want to start with one of the ideas you generated in your brainstorming activity, or you could begin your freewriting session with a prompt, such as "I am interested in _____ because . . ." Some writers set a timer and freewrite for five, ten, or fifteen minutes; others set a goal of a certain number of pages and keep writing until they meet that goal.

After brainstorming about the general topic of protecting marine life, Lauren focused her freewriting on her readers' purposes and interests. The following is an excerpt from Lauren's freewriting.

Everyone loves the ocean and has a general understanding of its significance to our global environment. My readers probably want to know about the challenges facing the health of our oceans and what can be done to protect them. They may want to know whether the problems are natural or caused by humans. They may also want to know what could happen if we don't take action. And they may want to know what they can do as individuals to make a difference.

Lauren did not edit her work or worry about spelling, grammar, or style.

My Research Project

Generate Ideas by Freewriting

In your research log, freewrite in response to one of the following prompts, replacing the blanks with the ideas for topics that you generated during your brainstorming session. Before you begin, set a goal of a certain number of minutes or a set amount of pages you will write.

- Writing about ____ will help me accomplish the following purposes . . .
- I am personally interested in ____ because . . .
- I am academically interested in ____ because . . .
- My readers need or would like to know about ____ because . . .

Blind Write or Dictate   If you find it difficult to freewrite without editing, try blind writing—freewriting on a computer with the monitor turned off—or dictating. Many smartphones and tablets allow you to speak your thoughts aloud and convert them immediately to text. These forms of freewriting can take your focus off generating text, because you carry them out without looking at a computer screen.

Use Looping   Looping is another form of freewriting. During a looping session, you write for a set amount of time (say, five minutes) and then read what you've written. As you read, identify one key idea in what you've written and then write for five minutes with the new key idea as your starting point. Lauren, for example, wrote in response to a sentence she had generated during freewriting, "And they may want to know what they can do as individuals to make a difference."

> My readers will be both my marine biology professor, who probably knows a lot about the causes and cures of damage to marine life, and my fellow students, who know the basic stuff that I know, such as the fact that both climate change and human pollution are affecting ocean life. But readers will want some specific information about steps we can take to decrease damage to the ocean. They'll need to see it as relevant to their own lives, even if they don't have the passion for sea life that I have.

My Research Project

Generate Ideas by Looping

In your research log, select a response from your freewriting activity and carry out the following looping exercise.

1. Paste the response at the top of your word processing file or write it at the top of a page in your notebook. Then freewrite for five minutes about the response.

2. Identify the best idea in this freewriting.

3. Freewrite for five more minutes about the idea you've identified.

Repeat the process until you've refined your idea into a potential topic.

Use Clustering   Clustering involves presenting your ideas about a potential topic in graphical form. Clustering can help you gain a different perspective on a topic by helping you map out the relationships among your ideas. It can also help you generate new ideas. Featured writer Nicholas Brothers used clustering to map out his ideas and further refine his topic (see Figure 1.4).

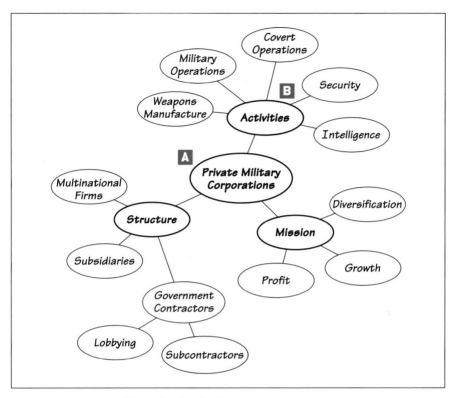

FIGURE 1.4 A Cluster of Ideas Created by Nicholas Brothers

A Nicholas listed a central idea and three key areas to explore.

B Key areas are also linked to related ideas.

My Research Project

Generate Ideas by Clustering

In your research log, generate additional ideas about your potential topic by using a clustering exercise.

1. In the middle of a sheet of paper, or in the center of a digital document (word processing file or graphics file), write your potential topic.

2. Identify ideas that are related to your central topic and list them near it. Think about the importance and relevance of each related idea, and draw lines and circles to show the relationships among your ideas.

3. Write additional ideas related to the ideas in Step 2. In turn, draw lines and circles to show their relationships to the other ideas in your cluster.

4. Repeat the process until you've created a cluster of ideas that represents your current understanding of the topic you are considering.

Use Sentence Starters   Sentence starters help you generate ideas by "filling in the blanks" in each sentence. The following sentence starter was used by featured writer Josh Woelfle to generate ideas about his writing assignment.

Sentence Starter   Although we know that ____, we also know that ____.

Although we know that conventional cancer treatments such as chemotherapy and radiation have significantly reduced deaths from cancer, we also know that they can bring with them a great deal of pain and have important and often painful side effects.

There are nearly as many sentence starters as there are ideas about how to structure a sentence. You can make up your own or you can try some of the following.

Exploring Interests

I would like to understand [how / why / whether] ____ happened.

I want to know more about ____.

I am interested in ____ because ____.

Explaining

There are three reasons this is [true / not true / relevant / important / essential]. First, ____. Second, ____. Third, ____.

We can [change / improve / fix] this by ____.

To accomplish ____, we must ____.

People do this because ____.

We were trying to ____, but we ended up ____.

Interpreting and Analyzing

This means that ____.

If we were starting over, we would ____.

It has always been the case that ____.

Understanding Causes and Effects

When I was ____, I decided ____. That decision has ____.

When I was ____, I believed ____. But now I believe ____.

The root cause of this problem is ____.

This happened because ____.

Predicting

When this happens, ____.

We would prefer that ____ were true, but we must recognize that ____.

Too often, we ____.

If we ____, then ____.

Stating Beliefs

I believe ____.

We have to ____.

I want to ____.

Exploring Possibilities

If this is [true / happening / important], then ____.

Sometimes, ____.

We could ____.

How can we ____?

Evaluating

The most important aspect of ____ is ____.

This is better because ____.

Comparing and Contrasting

Like ____, ____.

Unlike ____, ____.

I know ____, but I don't know ____.

When you have completed your brainstorming, freewriting, blind writing, dictating, looping, and clustering activities, and have tried using sentence starters, review what you've written. You'll most likely find that these prewriting techniques have generated a useful list of ideas for a topic.

Choose an Appropriate Topic [FRAMING MY ARGUMENT]

In the most general sense, your topic is what you will research and write about—it is the foundation on which your research writing project is built. An appropriate topic, however, is much more than a simple subject heading in an almanac or encyclopedia. It is a subject of debate, discussion, and discovery. As you prepare to choose a topic, consider your writing situation, the time and effort you'll put into your research writing project, and the characteristics of appropriate topics.

Look for Framing My Argument sections like this one throughout this book. They provide advice on developing sound arguments and using appropriate evidence.

Reflect on Your Writing Situation   After you've spent time thinking and generating ideas about potential topics for your research project, review the topics you've identified and see whether you're ready to choose a topic. As you carry out your review, think carefully about the level of interest you and your readers might have in the topic, the number of readers who will be interested in the topic, and the appropriateness of the topic for your assignment.

Think of Your Topic as a <u>Conversation</u> You'd Like to Join Thinking of your topic as a topic of conversation is critical to your success as a research writer. Research writing goes beyond merely locating and reporting information. Instead, it is an ongoing process of inquiry in which you must consider your purposes, your readers, and the conventions associated with the type of document you plan to write. Ultimately, research writing is about taking and sharing a position on your topic. In some cases, this will involve sharing your understanding or evaluation of a topic with your readers. In other cases, it will involve attempting to convince them to accept your argument about a topic. In still other cases, it will involve sharing your interpretation or analysis of a topic with your readers. Sharing your position—and the information, ideas, and arguments you draw on to support it—allows you to contribute to and advance a conversation about your topic.

Look for a Topic Appropriate to Your Writing Situation As you reflect on the list of potential topics you've generated, keep in mind the characteristics of topics that are well suited to research writing projects. In general, appropriate topics share the following qualities.

- **Relevance** A good topic will be relevant to your personal life, your academic discipline or profession, or the assignment you have been given. A great topic will be relevant to all of these.

- **Specificity** A good topic will be broad enough to interest you and your readers yet narrow enough to address within the length and time limitations of your assignment. If you begin with a broad topic, such as "food," you'll want to narrow it eventually to something more manageable, such as "organic food in fast-food restaurants."

- **Current Interest** Without exception, good topics are the subject of debate or discussion. A topic need not be controversial—it might simply be something readers want to learn about—but many topics certainly are, and generally the more controversial a topic the easier it will be to find sources that are relevant to your research writing project.

- **Accessible** Keep in mind that you need to be able to locate sources on your topic. If you choose a topic that is too cutting edge, technical, arcane, or obscure, you may have trouble doing your research within the parameters of the assignment.

Be Flexible As you consider your choice of topic, remember that your decision is subject to change. It's a starting point, not a final destination. As you explore your topic, you'll begin to focus on a specific issue—a point of disagreement, uncertainty, concern, or curiosity—that is being discussed by a community of readers and writers. As you learn about your topic, you might find that related topics are more appealing or more appropriate. You might even find that you need to rethink your choice completely.

QUICK REFERENCE

Getting Started

✔ Build confidence by thinking of writing as a form of conversation. (p. 4)

✔ Create a research log to manage information and ideas as you work. (p. 5)

✔ Increase confidence by understanding the rhetorical nature of writing situations. (p. 7)

✔ Learn about the role of genre and design in research writing. (p. 10)

✔ Gain confidence about research writing by becoming acquainted with research writing processes. (p. 11)

✔ Develop a project timeline to help manage your time. (p. 14)

✔ Begin working with your assignment by reflecting on your research writing situation. (p. 17)

✔ Generate ideas about appropriate topics by brainstorming, freewriting, blind writing, dictating, looping, clustering, and using sentence starters. (p. 20)

✔ Choose a promising and appropriate topic. (p. 25)

2

Exploring and Focusing

 Key Questions

2a. **How can I explore my topic?** 28
Create a plan to explore your topic
Discuss your topic with others
Conduct preliminary observations
Identify useful types of sources
Find sources

2b. **How can I focus on an issue?** 35
Identify conversations about issues in your topic
Assess your interest in the issues
Choose an issue

Exploring involves gaining a general understanding of the issues—points of disagreement, uncertainty, concern, or curiosity—within a topic. Focusing on a single issue lays the groundwork for developing the research question that will frame your thinking about that issue and guides your efforts to gain a comprehensive understanding of it.

2a

How can I explore my topic?

As you explore your topic, you'll find yourself listening in on conversations about several issues. Your goal will be to choose one that intrigues you and is well suited to your writing situation.

Step 1: Create a Plan to Explore Your Topic 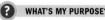 WHAT'S MY PURPOSE?

Before you start exploring your topic, create an informal research plan. Your plan should reflect your purpose for working on the project and provide directions for locating, collecting, and managing information. The most common elements of a research plan include:

- a list of people with whom you can discuss your topic, including people who know a great deal about or have been involved with the topic and people, such as librarians, who can help you locate information about your topic
- a list of questions to ask people who can help you explore your topic
- a list of settings you might observe to learn more about your topic
- a list of resources to search and browse, such as library catalogs, databases, Web search sites, and Web directories
- a system for keeping track of the information you collect

After you create your plan, use it to guide your work and to remind yourself of steps you might overlook. A note such as "talk to Professor Chapman about recent clinical studies" can come in handy if you've become so busy searching the Web or your library's catalog that you forget about your other plans for exploring your topic. After you've drafted your plan, share it with your instructor, your supervisor, or a librarian, who might suggest additional resources, shortcuts, and alternative strategies. Take notes on the feedback you receive and, if necessary, revise your plan.

My Research Project

Create a Plan to Explore Your Topic

In your research log, answer the following questions.

- Who can help me learn more about my topic?
- What questions should I ask people on my list?
- What settings can I observe to learn more about my topic?
- What resources can I search or browse through to learn more about my topic?
- How can I keep track of information I collect as I explore my topic?

Using your responses, write your plan as a series of steps and ask your instructor, your supervisor, or a librarian to review it.

Step 2: Discuss Your Topic with Others

Talking about your topic with people who know about it or have been affected by it can provide you with new insights. An instructor, a supervisor, or a librarian can help you identify resources you might not have thought of.

Featured writer Alexis Alvarez explored her topic — women and competitive sports — in part by talking with family members and friends who had competed in organized sports. These discussions helped Alexis better see the many different issues she could pursue within her topic.

You can also explore a topic by conducting formal interviews (p. 174) or by writing letters and e-mail messages (p. 186). If you are uncertain about how to find people you can interview about your topic, start by visiting a Web discussion forum, message board, or blog devoted to discussion of serious issues. (For an example, visit the *Huffington Post* blogs page at **huffingtonpost.com/politics/the-blog/**.)

Step 3: Conduct Preliminary Observations

Observation is a powerful tool, especially when you are just getting started on a writing project. Like discussing your topic with others, observing can provide you with valuable information that isn't available from other sources. You can learn how to plan, conduct, and analyze the results of an observation on pp. 179–82.

Featured writer Alexis Alvarez used observation to help explore her topic, the effects of competitive sports on adolescent girls. Alexis observed friends and relatives who are competitive athletes, and this provided her with a different perspective than she could have gained through other information-gathering techniques.

Step 4: Identify Useful Types of Sources

Depending on your topic, some types of sources will be more useful than others. For example, if you are interested in a topic such as featured writer Brandon Tate's (hydraulic fracturing) and want to learn about the latest developments in the debate about its use, you might focus on government and industry websites, trade and professional journals, newspapers, magazines, and blogs. If you are interested in a topic such as Shakespearean drama, as featured writer Cori Schmidtbauer was, you would focus on books and articles in scholarly journals. Note the following characteristics of sources you might collect and review.

- **Books** undergo a lengthy editorial process before they are published, and librarians evaluate them before adding them to a library collection.

- **Articles in scholarly journals** also undergo a lengthy editorial process before they are published. Most are reviewed—evaluated for accuracy, completeness, and methodological soundness—by experts in the field before they are accepted for publication. You can usually recognize a scholarly journal by its listing of an editorial board, the use of works cited lists and in-text citation in articles found in the journal, and the presence of the words *peer reviewed*, *blind reviewed*, or *refereed*.

- **Articles in trade and other professional journals** do not always go through a strict review process. You can find out whether articles are reviewed by looking at the submission policies printed in the journal.

- **Articles in magazines and newspapers** are usually reviewed only by the editors of the publication. Editorials typically represent an editor's or editorial board's opinion on an issue and are not subject to review. Similarly, opinion columns and letters to the editor seldom go through a review process.

- **Websites,** unlike sources found in a library, seldom go through a peer-review process. They are created by organizations, corporations, educational and government institutions, and individuals. Their purposes vary widely, as do their quality and reliability.

- **Blogs** are a specialized type of website that allows individuals and groups to post entries on a topic or an issue.

- **Media sites,** such as YouTube (**youtube.com**), provide access to video, music and audio, and animation.

- **Theses and dissertations** are final projects written by students in graduate programs. Theses and dissertations vary in quality and reliability, although they have been reviewed and approved by committees of professors.

- **Other sources** include maps, videotapes, audiotapes, and multimedia items such as CD-ROMs and DVDs. These can be found in many library collections.

WORKING TOGETHER

Plan Your Search for Sources

Before you visit the library, search a database, or browse the Web, sit down with a group of classmates to generate ideas for a search. To carry out this activity, follow these steps.

1 Explain your subject and discuss your purpose for informing readers. If your readers go beyond the instructor and your classmates, describe your readers and their needs, interests, knowledge, experiences, values, and beliefs. Talk briefly about specific ideas you have for gathering information on your subject.

2 Once you've explained your subject, the other members of your group should brainstorm ideas about useful resources for locating sources, such as the library catalog, specific databases, useful websites and directories, and relevant field research methods.

3 For each resource that has been identified, the group should brainstorm suggestions for using it effectively. For example, the group might generate a list of specific keywords and phrases to use in your search, create a list of good candidates for an interview and useful interview questions, and make suggestions about what to look for in an observation.

4 At the end of the discussion, ask any questions you have about the resources and search strategies your classmates have suggested.

5 If you are working face to face, take notes on the discussion. If you are using a chat or instant-messaging program, record a transcript of the session. The goal of the session should be to generate as many useful search resources and strategies as possible. Don't rule out any ideas, no matter how trivial or ridiculous they might seem at first. When the exchange is completed, turn to the next writer and repeat the process.

My Research Project

Record Your Search Results

As you explore your topic, record your searches.

1. Identify the library catalogs, databases, and websites you search.

2. List the words and phrases you use in your searches.

3. Note the quality and quantity of results produced by each search.

4. Recording search results will allow you to conduct these searches again or conduct the same searches on different search sites or databases.

Step 5: Find Sources

After you've talked with others about your topic and observed relevant settings, take advantage of the work other writers have done on the topic by finding and reviewing sources.

Search your library's catalog for sources using title, author, and subject words. Before you begin your search, generate a list of words and phrases related to the topic you want to explore. For more about searching the library catalogs, see p. 155.

Browse your library's shelves to find sources related to those you've already located (see Figure 2.2). Review the works cited lists, footnotes, endnotes, or in-text citations for particularly useful sources. Then find and review these cited sources.

The catalog allows you to locate books, journals, databases, media items, and other types of sources.

| Books + | Articles & Databases | Journal Titles | Reserves | Guides |

Discovery home

Find books, e-books, journals, Web pages, multimedia and CSU scholarly works

| hydraulic fracturing | All Fields ∨ | SEARCH |

Limit to: ☐ Library Catalog ☐ Digital Repository and Digital Collections ☐ CSU Libraries Website

More Options ▾ | Advanced Search | Classic Catalog (Sage) | Renew Books | Google Books ⊕

Several search options, including advanced search (p. 154), are provided.

A keyword search for *hydraulic fracturing* is conducted.

FIGURE 2.1 Library Catalog Search Page [Courtesy of Morgan Library, Colorado State University.]

FIGURE 2.2 Browsing the Shelves in a Library [Courtesy of Morgan Library, Colorado State University.]

A   If you located the book *Bolivia & Coca* . . .

B   . . . browse the shelves to find related works such as *The Coca Boom and Rural Social Change in Bolivia.*

C   Locate related sources by reading a book's works cited list, footnotes, endnotes, or in-text citations.

Browse newsstands and bookstores for specialty newspapers and magazines to which your library doesn't subscribe, and look at the books in a large bookstore or on a bookseller's website.

Search databases *i* **INFORMATION LITERACY** just as you would search an online library catalog (see Figure 2.3). Most databases provide publication information about articles in journals, magazines, and newspapers. To identify relevant databases, ask a reference librarian for assistance. To learn more about searching databases for sources, see p. 159. ▨

Search the Web using the search terms you used for your catalog and database searches. To start searching the Web, visit one of the leading search sites (see Figure 2.4), such as Ask (**ask.com**), Bing (**bing.com**), Google (**google.com**), or Yahoo! (**yahoo.com**). As you review your search results, remember that many Web-based sources will not have undergone the same review process applied to sources in library catalogs and databases.

Search social media to find tweets, Facebook posts, or blog posts about your topic. These items can lead to other relevant sources.

Brandon searched for *hydraulic fracturing*.

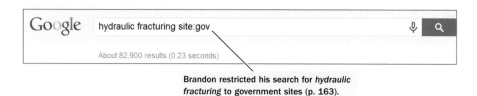

Brandon limited his search to full-text sources.

Brandon set a date range to locate only recent sources.

FIGURE 2.3 Brandon Tate's Initial Search in the Academic Search Premier Database

Google   hydraulic fracturing site:gov

About 82,900 results (0.23 seconds)

Brandon restricted his search for *hydraulic fracturing* to government sites (p. 163).

FIGURE 2.4 Brandon Tate's Initial Search on Google

Visit online discussion groups, such as e-mail lists, newsgroups, and Web discussion forums, to find everything from expert opinions to the musings of people who know little or nothing about a topic. If you read with a bit of skepticism, however, you can begin to learn about the issues surrounding a topic.

To learn more about finding sources, see Chapter 10.

My Research Project

Manage Sources in Your Research Log

A critical aspect of working with sources is deciding how to manage them so that you can easily locate information when you need it. You can choose from several options.

- Saving, downloading, or e-mailing sources

- Adding sources to cloud-based services such as DropBox, iCloud, or OneDrive

- Organizing your sources with Web-based tools, such as Google Drive or Delicious

- Printing sources and saving them in a notebook or folder

These and related strategies are discussed in Chapter 8.

My Research Project

Explore Your Topic

As you work through the strategies discussed in this chapter, keep track of your topic exploration by answering the following questions in your research log.

1. What is my topic?

2. Have I discussed my topic with others? If so, what have I learned? If not, who are likely candidates for interviews—such as librarians, instructors, and people involved with or affected by my topic—and what questions should I ask them?

3. Are there any preliminary observations I should conduct? Have I done so? If so, what have I learned?

4. Have I identified types of sources that are appropriate for my project? What kind of sources are they?

5. Have I found and reviewed sources? Have I searched the library catalog and browsed the shelves? Have I searched databases and the Web? Have I skimmed, marked, annotated, and taken brief notes on the sources I've found? If so, what have I learned about my topic?

2b

How can I focus on an issue?

Once you've explored your topic, your most important goal is to focus on a specific issue. Issues are points of disagreement, uncertainty, concern, or curiosity that are being discussed by communities of readers and writers.

As she explored the general topic of protecting marine life, Lauren Mack read sources, viewed films and videos, talked with her professor and other specialists about her topic, and kept a running list of ideas and information that interested her. Lauren started to make connections among the wide range of information, ideas, and arguments she encountered, and she was ultimately able to focus on the single issue that interested her most: the problems facing coral reefs.

Moving from your topic to a single issue about that topic involves identifying conversations about issues in your topic, assessing your interest in the issues, and asking whether writing about this issue will allow you to achieve your purposes as a writer.

Step 1: Identify Conversations about Issues in Your Topic

Identifying conversations about issues in your topic is the first step in determining which issue is most appropriate for your research project. As you work through this process, look for patterns in the information, ideas, and arguments you encounter in your sources.

Find Central Concepts Repeated in Your Sources   When several sources refer to the same idea, you can assume that this information is central to the topic. For instance, as Alexis Alvarez looked at articles and websites about the impact of competitive athletics on adolescent girls, she found repeated references to self-esteem, confidence, and performance-enhancing drugs. Noticing this repetition enabled Alexis to identify some of the important conversations about her topic.

Find Broad Themes Discussed in Your Sources   Sources that discuss the same general theme are most likely involved in the same conversation. Featured writer Elizabeth Leontiev found that some of the sources she explored focused on the history of the U.S. war on drugs, some focused on its cost, others focused on its effectiveness, and still others focused on the impact of the war on drugs both in Central and South America. By noting these broad themes, Elizabeth was able to identify some of the key conversations taking place about her topic.

Find Disagreements among Your Sources   Some sources will explicitly indicate that they disagree with arguments, ideas, or information in other sources. For example, Brandon Tate found that some sources reported on the economic value of fracking, while others argued that fracking posed unacceptable risks to drinking water supplies and local air quality. Looking for such explicit statements of disagreement helped Brandon identify a group of sources that were engaged in conversation with one another.

Find Recurring Voices in Your Sources   As you read sources, you might find that some authors write frequently about your topic or that some authors are referred to frequently by other writers. These authors might have significant experience or expertise related to the topic, or they might represent particular perspectives on the topic. Stay alert for these recurring voices.

Step 2: Assess Your Interest in the Issues

Determine your personal interest in each issue by asking yourself what interests you most about each one. Identifying personal connections between your sources and your own interests will help you focus on an issue that will sustain your interest throughout the course of your research writing project.

Alexis Alvarez, for example, drew on her personal experiences and her knowledge of the experiences of friends and family as she considered issues related to the topic of women and competitive sports. She had been surprised to learn about the use of performance-enhancing drugs among young athletes. She found herself wondering whether any of her friends or her sister's teammates might know of athletes who had used steroids. As she thought more about the topic, she found herself returning to the issue of performance-enhancing drugs.

TUTORIAL

How can I identify conversations in my sources?

You can identify conversations taking place in your sources by looking for patterns. Creating a four-column table like the one below can help you sort things out. In this example, Elizabeth Leontiev notes that three of her sources talk about the effectiveness of the U.S. war on drugs. She used this conversation as the basis for her research on the impact of U.S. drug policy on South American coca farmers.

1 Record the source. Here, Elizabeth uses the authors' last names.

2 Record concepts that are repeated in your sources.

3 Record other broad themes that you've noticed in your sources.

4 Note points on which the sources disagree.

5 Note the sources that these sources are citing. (You might use them later.)

Source	Gordon	Forero	Logan
Repeated Concepts	"zero cocaine, not zero coca"	"zero cocaine, not zero coca"	
Broad Themes	Overall effectiveness of U.S. war on drugs	Overall effectiveness of U.S. war on drugs	U.S. interference in affairs of other countries
Disagreements	U.S. policy of coca extermination— argues it has failed	U.S. policy of coca extermination— focuses on political issues	U.S. policy of coca extermination— argues policy is likely to change
Key Voices	Forero, Chipana, Morales	Morales	Morales, Reinicke

Step 3: Choose an Issue [FRAMING MY ARGUMENT]

After you've assessed the issues you've found during your exploration of your topic, select the strongest candidate and the one that interests you most. Think, too, about the level of interest your readers might have in the issue and whether writing about it will help you achieve your purposes as a writer.

Evaluate each issue by asking yourself the following questions. As you do so, you can follow Alexis Alvarez's responses to the questions.

Will selecting this issue help me achieve my purposes as a writer? Review your purpose and examine how each of the issues you have identified will help you best accomplish it.	As she reviewed her assignment, Alexis considered three issues she had identified as she explored her topic: parent-child relationships, the impact of competitive sports on social development, and the use of performance-enhancing drugs (PEDs) by younger athletes. She found herself drawn to the use of PEDs because her strong reaction to it suggested she might want to investigate and make an argument about it.
Will my readers want or need to read about this issue? Ask yourself which issue your readers would be most interested in or would most need to know about.	Her instructor had asked her to consider either her classmates or members of her home community as the audience for her essay. In part because she was surprised by the early age at which some athletes began using PEDs, Alexis thought that many of her readers would be as well. Even if they didn't need to know about it, she thought, they'd probably be as interested and surprised as she was.
Is this issue appropriate for my project's context? Consider the social and disciplinary contexts in which you are writing. If you are writing for a science class, for example, ask whether the issue will meet the expectations of your instructor and other readers.	Alexis felt that the issue was both significant and relevant enough to meet the needs of her assignment. She felt that the sources she had read so far — some published in scholarly journals and others on the Centers for Disease Control website — would be appropriate for her course context.
Is this issue appropriate for the type of document I plan to write? Some issues that are well suited for editorials and opinion columns in your school newspaper, for example, might not be suitable for an academic or a professional paper.	Alexis's assignment required her to use a range of sources, including scholarly books and articles. As she explored her topic, she found newspaper articles, books, scholarly journal articles, and government websites that addressed the use of PEDs in competitive youth soccer. To confirm that she was on the right track, Alexis checked in with her instructor, who agreed that the issue would be appropriate for her assignment.

Is this issue compatible with my requirements and limitations? Determine whether you can address an issue reasonably, given your assignment due date.	Based on her initial explorations, Alexis felt that she could work within the length limitations of her assignment and meet the assignment due date. Alexis's early research also showed her that she could meet the requirement to use a range of sources, including scholarly books and articles.
What opportunities do I have if I choose this issue? Identify any special resources that might be available to you, such as access to a special collection in a library, experts on an issue, or individuals who have been affected by it.	Alexis decided that, in addition to the sources she had been able to find in her library and on the Web, she could gain a firsthand perspective on the issue by talking with her sister and friends who played competitive sports.

Table 2.1 shows the topics explored by the featured writers and the issues they addressed.

TABLE 2.1 THE PROGRESSION FROM TOPIC TO CONVERSATION

Featured Writer	Topic	Issue
Alexis Alvarez	Women and competitive sports	Steroid use among adolescent girls involved in competitive sports
Nicholas Brothers	Private military corporations	Use of private military corporations to support the U.S. war on terror
Elizabeth Leontiev	The war on drugs	Impact of U.S. war on drugs on South American coca farmers
Lauren Mack	Protecting marine life	The problems facing coral reefs
Cori Schmidtbauer	William Shakespeare's dramas	Portia's unconventional role in *The Merchant of Venice*
Brandon Tate	Hydraulic fracturing ("fracking")	Impact of fracking on the environment and the economy
Josh Woelfle	A cure for cancer	Promising new treatments for cancer

My Research Project

Choose an Issue within Your Topic

In your research log, complete the following activity to focus your topic on a single issue.

1. What are the three most important issues I have identified so far?

2. Of these issues, which one will best help me sustain my interest in this project?

3. Which one will best help me achieve my purposes as a writer?

4. Which one will best address my readers' needs, interests, knowledge, experiences, values, and beliefs?

5. Which one is best suited to my context (social, cultural, historical, disciplinary, physical)?

6. Which one is most appropriate for the type of document I plan to write?

7. Which one best fits the requirements of my assignment?

8. Which one has the fewest limitations?

9. Which one allows me to best take advantage of opportunities?

10. Based on these answers, the issue I want to choose is . . .

QUICK REFERENCE

Exploring and Focusing

✔ Get organized by creating a plan to explore your topic. (p. 28)

✔ Discuss your topic with people who know about or have been affected by it. (p. 29)

✔ Conduct preliminary observations. (p. 30)

✔ Identify useful types of sources. (p. 30)

✔ Begin finding and managing written sources. (p. 32)

✔ Identify conversations about issues related to your topic. (p. 35)

✔ Assess your interest in the issues. (p. 36)

✔ Choose an issue. (p. 38)

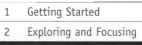

3

Developing Your Research Question

> **Key Question**
>
> **3a. How can I develop my research question?** 41
> Reflect on your issue and disciplinary context
> Focus on your role
> Focus on an aspect of your issue
> Choose and focus your research question
> Refine your research question

Your research question provides the foundation for developing your position—the main point you will make about your issue. It also guides your efforts to develop a research proposal, plan your search for information, and collect information.

3a

How can I develop my research question?

A research question directs your efforts to collect, critically read, evaluate, and take notes on your sources. Most research questions are narrowly focused, allowing writers to collect information in time to meet deadlines. Research questions are also subject to revision as writers learn more about an issue. It's best, at this early stage in your project, to think of your research question as a flexible guide.

Developing your research question involves reflecting on your issue and disciplinary context, focusing on your role, focusing on an aspect of your issue, and refining your question.

Step 1: Reflect on Your Issue and Disciplinary Context ❓ **WHAT'S MY PURPOSE?**

As you've explored your topic and focused on your issue, you've learned more about the conversation you've decided to join. The sources you've read have helped you gain an understanding of some of the most important information,

41

TABLE 3.1 DISCIPLINARY QUESTIONS

Discipline	Types of Questions	Examples
Humanities	Interpretive questions about literature, music, philosophy, rhetoric, and the arts	How did the acceptance of Manet's painting style open the door for Impressionism?
		What similarities does Toni Morrison's character Amy Denver in *Beloved* share with Twain's character Huck Finn?
Social Sciences	Questions about factors that affect human behavior, including "how" and "why" questions about various events	What is the significance of social networking sites such as Facebook and Twitter in protest movements?
		What factors contribute to a person becoming a mass murderer?
		Why did fascism ultimately fail in Italy in the 1940s?
Sciences	"How" and "why" questions about the natural world, including both the environment and living beings	How can we combat the obesity epidemic among school-age children?
		What are the preventable causes of climate change?

ideas, and arguments shaping the conversation. You might also have had the opportunity to talk with others about your issue and perhaps even to conduct observations. If you're like most research writers, your initial thoughts about your topic and issue have changed as you've carried out your investigations.

As you begin generating ideas for a research question, ask whether what you've learned about the issue has changed your understanding of your writing situation. Then ask yourself what you'd like to learn next. As you ask these questions, consider how disciplinary or professional contexts might shape the questions you can ask. If you are writing a research report for a biology class, for example, your understanding of the kinds of questions biologists typically ask about issues will come into play. That's true for virtually every discipline and profession, each of which has areas that are of interest to its members and each of which has particular ways of asking questions about those areas of interest (see Table 3.1).

Similarly, your understanding of the kinds of genres typically used to communicate within the discipline or profession—such as articles, presentations, and essays—will shape your work on your research question. Some genres, such as books and longer reports, are well suited to broader questions. Others, because of their comparative brevity (think of poster sessions, conference presentations, reports, and essays), are better suited to highly focused research questions.

Step 2: Focus on Your Role   [FRAMING MY ARGUMENT]

Your role as a writer—the manner in which you'll relate to your readers—will have a profound impact on your decisions about your research question. Writers who inform their readers, for example, develop strikingly different questions than those who seek to persuade them to take action. Had featured writer Brandon Tate decided to inform his readers about the impact of hydraulic fracturing on air and water quality, for example, he might have pursued questions such as the following.

> What are the effects of fracking on local air and water quality?
>
> What have recent scientific research studies indicated about the impact of fracking on air and water quality?

In contrast, had Brandon adopted the role of advocate, his research questions might have resembled the following.

> In light of recent findings about the impact of fracking on air and water quality, should Coloradoans enact legislation to ban fracking?
>
> Given scientific evidence that fracking has a negative effect on air and water quality, should the government establish regulations that might reduce or eliminate those effects?

The roles writers can adopt vary widely (p. 8). Table 3.2 provides a list of some of the most important roles you might adopt and offers examples of the kinds of questions writers adopting a particular role might ask (p. 44). These questions serve as sentence starters you can use to generate potential research questions (p. 24).

Step 3: Focus on an Aspect of Your Issue

You can begin to generate potential research questions by using freewriting (p. 21), looping (p. 22), the sentence starters found on p. 24 or in Table 3.2 (p. 44), and the question matrix found in the My Research Project activity on p. 48. As you generate potential questions, consider both your role and general areas of focus within the issue you've decided to address. The following areas often lead to useful lines of inquiry.

- **Information** What is known — and not known — about an issue?
- **History** What has occurred in the past that is relevant to an issue?
- **Assumptions** What conclusions — merited or not — have writers and readers already made about an issue?
- **Goals** What do the writers and readers involved in conversation about this issue want to happen (or not happen)?
- **Outcomes** What has happened so far? What is likely to happen?
- **Policies** What are the best procedures for carrying out actions? For making decisions?

With your issue and role in mind, you can generate questions using one or more of these areas as a starting point. In addition, you can narrow the focus of your questions by exploring the intersections between these areas and specific thinking processes, such as examining trends, similarities and differences, and cause/effect relationships.

TABLE 3.2 THE RELATIONSHIP AMONG ROLES AND RESEARCH QUESTIONS

Purpose	Role	General Questions
To Inform	Reporter	What is known—and not known—about _____?
		How might we define _____?
To Create and Share New Knowledge	Inquirer	What causes _____?
		What are the effects of _____?
		What can [cure / repair / prevent] _____?
To Reflect	Observer	What are the implications of _____?
		How can we learn from the example of an individual or a group?
		What can we gain from thinking about an idea, a work of art, a work of literature, or a performance?
To Evaluate	Evaluator	What conclusions—merited or not—have writers and readers already made about _____?
		What assumptions are shaping current thinking about _____?
		What are the best choices available for addressing _____?
		What are the relative strengths and weaknesses of _____?
To Analyze	Interpreter	What has occurred in the past that is relevant to _____?
		What causes _____?
		What are the effects of _____?
		Does the data suggest that _____ [is / is the result of] a trend?
		What is likely to happen [to / as a result of] _____?
		In what ways is _____ similar to _____?
		In what ways does _____ differ from _____?
To Solve Problems	Problem Solver	Why is _____ a problem?
		What is the best solution to _____?
		Why should we adopt _____ as a solution to _____?
To Convince (Change Readers' Beliefs or Attitudes), **Persuade** (Cause Readers to Take Action), **or Mediate** (Seek to Establish Common Ground among Readers)	Advocate	What are the origins of this argument?
		What is the status of this argument?
		Who has made the best arguments about _____?
		What do the writers and readers involved in conversation about _____ want to [see happen / not happen]?
		What should be done about _____?
		How should _____ be accomplished?
		How can we find common ground about _____?

	Definition (Describe specific aspects of the issue.)	Causes and Effects (Ask what leads to a specific result.)	Trends (Ask about sequences of events.)	Relationships (Examine connections between aspects of an issue.)	Similarities and Differences (Compare and contrast.)	Strengths and Weaknesses (Assess relative merits.)
Information: What is known—and not known—about an issue?						
History: What has occurred in the past that is relevant to an issue?						
Assumptions: What conclusions—merited or not—have writers and readers already made about an issue?						
Goals: What should happen (or not happen)?						
Outcomes: What has happened so far? What is likely to happen?						
Policies: What are the best procedures for carrying out actions? For making decisions?						

Step 4: Choose and Focus Your Research Question

Review your potential research questions and select a question that interests you and is appropriate for your research writing situation. You should be confident that you will be able to respond to the question in a substantive and useful way. You should also be confident that your response will be neither too simplistic nor too ambitious to address in an essay. Questions that can be answered with an unelaborated "yes" or "no" response, for example, are not generally pursued in a research writing project. It is also the case, however, that many initial research questions are far too broad to serve as the basis for a focused research project.

In general, a research question that is too broad will lead to answers requiring far more space to answer than most writing assignments allow, while a question that is too narrow will lead to answers that are so specific that they will fail to interest most readers. In both cases, the document that emerges will usually lack depth and fail to make a useful contribution to the conversation.

Too Broad

How did real estate development on the East Coast of the United States affect the environment during the twentieth century?

Too Narrow

In what ways has source-point pollution of the Minnesota River affected the profit margins of women-owned metal fabrication companies in the Mankato area?

Balanced Focus

How can we best address drinking-water problems caused by the dumping of polluted lake water into Florida rivers and estuaries?

Consider how specific question words can help you create a focused research question. If you are interested in conducting an analysis, for example, you might use the words *what, why, when, where, who,* and *how.* If you are interested in informing readers about the goals or outcomes associated with a particular issue, you might use the words *would* or *could.* If the conversation focuses on determining an appropriate course of action, as might be the case if you were adopting the role of an advocate, generate questions using the word *should.* Take a look at the differences in the following questions.

- **What** are the benefits of hydraulic fracturing?

- **Would** it be feasible to require oil and gas producers to reduce or eliminate the use of chemicals during hydraulic fracturing?

- **Should** the federal government pursue legislation to reduce the environmental and health impacts of hydraulic fracturing?

Each question would lead to differences in how to search for sources of information, which sources to use in a project document, what role to adopt as a writer, and how to organize and draft the document.

TUTORIAL

How do I generate research questions consistent with my role?

Each role listed in Table 3.2 is associated with sentence starters you can use to generate potential research questions. Once you've identified your purpose and chosen the role you'll adopt as you work with your readers, you can use these sentence starters to generate potential research questions.

Adopting the role of interpreter, for example, featured writer Lauren Mack might have generated the following research questions about her issue, the problems facing coral reefs.

Interpreter	**What has occurred in the past that is relevant to ____?** • the potential extinction of many forms of coral? • efforts by state and local governments to preserve coral reefs? **What causes ____?** • individuals to act in ways that contribute to the demise of coral reefs? • nonprofit organizations to work to preserve coral reefs? • government agencies to adopt regulations that might lead to the demise of coral reefs? **What are the effects of ____?** • damaging or destroying coral reefs? • commercial activity on coral reefs? • overfishing on coral reefs? **Does the data suggest that ____ [is / is the result of] a trend?** • the die-off of coral reefs? • individual action to preserve coral reefs? **What is likely to happen [to / as a result of] ____?** • the communities that rely on coral reefs for commercial benefits? • aquatic species that rely on the ecosystem provided by coral reefs? **In what ways is ____ similar to ____?** • damage to coral reefs similar to the systematic killing of the plains bison in the 1800s? **In what ways does ____ differ from ____?** • the commercial exploitation of coral reefs differ from past exploitation of old-growth forests?

WORKING TOGETHER

Craft Focused Research Questions

Working with a small group of writers, use question words to focus potential research questions. To prepare for the activity, review your list of potential research questions and identify two or three that interest you most. Then carry out the following activities.

1 Taking turns with other members of the group, **share a research question** and ask the other members of the group to brainstorm variations on the question that use the question words *who, what, where, when, how, why, would, could,* and *should.* Take notes on the variations.

2 After you have each shared your best research questions, **review your notes.** Highlight the variations on the questions that will help you best accomplish your purpose and address the needs and interests of your readers.

3 Taking turns, **share your conclusions** with the group. Ask for reactions and additional suggestions. Take notes.

4 After the activity, **review your notes** and determine whether you should revise your research question.

Step 5: Refine Your Research Question

Choose the research question that emerged from the research project activity "Craft Focused Research Questions." Refine your question by referring to shared assumptions and existing conditions, narrowing its scope, and conducting preliminary searches.

Refer to Shared Assumptions and Existing Conditions   You can refine your research question by using qualifying words and phrases to narrow its scope, by calling attention to assumptions that have been made by the community of

My Research Project

Generate a Matrix of Research Questions

Use the table on p. 45 to generate potential research questions. You need not complete every cell in the table and you can create more than one question in each cell. To complete the activity, choose a column, such as "Information," and then generate questions to focus on—for example, defining what is known about the issue, tracing causes and effects, charting trends, and so on.

To generate questions, use freewriting or the sentence starters found on pp. 24–25.

writers and readers who are addressing your issue, or by referring to existing conditions relevant to your issue. Note the difference between the following three versions of featured writer Alexis Alvarez's research question.

Original Question

What should be done about steroid use by adolescent girls involved in competitive sports?

Alternative 1

Even though we know that widespread drug testing of all athletes, younger and older, is impossible, what should be done about steroid use by adolescent girls involved in competitive sports?

Alternative 2

Given the lack of knowledge among athletes and their parents about the health consequences of steroid use, what should be done about steroid use by adolescent girls involved in competitive sports?

As you refine your research question, you might use conditional words and phrases such as the following.

Mix . . .	and Match
Although	we know that . . .
Because	it is uncertain . . .
Even though	it is clear that . . .
Given that	studies indicate . . .
In light of	recent events . . .
Now that	it has been shown . . .
Since	the lack of . . .
While	we cannot . . .

Narrow the Scope of Your Research Question   Early drafts of research questions typically suffer from lack of focus. You can narrow the scope of your question by looking for vague words and phrases and replacing them with more specific words or phrases. The process of moving from a broad research question to one that might be addressed effectively in a research essay might produce the following sequence.

Original Research Question

What is behind the increased popularity of women's sports?

Refined

What has led to the increased popularity of women's sports in colleges and universities?

Further Refined

How has Title IX increased opportunities for women athletes in American colleges and universities?

TUTORIAL

How do I refine my research question?

The first draft of your research question might be too broad, which can make it difficult for you to focus your research efforts. Refine your initial research question so that you can collect information efficiently.

In this example, Brandon Tate refines his research question about the impact of hydraulic fracturing on local air and water quality. He used his research question as he collected and worked with sources, and later, he developed his thesis statement to answer his question.

Preliminary Research Question
What should we do about hydraulic fracturing?

1 Refer to shared assumptions and existing conditions by using phrases such as *although it is clear that . . .* , *because we cannot . . .* , and *given that studies have shown. . . .*

Given the national commitment to reducing our reliance on foreign oil, what should we do about hydraulic fracturing?

2 Identify vague words and phrases, such as *what should we do about*, and replace them with more specific language.

Given the national commitment to reducing our reliance on foreign oil, what steps can U.S. citizens take to ensure that environmental concerns play an important role in the regulation of hydraulic fracturing?

3 Using these specific terms, conduct preliminary searches in your library catalog, in databases, and on the Web. If you get too many results, narrow your focus even further. (Here, Brandon narrows his target audience from U.S. citizens to Colorado citizens and focuses on passing a statewide referendum.)

Given the national commitment to reducing our reliance on foreign oil, what steps can Colorado citizens take to pass a statewide referendum regulating hydraulic fracturing?

In this example, the writer has narrowed the scope of the research question in two ways. First, the writer has shifted its focus from women's sports in general to women's sports in American colleges and universities. Second, the writer has moved from a general focus on increased popularity of women's sports to a more specific focus on opportunities brought about by Title IX, federal legislation that mandated equal opportunities for women athletes. Table 3.3 shows the featured writers' progress from a general topic to a focused issue to a refined research question.

Conduct Preliminary Searches One of the best ways to test your research question is to conduct some preliminary searches in a library catalog or database or on the Web. If you locate a vast amount of information in your searches, you might need to revise your question so that it focuses on a more manageable aspect of the issue. In contrast, if you find almost nothing in your search, you might need to expand the scope of your research question.

TABLE 3.3 THE FEATURED WRITERS' RESEARCH QUESTIONS

Featured Writer	Topic	Issue	Initial Research Question	Final Research Question
Alexis Alvarez	Women and competitive sports	Steroid use among adolescent girls involved in competitive sports	What are the effects of competitive sports on adolescent girls?	What should be done about steroid use by adolescent girls involved in competitive sports?
Nicholas Brothers	Private military corporations	Use of private military corporations to support the U.S. war on terror	How important have private military corporations become for the U.S. military?	What roles do private military corporations play in the U.S. war on terror?
Elizabeth Leontiev	The war on drugs	Impact of U.S. war on drugs on South American coca farmers	What are the effects of the U.S. war on drugs on South America?	How can we reduce the economic impact of the war on drugs on South American coca farmers?
Lauren Mack	Protecting marine life	The problems facing coral reefs	What are the threats to coral reefs?	Why are coral reefs important, and what can be done to protect them from destruction?

(continued)

TABLE 3.3 *CONTINUED*

Featured Writer	Topic	Issue	Initial Research Question	Final Research Question
Cori Schmidtbauer	William Shakespeare's dramas	Portia's unconventional role in *The Merchant of Venice*	How are women portrayed in Shakespeare's plays?	How does Portia's character in *The Merchant of Venice* fit the ideal of an Elizabethan woman?
Brandon Tate	Hydraulic fracturing	Impact of fracking on local air and water quality	What do readers need to know to form an educated opinion about hydraulic fracturing?	What do individuals need to know to develop an informed opinion about the controversial issue of hydraulic fracturing?
Josh Woelfle	A cure for cancer	Promising new treatments for cancer	What new treatment options are available for cancer patients?	What makes new cancer treatments potentially superior to traditional treatments such as chemotherapy and radiation?

> **QUICK REFERENCE**

Developing Your Research Question

✔ Reflect on your issue and disciplinary or professional context. (p. 41)

✔ Consider how your role will shape your research question. (p. 42)

✔ Focus on specific aspects of your issue. (p. 43)

✔ Choose and focus your research question. (p. 46)

✔ Refine your research question. (p. 48)

PART II

Working with Sources

As you work with sources, you'll read critically, evaluate sources, take notes, work with information and ideas, manage the sources you collect, and guard against unintentional plagiarism. The next six chapters lead you through the process of engaging with the information, ideas, and arguments you will encounter as you work on your research writing project.

4

Reading Critically and Actively

> **Key Questions**
>
> **4a. How can I read sources critically?** 56
> Read with an attitude
> Distinguish between critical reading and evaluating
> Approach a source with your writing situation in mind
> Read promising sources more than once
> Develop a position on your research question
>
> **4b. What strategies can I use to read actively?** 61
> Skim for organization and content
> Mark and annotate sources
> Take notes
>
> **4c. What should I pay attention to as I read?** 66
> Identify the genre
> Note illustrations
> Identify primary and secondary sources
> Identify main points
> Identify reasons and evidence
> Identify interpretive frameworks
> Identify new and hard-to-understand information
> Identify similarities and differences

As you've explored your topic, you've almost certainly read—or, more likely, skimmed—several sources. As you focus your attention on a particular issue, you'll begin to read more carefully, both to learn more about the issue and to understand how you might position your contribution to the issue in light of what others have written. In this chapter, you'll learn how to read sources critically and actively.

4a

How can I read sources critically?

Reading critically means reading with an attitude. It also means reading with your writing situation and research question in mind. Unlike evaluation, which focuses on the suitability of a source for your argument, critical reading is a flexible process that will differ at various points in your research writing process. Through critical reading, you can quickly recognize the questions—points of disagreement, uncertainty, concern, or curiosity—that are under discussion in a written conversation as well as think about how you'll respond to one of these questions.

Read with an Attitude

Reading critically means reading with an attitude. Your attitude will change during your research writing process. As you begin to read your sources critically, your attitude might be one of curiosity. You'll note new information and mark key passages that provide you with insights into the conversation you're joining. You'll adopt a more questioning attitude as you try to determine whether sources fit in your project or are reliable. Later, after you begin to draw conclusions about the conversation, you might take on a more skeptical attitude, becoming more aggressive in challenging arguments made in sources than you were at first.

Regardless of where you are in your research writing process, you should always adopt a critical attitude. Accept nothing at face value; ask questions; look for similarities and differences among the sources you read; examine the implications of what you read for your research project; be on the alert for unusual information; and note relevant sources and information. Most important, be open to ideas and arguments, even if you don't agree with them. Give them a chance to affect how you think about the conversation you've decided to join.

Distinguish between Critical Reading and Evaluating

At first glance, reading critically might seem to be the same as evaluating, which is discussed in detail in the next chapter. Although the two processes are related, they're not identical. Critically reading a source—questioning what it says and thinking about what it means—focuses your attention on making sense of the source. In contrast, evaluation focuses your attention on determining how reliably a source presents its information and how well it meets your needs as a research writer.

Approach a Source with Your Writing Situation in Mind ❓ **WHAT'S MY PURPOSE?**

One way to get into the habit of reading critically is to approach a source with your writing situation in mind (see Table 4.1). As you read, remember that you

TABLE 4.1 READ A SOURCE WITH YOUR WRITING SITUATION IN MIND

Reflect on . . .	By asking . . .
Your Research Question and Position Statement	Are the information, ideas, and arguments in this source relevant to my research question and position statement?
	Does this source present information, ideas, and arguments that make me reconsider my research question or position statement?
	Does it provide any information, ideas, or arguments?
	Does it offer a new perspective on the issue?
Your Purpose and Role	Will the information in the source help me accomplish my purpose? Can I use the information in this source as support for points I want to make? Can I use it to illustrate ideas that differ from mine?
	Is the information in this source more useful for my purpose than what I've found in other sources?
	Does the source provide a good model of a convincing argument or an effective presentation of information? Can I learn anything from the presentation of the points and evidence in this source?
Your Readers	Would my readers want to know about the information, ideas, and arguments found in this source?
	Would my readers find the source's information convincing or compelling?
	Would my readers benefit from a review of the argument and evidence presented in this source?
	How will my readers react to the argument and evidence presented in this source?
Genre	What type of evidence is usually provided in this type of document?
	How are documents of this type typically organized? Can I find examples of effective organizational strategies in the sources I read?
Design	Does this source provide a useful model for designing my document?
	Will I be expected to provide charts, graphics, photographs, or other types of illustrations? If so, can I learn anything from how illustrations are used in the source?
	Does this source help me understand how I might address the context in which my document will be read?
Requirements and Limitations	If I find useful information in a source, will I be able to follow up on it with additional research? Will I have enough time to follow up on that information?
	How much information can I include in my document? Will my readers be looking for an overview or a detailed report?

II Working with Sources

are working on your research writing project to make a contribution, to shape your readers' thinking about your issue. Don't hesitate to question the authors who have written before you. You should respect their work, but you shouldn't assume that their conclusions are the last word. Be prepared to challenge their ideas and arguments. If you don't do this, you'll simply repeat the ideas of others instead of advancing your own.

Read Promising Sources More Than Once

As you work through your sources, you'll find that some are worth reading more carefully than others. When a source offers what appears to be good information, ideas, or arguments, spend additional time marking and annotating relevant passages in the text and taking notes. Identify passages that are either particularly promising or difficult to understand and return to them later in your project.

Develop a Position on Your Research Question   [FRAMING MY ARGUMENT]

Your research question focuses your attention on your issue and directs you to specific sources as you collect information. Your research question also provides the basis for developing a position on your issue, which you can also use to guide your critical reading.

The position you develop on your issue serves as an answer to your research question. At this point in your research writing process, your position is likely to be tentative and incomplete. As you learn more about your issue by reading critically, you'll develop and refine your position. You might even change your position entirely. Eventually, your position will serve as a foundation for your thesis statement—a formal statement of the main point you want to make about your issue. Figure 4.1 shows the progression from research question to position statement to thesis statement in the context of the research writing process.

As a response to your research question, your position can help you decide whether you agree or disagree with an author—and, thus, whether you want to align yourself with his or her position on the issue. It will also help you judge whether the evidence provided in a source might be of use to you as you develop your argument—either to support your own argument or to illustrate an alternative approach to the issue.

To develop a statement about your position on your issue, brainstorm or freewrite in response to your research question. After reviewing your response, draft a brief statement of your position and use this to guide your critical reading.

II Working with Sources

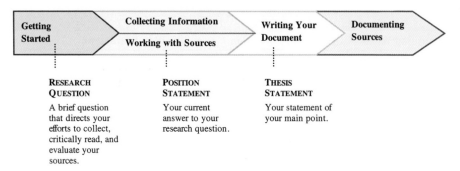

FIGURE 4.1 Moving from a Research Question to a Position Statement
to a Thesis Statement

Featured Writer Alexis Alvarez's Research Question

What should be done about steroid use by adolescent girls involved in competitive sports?

Alexis Alvarez's Response to Her Research Question

The typical response to steroid use in sports, such as the Olympics or professional football, seems to be some sort of punishment—losing a medal or being banned from competition for a period of time. But will this work with kids—especially kids who don't seem to have the same level of maturity as older athletes? And what about parents who encourage kids—and most likely provide the funds—to use steroids to get ahead (parents with college scholarship dollars in their eyes, no doubt)? So ... maybe punishment isn't the answer—or at least it's only part of the answer. It seems from my reading so far that most kids don't understand the negative consequences of using steroids. They only see the potential benefits (making a team, performing at a higher level, getting famous, getting a scholarship, etc.). And parents might not understand those consequences as well. And then some coaches might even get into the act, "helping" kids compete at a higher level, and getting the wins they "need." If kids don't understand the consequences, then education might be useful. And most kids don't like to cheat, so maybe part of the answer is putting more of an emphasis on fair play. And you need to get parents and coaches into some sort of solution too.

Alexis Alvarez's Initial Position Statement

Steroid use by adolescent girls involved in competitive sports might be addressed by educating athletes, parents, and coaches about health consequences and emphasizing fair play.

This position statement is too vague to use as a thesis statement, but it would serve as an effective guide for reading sources critically. If Alexis had read a source that argued for a solution to the problem of steroid use by young athletes, for example, her position statement would provide a basis for asking

TABLE 4.2 THE FEATURED WRITERS' POSITION STATEMENTS

Featured Writer	Research Question	Position Statement
Alexis Alvarez	What should be done about steroid use by adolescent girls involved in competitive sports?	Steroid use by adolescent girls involved in competitive sports should be addressed by educating athletes, parents, and coaches about health consequences and emphasizing fair play.
Nicholas Brothers	What dangers are associated with U.S. reliance on private military corporations in its war on terror?	The overreliance of the United States on private military corporations is a danger to national and international security.
Elizabeth Leontiev	How can we reduce the economic impact of the war on drugs on South American coca farmers?	The U.S. and South American governments should adopt the "zero cocaine, not zero coca" policy.
Lauren Mack	Why are coral reefs important, and what can be done to protect them from destruction?	Preserving the many benefits of coral reefs—which range from recreational uses, sea life habitats, and potential medical benefits from the species who live in and around them—can be accomplished by working to stop climate change.
Cori Schmidtbauer	How does Portia's character in *The Merchant of Venice* fit in with Elizabethan ideas of women?	Portia appears to rebel against the expectations of Elizabethan culture.
Brandon Tate	What do individuals need to know to develop informed opinions about the controversial issue of hydraulic fracturing?	Voters should understand the impact of hydraulic fracturing on the environment, the oil and gas industry, and the economy.
Josh Woelfle	What makes new cancer treatments potentially superior to traditional treatments such as chemotherapy and radiation?	In combination with efforts to address multidrug-resistant strains of cancer, enzyme inhibitor-based drugs can combat the disease with far fewer and far less serious side effects.

whether the solution is consistent with those offered in other sources or whether it is based on a different set of assumptions.

Table 4.2 presents the movement from research question to position statement in the featured writers' projects. Note how each position statement attempts to answer the writer's research question. This marks a significant step for the

My Research Project

Draft a Position Statement

In your research log, complete the following activity to draft your position statement.

1. Write your current research question.
2. Brainstorm or freewrite in response to your research question.
3. Select the response that best reflects your current understanding of the conversation you have decided to join. If appropriate, combine responses into one position statement.
4. Write your position statement.

featured writers in their research writing projects: a shift from learning about the conversations they had decided to join to starting to develop their contributions to those conversations.

4b

What strategies can I use to read actively?

Once you have thought about your writing situation, drafted your position statement, and decided what to focus on, you're ready to start reading actively. Reading actively means interacting with sources and considering them in light of the conversation you've decided to join. When you read actively, you might do one or more of the following.

- Identify key information, ideas, and arguments by skimming and marking.
- Write questions in the margins.
- Jot down reactions to information, ideas, and arguments.
- Record quotations, paraphrases, and summaries in the form of notes.
- Take notes about how you might use information, ideas, and arguments in your project document.
- Link one part of the source to another visually.
- Identify important passages for later rereading.

As you read sources, use three active-reading strategies: skimming, marking and annotating, and taking notes.

Skim for Organization and Content

Before investing too much time in a source, skim it. Skimming—reading just enough to get a general idea of what a source is about—helps you understand how a source is organized, which can help you more quickly assess its usefulness and relevance. If the source uses a familiar organizational pattern, you'll find it easier to locate key information.

To skim most genres (print and digital), use the strategies shown in Figure 4.2. If you are skimming a longer document, such as a book or report, consider these additional strategies.

- **Check the table of contents,** if one is provided. It will give you a useful overview of the document's content and organization.

- **Check the index,** if one is provided, to learn more about the content of the document.

- **Check the glossary,** if one is provided. The terms that are defined can provide clues about the focus of the document.

Check the title for clues about content.

Skim opening paragraphs for the purpose and scope of the document.

Check headings and subheadings to learn more about the content and organization.

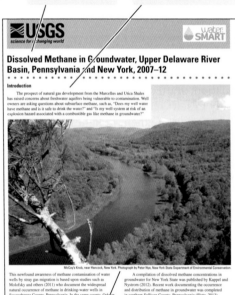

Skim captions of photos and figures, which often highlight important information, ideas, and arguments.

Read the first and last sentences of paragraphs to find key information.

FIGURE 4.2 Skimming a Document [USGS.]

Scan for boldface, colored, or italic text. Important information is often highlighted in some way on the page.

Check the URL to learn about the purpose of a Web page. Look for cues such as .edu for education, .gov for government, and .com for commercial and business sites.

Check the page title in the tab or title bar of the browser for the purpose and content of the page.

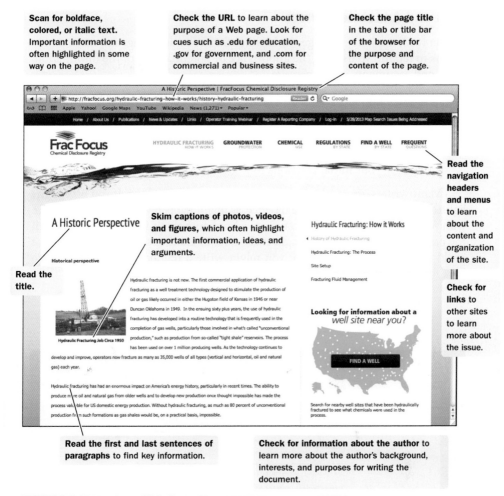

Read the navigation headers and menus to learn about the content and organization of the site.

Check for links to other sites to learn more about the issue.

II Working with Sources

Read the title.

Skim captions of photos, videos, and figures, which often highlight important information, ideas, and arguments.

Read the first and last sentences of paragraphs to find key information.

Check for information about the author to learn more about the author's background, interests, and purposes for writing the document.

FIGURE 4.3 Skimming a Web Page [Copyright GWPC & IOGCC, 2016.]

- Check the works cited list, if one is provided, to learn about the types of evidence used in the document.

- Check for pull quotes (quotations or brief passages pulled out of the text and set in larger type elsewhere on the page), which often call attention to important information, ideas, and arguments in a document.

- Check for information about the author to learn about the writer's background, interests, and purposes for writing the document.

Mark and Annotate Sources

As you read, mark key passages by highlighting or underlining, and make annotations to remind yourself of the importance or potential uses of the information, ideas, and arguments in the passage.

- **Mark important passages with highlighting or underlining** so that you'll be able to locate key passages easily later in your writing process. You can also attach notes or flags to printed pages.

- **Annotate passages** by briefly recording, in the margins or in digital comments, your initial reactions to a source.

Many writers use annotations in combination with marking. If you have highlighted a passage with which you disagree, as might happen when you read a source with your position in mind, you can write a brief note about why you disagree with the passage (annotating). You might make note of another source you've read that could support your argument, or you might write a reminder about the need to look for information that will help you argue against the passage.

FIGURE 4.4 Marking and Annotating Sources with Your Argument in Mind

Take Notes

Notes provide a compact, easy-to-review record of the most important information, ideas, and arguments you've found in your sources. Notes can help you keep track of your ideas about significant patterns you've seen in your sources, such as similarities and differences, repeated ideas and arguments, and frequently cited information. Notes can also help you keep track of your thoughts about planning your document. Equally important, careful note taking helps you avoid plagiarism. For these reasons, note taking is one of the most important research writing skills you can draw on as you work on your research writing project.

Notes can include direct quotations, paraphrases, and summaries, as well as your thoughts about your sources as a group and your plans for your document. You can read more about taking notes in Chapter 6. You can read about avoiding plagiarism in Chapter 9.

Working with Sources

Page number ——— Source information

Source: Singer, P. W. *Corporate Warriors: The Rise of the Privatized Military Industry*. Cornell UP, 2008.

Page 157:

The U.S. Defense Science Board estimated that the Department of —— Defense would save over $6 billion by privatizing and outsourcing in the early 1990s, but these savings have not been demonstrated. One report (RAND) claimed there were no cost savings at all; another (GAO) stated that the estimate was inflated by a minimum of $4.5 billion.

Paraphrase, written in student's own words

"The recurring pattern is that the military has set a policy of becoming—— more businesslike. It has not, however, fully examined whether doing so saves money or improves operations."

Direct quotation from the source clearly marked with quotation marks

FIGURE 4.5 Notes on a Source

CHECKLIST FOR ACTIVE READING

To read actively, follow these guidelines.

✔ Skim sources to identify key information, ideas, and arguments.

✔ Highlight, underline, add arrows, or draw circles around important passages.

✔ Write questions, jot down reactions, and add reminders in the margins or in digital comments.

✔ Take notes.

4c

What should I pay attention to as I read?

Different research writing projects will require you to pay attention to different things as you read. In general, however, you should pay attention to the following:

- the type of source — or genre — you are reading
- illustrations
- whether the source is a primary or secondary source
- the author's main point
- reasons and evidence offered to support the main point
- any analytical or interpretive approaches used by the author
- new information (information you haven't read before)
- ideas and information that you find difficult to understand
- ideas and information that are similar to or different from those you have found in other sources

Noting these aspects of a source during your active reading will help you better understand the source, its role in the conversation you've decided to join, and how you might use it in your document.

Identify the Genre

One of the most important things to pay attention to as you read is the type of source — or genre — you are reading. If a source is an opinion column rather than an objective summary of an argument, for example, you'll be less likely to be taken in by a questionable use of logic or analysis. If an article comes from a peer-reviewed scholarly journal, you'll be sure that it's been judged by experts in the field as well founded and worthy of publication.

Recognizing the type of source you are reading will help you create a context for understanding and questioning the information, ideas, and arguments presented in the source.

Note Illustrations

Illustrations — such as photographs and other images, charts, graphs, tables, animations, audio clips, and video clips — are typically used to demonstrate or emphasize a point, help readers better understand a point, clarify or simplify the presentation of a complex concept, or increase the visual appeal of a document. Illustrations can also serve as a form of argument by presenting a surprising or

TUTORIAL

How can I read actively?

Marking and annotating allow you to identify key information, ideas, and arguments; record your reactions to a source; question the source; connect the source to other sources; and note how you might use information, ideas, and arguments.

In this example, featured writer Josh Woelfle marks and annotates a fact sheet from the National Cancer Institute's website. Later, he will use information from the fact sheet to shape his argument about the advantages of promising alternative treatments for cancer.

1 Identify key information, ideas, and arguments.

2 Write questions in the margins.

3 Record your reactions to information, ideas, and arguments in the margins.

4 Note how you might use information, ideas, and arguments in your project document.

5 Link parts of the text visually.

6 Identify important passages for later rereading.

[National Cancer Institute]

even shocking set of statistics or setting an emotional tone. As you read, be aware of the types of illustrations and the effects they produce. The types of illustrations you are likely to encounter include the following.

- **Photographs and images,** such as drawings, paintings, and sketches, are frequently used to set a mood, emphasize a point, or demonstrate a point more fully than is possible with text alone.

- **Charts and graphs** provide a visual representation of information. They are typically used to present numerical information more succinctly than is possible with text alone or to present complex information in a compact and more accessible form.

- **Tables** provide categorical lists of information. Like charts and graphs, they are typically used to make a point succinctly. Tables are frequently used to illustrate contrasts among groups, relationships among variables (such as income, educational attainment, and voting preferences), or change over time (such as growth in population during the past century).

- **Digital illustrations** are found in sources such as PowerPoint presentations, Web pages, and word processing documents. Illustrations such as audio, videos, and animations differ from photographs and other images, charts, graphs, and tables in that they don't just appear on the page — they do things.

You can read more about the uses of illustrations in Chapter 16.

Identify Primary and Secondary Sources

Primary sources are either original works or evidence provided directly by an observer of an event. Primary sources include:

- poems, short stories, novels, musical recordings, paintings, and other works of art or literature
- diaries, journals, memoirs, and autobiographies
- interviews, speeches, government and business records, and letters
- drawings, photographs, films, or video and audio recordings of an event
- physical artifacts, such as a weapon used in a crime

Secondary sources comment on or interpret an event, often using primary sources as evidence (see Table 4.3).

As a research writer, your goal is to develop your own ideas about an issue so that you can create an original, well-supported contribution to the conversation you've decided to join. If you rely entirely or mostly on secondary sources, you'll be viewing the issue through the eyes of other researchers. Be sure to ask

TABLE 4.3 EXAMPLES OF PRIMARY AND SECONDARY SOURCES

Primary Sources	Secondary Sources
A play by William Shakespeare	An article that presents an analysis of the play
A transcript of the statement made by President George W. Bush on September 11, 2001	A recording of an interview in which a historian discusses the significance of the statement
A report of a laboratory study concerning the benefits of strength training for women with osteoporosis	A website that presents a review of recent research about prevention and treatment of osteoporosis

yourself, when you read a secondary source, what factors might have affected the author's argument, presentation, or analysis.

Identify Main Points

Most sources, whether they are informative or argumentative, make a main point that you should pay attention to as you read critically. For example:

- an editorial in a local newspaper urges voters to approve financing of a new school
- an article reports a new advance in automobile emissions testing
- a Web page provides information about the benefits of a new technique for treating a sports injury

Usually, but not always, the main point will be expressed in the form of a thesis statement (p. 193). As you read critically, make sure you understand what the author of the source wants readers to know, accept, believe, or do as a result of reading the document.

Identify Reasons and Evidence

Once you've identified the main point, look for the reasons given to accept it. If an author is arguing, for instance, that English should be the only language used for official government business in the United States, that author might support his or her argument with the following reasons.

The use of multiple languages erodes patriotism.

The use of multiple languages keeps people apart—if they can't talk to one another, they won't learn to respect one another.

The use of multiple languages in government business costs taxpayers money because so many alternative forms need to be created.

Reasons can take a wide range of forms and are often presented in ways that appeal to emotions, logic, principles, values, or beliefs (p. 209). As persuasive as these reasons might seem, they are only as good as the evidence offered to support them. In some cases, evidence is offered in the form of statements from experts on a subject or people in positions of authority. In other cases, evidence might include personal experience. In still other cases, evidence might include firsthand observations, excerpts from an interview, or statistical data.

When you find empirical evidence used in a source, consider where the evidence comes from and how it is being used. If the information appears to be presented fairly, ask whether you might be able to use it to support your own ideas, and then try to verify its accuracy by consulting additional sources.

Identify Interpretive Frameworks

Writers frequently analyze and interpret the evidence they've presented. As you read a source, keep in mind that any analysis or interpretation, no matter how well grounded in evidence, is subject to the writer's purpose, interests, values, beliefs, and experiences. Try to understand what sort of interpretive framework is being used to analyze and make claims about the evidence the writer presents in the document.

An interpretive framework is a set of strategies for identifying patterns. Typically, these frameworks have been used successfully and refined over time by

---

WORKING TOGETHER

Follow the Writer's Argument

Working with a group of classmates, identify the main point, reasons, and evidence in Edwin J. Feulner's article "The Energy Potential of Fracking" (available at www.heritage.org/research/commentary/2013/2/the-energy -potential-of-fracking).

1 List the main point at the top of your page. Determine what the writer is asking you to know, believe, or do.

2 Briefly list each reason to accept the main point in the order in which it appears in the source. You might want to brainstorm these lists individually based on your reading of the article and then share your ideas to create the group's list.

3 Once you've agreed on the reasons, work together to identify the most important evidence used to support each reason.

writers interested in a given subject area or working in a particular field. Writers can choose from hundreds (perhaps thousands) of specialized frameworks used in disciplines across the arts, sciences, social sciences, humanities, engineering, and business. A historian, for example, might apply a feminist or cultural analysis to interpret diaries written by women who worked in defense plants during World War II. As you read sources, pay particular attention to writers who use five broad interpretive frameworks: trend analysis, causal analysis, data analysis, text analysis, and rhetorical analysis.

Trend Analysis   Trends are patterns that hold up over time. Trend analysis, as a result, focuses on sequences of events and the relationships among them. It is based on the assumption that understanding what has happened in the past will allow us to make sense of what is happening in the present and to draw inferences about what is likely to happen in the future.

Trends can be identified and analyzed in nearly every field, from politics to consumer affairs to the arts. Economists interested in the effects of fuel pricing fluctuations, for example, often turn to historical accounts of fuel crises in the 1970s to understand potential impacts. Sports and entertainment analysts, as well, frequently turn to trend analysis — in attempts to forecast the next NBA champion, for instance, or to explain the reemergence of superheroes in popular culture during the last decade.

As you read sources that use trend analysis, keep in mind that claims based on this form of analysis typically present historical information (sometimes in the form of statistics), argue that a trend exists, and then draw conclusions based on the existence of that trend. Ask yourself, as you read sources using this form of analysis, whether sufficient evidence exists to establish a trend, whether appropriate evidence has been used, and whether alternative conclusions might be drawn from the same evidence.

Causal Analysis   Causal analysis focuses on the factors that bring about a particular situation, such as the dot-com collapse in the late 1990s, the rise of terrorist groups, or the impact of calorie restriction on longevity. Writers use causal analysis when they believe that understanding the underlying reasons for a situation will help people address the situation, influence the likelihood of it happening again, or appreciate its potential consequences.

As you read sources that use causal analysis, ask whether the writer has identified multiple causes (since most effects are the result of more than a single cause), whether the writer has identified important causes (since some causes are far more important than others), and whether the writer has confused correlation with causation. Correlation is the observation that two things are related. It's been shown, for example, that people who own large, expensive homes often drive luxury cars. Most people would agree, however, that it would be foolish to think that the best way to get a nice new home is to buy an expensive car. Instead, they'd point out that there are other factors — such as a high income combined with a desire to live in a nice home and drive an expensive car — that are the likely causes.

II Working with Sources

Data Analysis Data can include a wide range of evidence, including facts, observations, survey responses, statistics, and other forms of numerical information, such as measurements or test scores. Writers frequently use data to make claims about an issue.

Data analysis is something most people do on a regular basis. If you've looked at the percentage of people who favor one particular political candidate over another, for example, you've engaged in data analysis. Similarly, if you've checked your bank account to determine whether you have enough money for a new coat, you've carried out a form of data analysis. Writers typically analyze numerical information to help readers better understand an issue, to look for differences, and to explore relationships.

As you read sources that use this form of analysis, ask whether the writer has presented sufficient evidence to support his or her analysis and whether the reasoning presented by the writer is rigorous and fair. For example, if someone is arguing that a recent survey provides enough evidence for the adoption of a new policy, ask how many people were surveyed and whether they represent a broad cross section of the population. You should also ask whether the writer has described the statistical methods used to make the claim and, if so, whether the methods are appropriate.

Keep in mind as well the common problems that sources relying on data analysis can suffer from, such as base-rate fallacies and cherry-picking. An example of a base-rate fallacy would be a claim that drinking a particular drink, such as coffee, can double your risk of developing cancer. If the initial risk was one in ten million, this means that the new risk is two in ten million—far less than the chance of getting in an accident as you drive to the coffee shop. Cherry-picking involves selecting only those findings that support a writer's conclusions, rather than reporting all of the relevant findings.

Text Analysis Today, the word *text* can refer to a wide range of printed or digital works. Texts open to interpretation include novels, poems, plays, essays, articles, movies, speeches, blogs, songs, paintings, photographs, sculptures, performances, Web pages, videos, television shows, and computer games.

Many writers use the elements of literary analysis to analyze texts. In this form of analysis, interpreters focus on theme, plot, setting, characterization, imagery, style, and structure as well as the contexts—social, cultural, political, and historical—that shape a work. Writers who use this form of analysis focus both on what is actually presented in the text and what is implied or conveyed "between the lines." They rely heavily on close reading of the text to discern meaning, critique a writer's technique, and search for patterns that will help them understand the text as fully as possible. They also tend to consider and include in their analysis other elements of the wider writing situation in which the text was produced—in particular, the writer's purpose, intended audience, use of sources, and choice of genre.

As you read sources that use text analysis, ask whether the claims made about the text are supported by evidence drawn from the text itself. Be wary of situations in which the writer simply uses the text as a point of departure, rather than offering evidence in the form of quotations, paraphrases, and summaries. Ask as well whether the writer is considering the text in its entirety.

Rhetorical Analysis　In much the same way that writers assess the writing situations that shape work on their documents, they can use rhetorical analysis to contribute to a conversation. In response to the argument in a particular document (written, visual, or some other form), for example, a writer might use rhetorical analysis to explain the origins or purposes of the argument.

As you read sources that use rhetorical analysis, focus on how the various aspects of the rhetorical situation—writers and purpose, writers' roles, readers/audience, sources, and contexts—contribute to the argument used in a document. Determine as well whether the analysis focuses on argument. Many sources that employ rhetorical analysis address the structure of an argument (p. 215), focusing on the writer's use of appeals—such as appeals to logic, emotion, character, and so on (p. 208)—and the quality of the evidence that was provided. Similarly, sources that use rhetorical analysis sometimes criticize an argument by exposing its use of logical fallacies (p. 212). In general, when argument is a key part of a rhetorical analysis, the writer will typically connect the analysis to one or more of the major elements of the rhetorical situation.

Identify New and Hard-to-Understand Information

As you read, mark and annotate passages that contain two types of information: new information and information that you initially find hard to understand. Keep track of new information in your research log in the form of a list or as a series of brief descriptions of what you've learned and where you learned it.

You might be tempted, as many writers are, to ignore information that's hard to understand. If you skip over this information, however, you might miss something that is critical to the success of your research project. When you encounter information that's difficult to understand, mark it and make a brief annotation reminding yourself to check it out later.

Sometimes you'll learn enough from your reading of other sources that the passage won't seem as difficult when you come back to it later. And sometimes you'll still be faced with a passage that's impossible to figure out on your own. In this case, turn to other resources or someone else for advice.

> Search a database, library catalog, or the Web using words you didn't understand in the source.
>
> Ask your instructor or a librarian for help.
>
> Ask a question about the passage on a newsgroup or electronic mailing list.
>
> Interview an expert in the area.

Identify Similarities and Differences

You can learn a lot by looking for similarities and differences among the sources you read. For example, you might identify a group of authors who take a similar approach to an issue, such as favoring increased government support for research on alternative forms of cancer treatment. You could then contrast this group with other groups of authors, such as those who argue that we should focus on improving conventional treatments and those who believe that government funding would be better spent on seeking cures for cancer. Similarly, you can make note of information in one source that agrees or disagrees with information in another. These notes can help you build your own argument and identify information that will allow you (and potentially your readers) to better understand the issue.

CHECKLIST FOR CRITICAL READING

To read critically, pay attention to the following aspects of a source.

✔ Identify the genre.

✔ Note useful illustrations.

✔ Note whether the document is a primary or secondary source.

✔ Identify the main point.

✔ Identify reasons and evidence.

✔ If analysis is used, identify the type of interpretive framework that is used.

✔ Identify new and hard-to-understand information.

✔ Compare the source with the other sources you've read.

My Research Project

Note Connections among Sources

In your research log, identify connections among your sources.

1. Do your sources tend to fall into one or more genres, such as scholarly articles, books, blog entries, or Web pages? If so, identify the most common genres.

2. Do your sources tend to be primary or secondary sources or a mix of the two types? Why do you think you're seeing this pattern?

3. Do the authors of your sources tend to agree with one another? Disagree? Fall into various groups? Describe the pattern you see.

4. Does the information in one or more sources contradict information in other sources? If so, where are you seeing the contradiction and what do you think is causing it?

5. Do authors tend to rely on similar arguments and evidence? If so, describe the arguments and evidence.

6. Are any sources cited frequently by the authors of your sources? If so, identify the source.

7. What interpretive frameworks are found in your sources? Are any of them used in more than one source? If so, why do you think the authors are relying on this framework or these frameworks?

QUICK REFERENCE

Reading Critically and Actively

☑ Read with an attitude, keeping in mind the following: your research question and position statement; your purpose; your readers' needs, interests, knowledge, experiences, values, and beliefs; the type of document you will write and the context in which it will be read; and your requirements and limitations. (p. 56)

☑ Read promising sources multiple times, first skimming, then reading actively, then rereading important passages. (p. 58)

☑ Draft a position statement. (p. 58)

☑ Mark, annotate, and take notes on your sources. (p. 64)

☑ Identify the genre of a source, useful illustrations, primary and secondary sources, main points, reasons and evidence, interpretive frameworks, new and hard-to-understand information, and similarities and differences among sources. (p. 66)

II Working with Sources

5

Evaluating Sources

 Key Questions

5a. **What factors should I use to evaluate a source?**   76
Evaluate relevance
Evaluate evidence
Evaluate the author
Evaluate the publisher
Evaluate timeliness
Evaluate comprehensiveness
Evaluate genre

5b. **Should I evaluate all types of sources in the same way?**   81
Evaluate the relevance and credibility of digital sources
Evaluate the relevance and accuracy of field sources

At the beginning of a research project, you'll most likely make quick judgments about your sources. Skimming an article, a book, or a website might be enough to tell you that spending more time with the source would be wasted effort. As you encounter a new source, determine how well it meets your needs as a research writer and how reliably it presents information, ideas, and arguments.

5a

What factors should I use to evaluate a source?

Evaluating a source means examining its relevance, evidence, author, publisher, timeliness, comprehensiveness, and genre.

Evaluate Relevance   WHAT'S MY PURPOSE?

Relevance is the extent to which a source provides information you can use in your research writing project. The most important questions you should ask to determine the relevance of a source are about your purpose and readers.

In the course of your research, you might find a number of information-filled sources. If the information is not relevant, however, it won't help you fulfill your purpose. For example, a review of Apple's iOS operating system might contain accurate and up-to-date information, but if you're writing about the monopolistic practices of leading hardware manufacturers, this source probably won't be of much use to you.

The information in a source should also be useful to your readers. You might be tempted to include a beautifully worded quotation, but if your readers won't see how it contributes to your document, don't use it. Your readers will expect information that meets their needs. If they want to read about inexpensive mobile technologies for college students, for instance, pass up sources that focus on the latest enterprise technologies.

Evaluate Evidence

Evidence is information offered to support an author's reasoning about an issue (p. 69). Evidence is connected to reasons through appeals to authority, emotion, principles, values, beliefs, character, and logic. It can also include measurements and observations, typically referred to as empirical evidence. For example, an argument in favor of charging local sales tax on Web-based purchases might use statistics — a form of empirical evidence. It could calculate the revenue a town of fifty thousand might lose if 5 percent of its citizens made fifteen online purchases in a given year. As a research writer, you can evaluate not only the kind of information used in a source but also the quality, amount, and appropriateness of that evidence. Ask the following questions about each source.

- **Is enough evidence offered?** A lack of evidence might indicate fundamental flaws in the author's argument.

- **Is the right kind of evidence offered?** More evidence isn't always better evidence. Ask whether the evidence is appropriate for the reasons offered and whether more than one type of evidence is used. Many sources rely far too heavily on a single type of evidence, such as personal experience or quotations from experts.

- **Is the evidence used fairly?** Look for reasonable alternative interpretations, questionable or inappropriate use of evidence, and evidence that seems to contradict points made elsewhere in a source. If the source uses statistics, are they interpreted fairly and presented clearly? If a quotation is offered to support a point, is the quotation used appropriately or out of context?

- **Are sources identified?** Knowing the origins of evidence can make a significant difference in your evaluation of a source. For example, if a writer quotes a political poll but doesn't say which organization conducted the poll, you might reasonably question the reliability of the source.

Evaluate the Author

The significance of authorship is affected by context. Take, for example, two editorials that make similar arguments and offer similar evidence. Both are published in your local newspaper. One is written by a fourteen-year-old middle school student, the other by a U.S. senator. You would certainly favor the senator's editorial if the subject was U.S. foreign policy. If the subject was student perceptions about drug abuse prevention in schools, however, you might value the middle school student's opinion more highly.

Ask the following questions about the author of a source.

- **Is the author knowledgeable?** An author might be an acknowledged expert in a field, a reporter who has written extensively about an issue, or someone with firsthand experience. Then again, an author might have little or no experience with a subject beyond a desire to say something about it. How can you tell the difference? Look for a description of the author in the source. If none is provided, look for biographical information on the Web or in a reference such as *Who's Who.*

- **What are the author's biases?** We all have biases — a set of interests that shapes our perceptions. Try to learn about the author's affiliations so that you can determine the extent to which his or her biases affect the presentation of arguments, ideas, and information in a source. For instance, you might infer a bias if you know that an author writes frequently about gun control and works as a regional director for the National Handgun Manufacturers Association.

Evaluate the Publisher

A publisher is a person or group that prints or produces the documents written by authors. Publishers provide access to print or digital sources, including books, newspapers, journals, websites, sound and video files, and databases. Some documents — such as personal blog posts or sources obtained through field research — have no publisher.

You can make informed judgments about publishers in much the same way that you can evaluate authors. Ask the following questions about the publisher of a source.

- **How can I locate information about the publisher?** If a publisher is listed in a print document, search for information about the publisher on the Web. You can often tell whether a publisher is reputable by looking at the types of material it publishes. If you are viewing a document on the Web, search for a link to the site's home page.

- **How do the publisher's biases affect the information, ideas, and arguments in the source?** Like authors, publishers have biases. Unlike authors, they often advertise them. Many publishers have a mission statement on their websites, while others present information on their Web pages that can help you figure out their biases. You might already know a fair amount about the biases of a publisher, particularly if the publisher is a major newspaper or magazine, such as the *New York Times* (regarded as liberal) or the *Wall Street Journal* (regarded as conservative). If the publisher is a scholarly or professional journal, you can often gain an understanding of its biases by looking over the contents of several issues or by reading a few of its articles.

Evaluate Timeliness

The importance of timeliness — a source's publication date — varies according to your writing situation. If your research project would benefit from sources that have recently been published, then evaluate recent sources more favorably than dated ones. If you're writing an article on the use of superconducting materials in new mass transportation projects, you probably won't want to spend a lot of time with articles published in 1968. On the other hand, if you're writing about the 1968 presidential contest between Hubert Humphrey and Richard Nixon, sources published during that time period will take on greater importance.

Print sources usually list a publication date. It can be more difficult, however, to tell when Web sources were created. When in doubt, back up undated information found on the Web with a dated source.

Evaluate Comprehensiveness

Comprehensiveness is the extent to which a source provides a complete and balanced view of a topic. Like timeliness, the importance of comprehensiveness varies according to the demands of your writing situation. If you are working on a narrowly focused project, such as the role played by shifts in Pacific Ocean currents on snowfall patterns in Colorado in the winter of 2008, you might not find this evaluation criterion as useful as the others. However, if you are considering a broader issue, such as the potential effects of global climate change on agricultural production in North America, or if you are still learning as much as you can about your issue, give preference to sources that provide more complete treatment.

Evaluate Genre

Understanding the typical characteristics of a genre can help you identify the roles authors take on as they develop their contributions to a written conversation. This is true not only for individual genres, such as articles and blogs, but also for more general categories, such as scholarly publications, trade and professional publications, and popular publications (see Table 5.1). Sources in these general categories typically are written for distinctly different purposes, are directed toward readers who have strikingly diverse levels of expertise on a subject, and undergo widely varying levels of review by experts on a subject. As you evaluate your sources, consider the characteristics of these three types of publications.

II Working with Sources

TABLE 5.1 GENERAL GENRE CHARACTERISTICS	Scholarly Publications	Trade and Professional Publications	Popular Publications
Purposes	Report original research, review original research, or analyze trends in recent research	Focus on new developments within a field but are not usually as technically challenging as scholarly publications	Report or comment on events, individuals, groups, or activities
Writers	Have significant expertise in a given field	Usually have expertise on an issue but can be freelancers hired by a company or professional organization	Know a great deal about a subject but would be more accurately characterized as generalists
Readers	Possess specialized knowledge about the subject	Members of a profession interested in developments in the field	General audience; most are written at a reading level appropriate for an eighth- to tenth-grade education
Sources	Extensive in-text citations and works cited lists or bibliographies	Sources are cited but often less thoroughly than in scholarly publications	Seldom include citations, although newspapers, magazines, and blogs often identify sources in general terms or by using hyperlinks
Review	Almost always reviewed by other experts in the same field	Sometimes peer-reviewed but usually reviewed only by editorial staff	Not peer-reviewed and not always carefully reviewed by editorial staff
Genres	Journal articles, books, conference papers	Journal articles, newsletter articles, blogs, websites	Newspaper and magazine articles, blogs, websites, Wikis, videos

---

CHECKLIST FOR EVALUATING SOURCES

✔ **Determine whether the source is relevant.** Will the source help you accomplish your purpose and address your readers' needs and interests?

✔ **Determine whether the source provides evidence and uses it appropriately.** Is enough evidence of the right kind offered? Is evidence used fairly, is it convincing, and is its source provided?

CHECKLIST FOR EVALUATING SOURCES (*continued*)

☑ **Learn about the author of the source.** Ask whether the author is knowledge-able. Try to determine the author's affiliation and consider how the author's biases affect the information, ideas, and arguments in the source.

☑ **Learn about the publisher of the source.** Try to locate information about the publisher, and reflect on how the publisher's biases affect the information, ideas, and arguments in the source.

☑ **Think about the timeliness of the source** and its impact on and relevance to your project.

☑ **Consider the comprehensiveness of the source** and its impact on and relevance to your project.

☑ **Consider the genre of the source** and its impact on the kind of information included in the source, the manner in which information is used by the author, and the likely audience for which the source was written.

b

Should I evaluate all types of sources in the same way?

You can apply the general evaluative criteria discussed in the previous section to most types of sources. As you do so, keep in mind the specific challenges that digital and field sources can pose during evaluation.

Evaluate the Relevance and Credibility of Digital Sources

ⓘ **INFORMATION LITERACY**   Because anyone can create a website, start a blog, contribute to a Wiki, or post a message to a social networking site, e-mail list, Web discussion forum, message board, or comments list, approach these sources with more caution than you would reserve for print sources such as books and journal articles, which are typically published only after a lengthy editorial-review process. ▥

Websites and Blogs   To assess the relevance and credibility of a website or a blog, examine its domain (.edu, .com, and so on) and look for information about the site (often available through an About page). The tutorial on p. 83 provides information about evaluating websites.

Social Networking Sites and Discussion Venues   To assess the relevance and credibility of a message on one of these online venues, try to learn something about the author.

- On social networking sites, you can usually link back to authors' personal pages.
- In e-mail lists, discussion forums, and message boards, check for a "signature" at the end of the message and try to locate a Frequently Asked Questions (FAQ) list.
- In comments lists following articles and blogs, look for signed comments that reveal more information about the author regarding his or her level of expertise or bias.

Wikis   Wikis are websites that can be added to or edited by visitors to the site. Wikis such as Wikipedia (**en.wikipedia.org**) have grown in importance on the Web, and many Wikipedia pages are highly ranked by Web search sites. Wikis can be good resources as you start a research writing project because they help you gain an initial understanding of an issue. In some cases, people who are experts on an issue contribute to Wikis and provide information and analyses. Wikis can also link to other resources that can help you learn about the issue. Unfortunately, it can be difficult to evaluate the credibility of Wiki pages because their creators and editors are often not known and because changes to Wiki pages can occur quickly. Some entries are edited so frequently, in fact, that they become the subject of "edit wars," in which edits to a page are undone almost instantly by those who disagree with the edits. In some cases, the entry you found yesterday might have little or no resemblance to the entry you could read today.

With this in mind, it is best to use Wikis when you are beginning to learn about an issue. Avoid citing them as the "last word" on a topic because those last words might change before you submit your final draft.

Evaluate the Relevance and Accuracy of Field Sources

With some adjustment, most of the criteria discussed in this chapter can be applied to field sources such as interviews, correspondence, observations, and surveys. The relevance and the accuracy of the information you collect deserve additional attention. Ask the following questions as you evaluate information collected through field research.

- Are the questions you asked in an interview, in a survey, or through correspondence still relevant to your research project?
- Is the information you collected in an observation still relevant? Are your observation notes as complete as you had hoped they would be?
- Are the individuals you interviewed or corresponded with as qualified and knowledgeable as you expected?
- Were questions in interviews, surveys, and correspondence answered fully and honestly?
- Did survey respondents have adequate time to complete the survey? Did they appear to believe their privacy would be respected?

How do I evaluate a website?

Because websites can be published without having gone through a rigorous review process, you'll want to evaluate them carefully. Evaluate a website by learning about its author, publisher, purpose, publication date, use of evidence, relevance, timeliness, and credibility. This example shows how you can evaluate a Web page for the value it might have as a potential source for your topic.

1 Check its domain (.com, .edu, .gov, and so on) to learn about its purpose and publisher:

.biz, .com, .coop	business	**.name**	personal
.edu	higher education	**.net**	network organization
.gov	government	**.org**	nonprofit organization
.mil	military	**.pro**	professional

2 Check the title bar, page header, and page titles to learn about the site's purpose, publisher (p. 78), and relevance (p. 76).

3 Search for information—on the site or through a separate Web search—about the author (p. 78) or publisher (p. 78), if identified.

4 Check timeliness (p. 79) by looking for a publication or "last modified" date.

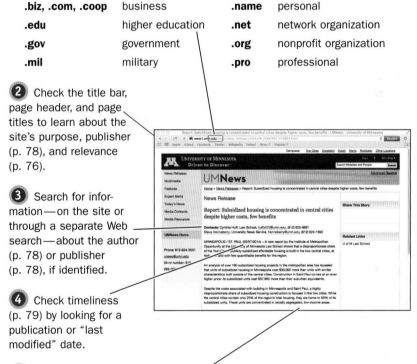

5 Read the body text and review illustrations to evaluate relevance (p. 76), evidence (p. 77), and comprehensiveness (p. 79).

6 Check page footers for information about the publisher and author. Look for About This Site or Contact links (not shown).

II Working with Sources

My Research Project

Conduct a Source Evaluation

A source evaluation applies the evaluation criteria you've read about in this chapter to a single source. You should consider each criterion in light of your writing situation and then determine the suitability of the source for your research writing project. To carry out a source evaluation, respond to the following prompts.

1. Provide the complete citation for the source.

2. In what ways are the information, ideas, and arguments in the source relevant to your research writing project?

3. Is the line of argument in the source sound and well supported? In what ways can you use it in your project?

4. What have you learned about the author and publisher that would lead you to accept, question, or reject the line of argument presented in the source?

5. In what ways does the publication date of the source affect your judgment of its usefulness for your project?

6. In what ways does the comprehensiveness of the source affect your judgment of its usefulness for your project?

7. In what ways does the genre of the source affect your judgment of its usefulness for your project?

8. In what ways could this source help you achieve your purpose and address the needs and interests of your readers?

9. How are you likely to use this source in your project?

 QUICK REFERENCE

Evaluating Sources

✔ Evaluate the relevance, evidence, author, publisher, timeliness, comprehensiveness, and genre of your sources. (p. 76)

✔ Evaluate Web sources for relevance and credibility. (p. 81)

✔ Evaluate field research for relevance and accuracy. (p. 82)

6

Taking Notes

 Key Questions

Taking notes early in your work on a research writing project allows you to keep track of what your sources have to offer. Later, as you begin to focus on planning and drafting your document, you'll be able to review your notes to determine whether to reread a source or set it aside and save time for other, more relevant sources.

6a

Why should I take notes?

Taking notes benefits research writers in two ways. First, it helps you keep track of the most important information, ideas, and arguments you've encountered in your sources. Although you can also do this by saving copies of each of your sources, notes help you zero in on the passages, images, tables, and other parts of your sources that you'll find most useful as you plan and draft your document. If you are working on a project that involves more than a few sources, taking notes will save you a great deal of time searching across your sources for a specific passage.

Second, and more important, taking notes helps you understand your sources more thoroughly than if you simply saved and highlighted copies of them. By paraphrasing or summarizing a source, for example, you force yourself to present passages from the source in your own words (p. 89). This process of putting things in your own words requires you to connect the source to what you already know, which can help you learn more about the issue you're addressing in your research writing project.

Taking notes, as a result, plays a much more vital role in your research writing project than simply keeping track of information. It helps you better understand the issue and lays the groundwork for your own contribution to the conversation you've decided to join.

6b

How can I take notes?

The methods you use to take notes — such as using note cards, a paper notebook, a word processing program, Web-based tools, or an app on a smartphone or tablet, for example — should reflect how you like to work with information. If you're uncertain about which method might suit you, talk to other writers, your instructor, or a librarian and then try a few of the most promising methods. Each method has its own advantages and disadvantages, and no single method is right for every situation.

You should take notes when a source:

- features an idea that surprises or interests you or that you think you might want to argue for or against
- provides a statement that enhances your understanding of the issue
- offers insights into how an authority or expert understands the issue
- conveys an understanding of someone else's firsthand experience with an issue or event

As you take notes, remember that they should help you accomplish your purposes as a writer and address your readers effectively. Ensure that you quote your sources accurately, paraphrase passages fairly and appropriately, and summarize clearly and fairly. In every case, provide enough source information to allow you to locate the original source — useful when you need to check for accuracy or want to find additional information.

Your notes will be most useful if you take them systematically and consistently. For example, instead of taking some notes on Post-it Notes, some on note cards, and the rest in a word processing file, take all your notes in one form. This will make it easier to find information later and reduce the time and effort required to organize and draft your document. It will also reduce the chances that you'll plagiarize unintentionally (p. 128).

Quote Directly

A direct quotation is an exact copy of words found in a source. You should take direct-quotation notes in the following cases:

- when a passage in a source features an idea that you want to argue for or against
- when a passage in a source provides a clear and concise statement that would enhance your project document
- when you want to use the exact words of an authority or expert
- when you want to use the exact words of someone who has firsthand experience with the issue you are researching
- when you want to set a mood

You can read about these and other reasons to use quotations in your document in Chapter 15.

Remember that, no matter how you might use a quotation later, your notes must be accurate. When you quote directly in your notes, you should enclose the passage in quotation marks, identify the source, and list the number of the page (or paragraph, if you are using a digital source that does not indicate page numbers) where the quotation can be found. Proofread what you have written to make sure it matches the original source exactly—including wording, punctuation, and spelling.

Using quotation marks as you take notes is critically important. If you don't use quotation marks, you might later think the passage is a paraphrase or summary and unintentionally plagiarize it when you draft your document. To learn more about avoiding plagiarism, see Chapter 9.

In some cases, it makes sense to modify a direct quotation while you're taking notes. You might want to quote only parts of a passage, add clarifying information to a note, or correct an error in the original text.

Modifying a Direct Quotation Using Ellipsis Marks When only part of a passage relates to your project, you might want to quote only that part in your notes. To indicate that you have changed a quotation by deleting words, use three spaced periods, or ellipsis marks (. . .). If you don't use ellipsis marks, your readers will assume that a quotation you are presenting is identical to the text found in the source.

Original Passage

Anderson is convinced that this is the right way to do it because he's seen all of the ways that aren't. A girls' basketball coach for more than two decades, he'd already experienced firsthand all that modern youth sports had to offer. It wasn't pretty: Screaming, red-faced parents who shuffle their children from program to program because Junior or Jane doesn't get enough court time. Elite squads that serve as showcases for a few superstar players trying to attract the attention of a Division 1 program. Eight-year-old prima donnas factory-installed with a sense of entitlement simply because they know their way around a ball and a pair of high-tops.

Source: Eric Dexheimer, "Nothing to Lose," retrieved from www.westword .com/news/nothing-to-lose-5079313, paragraph 15.

Quotation Modified Correctly Using Ellipsis Marks

"Anderson is convinced that this is the right way to do it because he's seen all of the ways that aren't. A girls' basketball coach for more than two decades, he'd already experienced firsthand all that modern youth sports had to offer. . . . Screaming, red-faced parents who shuffle their children from program to program. . . . Elite squads that serve as showcases for a few superstar players. . . . Eight-year-old prima donnas . . . with a sense of entitlement simply because they know their way around a ball and a pair of high-tops" (paragraph 15).

Three periods indicate material deleted from a sentence.

Four periods indicate the deletion of a full sentence or more.

Modifying a Direct Quotation Using Brackets   To modify a direct quotation by changing or adding words, use brackets: [ ]. If you don't use brackets when you change or add words, readers will assume the quotation you are presenting is identical to the text found in the source.

Quotation Modified Correctly Using Brackets

"The [Corporation for National Service] is an independent agency with a 15-member board of directors that is appointed by the president and confirmed by the Senate" (Lenkowsky and Perry 299).

[Corporation for National Service] replaces the original text's use of the acronym *CNS.*

Remember that using brackets and ellipsis marks does not entitle you to change the meaning of a quotation. Check your notes against the original passages to be sure you aren't misrepresenting the source.

Modifying Quotations Using "Sic"   If a passage you are quoting contains a misspelled word or an incorrect fact, use the word "*sic*" in brackets to indicate that the error occurred in the original passage. If you don't use "*sic*," your readers will think that the mistake is yours.

Quotation Modified Correctly Using "Sic"

"George W. Brush's [sic] interest in faith-based initiatives strongly shaped his national service agenda" (Vincent 221).

To avoid unintentional plagiarism when quoting from sources, take careful notes by using the following checklist. Be aware, however, that mistakes can happen, particularly if you are taking notes in a hurry. As you draft your document, remember to look for notes that differ from your usual style of writing. More often than not, if a note doesn't sound like your own writing, it isn't.

> **CHECKLIST FOR QUOTING**
>
> To quote accurately when taking notes, follow these guidelines.
>
> ✔ Identify the author, the title, and the page or paragraph where the passage can be found.
>
> ✔ Avoid unintentional plagiarism by using quotation marks.
>
> ✔ Use ellipsis marks, brackets, and "*sic*" as necessary.
>
> ✔ Check your note against the original passage to be sure you aren't introducing errors or misrepresenting the source.

Paraphrase

When you restate a passage from a source in your own words, you are paraphrasing the source. Writers use paraphrases in their documents for some of the same reasons they use quotations:

- to illustrate or support points they plan to make in their document
- to cite authorities on an issue
- to share the experiences of people who have been affected by an issue
- to refer to ideas with which they disagree

Using paraphrases in your notes serves three purposes. First, restating a passage in your own words can help you remember it better than if you simply copy and paste a quotation. Second, because paraphrases are written in your own words, they're usually easier to understand later, when you're drafting. Third, paraphrasing as you take notes will help you save time during drafting, particularly if you find — as many writers do — that you don't want to rely exclusively on quotations from your sources.

Paraphrasing is a useful skill that takes practice. The challenges that typically face writers as they paraphrase include mirroring the source material too closely — that is, making such minor changes to the words and sentence structure of a source that the paraphrase remains nearly identical to the original passage — and distorting the meaning of the source.

Consider the differences among the original passage below and the appropriate and inappropriate paraphrases that follow it.

Original Passage

If, after three decades, I'm more surefooted about teaching writing and more passionate about it, I imagine it is because I teach not from a set of secret codes or passwords, but from my own work as a writer, waiting to be surprised by the alphabet's infinite possibilities; and from encouraging students to write as if they have an audience, a gathering, waiting to receive their words.

Source: Nancy Sommers, "Living Composition," p. 34.

Inappropriate Paraphrase

Sommers notes that, after roughly thirty years, she is more confident about teaching writing and more excited about it, not because she draws on a sort of secret sauce for teaching, but because of her experiences working as a writer. She is always ready to be surprised by the possibilities of language and wants to help students write as if they are addressing readers who care about the words they have to share (34).

> Does not differ sufficiently from the original; uses similar sentence structures and changes only some key words.

Inappropriate Paraphrase

Sommers writes that she continues to be passionate about teaching writing because she remains open to the infinite possibilities of language and its power to reach an audience (34).

> Distorts the meaning of the original passage.

Appropriate Paraphrase

Sommers's growth as a teacher has little to do with some sort of privileged, insider knowledge and everything to do with her own work as a writer who loves language and her desire to help students understand that they write best when they write for an interested and receptive group of readers (34).

> Preserves the meaning of the original passage without replicating the sentence structure and wording.

Remember that paraphrases are generally about as long as the original passages on which they are based. Keep in mind as well that, even though you are using your own words when you paraphrase, you must still cite the source because the paraphrase presents ideas and information that are not your own.

When paraphrasing, focus on understanding the key ideas in the passage and then restate them in your own words. Begin a paraphrase with the phrase "In other words." This strategy reminds you that it's important to do more than

---

CHECKLIST FOR PARAPHRASING

To paraphrase, follow these guidelines.

✔ Be sure that you understand the passage by reading it and the surrounding text carefully.

✔ Restate the passage in your own words. Make sure that you do more than simply change a few key words.

✔ Compare the original passage with your paraphrase. Make sure that you've conveyed the meaning of the passage but that the wording and sentence structure differ from those in the original passage.

✔ Note the author, the title, and the page or paragraph where the passage can be found.

TUTORIAL

How do I paraphrase a source?

Paraphrasing a source involves restating the ideas and information in a passage in your own words. Use different words and sentence structure to ensure that your paraphrase isn't too close to the original passage. In this example, Alexis Alvarez identifies a relevant passage in one of her sources and creates a note that paraphrases the passage.

1 Select the passage you want to paraphrase.

Original Passage: Why do athletes risk chronic debilitating diseases and death by taking steroids? Because these drugs work. In very short order, they pack on pounds of muscle and increase strength dramatically. Weight training while using steroids maximizes your gains.

Source: Kendrick, C. (n.d.). Seduced by steroids. Retrieved from www.familyeducation.com/drugs-and-alcohol/sports/36182.html.

2 Identify relevant information and ideas in the passage.

Why do athletes risk chronic debilitating diseases and death by taking steroids? Because these drugs work. In very short order, they pack on pounds of muscle and increase strength dramatically. Weight training while using steroids maximizes your gains.

3 Draft a paraphrase that identifies the source and includes the information.

Kendrick (n.d.) asks why athletes use steroids, which can lead to serious illness and death. He responds to his own question by noting that steroids increase muscle mass and strength and are particularly effective when used with weight training.

4 Revise the paraphrase so that it uses wording and sentence structure that differs from the original passage.

Kendrick (n.d.) notes that, despite long-term and potentially lethal health risks, athletes use steroids because, in combination with weight training, they can dramatically increase strength and muscle mass.

simply change a few words in the passage. You might also want to set the original source aside while you paraphrase so that you won't be tempted to copy sentences directly from it. After you've completed your paraphrase, check it for accuracy.

Summarize

A summary is a concise statement of information in a source. Research writers often summarize an entire source, but they can also summarize lengthy passages. You can write summaries to capture the overall argument and information in a source and to record a writer's argument so that you can later refute it.

Unlike paraphrases, which are generally about as long as the passages on which they are based, summaries are as a rule shorter than the source or passage that is being summarized. Like paraphrases and quotations, you should always cite the source of the summary in your note.

Here is an original passage from *Scientific American*, a source one might consult while researching television addiction. Two notes containing summaries of the passage, one inappropriate and the other appropriate, follow the original.

Original Passage

What is more surprising is that the sense of relaxation ends when the set is turned off, but the feelings of passivity and lowered alertness continue. Survey participants commonly reflect that television has somehow absorbed or sucked out their energy, leaving them depleted. They say they have more difficulty concentrating after viewing than before. In contrast, they rarely indicate such difficulty after reading. After playing sports or engaging in hobbies, people report improvements in mood. After watching TV, people's moods are about the same or worse than before.

Source: Robert Kubey and Mihaly Csikszentmihalyi, "Television Addiction," p. 76

Inappropriate Summary

Although watching television may relax a viewer, viewers report that turning off the television set makes them feel moody and depressed. (summary)

\

> The summary misrepresents the main point of the article and does not identify the authors.

Appropriate Summary

Kubey and Csikszentmihalyi, "Television Addiction," p. 76

Kubey and Csikszentmihalyi report that although watching television may relax a viewer, studies have shown it does little to improve a viewer's alertness, energy level, or mood. (summary)   \

> The summary conveys the main point of the article and clearly identifies its authors.

To avoid unintentional plagiarism when summarizing a source, begin your summary with "The author argues that" or "The author found that." Set the original source aside while you write your summary so that you won't be tempted to copy sentences directly from it. After you've completed your summary, check it for accuracy.

CHECKLIST FOR SUMMARIZING

To summarize, follow these guidelines.

✔ Be sure that you understand the source by reading it carefully.

✔ Summarize main points and reasons in your own words. Make sure that you do more than string together a series of close paraphrases of key passages.

✔ Check for unintentional plagiarism by comparing the original source with your summary.

✔ Note the author, the title, and, if you are summarizing only part of a source, the page(s) or paragraph(s) where the information can be found.

WORKING TOGETHER

Quote, Paraphrase, and Summarize

Form a small group and read Edwin J. Feulner's article, "The Energy Potential of Fracking" (available at www.heritage.org/research/commentary/2013/2/the -energy-potential-of-fracking). Each member of the group will be responsible for one of the following activities: identifying useful quotations, creating paraphrases, or summarizing all or part of the article.

1 Read the article.

2 Return to the article and **take notes** in the form of quotations, paraphrases, or summaries.

3 Take turns sharing the notes that were taken. Each group member should explain why the notes were taken and how they might be used in a writing project.

4 As each report is given, the other members of the group should **jot down any new ideas** that emerge from the discussion. Pay attention to useful strategies for identifying useful information, ideas, and arguments and record any good ideas about how to make use of notes.

5 As a group, **prepare a report** that identifies strategies for selecting useful passages; explains how notes can incorporate quotations, paraphrases, and summaries; and reflects on how notes might be used to make progress on a research writing project.

6c

How can I use my notes to improve my understanding of an issue?

Notes can do far more than record useful information, ideas, and arguments for later use. Because taking notes requires thought and effort, the process of choosing quotations, creating paraphrases, and summarizing sources can help you gain a deeper understanding of an issue. Yet taking notes can do far more than simply help you remember and understand your sources. It can help you keep track of ideas that occur to you as you work with sources and gain insights into how your sources are related to each other. Taking notes, in a real sense, plays an important role in developing your plan for making a contribution to the conversation you've decided to join.

Record Your Reactions and Impressions

You can use your notes to keep track of your reactions and impressions (see Figure 6.1). If you've read a source before and jotted down brief notes in the margins or added comments using a word processor, look for those now and use them as the basis for a more substantial reflection on the information, ideas, or arguments in a source. For example, you might have written, "This makes sense" in the margin. If so, take some time to create a note that explains why it makes sense and what the source adds to your understanding of the issue. Learn more about annotating sources during critical reading on p. 64.

If you are reading or viewing a source for the first time, use your notes to record your initial impressions, ask questions, and respond to claims made by the author. Then review your notes and expand them by reflecting in more detail on the points raised in your first set of notes.

Compare Sources   ❓ **WHAT'S MY PURPOSE?**

Your notes can indicate connections among your sources by identifying relationships among information, ideas, and arguments. Paying attention to your sources as a group—not just to individual sources—helps you gain a more complete understanding of your issue. It also can be useful when you begin planning and organizing your document, since those connections can help you frame your argument. To compare sources, use the following techniques.

Look for Similarities   As you take notes, identify similarities among your sources. Later, those comparisons can help you define groups of authors that you

The title of the source is listed at the top of the note. —— Notes on *Blackwater: The Rise of the World's Most Powerful Mercenary Army* by Jeremy Scahill

Quotes	Notes and Reactions
The quotation is surrounded by quotation marks. → "On April 28, 2004, the Abu Ghraib prison scandal was blown into the open when CBS's *60 Minutes II* broadcast graphic images depicting U.S. soldiers torturing and humiliating Iraqi prisoners. It soon emerged that private contractors from two U.S. corporations—the San Diego–based firm Titan Corporation and the Virginia-based CACI—were allegedly involved in the torture, having provided interrogators for use at the prison during the period of alleged abuse." (p. 157)	This is a key event in the Iraq War and this passage will surely be a linchpin in the section of my paper regarding PMC malfeasance and crimes.
"In late 2006, Senator Lindsey Graham quietly inserted language into the 2007 defense authorization bill, which Bush subsequently signed, that sought to place contractors under the Pentagon's UCMJ [Uniform Code of Military Justice], but what effective impact—if any—this could have remains unclear, with experts predicting resistance from the private war industry." (p. 360)	I'd like to do some more research to see if the UCMJ has been effectively applied to a contractor in the years between the publication of this book and now. Personally, I'd doubt it. This is a powerful industry with plenty of lawyers to challenge this language.

Nicholas writes down his reactions to the quotations.

Page numbers follow quotations.

FIGURE 6.1 An Example from Nicholas Brothers's Notes and Reactions [From *Blackwater: The Rise of the World's Most Powerful Mercenary Army*, by Jeremy Scahill, copyright © 2007. Reprinted by permission of Nation Books, an imprint of Perseus Books, LLC, a subsidiary of Hachette Book Group, Inc.]

can use to support your argument, point to as misguided for the same general reason, or illustrate a particular point. Featured writer Lauren Mack reviewed her notes and identified connections she saw between what she'd read on educational websites and what she'd learned from her interviews with colleagues at her New England Aquarium internship. In her interview notes, Lauren added a comparison note: "This ties in with the Smithsonian article."

Look for Disagreements   Taking note of disagreements among your sources can help you determine the sticking points in the conversation you've decided to join. In turn, understanding where your sources disagree can help you decide where to make your contribution to the conversation (see Figure 6.2).

Look for Common Citations   Any source that is being referenced frequently is likely to contain important information, ideas, or arguments. Take note of frequently cited sources and consult them later.

46   THE RISE

The second implication is that this new private military actor is driven by business profit rather than individual profit. PMFs function as registered trade units, not as personal black-market ventures for individual profit or adventure. As firms, they can make use of complex corporate financing, ranging from sale of stock shares to intra-firm trade, meaning that a wider variety of deals and contracts can be worked out. For good reason, individual mercenaries tend only to trust payments in cash and, in turn, cannot be trusted for anything beyond the short-term.

The key is that it is not the person that matters, but the structure that they are within. Many PMF employees have been mercenaries both before and after their employ, but their processes, relationships, and impacts within local conflicts were completely different.

The third distinguishing characteristic of the privatized military industry is that the arena they compete on is the open global market. That is, unlike the activities of the White Legion or similar mercenary units, PMFs are considered legal entities bound to their employers by recognized contracts and in many cases at least nominally to their home states by laws requiring registration, periodic reporting, and licensing of foreign contracts.[17] Rather than denying their existence, private military firms are registered businesses and, in fact, often publicly advertise their services—including many even having corporate websites on the Internet.[18] This status differentiates them not only from mercenaries, who had to hide from the law, but also from past entities, such as the charter companies, that did not coexist with any state law, but rather made their own laws.

New military firms also provide a much wider offering of services and, importantly, to a much wider variety of clients. As the head of Sandline was proud to note, firms in the privatized military industry are "structured organi-

> Line up this argument against Scahill's virtually interchangeable use of the terms "private military corporation" and "mercenary"

FIGURE 6.2 An Annotation about a Disagreement among Sources *Nicholas Brothers reminds himself about the differences among his sources.* [Information from *Corporate Warriors*, by P. W. Singer. Copyright © 2003 Cornell University. Used by permission of the publisher, Cornell University Press.]

Classify Sources

As you take notes, use them to classify your sources. Among other purposes, you can keep track of sources that might be used to support particular points in your document, that represent various approaches to your issue, and that include important information or ideas. Strategies for classifying sources include tagging, labeling, grouping, listing, and visualizing.

- **Tagging and Labeling**   ⓘ **INFORMATION LITERACY**   Tags are words or phrases that can be associated with digital notes. When tags are used, it is common to apply more than one tag to a note. Labels, in turn, can be applied to print notes. You can use tags and labels to remind yourself about the purpose or content of a note or to help you remember something about the source. You might tag a note with one of the reasons you're planning to use in your document, for example, or you might label a note as useful for your introduction. Later, as you're working on your introduction or fleshing out that reason, you can quickly call up all your relevant tagged notes. Similarly, you might label a note to remind yourself about the approach taken in the source to which it refers and later, as you draft, look for notes with that label. ▨

- **Grouping** As you read and take notes on your sources, you can begin to classify them into groups — organized, perhaps, by the part of the document in which you plan to refer to the source, the approach advanced in the source, or the kind of evidence contained in the source. If you are working with print notes, you can put them in piles, envelopes, or folders. If you are working with digital notes, you might drag each note into a group (within, for example, a word processing file) or into a folder (if you are saving each note as a distinct file).

- **Listing** Listing is similar to grouping, but this strategy does not require you to move your notes into a particular location. Instead, you can create notes that list your sources. You might, for example, list all the sources that contain information that might be used to support your position and then list sources that contain information that contradicts your position.

- **Visualizing** You can use the same clustering and mapping techniques as you take notes that you use as you generate ideas and organize your document (p. 22 and p. 121). For example, you can create notes that contain a sketch of the relationships among the sources you've read so far. Similarly, you could draw clusters of sources that support or illustrate a particular approach to your issue and then write brief notes about what they have in common, how the clusters of sources differ from each other, and so on.

Plan Your Document [FRAMING MY ARGUMENT]

Planning notes are directions to yourself about how you might use a source in your project document, how you might organize the document, or what ideas you should remember later. You can use planning notes to keep track of your ideas about the role that might be played in your document by the information, ideas, and arguments you encounter. Featured writer Lauren Mack wrote planning notes — such as, "How will this tie in? Use on opening screen?" — as she prepared to write her multimodal essay.

Working with Sources

II Working with Sources

My Research Project

Respond to Sources

As you take notes, you'll gain a deeper understanding of your sources, both individually and collectively. Use your knowledge of your sources to create a response. Your response can be useful later as you plan and draft your project document. Use one or more of the following prompts as the basis for your response.

- What do you agree with in one or more of your sources? Briefly summarize the idea or argument and then explain why you agree with it.

- What do you disagree with in one or more of your sources? Briefly summarize the idea or argument and then explain why you disagree with it.

- What do you see as the most important idea emerging from your research so far? Briefly summarize the idea and then explain its importance.

- Why do you think one or more of the authors you've taken notes on so far approach the issue as they have? Briefly describe their approaches and then explain why they are taking them.

- What approach do you think should be taken on this issue? Briefly describe the approach and then explain its importance.

QUICK REFERENCE

Taking Notes

✔ Decide how you will record your notes; then take notes systematically and consistently. (p. 86)

✔ Take notes to quote passages directly. (p. 87)

✔ Take notes to paraphrase key ideas. (p. 89)

✔ Take notes to summarize whole sources or lengthy passages. (p. 92)

✔ Take notes to record your reactions and impressions. (p. 94)

✔ Take notes to compare the information, ideas, and arguments in sources. (p. 94)

✔ Take notes to classify sources. (p. 96)

✔ Take notes to help plan your document. (p. 97)

7

Engaging with Information, Ideas, and Arguments

Key Questions

As you make progress on your writing project, you'll begin to summarize, synthesize, reflect on, and develop positions on the issue you're planning to address. This chapter considers how, as an academic writer, you can use intermediate genres — such as summaries, responses, literature reviews, and proposals — to develop your contribution to the conversation you've decided to join.

7a

What should I know about academic writing?

Academic writing, like the kind of writing carried out in professional settings and civic life, requires an understanding of how to adapt to a writing situation and how to work with the documents typically used in academic conversations. Equally important, it requires an understanding of how to share information and ideas and how to make arguments.

Understand Academic Genres

When writers and readers form a community — such as an academic discipline, a professional association, or a group that shares an interest in a particular topic or activity — they develop characteristic ways of communicating with one another. Over time, members of a community will come to agree about the type of evidence generally accepted to support arguments, the style in which sources should be cited, and how documents should be designed and organized. As the needs of a community evolve, the genre will adapt as well. The organization of articles in academic journals in biochemistry, for example, differs in important ways from that of articles in academic journals in philosophy and literature. Similarly, the evidence used in scholarly articles will differ widely across academic disciplines.

As the needs and interests of a community change, the genres used will change as well. Academic essays, for example, might begin to make greater use of color and illustrations. In other cases, a single genre might evolve into several distinct genres. Similarly, as the number of readers on the Web has exploded over the past two decades, websites have become far more specialized. In the mid-1990s, most websites looked alike. Today, characteristic differences can be seen among personal blogs, commercial websites, government websites, and entertainment websites.

In addition to widely published academic genres, such as articles, essays, and reports, academic writers make extensive use of a number of "intermediate" genres — documents that help them develop their ideas and prepare to share them in more public forms. Academic writers frequently create working bibliographies, which allow them to keep track of their sources. They are also likely to create summaries of sources, source evaluations, and responses to sources. Academic writers who wish to gain a general understanding of the key ideas that are being discussed in a given conversation often turn to literature reviews to organize their thinking about those ideas. And it is not uncommon for writers to write proposals to gain feedback before they embark on larger projects such as research essays, reports, or websites.

Understand How to Develop an Academic Argument

Academic writing is concerned largely with the exchange of information, ideas, and arguments. The writer's purpose is typically to make a point and support it with reasoning and evidence. In the case of scientific reports, the evidence might take the form of data gained through a study. In the case of scholarly articles in political science or philosophy or essays in a composition course, the evidence might consist primarily of textual evidence from sources.

In longer documents, such as articles, essays, and reports, writers usually present several reasons for readers to accept or act on the writers' thesis statements. The reasons they choose will vary according to the type of document they are writing. In an argumentative essay, for example, writers usually offer a series of claims that will lead readers to accept their argument or take action in response to it. You can read about developing reasons to support your main point on p. 205.

For every reason you offer to support your main point, you'll also need evidence—such as details, facts, personal observations, and expert opinions—to back up your assertions and help your readers understand your ideas. Your evidence can take the form of quotations, paraphrases, summaries, numerical data, and visual images. It can also come from interviews, observations, and surveys. And it can come from your personal experience. You can read more about using evidence on p. 207.

As you choose evidence to support your reasons, think about how you will show the connections between your reasons and evidence. These connections, called *appeals*, help readers understand why a reason is appropriate and valid. Common appeals include appeals to logic, to character, and to emotion. You can learn more about appeals on p. 208.

Understand the Role of "Intermediate" Genres

As you learn more about your issue, you'll find yourself beginning to develop your own ideas about how best to address it. By reading, taking notes, and evaluating your sources, you'll gain a deeper understanding of the issue. Early in your writing project, however, your ideas are likely to be tentative and somewhat undeveloped. Creating intermediate genres, such as annotated bibliographies, summaries, source evaluations, responses, literature reviews, and proposals, can help you clarify and refine your ideas. By writing summaries and source evaluations, for example, you focus on a single source. Crafting reviews of literature can help you synthesize the information and ideas found in several sources. And drafting proposals can help you create a plan for carrying out a major research writing project.

7b

How can I create and use a bibliography?

A bibliography is a list of sources with complete publication information, usually formatted according to the rules of a documentation system such as those created by the Modern Language Association (see Chapter 20), the American Psychological Association (see Chapter 21), or the Council of Science Editors (see Chapter 23), or found in books such as the *Chicago Manual of Style* (see Chapter 22). As you take notes on your sources, use a working bibliography or an annotated bibliography to keep track of the sources you've consulted.

Create a Working Bibliography

A working bibliography is a running list of the sources you've explored and plan to use as you work on your research writing project. Publication information is provided for each source. The organization of your working bibliography can vary according to your needs and preferences. You can organize your sources in any of the following ways:

- in the order in which you collected your sources
- in categories
- by author
- by publication title
- according to how the information, ideas, and arguments in the source align with your position on your issue
- according to an outline of your project document

The entries in a working bibliography should include as much publication information about a source as you can gather (see Table 7.1).

Your working bibliography will change significantly as you work on your research writing project. As you explore your topic, choose an issue, collect sources, read them critically, evaluate them, and take notes, you will add potentially useful sources and delete sources that are no longer relevant. Eventually, your working bibliography will become one of the following:

- a *works cited* or *reference list* — a formal list of the sources you have referred to in a document
- a *bibliography* or *works consulted list* — a formal list of the sources that contributed to your thinking about an issue, even if those sources were not referred to explicitly in the text of the document

Keeping your working bibliography up-to-date is a critical part of your research writing process. It helps you keep track of your sources and increases the likelihood that you will cite all the sources you use in your document — an important contribution to your efforts to avoid plagiarism (see Chapter 9). Bibliography

| TABLE 7.1 INFORMATION YOU SHOULD LIST IN A WORKING BIBLIOGRAPHY ||
Type of Source	**Information You Should List**
All Sources	Author(s) Title Publication year Medium consulted
Book	Editor(s) of book (if applicable) Publication city Publisher Series and series editor (if applicable) Translator (if applicable) Volume (if applicable) Edition (if applicable)
Chapter in an Edited Book	Publication city Publisher Editor(s) of book Book title Page numbers
Journal, Magazine, or Newspaper Article	Journal title Volume number or date Issue number or date Page numbers
Web Page, Blog Entry or Reply, Discussion Forum Post, E-mail Message, or Chat Transcript	URL Access date (the date you read the source) Sponsoring organization (if listed)
Field Research	Title (usually a description of the source, such as "Personal Interview with Jessica Lynn Richards" or "Observation of June Allison's Class at Tavelli Elementary School") Date (usually the date on which the field research was conducted)

II Working with Sources

tools allow you to create, organize, and update a working bibliography formatted in a style such as MLA or APA.

The first three sources from Elizabeth Leontiev's working bibliography are found in Figure 7.1.

Create an Annotated Bibliography [FRAMING MY ARGUMENT]

An annotated bibliography provides a brief note about each of the sources you've listed, in addition to its complete citation information. These notes, or annotations, are typically no longer than two or three sentences. The content, focus, and length of your annotations will reflect both your purposes for creating an annotated bibliography and the needs and interests of your readers (see Table 7.2).

Entries follow MLA style
(p. **326**).

"US Weighs Cost of Plan Colombia." *BBC News*, 5 July 2005, news.bbc
.co.uk/2/hi/4627185.stm.

Forero, Juan. "Coca Advocate Wins Election for President in Bolivia."
The New York Times, 19 Dec. 2005, www.nytimes.com/2005/12/
19/world/americas/coca-advocate-wins-election-for-president-in
-bolivia.html.

United States, Office of National Drug Control Policy. *Coca in the
Andes*, www.whitehouse.gov/ondcp/targeting-cocaine-at-the
-source. Accessed 29 May 2015.

Use access
date when no
publication
date is given.

FIGURE 7.1 Part of Elizabeth Leontiev's Working Bibliography

The following examples show how the same source might be annotated for different readers.

For You or an Instructor

This Web page discusses everything about the hydraulic fracturing process and is one of very few sources that give specific numbers for the amount of water being used in fracking. I will use this information in the section on the disadvantages of fracking.

For Classmates in a Writing Group

This Web page discusses everything about the hydraulic fracturing process and is one of very few sources that give specific numbers for the amount of water being used in fracking. We can use this site to get a good understanding of the disadvantages (environmental and economic) of fracking.

For an External Audience, such as Visitors to a Website

The Explore Shale Web page provides an easy-to-understand overview of hydraulic fracking. Its graphical images allow visitors to see how the process works. It also provides details about the hydraulic fracturing process, including the amount of water being used in fracking.

An annotated bibliography is a useful tool even if it's not something you'll be expected to submit for a grade or share with other readers. By turning your

TABLE 7.2 PURPOSES AND FEATURES OF ANNOTATED BIBLIOGRAPHIES

		Your Readers		
	You	**An Instructor**	**A Writing Group**	**An External Audience**
Purpose	Keep track of sources; plan your document	Show progress on a project; serve as an intermediate assignment	Show how a source might be useful for a group project	Share information about important sources addressing an issue
Features				
Include complete source citation, using proper formatting.	✔	✔	✔	✔
Summarize the source, noting significant findings and key information.	✔	✔	✔	✔
Evaluate the source, including how it is relevant as well as background information on the author and publisher.	✔	✔	✔	✔
Compare sources.	✔			
Identify passages containing useful information, ideas, and arguments.	✔		✔	
Reflect on how the source could be used in a project document.	✔	✔	✔	
Note how readers might react to information, ideas, and arguments in the document.	✔			
Respond to the source with your own reaction or analysis.	✔			

II Working with Sources

working bibliography into an annotated bibliography, you can remind yourself of important information, ideas, and arguments in your sources; record your reflections, evaluations, and analyses of each source; note your responses to your sources; and record your ideas about how the source might be used to advance your position on your issue.

Costello, B. (2004, July 4). Too late? Survey suggests millions of kids could be juicing. *New York Post*. Retrieved from http://www.nypost.com

> Entries follow APA style (p. 355).

This article discusses steroid and other performance-enhancing drugs used by eighth- through twelfth-grade boys and girls and provides a number of relevant statistics. I'll use this source to support statements about steroid use among young female athletes.

Davies, D., & Armstrong, M. (1989). *Psychological factors in competitive sport*. New York, NY: Falmer Press.

> Annotations provide brief summaries of the purpose and content of the sources.

This book addresses various psychological factors in sports, including learning, motivation, anxiety, stress, and performance. I'll use it to support my discussion of why sports can have negative effects on girls.

DeNoon, D. (2004, August 4). *Steroid use: Hitting closer to home*. Retrieved from http://webmd.com/fitness-exercise/features/steroid-use-hitting-closer-to-home

> Annotations are intended for Alexis and her teacher. They indicate how and where Alexis will use the sources in her document.

This Web page provides information about increasing steroid use in America as well as the latest statistical figures regarding this use. I'll use it for statistical evidence and to drive home the point that this problem needs to be addressed.

FIGURE 7.2 Part of Alexis Alvarez's Annotated Bibliography, Written for Herself and Her Teacher

My Research Project

Create a Working or an Annotated Bibliography

Create a bibliography to keep track of your sources as you work on your research writing project. Your bibliography should include complete citation information for the sources you are considering for use in your project. You may also include annotations that contain source descriptions, source evaluations, reflections on the source, and plans for using the source in your project.

You can create a bibliography in print form (such as in a notebook) or in digital form (for example, in a word processing file). You can also use bibliography tools, which allow you to create entries for new sources, annotate sources, evaluate sources, copy and save some or all of the text from a source, and display your working bibliography in various citation styles (see Part V).

7c

How can I summarize sources?

Summaries focus on an individual source. Through summarizing, you can gain a thorough knowledge of the information found in a source, a deeper understanding of a compelling idea, or a detailed analysis of an argument. Summarizing is useful early on in a writing project, when you are learning about the issue and attempting to identify key ideas, arguments, and voices.

Many writers believe that a summary should be objective. It would be more precise to say that a summary should be accurate and fair. That is, you should not misrepresent the information, ideas, or arguments in a source. Achieving accuracy and fairness, however, does not necessarily mean that your summary will be an objective presentation of the source. Instead, your summary will reflect your purpose, needs, and interests and—if you're writing for an audience—those of your readers. You'll focus on information, ideas, and arguments that are relevant to your writing situation. As a result, your summary is likely to differ from one written by another writer. Both summaries might be accurate and fair, but each one will reflect a different writing situation.

As you read a source with the goal of writing a summary, highlight key points and note passages that include useful quotations or information you might use to add detail to your summary. If you are writing a summary for a class, it will typically take one of three forms: a main-point summary, a key-points summary, or an outline summary.

Write a Main-Point Summary

A main-point summary reports the most important information, idea, or argument presented in a source. You can use main-point summaries to keep track of the overall claim made in a source, to introduce your readers to a source, and to place the main point of that source into the context of an argument or a discussion of a subject. A student writing about the education provided to future writing teachers might have written the following main-point summary of the scholarly article "Living Composition," which was written by Nancy Sommers and which is readily available online at **ncte.org/library/NCTEFiles/Resources/Journals/TETYC/0431-sep2015/TETYC0431Living.pdf**.

> In her article "Living Composition," Nancy Sommers reflects on how her work as a writer and as a teacher of writing have combined to keep her "exhilarated" to return to the classroom.

Main-point summaries are brief. They identify the source and its main point.

Write a Key-Points Summary

Like a main-point summary, a key-points summary reports the most important information, idea, or argument presented in a source. However, it also includes the reasons (key points) and evidence the author uses to support his or her main point. Key-points summaries are useful when you want to keep track of a complex argument or understand an elaborate process.

> In her article "Living Composition," Nancy Sommers reflects on how her work as a writer and as a teacher of writing have combined to keep her "exhilarated" to return to the classroom. Recounting how her varied experiences as a teacher, mother, and writer have shaped her understanding of writing, she notes the shift in her perspective over the many years since she first began to teach writing.

The author, source, and main point are identified.

"I see that it's clear how much that [first] year was a song of myself, more . . . my performance than the students'," she writes. "It would take a decade or more for me to understand that teaching requires both humility and leaps of faith, and most importantly, a willingness to listen to, and learn from, students" (33). Looking back on her experiences with her students, she notes her hope that they've left her classrooms to become active writers, participating in public and professional discourse as well as in the kind of personal writing that she has enjoyed.

Quotations from the article are provided.

No matter what her students have done, however, she points out that "our narratives are inevitably woven together—that during our time together, we've helped each other find something to say, and a reason to say it" (36).

Key lessons learned over a lifetime of teaching are identified.

Write an Outline Summary

Sometimes called a plot summary, an outline summary reports the information, ideas, and arguments in a source in the same order used in the source. In a sense, an outline summary presents the overall "plot" of the source by reporting what was written in the order in which it was written. Outline summaries are useful when you need to keep track of the sequence of information, ideas, and arguments in a source.

> In her article "Living Composition," Nancy Sommers reflects on how her work as a writer and as a teacher of writing have combined to keep her "exhilarated" to return to the classroom. Recalling her early life as a writer and reader, she points out that despite growing up in a family where reading was considered "fine, in moderation, but too much reading could be dangerous" (32), she would go on to study literature in college and eventually find herself teaching writing to eighth graders in Chicago. Noting her "naïveté and youthful arrogance" (33), she points out that in retrospect her first year of teaching "was a song of myself, more soliloquy than exchange of voices, more my performance than the students'" (33).
>
> Over the years, Sommers would grow as a teacher and writer, balancing writing, the teaching of writing, and family life.

The author, source, and main point are identified.

Along the way, she encountered the—at the time—normal challenges facing women pursuing a career, including losing a teaching position when she became pregnant and dividing time between caring for her family, teaching her students, and pursuing her work as a writer and writing scholar.

The summary identifies each of the major points made in the article in the order in which they were made.

Yet Sommers also notes that it was through writing and the teaching of writing that she found a professional community of writing teachers, the Conference on College Composition and Communication, where she could share her ideas and benefit from a larger audience of writing scholars.

Sommers shares how she developed her own authorial voice and how she passes the lessons of that journey on to her students, encouraging them to participate in public and professional discourse as well as in the kind of personal writing that she has enjoyed.

\
The author's name is mentioned whenever information from the source is used.

She concludes, however, that no matter what her students have done as writers, "our narratives are inevitably woven together—that during our time together, we've helped each other find something to say, and a reason to say it" (36).

\
Phrases and terms such as "pointing to" and "conclude" provide a sense of movement through the source.

II Working with Sources

My Research Project

Summarize a Source

Using the following guidelines, write an outline summary of the article "Guiding the Budding Writer" by Peter Johnson, available online at citeseerx.ist.psu.edu/viewdoc/download?doi=10.1.1.455.9118&rep=rep1&type=pdf.

1. Record the authors and title of the source.

2. Identify the main point and key points made by the writers. Present the main point and key points in the order in which they appear in the source. For each point, briefly describe the evidence provided to back it up.

3. Clearly credit the authors for any information, ideas, and arguments you include in your summary: use quotation marks for direct quotations, and identify the page from which you've drawn a paraphrase or quotation. (See Chapters 19–23 for guidelines on citing sources.)

7d

How can I respond to sources?

Responding to a source can help you focus your reactions to the information, ideas, and arguments you've encountered in it. To prepare to write a response to a source, note passages with which you agree or disagree, reflect on interesting information and ideas, and record your thoughts about the effectiveness and relevance of the information and argument in the source.

Write an Agree/Disagree Response

If you want to explore an idea or argument in a source, try freewriting about why you agree or disagree with it. In your response, clearly define the idea or argument to which you are responding. Then explain whether you agree or disagree with the idea or argument—or whether you find yourself in partial agreement with it—and why.

Write a Reflective Response

A reflective response allows you to consider the meaning or implications of what you read. You might focus on a key passage or idea from a source, explaining or elaborating on it. Or you might reflect on your own experiences, attitudes, or observations in relation to a piece of information, an idea, or an argument. You can also use a reflective response to consider how an idea or argument might be interpreted by other readers, how it might be applied in a new context, or how it might be misunderstood.

Write an Analytic Response

An analytic response focuses on the important elements of a source, such as its purpose, ideas, argument, organization, focus, evidence, and style. For example, you might ask whether the main point is stated clearly or whether appropriate types of evidence are used to support an argument. You might also analyze the logic of an argument or map its organization. Or you might offer suggestions about how an author could have made the source more effective.

Write an Evaluative Response

Writers often respond to a source by evaluating its effectiveness. Often called a source evaluation, this type of response is sometimes assigned as an intermediate step in a larger research writing project. Evaluative responses use the evaluation criteria discussed in Chapter 5 as the basis for assessing the effectiveness of a source and the role it might play in the research writing project document. The My Research Project activity on p. 84 in Chapter 5 provides guidance on writing a source evaluation.

Even when writers choose one type of response, they often draw on other types to flesh out ideas. For example, you might consider why you disagree with an argument by analyzing how effectively the source presents the argument. Or you might shift from agreeing with an idea to reflecting on its implications.

My Research Project

Respond to a Source

Putting your response into words can help you sort out your reactions to the ideas, information, and arguments in a source. Use the following guidelines to write an informal response to one of the selections referenced above: Peter Johnston's article, "Guiding the Budding Writer," or Nancy Sommers's article, "Living Composition."

1. Identify a focus for your response. You might select important information, an intriguing idea, or the author's overall argument.

2. Decide what type of response you are going to write: agree/disagree, reflective, analytical, or some combination of the three types.

3. Write an introduction that identifies the information, idea, argument, or source to which you are responding, lays out your overall response (your main point), and identifies the source's author and title.

4. Provide reasons to support your main point and evidence to support your reasons.

5. Clearly credit the sources of any information, ideas, or arguments you use to support your response: use quotation marks for direct quotations, and identify the page or paragraph from which you've drawn a paraphrase or quotation. (See Chapters 19–23 for guidelines on documenting sources.)

7e

How can I explore connections among sources?

Explore Ideas through Informal Writing

You can use informal writing, such as freewriting (p. 21), to explore connections among the information, ideas, and arguments in your sources. Jot down notes in the margins of your sources or in your writer's notebook. Each time you read a new source, keep in mind what you've already read, and make note of similarities and differences among your sources. You can also spend time creating a brief essay that defines each group, identifies which authors belong to each group, and reflects on the strengths, weaknesses, and appropriateness of the approach taken by each group.

Create a Review of Literature

A review of literature presents a synthesis of the key information, ideas, and arguments in the sources you've collected so far. You should identify the most useful sources you found during your exploration of your topic and explain why you found them useful. Keep in mind, however, that a review of literature goes beyond the simple list of sources that are typically found in a working bibliography by offering a discussion of important approaches to your issue. That is, a review of literature focuses not so much on individual sources as on groups of sources and the shared ideas or positions taken by groups of sources. For example, you might find that the work you've read about the use of social media in writing instruction focuses on three areas: (1) supporting interaction among members of a given writing class, (2) allowing instructors to share

WORKING TOGETHER

Make Connections among Sources

Work together with a group of classmates to identify general approaches to the subject of how writing is taught. To prepare for the group activity, each member should read, mark, and annotate the articles, Web pages, and blog posts in this chapter. During class, you should carry out the following activities.

1 Members of the group should take turns reporting what they've learned about one of the sources.

2 As each report is made, the other members of the group should take notes on the key ideas highlighted by the reporter.

3 When the reports have been completed, the group should create an overall list of the key ideas discussed in the individual reports.

4 Identify sources that seem to share similar approaches to the issue. Give each group of sources a name, and provide a brief description of the ideas its authors have in common.

5 Describe each group of sources in detail. Explain what makes the authors part of the same group (their similarities) and how each group differs from the others you've defined.

Once you've completed the activity, consider how you would respond to each group of authors. Ask whether you agree or disagree with their approaches, and describe the extent to which you agree or disagree. Consider whether you would want to join a group, whether you would want to refine a particular approach to better fit your understanding of the subject, or whether you would rather develop a new approach.

---

course materials with students, and (3) helping instructors and students share feedback on writing projects.

Focusing on general approaches to an issue, as opposed to the individual positions adopted in particular sources, can help you understand the major ideas that are being considered in the conversation you are planning to join. By understanding existing approaches to an issue, you can determine whether you agree with any of those approaches or whether you want to introduce a completely new approach. In turn, this will help you develop your own individual position on the issue.

Reviews of literature can be written as an intermediate genre intended not only for your own use but also for use by other readers. Some academic journals publish reviews of literature on a regular basis, providing their readers with syntheses of and commentary on new work in a given area, such as teaching with technology or teaching English as a second language. Reviews of literature can also serve as important sections within research proposals (see below). When used in this way, reviews of literature help readers understand that the writer is knowledgeable about and well positioned to make a strong contribution to the conversation.

For an example that illustrates how key approaches to an issue can be discussed, see featured writer Nicholas Brothers's review of literature on p. 116.

My Research Project
Write a Review of Literature

Complete a literature review for your project. To prepare for the review, read your sources carefully and identify general approaches to your issue. Provide an overview of each approach you've identified; then discuss some of the most important or representative sources. Use quotations, paraphrases, and summaries to share information from the sources with your readers. Use in-text citation and a works cited list to identify your sources.

II Working with Sources

7f

How can I create a research proposal?

A research proposal—sometimes called a prospectus—is a formal presentation of your plan for your research writing project. A proposal helps you pull together the planning you've done on your project, identify areas where you need additional planning, and assess the progress you've made so far.

Unlike a research plan (p. 28), which is designed primarily to help *you* decide how to collect information, a research proposal is addressed to someone else, usually an instructor, a supervisor, or a funding agency. Although the specific format for research proposals can vary widely across disciplines, a research proposal typically includes the following parts:

- a title page
- an introduction that identifies your topic, issue, and/or research question
- a review of literature
- an explanation of how you will collect information
- a project timeline
- a working bibliography

In addition to these core elements, you can also provide an abstract or executive summary, offer an overview of key challenges, and include a funding request. You can read about how to develop each of these core and optional elements below.

Identify Your Topic, Issue, and Research Question

A title page and introduction offer your readers an overview of the topic and issue you'll address in your project document. Your title page should include the working title of your research writing project, your name and contact information, and the date. Your introduction should identify the topic you've chosen and the issue you've decided to address; state your research question and, if you have created one, your position on the issue (p. 58); describe your purpose; and identify and describe your readers. It should also identify the type of document you'll create and explain how your choice of genre reflects your purpose, your understanding of your readers, and the contexts that will shape your work on your research project.

Provide a Review of Literature

A review of literature will help you identify important arguments and approaches to your issue. See p. 111 to learn more about creating your review.

Explain How You'll Collect Information

Your research proposal should help your reader understand how you will collect information. Your plan should identify:

- the types of sources you intend to collect (such as books, journal articles, or opinion columns). Read about types of sources on p. 30.
- the types of search tools (such as library catalogs, databases, and Web search sites) and research methods (such as browsing library shelves, consulting librarians, or conducting surveys) you want to use. You can learn about locating sources in Chapter 10 and conducting field research in Chapter 11.
- the types of strategies (such as simple and advanced database searches or field research) that you intend to use in your searches (pp. 148–55).
- the schedule you will follow as you carry out your searches.

ⓘ INFORMATION LITERACY   Your research question will influence your decisions about how you will collect information. For example, you can use your research question—and, if you've developed one, your position on your issue (p. 58)—to help identify keywords and phrases that might be used in database, catalog, and Web searches. ▮

Develop a Project Timeline

A project timeline will give your reader an indication of the range of days, weeks, or months over which you will be completing your research and writing your document. Your timeline can range from a general description of the number of days or weeks you'll devote to your project to a detailed list of key project activities and the amount of time devoted to completing them. If you are working on a group project, a project timeline can be especially useful, since it will require discussion of individual responsibilities for completing tasks and deadlines for completing them.

Compile a Working or an Annotated Bibliography

A working bibliography lists the sources you've collected so far. Sometimes you will be asked to create an annotated bibliography, which contains a brief description of each source. Your working or annotated bibliography should conform to the documentation system (such as MLA, APA, *Chicago*, or CSE) specified by your instructor, supervisor, or funding agency. For more information on bibliographies, see p. 102.

Clarify and Elaborate on Your Core Proposal

Depending on your purpose, your reader, and the scope of your research writing project, you can choose to include several optional elements.

- **An abstract or executive summary** provides a brief summary—usually fifty to two hundred words—of your project. It should allow your reader to gain a general understanding of your project and your plans for completing it. Writers who wish to provide additional information, such as explanations of their personal interest in an issue, can provide an introduction, as Nicholas Brothers does in his research proposal (p. 116).

- **An overview of key challenges** allows you to share your thoughts about potential problems you'll need to address as you work on your project. This section of your research proposal might discuss difficulties you're likely to encounter, such as locating or collecting specific types of sources, gaining enough knowledge about an issue to develop a credible position, or finding enough respondents for a survey. It also provides an opportunity for your instructor, supervisor, or potential funder to respond by suggesting strategies for meeting specific challenges.

- **A funding request and rationale** provides a budget that identifies costs for key project activities, such as conducting your search, reviewing the sources you collect, writing and designing the document, and publishing or distributing the document.

Writing a formal research proposal allows you to reflect on the work you've done so far and get feedback on your plans to carry out your project. Perhaps more important, it requires you to make decisions about the best strategies for completing your project.

II Working with Sources

Brothers 1

Nicholas Brothers

English 108: College Writing and Research

Dawn Terrick

September 17, 2013

Research Proposal: Private Military

Corporations and the War on Terror

Introduction: For my research project, I would like to explore the world of the modern private military corporation (PMC). Mercenaries have been used throughout history by countries all over the world. With few exceptions, they have suffered a poor reputation; seen as unprofessional and unreliable, they went unused by many first-world nations in the age of standing professional armies. Yet, in recent years, PMCs have morphed into corporate entities and gained new respect. But is this respect deserved? Throughout the Afghanistan and Iraq conflicts, the United States' use of private military corporations has increased to what I consider startling levels.

While I will strive to be as objective as possible when conducting my research, my prior personal interest in this issue has always put me at odds with the supporters of PMCs. Fundamentally, I believe that overreliance on contractors is a danger to national and international security. However, it is entirely possible that, with further study, I will gain a new appreciation for PMCs and their personnel.

> Position statement is clear and concise.

My purpose is ultimately to build an argument about the United States' continued use of PMCs. To present my position on the issue, I will need to inform my readers about the history of PMCs and analyze the corporations' evolving role in our country's military engagements. My readers are my class peers (from many different backgrounds and studying different subjects) and my instructor. Although there is a wide range of scholarship and reportage on this topic, I believe the general public remains unaware of the pervasiveness of these corporations. It's my hope that upon reading my paper, the layperson will have a better understanding of how and why PMCs are involved in the wars in Iraq and Afghanistan. I will be creating an academic essay and a brief presentation to convey my research and argument to my readers. The print format of the essay will allow readers to follow my logic at their own pace and reread sections of the essay as needed, and it will also provide them an easy way to look up the sources I use if they want to explore the topic further — which I hope they will. The presentation will allow me to explain a complicated issue in a more conversational format and answer any questions.

> Discussion of purpose addresses the writer's intent and the readers' needs.

Brothers 2

I plan to begin my paper with background information — mostly recent history unless I find something compelling from the distant past that I feel readers must know to better understand the present. I would like to explore the practical and moral costs of using PMCs. In doing so, I will likely focus on specific companies and incidents during the "War on Terror" years.

Research Question: What roles do private military corporations play in the U.S. military's war on terror?

The research question is open-ended but focuses on a specific time and place.

Review of Literature: The book that originally piqued my interest in this topic was Jeremy Scahill's *Blackwater: The Rise of the World's Most Powerful Mercenary Army*, which depicts PMCs as very dangerous entities. Articles I've come across in publications such as *Salon.com* and *Mother Jones* also strongly criticize PMCs. On the complete opposite end of the spectrum are the corporate websites of the PMCs, which of course paint their contractors in only the most positive light. I found a more evenhanded approach to the topic in P. W. Singer's *Corporate Warriors: The Rise of the Privatized Military Industry*, which provides a solid overview of the history of PMCs and explains their structure and functions.

The literature review helps Nicholas think about his sources' different positions.

Search Plan and Relevant Sources: I will need to continue to seek out a range of perspectives on PMCs as I develop my own argument. I plan to conduct some field research by interviewing people who have firsthand experience with or expertise on PMCs. My brother, Michael Brothers, is in the military and might agree to an interview, and I plan to look at the research interests of the political science professors at Missouri Western to see if anyone might be able to provide me with insight on the wars from an academic perspective.

I have already located three books on the subject through the library's catalog, and by reading through the citations and sources used by the authors of these books, I have identified several other books that I might explore. In addition, I have used simple keyword and advanced searches on EBSCOhost, LexisNexis, and *NYTimes.com* to find several magazine, newspaper, and scholarly journal articles that provide contrasting viewpoints on the use of PMCs. They range from first-person accounts of PMC operations to academic articles analyzing the history and current use of PMCs.

I'd also like to take a look at some official government reports and read the actual language of some of the laws that surround PMCs. The Department of Defense website as well as senators' and representatives' websites might be good places to start.

Nicholas identifies both a general search idea and a specific plan to carry out the search.

II Working with Sources

Brothers 3

Once my first draft is complete, I might conduct another round of research to help answer any new questions or expand on new supporting points that I've developed.

Project Timeline: I have a little more than one month to complete this project. I already have several solid sources and plan to have my first assignment (the background paper based on what I know so far) completed one week from today. The next week, I'll conduct my interviews and write an interview paper based on my conversations. From there, I will combine the background paper and the interview paper, synthesizing these two drafts along with any new sources I've found. I will receive feedback on my first draft from my classmates and instructor. Then, I'll conduct any additional research needed and revise the draft by the due date of Oct. 20. After the final draft is submitted, I'll create a reverse outline and summarize my paper's most important points for a brief in-class presentation the following week.

A general project timeline indicates the time devoted to each stage of the process.

Key Challenges: Finding knowledgeable firsthand sources will be the main problem I will encounter, but I have some candidates in mind in helping me to understand the perceptions of U.S. military personnel, the history of mercenaries, and the political ramifications of their present-day use by the United States. I will contact them soon to inquire about their willingness and availability. I feel that I have already amassed a good deal of research material and plans, but I am wary that my sources so far might be geared toward my inherent bias toward the subject. I would like to make sure I have real opposing views to explore and not just straw men; this is a goal I will continually have to work toward.

Writing down key challenges helps Nicholas avoid potential problems.

Time is another challenge. I have to conduct field research quickly and synthesize the results of the interview paper with the rest of my research in a short amount of time to create a first draft. I'm also concerned about focusing my topic enough for the paper to make sense — there are a lot of issues related to my topic that are intriguing, from the history of mercenaries to the legal status of PMCs and their lack of culpability for their crimes. Limiting the scope of my project could be difficult given the many aspects of the topic that seem worth addressing.

Working Bibliography

Scahill, Jeremy. *Blackwater: The Rise of the World's Most Powerful*
    Mercenary Army. 2nd ed., Nation Books, 2007.

This book details the history of the private military corporation
formerly known as Blackwater, with a focus on its controversial
operations in Iraq and Afghanistan. Scahill is a reporter for the
Nation and has reported extensively on Blackwater. I will use this
book throughout my research project, as Blackwater (now Xe Services)
remains one of the most powerful, visible, and divisive PMCs in the
world.

Singer, P. W. *Corporate Warriors: The Rise of the Privatized Military*
    Industry. 2nd ed., Cornell UP, 2008.

This scholarly look at the issue takes a balanced view: Singer is able
to see the opportunities that PMCs provide while casting a critical
eye at the potentials for abuse. I believe this will be an essential
resource due to its balanced viewpoint and thoroughness.

The working bibliography summarizes sources and evaluates their usefulness.

Smith, Eugene B. "The New Condottieri and US Policy: The
    Privatization of Conflict and Its Implications." *Parameters: US*
    Army War College, vol. 32, no. 4, 2012, p. 104. *Academic Search*
    Premier, EBSCO, pdc-connection.ebscohost.com/c/articles/
    8640772/new-condottieri-us-policy-privatization-conflict
    -implications.

Written before the invasion of Iraq, this academic article briefly
outlines the history of the privatization of warfare and concludes
that the United States should employ PMCs due to their track record.
At the time of this article's writing, Eugene B. Smith was a lieutenant
colonel in the United States Army and served in the United States
Central Command area of operations. This article might be useful
in understanding the military command that has increasingly
employed private contractors in the last decade.

My Research Project

Create a Research Proposal

Use the following activity to create a formal research proposal.

1. Provide the working title for your project.

2. Describe your issue.

3. Describe your purpose for working on this project.

4. Describe your readers' needs, interests, knowledge, experiences, values, and beliefs.

5. State your research question.

6. Briefly review key findings about your issue from the sources you found as you explored your topic.

7. Indicate how you'll locate additional information, ideas, and arguments about your issue.

8. Include your project timeline.

9. Include your working bibliography.

10. Discuss the key challenges you face (optional).

11. Identify specific funding requests (optional).

QUICK REFERENCE

Engaging with Information, Ideas, and Arguments

✔ Understand academic writing, academic argument, and the role of intermediate genres. (p. 100)

✔ Create working bibliographies and annotated bibliographies. (p. 102)

✔ Summarize sources. (p. 106)

✔ Respond to sources. (p. 109)

✔ Explore connections among sources by developing a review of literature. (p. 111)

✔ Develop a research proposal. (p. 113)

8

Managing Information

Key Questions

Even with a narrowly defined research question, it's likely that your searches will produce a large number of relevant sources. To use those sources most effectively, decide how to save, organize, and keep track of your sources. Doing so will help you work with your sources more easily as you plan and draft your document.

8a

How can I save and organize print information?

During your research project, you might accumulate a great deal of print information, such as:

- your written notes (in a notebook, on loose pieces of paper, on Post-it Notes, and so on)
- printouts from Web pages and databases
- printed word processing documents, such as your outline and rough drafts
- books, magazines, newspapers, brochures, pamphlets, and government documents
- photocopies of articles, book chapters, and other documents
- letters, printed e-mail messages, survey results, and so on

Rather than letting all this material build up in messy piles on your desk, create a filing system to keep track of your print documents. Filing systems can range from well-organized piles of paper labeled with sticky notes to three-ring binders to file cabinets filled with neatly labeled folders.

Regardless of the approach you take, keep the following principles in mind.

- **Make it easy to locate your print materials.** Decide whether you want to group material by topic, by date, by pro versus con, by type of material (Web pages, photocopies, original documents, field sources, and so on), or by author.

- **Stick with your organizing scheme.** You'll find it difficult to locate materials if you use different approaches at different points in your research project.

- **Always include complete publication information.** If a source doesn't contain publication information, write it on the document yourself. You'll need it later. Publication information includes author, title, publisher, place and date of publication, and—for a Web source—sponsoring organization and URL.

- **Write a brief note on each of your print materials.** Indicate how it might contribute to your project.

- **Record the date.** Indicating dates when you found a source can help you reconstruct what you might have been doing at the time. Dates are also essential for documenting Web sources and other online sources (see Chapters 19–23).

8b

How can I save and organize digital information?

i **INFORMATION LITERACY**   As you save digital information, keep it organized. The simplest organizational strategy is to save your work in a single folder. As you save your work, use descriptive file names. Rather than naming a file "Notes 1," for instance, name it "Interview Notes from John Garcia, April 22." Keep in mind that the single-folder approach might not work well for larger projects. At some point, the sheer number of files in the folder makes it difficult to find a single file easily. Rather than scrolling through several screens of files, you might find it more efficient to create multiple folders to hold related files (see Figure 8.1). ▥

Downloading   Downloading digital sources to a hard drive, a flash drive, or a Cloud-based service such as OneDrive, DropBox, or iCloud allows you to open them later in a Web browser or word processing program. Downloading sources can save you time toward the end of your writing project, particularly when you are drafting or revising your document (see Figure 8.2).

How you save your sources will vary according to the type of digital source you're viewing.

- To download entire Web pages, right-click (for Windows), Command-click (for Mac), or press and hold a finger (on phones and tablets) on the page and choose the Save or Save as command. Or use the options icon or menu to save the page (see Figure 8.2).

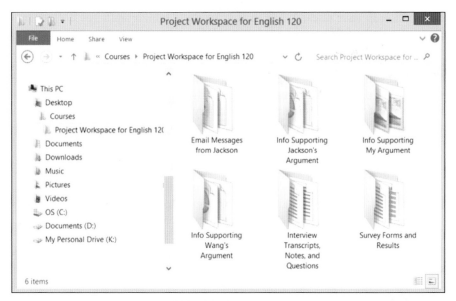

FIGURE 8.1 A Project Workspace Using Multiple Folders

- To download images and other media materials from the Web, click or press and hold on the item you want and select the appropriate command.
- To download records from a database, check the online help pages. Most databases allow you to mark and save records returned by a search. To download full-text sources from databases, you can open and save the file (often a PDF file or a text file) or download it in the same way you would download an image.

Remember that downloading a source does not automatically record the URL or the date on which you viewed the source for the first time. Be sure to record that

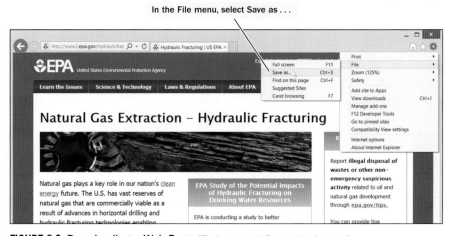

FIGURE 8.2 Downloading a Web Page [Environmental Protection Agency.]

information in your research log, in your working bibliography (p. 102), or in a document in the folder where you've saved your files.

Copying and Pasting You can save text from relevant sources as notes in a word processing document or programs such as EverNote and OneNote. Be sure to keep track of source information, such as the URL and the date you viewed a source, so that you can return to it if necessary and cite it appropriately. You can also use Web clipping tools, which work with your browser as toolbars or "add-ons" (a term used for programs that work within browsers) to copy all or part of a Web page. Leading, no-fee Web capture tools include Diigo (**diigo.com**) and Zotero (**zotero.org**).

Using E-mail You can e-mail yourself messages containing digital documents you've found in your research. Some databases, such as those from EBSCO and OCLC/FirstSearch, allow you to e-mail the text of selected records directly from the database (see Figure 8.3). You can also use e-mail as a form of file folder by sending messages to yourself that include copies of documents in the form of pasted text or attached files. If you use a subject line such as "My Comp 110 Research Project," you can sort your messages by subject line and easily view all the information you've collected or you can simply search for messages containing the phrase *research project.*

Taking Photos, Making Recordings, and Saving Notes If you have a smartphone or a tablet, you can record conversations with others, record voice memos that contain ideas about your project, save video, take photos of sources you find in the periodicals room (p. 167), and surf the Web to locate sources. Most phone and tablet operating systems provide access to "apps" (or applications), often at

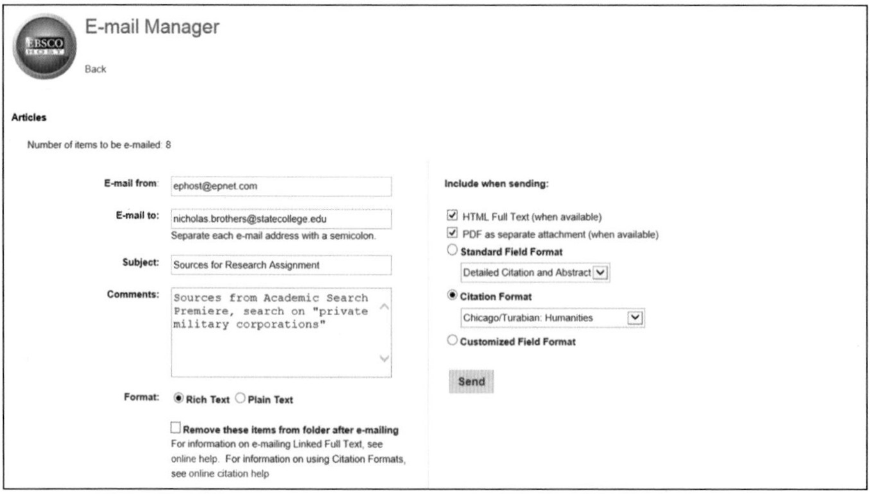

FIGURE 8.3 Sending E-mail from a Database

no or low cost, that allow you to collect and organize information the same way you would on a laptop or desktop computer (see Figure 8.4).

As you save information with these tools, keep your work well organized. Use descriptive names, save work in folders or albums, and add information about where and when you found the information. Be sure to talk with other writers about the apps they've found useful and, if they're free, try them out yourself.

Saving Bookmarks and Favorites in Your Browser   You can use a Bookmarks or Favorites list in a Web browser to keep track of online sources. Keep these lists organized by putting related items into folders and giving the items on your list descriptive names. If you use this strategy, however, remember that pages on the Web can and do change—and perhaps might do so even before you finish your writing project. Be aware as well that some Web pages are generated by database programs, which can result in unwieldy URLs, such as

> newfirstsearch.oclc.org/WebZ/FSFETCH?fetchtype=fullrecord:sessionid=fsapp2
> -49320-imjmp9sc-hoge4g:entitypagenum=9:0:recno=4:resultset=3:format=FI:next
> =html/record.html:bad=error/badfetch.html:entitytoprecno=4:entitycurrecno=4
> :numrecs=1

Although this long string of characters starts out looking like a normal URL, the majority of the characters are used by the database program to determine which records to display on a page. In many cases, the URL works only while you are conducting your search. If you add such a URL to your Bookmarks or Favorites list, there's a good chance it won't work later.

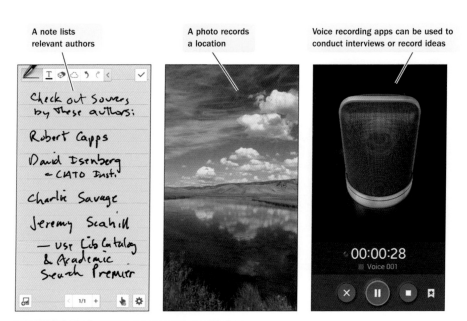

A note lists relevant authors

A photo records a location

Voice recording apps can be used to conduct interviews or record ideas

FIGURE 8.4 Saving Digital Information with Apps

Backing Up Your Files Whatever strategies you use to save and organize digital materials, replacing lost information takes time and effort. Avoid the risk of lost information by taking the time to make copies of your digital files and downloads, e-mail messages, saved Web pages and clippings, and Bookmarks or Favorites list.

QUICK REFERENCE

Managing Information

✔ Decide how you will save and organize print information. (p. 121)

✔ Decide how you will save and organize digital information. (p. 122)

‖ Working with Sources

9

Avoiding Plagiarism

Key Questions

Few writers intentionally try to pass off the work of others as their own. However, deadlines and other pressures can lead writers to take notes poorly and cite sources improperly. In addition, easy access to documents through the Web and full-text databases has made it all too easy to copy and paste work from other writers without acknowledging its source.

Failing to cite your sources can lead to serious problems. Your readers will not be able to determine which ideas and information in your text are your own or which are drawn from your sources. If they suspect you are failing to acknowledge your sources, they are likely to doubt your credibility and suspect your competence, and they might even stop reading your document. More seriously, submitting academic work that does not include proper identification of sources might result in failure in a course or some other disciplinary action.

127

9a

What is plagiarism?

Plagiarism is a form of intellectual dishonesty. It involves either unintentionally using someone else's work without properly acknowledging where the ideas or information came from (the most common form of plagiarism) or intentionally passing off someone else's work as your own (the most serious form of plagiarism).

Plagiarism is based on the notion of "copyright," or ownership of a document or an idea. Like a patent, which protects an invention, a copyright protects an author's investment of time and energy in the creation of a document. Essentially, it assures authors that, when they create a document, someone else won't be able to steal ideas from it and profit from that theft without penalty.

In this sense, plagiarism in academic writing differs in important ways from the kind of mixing and remixing that can take place in popular culture. The expectations of readers of source-based documents differ, for instance, from those of people who listen to music. While listeners enjoying a song on the radio might not be surprised to hear part of another song added to a mix, readers of an article in *Time* magazine or an academic journal might be alarmed to read an unattributed passage that they recognize as the work of another writer. Context matters, and in this case the context of academic writing differs significantly from that of popular culture.

Unintentional Plagiarism

In most cases, plagiarism is unintentional, and most cases of unintentional plagiarism result from taking poor notes or failing to use notes properly. You are plagiarizing if you:

- quote a passage in a note but neglect to include quotation marks and then later insert the quotation into your document without remembering that it is a direct quotation

- include a paraphrase that differs so slightly from the original passage that it might as well be a direct quotation

- don't clearly distinguish between your ideas and ideas that come from your sources

- neglect to list the source of a paraphrase, quotation, or summary in your text or in your works cited list

Although unintentional plagiarism is, by definition, something that the writer hasn't planned to do, it is nonetheless a serious issue and, when detected, is likely to have consequences. Some instructors might require that an assignment be rewritten; others might impose a penalty, such as a lowered grade or failure on the assignment.

TUTORIAL

How can I avoid unintentional plagiarism?

Unintentional plagiarism is the use of another writer's work without properly acknowledging the source of the ideas or information. Unintentional plagiarism is often the result of rushed work on a project. It can sometimes result from inadequate research writing skills or honest mistakes. In this example, Cori Schmidtbauer checks her rough draft for unintentional plagiarism.

To avoid unintentional plagiarism, follow these steps.

1 Check for a works cited or reference list.

2 Identify each quotation, paraphrase, and summary.

3 Check for appropriate attributions.

4 Check for appropriate in-text citation.

5 Ensure that each source is included in your works cited or reference list.

6 Check for changes in writing style. If you find changes, check your notes to identify the source of the passage and ensure that you haven't neglected to include quotation marks or paraphrased too closely.

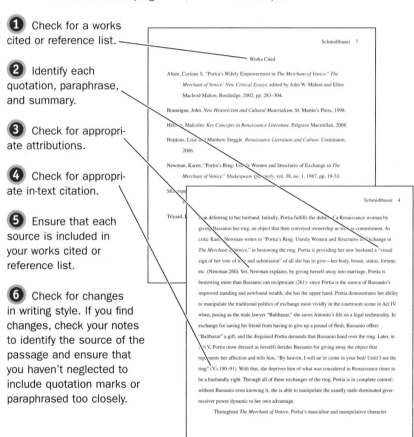

Schmidtbauer 7

Works Cited

Abate, Corinne S. "Portia's Wifely Empowerment in *The Merchant of Venice*." *The Merchant of Venice: New Critical Essays*, edited by John W. Mahon and Ellen Macleod Mahon, Routledge, 2002, pp. 283–304.

Brannigan, John. *New Historicism and Cultural Materialism*. St. Martin's Press, 1998.

Hebron, Malcolm. *Key Concepts in Renaissance Literature*. Palgrave Macmillan, 2008.

Hopkins, Lisa, and Matthew Steggle. *Renaissance Literature and Culture*. Continuum, 2006.

Newman, Karen. "Portia's Ring: Unruly Women and Structures of Exchange in *The Merchant of Venice*." *Shakespeare Quarterly*, vol. 38, no. 1, 1987, pp. 19-33.

Schmidtbauer 4

in deferring to her husband. Initially, Portia fulfills the duties of a Renaissance woman by giving Bassanio her ring, an object that then conveyed ownership as well as commitment. As critic Karen Newman writes in "Portia's Ring: Unruly Women and Structures of Exchange in *The Merchant of Venice*," in bestowing the ring, Portia is providing her new husband a "visual sign of her vow of love and submission" of all she has to give—her body, house, status, fortune, etc. (Newman 260). Yet, Newman explains, by giving herself away into marriage, Portia is bestowing more than Bassanio can reciprocate (261): since Portia is the source of Bassanio's improved standing and newfound wealth, she has the upper hand. Portia demonstrates her ability to manipulate the traditional politics of exchange most vividly in the courtroom scene in Act IV when, posing as the male lawyer "Balthazar," she saves Antonio's life on a legal technicality. In exchange for saving his friend from having to give up a pound of flesh, Bassanio offers "Balthazar" a gift, and the disguised Portia demands that Bassanio hand over the ring. Later, in Act V, Portia (now dressed as herself) derides Bassanio for giving away the object that represents her affection and tells him, "By heaven, I will ne'er come in your bed/ Until I see the ring" (V.i.190–91). With that, she deprives him of what was considered in Renaissance times to be a husbandly right. Through all of these exchanges of the ring, Portia is in complete control; without Bassanio even knowing it, she is able to manipulate the usually male-dominated giver-receiver power dynamic to her own advantage.

Throughout *The Merchant of Venice*, Portia's masculine and manipulative character

■■ Working with Sources

Intentional Plagiarism

Intentional plagiarism, although less common than unintentional plagiarism, can lead to academic penalties ranging from a reduced grade on an assignment to failure of a course to expulsion. Intentional plagiarism includes:

- engaging in "patchwork writing," which involves piecing together passages from two or more sources without acknowledging the sources and without properly quoting or paraphrasing
- creating fake citations to mislead a reader about the sources of information used in a document
- copying or closely paraphrasing extended passages from another document and passing them off as the writer's original work
- copying an entire document and passing it off as the writer's original work
- purchasing a document and passing it off as the writer's original work

Plagiarism in Group Projects

Peer review and other collaborative activities raise important, and potentially confusing, questions.

- If another writer suggests changes to your document and you subsequently incorporate them into your document, are you plagiarizing?
- What if those suggestions significantly change your document?
- If you work with a group of writers on a project, do you need to identify the parts that each of you wrote?
- Is it okay to list yourself as a coauthor if another writer does most of the work on a collaborative writing project?

The answers to these questions will vary from situation to situation. In general, it's appropriate to use comments from reviewers in your document without citing them. If a reviewer's comments are particularly helpful, you might acknowledge his or her contributions in your document; writers often thank reviewers in a footnote or an endnote or in an acknowledgments section. It is usually appropriate to list coauthors on a collaboratively written document without individually identifying the text that was written by each, although some instructors ask that individual contributions be noted in the document or on a cover page. If you are uncertain about what is appropriate, ask your instructor.

9b

What are research ethics?

Research ethics are based on the notion that writing — and in particular research writing — is an honest exchange of information, ideas, and arguments among writers and readers who share an interest in a certain issue. As a research writer, then, you'll want to behave honestly and ethically. In general, you should:

- acknowledge the sources of the information, ideas, and arguments used in your document—to show respect for the work that others have done before you

- accurately and fairly represent the information, ideas, and arguments— to ensure that you do not misrepresent that work to your readers

- provide citation information for your sources—to help your readers understand how you have drawn your conclusions and where they can locate those sources should they want to consult them

These three rules are the essence of research ethics. Ultimately, failing to act ethically—even when the failure is unintentional—can reflect poorly on you and your document. If your readers suspect that you have acted unethically, they will question the accuracy and credibility of the information, ideas, and arguments in your document. If they suspect you've sacrificed research ethics altogether, they'll probably stop reading your document. Figure 9.1 shows how Cori Schmidtbauer attended to research ethics in her essay about Portia's role in *The Merchant of Venice*.

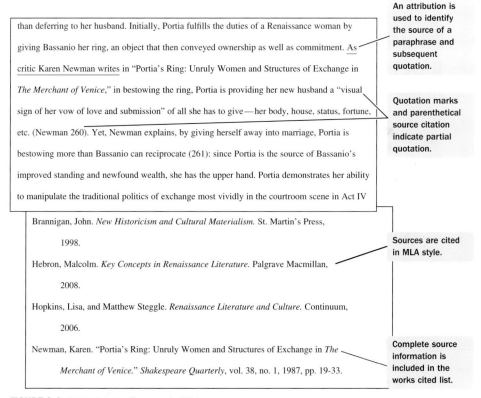

than deferring to her husband. Initially, Portia fulfills the duties of a Renaissance woman by giving Bassanio her ring, an object that then conveyed ownership as well as commitment. As critic Karen Newman writes in "Portia's Ring: Unruly Women and Structures of Exchange in *The Merchant of Venice*," in bestowing the ring, Portia is providing her new husband a "visual sign of her vow of love and submission" of all she has to give—her body, house, status, fortune, etc. (Newman 260). Yet, Newman explains, by giving herself away into marriage, Portia is bestowing more than Bassanio can reciprocate (261): since Portia is the source of Bassanio's improved standing and newfound wealth, she has the upper hand. Portia demonstrates her ability to manipulate the traditional politics of exchange most vividly in the courtroom scene in Act IV

Brannigan, John. *New Historicism and Cultural Materialism*. St. Martin's Press, 1998.

Hebron, Malcolm. *Key Concepts in Renaissance Literature*. Palgrave Macmillan, 2008.

Hopkins, Lisa, and Matthew Steggle. *Renaissance Literature and Culture*. Continuum, 2006.

Newman, Karen. "Portia's Ring: Unruly Women and Structures of Exchange in *The Merchant of Venice*." *Shakespeare Quarterly*, vol. 38, no. 1, 1987, pp. 19-33.

An attribution is used to identify the source of a paraphrase and subsequent quotation.

Quotation marks and parenthetical source citation indicate partial quotation.

Sources are cited in MLA style.

Complete source information is included in the works cited list.

FIGURE 9.1 Attending to Research Ethics

II Working with Sources

9c

What is common knowledge?

Although crediting other authors for their work is important, you almost certainly won't need to document every fact and idea used in your document because some of the information you'll use falls under the category of common knowledge. Common knowledge is information that is widely known, such as the fact that the Declaration of Independence was signed in 1776. Or it might be the kind of knowledge that people working in a particular field, such as petroleum engineering, use on a regular basis.

If you're relatively new to your topic, it can be difficult to determine whether information in a source is common knowledge. As you explore your topic, however, you will begin to identify what is generally known. For instance, if three or more sources use the same information without citing its source, you can assume that the information is common knowledge. If those sources use the information and cite the source, however, make sure you cite it as well.

9d

What is fair use and when should I ask permission to use a source?

The concept of fair use deals with how much of a source you can borrow or quote. According to Section 107 of the Copyright Act of 1976—the fair use provision, available at **copyright.gov/title17/**—writers can use copyrighted materials for purposes of "criticism, comment, news reporting, teaching (including multiple copies for classroom use), scholarship, or research." In other words, writers generally don't need to seek permission to make brief quotations from a source or to summarize or paraphrase a source.

ⓘ **INFORMATION LITERACY**   If you are working on an assignment for a course—and do not plan to publish the assignment on the Web or in print—you generally can use material from another source without seeking permission. Remember, however, that in all cases you must still cite the source of the material you use.

Writers who plan to publish their work should seek permission to use material from a source if they want to quote a lengthy passage or, in the case of shorter works such as poems and song lyrics, if they want to quote a significant percentage of the source.

If you seek permission to use a source, explain why and how you want to use it. Many authors and publishers allow academic use of their work but frown on commercial uses. When you contact an author or a publisher, include your name

Dear Ms. Jackson:

I am a student and am completing a research project for my writing class, English Composition 200, at Colorado State University. The research project will be used only for educational purposes and will be distributed only to my instructor and members of my class for a period of three weeks during April and May of this year.

I would like to include in my project the following image, which is displayed **B** on your site at westernliving.org/images/2302a.jpg, and would greatly appreciate your permission to do so:

If you are able to grant me the requested permission, please respond to this **C** e-mail message. My deadline for completing my project is April 22nd. I appreciate your quick response.

If you are not the copyright holder or do not have authority to grant this request, I would appreciate any information you can provide concerning the current copyright holder.

Thank you for considering this request.

Sincerely,

Glenn Choi **D**

GlennChoi@students.colostate.edu

(970) 555–1515

FIGURE 9.2 Sample Permission Request

A Or ". . . on the Web at myschool.edu."

B Insert or describe passage or image. For example: "paragraphs 3 through 5 of the article," a thumbnail of the image, the URL of a document or image on the Web.

C Or ". . . sign the enclosed copy of this letter and return it to me."

D Provide contact information, such as name, address, e-mail address, phone number, fax number.

and contact information, the source you wish to use, the purpose for which you will use the source, and the time during which it will be used (see Figure 9.2).

If you contact an author or a publisher by mail, include a self-addressed, stamped envelope. It saves the author or publisher the cost of responding by mail, indicates that you are serious, and perhaps most important, shows good manners. ▇

II Working with Sources

9e

How can I avoid plagiarism?

In most cases, writers who plagiarize do so unintentionally. You can avoid unintentional plagiarism by learning how to:

- conduct a knowledge inventory
- take notes carefully
- distinguish between your ideas and those drawn from your sources
- cite sources in the text and in a works cited or reference list
- recognize misconceptions about intentional plagiarism

Conduct a Knowledge Inventory

You can avoid unintentional plagiarism by ensuring that you have a clear understanding of your issue. When you are just beginning to learn about an issue, you might find it difficult not only to express your own ideas clearly and effectively, but also to restate or reframe the information, ideas, and arguments you've encountered in your sources. The result might be a document composed of passages that have been copied without attribution or paraphrased too closely. To address difficulties understanding an issue, conduct a knowledge inventory to gain insights into what you do and don't understand about the issue. Conducting a knowledge inventory involves answering three questions.

1. What do you already know about the issue?
2. What don't you know?
3. What do you want to know?

My Research Project

Conduct a Knowledge Inventory

In your research log, answer the following questions about the issue you've decided to address in your project document.

1. What do I already know about the issue?

2. What don't I know?

3. What do I want to know?

Review your answers and then identify the concepts that, if you understood them more fully, would allow you to work on your assignment more effectively. Learn about those concepts by discussing them with your instructor, a librarian, or someone who knows about or has been affected by the issue.

Your answers can provide a starting point for brainstorming, collecting and working with sources, and planning. They can also serve as a guide for discussing the issue with others. Once you've completed your knowledge inventory, meet with your instructor, consult a librarian, or talk with people who are knowledgeable about the issue. Ideally, your discussions will help you determine the most productive way to learn more about your issue. You might, for example, identify key concepts that, if you understood them more fully, would help you write about your issue more effectively.

Take Notes Carefully

Unintentional plagiarism occurs most often when a writer takes poor notes and then uses information from those notes in a document. Notes might contain direct quotations that are not surrounded with quotation marks, paraphrases that differ in only minor ways from the original passage, and summaries that contain original passages from a source. Taking notes accurately and appropriately is the first—and arguably the most important—step in avoiding unintentional plagiarism. For guidance on quoting, paraphrasing, and summarizing during note taking, see Chapter 6. For guidance on integrating quotations, paraphrases, summaries, numerical information, and illustrations into your document, see Chapter 15.

To avoid plagiarizing as you take notes, keep the following guidelines in mind.

- Surround every quotation with quotation marks.
- Ensure that every paraphrase differs in both wording and sentence structure from the original passage.
- Avoid creating summaries that are little more than a patchwork of sentences pulled from the original source.
- Include publication information—in particular, author information and the location of passages that are quoted or paraphrased—about the source on every note.
- Double-check your notes to be sure that they are accurate and do not include problems that might lead to unintentional plagiarism when you integrate source information into your project document.

The tutorial on p. 138 illustrates some of the problems that can arise as you take notes on your sources.

As You Draft, Distinguish between Your Ideas and Ideas in Your Sources   [FRAMING MY ARGUMENT]

To distinguish between your ideas and those obtained through your sources, use attributions—words and phrases that alert your readers to the source of the information or ideas you are using. To avoid plagiarizing as you integrate information from your notes into your document, use these guidelines.

- Look for notes that differ from your usual style of writing. More often than not, if a note doesn't sound like your own writing, it isn't. If you find a note that might be a direct quotation, a close paraphrase, or a patchwork summary, double-check the note against the original source.

- Use author attributions to clearly distinguish information, ideas, and arguments drawn from your sources. Failing to do so is likely to lead your readers to think the information, ideas, and arguments are your own. To avoid this problem, attribute source information using phrases such as "according to Jessica Richards" and "Sandra Chapman argues."

You can learn more about using attributions to identify the origin of quotations, paraphrases, and summaries in Chapter 15.

Identify Sources in Your Document

Include a complete citation for each source you refer to in your document. The citation should appear both in the text of the document (as an in-text citation) and in a works cited or reference list.

In the following examples, the writer includes MLA-style parenthetical citations that refer readers to a list of works cited at the end of the document. Note that MLA style, as well as APA, *Chicago*, and CSE styles, allow for a combination of attributions and parenthetical information to refer to sources (see Chapters 20–23).

> Jessica Richards argues, "We need to develop an efficient, cost-effective means of distributing hydrogen fuels before we can move to a hydrogen economy. If we don't we'll be operating in crisis mode when the next serious oil shortage arrives" (322).

> "We need to develop an efficient, cost-effective means of distributing hydrogen fuels before we can move to a hydrogen economy" (Richards 322).

Be sure to cite page or paragraph numbers for paraphrased and summarized information as well as for direct quotations. The following paraphrase of Jessica Richards's comments about energy needs includes the page number of the original passage in parentheses.

> Jessica Richards argues that we need to create an "efficient, cost-effective" system for delivering hydrogen fuel now, instead of while we are facing a critical oil shortage (322).

To learn more about identifying sources in your document, see pp. 251–61, in Chapter 15. To learn how to document sources using the MLA, APA, *Chicago,* and CSE documentation systems, see Chapters 20–23.

Understand Why Writers Plagiarize

Although most plagiarism is unintentional, some students do plagiarize deliberately. The causes of intentional plagiarism range from running out of time to seeing little value in a course. The most common reasons offered to explain intentional plagiarism—and steps you can take to avoid falling victim to its temptation—are listed below.

"It's easier to plagiarize." Some people believe it takes less work to cheat than to create an original document. That's probably true—but only in the short term. If you are pursuing a college degree, the odds are high that your profession will require writing ability or an understanding of how to work with information. When you're assigned a report or a proposal down the road, you might regret not taking the time to hone your writing and research skills.

"I ran out of time." Most writers occasionally find themselves wondering where all the time has gone and how they can possibly complete an assignment on schedule. If you find yourself in this situation, contact your instructor about a revised deadline. You might find that you'll face a penalty for turning in work late, but that penalty will almost certainly be less severe than a penalty for intentional plagiarism.

"I couldn't care less about this assignment." It's not unusual to put off assignments that don't interest you. Rather than avoiding the work, try to approach the assignment in a way that interests you (p. 36). If that fails, contact your instructor to see if you can customize the assignment so that it better aligns with your interests.

"I'm no good at writing." A lot of people have doubts about their ability to earn a good grade in a writing course. Occasionally, however, some students convince themselves that plagiarizing is a reasonable alternative to writing their own documents. If you lack confidence, seek assistance from your instructor, a campus writing center, a tutoring center, one of the many online writing centers on the Web (such as the Writing@CSU website at **writing.colostate.edu**), or a friend or family member. You're likely to find that, even with only modest support, you'll be able to do well.

"I didn't think I'd get caught." Some students believe—and might even have experiences to support their belief—that they won't get caught plagiarizing. Most writing instructors, however, become familiar with their students' writing styles. If they notice a sudden change in style, or encounter varying styles in the same document, they might become suspicious. The availability of plagiarism detection software also increases the likelihood that plagiarism will be discovered.

"Everybody cheats." Some people plagiarize because they believe that many of their classmates are doing so. They fear that, if they don't plagiarize, they'll be at a competitive disadvantage. In fact, however, the number of students who plagiarize is quite low. Don't be persuaded by dramatic statistics that plagiarism is the norm in writing classes. The reality is that few students plagiarize intentionally, and those who do still tend to earn lower grades than their peers.

II Working with Sources

TUTORIAL

How do I avoid plagiarism as I take notes?

You can avoid plagiarism at the earliest stage of research by taking notes that quote, paraphrase, and summarize sources accurately and by recording the source of the information.

Original Passage: Coral reefs are one of the most important marine habitats in shallow tropical seas. Reefs provide structure and act as focal points for secondary production. As a consequence, coral reefs provide a number of important ecosystem services (Moberg and Folke 1999). Reefs protect shorelines from coastal erosion and provide habitat for fish and millions of other organisms making them the most biodiverse marine ecosystem. These in turn support commercial and recreational fishing, diving and boating activities, tourist activities, shelter harbors and are a source of biomedicinal compounds.

Source: Richard S. Appeldoorn, Paul M. Yoshioka, and David L. Ballantine, "Coral Reef Ecosystem Studies: Integrating Science and Management in the Caribbean," p. 134.

1 Quote appropriately by identifying your source, using quotation marks around quoted material, and providing a page number for the quotation.

Quotation

Appropriate

Coral reefs play important roles in the Caribbean ecosystem. As Appeldoorn, Yoshioka, and Ballantine note, "Reefs protect shorelines from coastal erosion and provide habitat for fish and millions of other organisms" (134).

2 Avoid quoting inappropriately by checking your notes for quotation marks and proper citation of the source's information. Be sure that you've quoted the source accurately using ellipsis marks and brackets to show any deletions (p. 87).

Inappropriate

Coral reefs play important roles in the Caribbean ecosystem, since they protect shorelines from coastal erosion and provide habitat for fish and millions of other organisms.

3 When you paraphrase information from a source in your notes, be sure to use your own words to record the meaning of the passage and provide a page number to help you locate the information (and create a full citation) later on.

Paraphrase

Appropriate

According to Appeldoorn, Yoshioka, and Ballantine, coral reefs play important roles in the Caribbean ecosystem, serving as habitat for a wide range of ocean species and protecting shorelines from erosion (134).

④ Avoid inappropriate paraphrases by reviewing your notes against the source's wording to make sure they aren't a close match. If the source's wording is compelling and you want to capture it, consider using a quotation instead.

Inappropriate

According to Appeldoorn, Yoshioka, and Ballantine, coral reefs protect shorelines from coastal erosion and offer habitat for fish and multitudes of other organisms.

⑤ When summarizing, use your own words to create an overview of the source's line of argument. Make sure you record the author and title of the source in your notes or following the summary.

Summary

Appropriate

In the article "Coral Reef Ecosystem Studies: Integrating Science and Management in the Caribbean," Appeldoorn, Yoshioka, and Ballantine point out the important roles that coral reefs play in the Caribbean ecosystem. They note that reefs protect shorelines from erosion and provide habitat for fish and a multitude of other aquatic organisms. In addition, they point out, reefs provide important economic and recreational benefits to people, serving as sites for commercial fishing, sources of biomedical compounds, and opportunities for diving, boating, and other tourist activities

⑥ Avoid inappropriate summaries by citing the source of your information. Review your notes to be sure you haven't used the source's wording in your summary.

Inappropriate

Coral reefs are one of the most important marine habitats in shallow tropical seas. They provide a number of important ecosystem services, including protecting shorelines from coastal erosion and serving as habitat for fish and millions of other organisms. These in turn support commercial and recreational fishing, diving and boating activities, tourist activities, shelter harbors and are a source of biomedicinal compounds.

II Working with Sources

"This course is a waste of my time." If you view a course as little more than a box that needs to be checked, it might seem reasonable to check that box with as little effort as possible. Turning in work that isn't your own, however, can backfire. If you are caught plagiarizing, you'll most likely receive a reduced—or failing—grade for the assignment or the course. Instead of plagiarizing, talk with the instructor or an academic advisor about your lack of interest. You might find that the course actually has some relevance to your interests and career plans.

9f

What should I do if I'm accused of plagiarism?

If your instructor expresses concerns about the originality of your work or the manner in which you've documented your use of information, ideas, and arguments from sources, ask for a meeting to discuss the situation. To prepare for the meeting, take the following steps.

- Review your document to identify passages that might have raised suspicions.
- Collect the materials you've used in your writing project, such as copies of your sources, responses to surveys, interview transcripts, and so on.
- Collect materials you've written during the project, such as the results of brainstorming and freewriting sessions; organizational materials you've created, such as clusters, maps, and outlines; and rough and final drafts of your document.
- Reflect on your research writing process.

During the meeting, listen to the concerns of your instructor before responding. It will be natural to feel defensive about the situation, but you'll probably be more comfortable if you take notes and try to understand why your instructor has concerns about your document. Once your instructor is finished expressing his or her concerns, think carefully about what has been said and respond as clearly as possible. You'll probably find that your instructor will have follow-up questions, most likely about the sources you've used, your research writing process, and the document you've written.

If you find that you have engaged in unintentional plagiarism, ask your instructor for guidance about how to avoid it in the future and ask what sort of penalty you will face for your error. Ask, as well, what consequences you might face should it be determined that you have plagiarized intentionally.

If you and your instructor are unable to resolve the situation, you might face a disciplinary process. To prepare for that process, learn as much as you can about the academic integrity policies at your institution.

QUICK REFERENCE

Avoiding Plagiarism

✔ Understand the definition of plagiarism and the concept of copyright. (p. 128)

✔ Understand the meaning of research ethics. (p. 130)

✔ Understand the concept of common knowledge. (p. 132)

✔ Understand the concept of fair use and, if necessary, seek permission to use sources. (p. 132)

✔ Understand how to reduce the chance that you'll plagiarize unintentionally. (p. 134)

✔ Understand why you might be tempted to plagiarize intentionally and reflect on strategies for avoiding temptation. (p. 136)

✔ Understand what to do if you are accused of plagiarism. (p. 140)

II Working with Sources

PART III

Collecting Information

Learning how to collect information provides you with the foundation for a successful research project. As you begin to answer your research question, you'll want to know more about how and where to look for useful sources of information. In this section, you'll learn how to search for information using digital resources, print resources, and field research.

10

Searching for Information

The primary challenge you will face as you search for information is not finding enough sources; it is finding the right sources. This chapter addresses the important differences among library catalogs, databases, Web search sites, and media search sites that you can use to locate relevant, useful information. You'll also find discussions of how to use the resources in your library to locate sources.

10a

How can I prepare to search digital resources?

To increase your chances of obtaining good results from searches of digital resources, reflect on the work you've done so far, identify search terms related to your issue, learn about the types of searches you might conduct, and get feedback on your plans to carry out those searches.

Review Your Research Plan and Proposal ❓ WHAT'S MY PURPOSE?

As you prepared to explore your topic, you might have created an informal research plan. Later, after you chose your issue, you might have created a research proposal (sometimes called a prospectus). If these documents are available, review them. You're likely to find that they'll provide useful guidance for planning your search of digital resources.

You should also spend time reflecting on the progress you've made so far in identifying useful sources. If you searched library catalogs, databases, or the Web, you probably noticed that one or more of these resources produced better results than others. You might also have noticed that some search terms produced better results than others. Be sure to consider what you've learned so far about useful digital resources and promising search terms.

Consider as well potential links between your issue and specific disciplines or professions. An issue of general interest, such as research on stem cells, which raises a host of ethical and moral issues and has been the subject of debate within the popular media, has also been a topic of discussion within the biological sciences, the social sciences, philosophy, and theology, among several others. Exploring discussions taking place within disciplinary and professional publications allows you to examine your topic from important perspectives.

Identify Keywords and Phrases

You can identify useful search terms by using a range of idea-generating techniques, such as brainstorming and clustering, and by building on your research question (p. 41), position statement (p. 58), or thesis statement (p. 193). Brainstorming, freewriting, looping, clustering, and completing sentence starters (pp. 20–25) can help you come up with words and phrases that you can use in your searches. Elizabeth Leontiev, for example, used freewriting to generate ideas for her searches. When she completed her freewriting session, she highlighted promising words and phrases.

> The best source I've read so far is Gutierrez, who said that the best way to improve quality of life for coca farmers is planting alternative crops, like bananas, or even going into dairy farming. There are probably a lot of alternatives — maybe coffee is an option. But there are a lot of obstacles, such as FARC, which is heavily involved in the drug trade, and they prevent farmers from shifting to alternative crops. These groups don't want to lose money by reducing the amount of coca produced. So the farmers find themselves and their families caught between the drug cartels and the government.

You can also generate search terms by using your research question, position statement, or thesis statement as a starting point. Alexis Alvarez, for example, typed her research question in a word processor, formatted the most important words and phrases in the question in boldface, and then brainstormed a list of related words and phrases.

What should be done about **steroid use** by **adolescent girls** involved in **competitive sports**?

solutions	illegal drugs	girls	athletics
resolutions	performance-	teenagers	competition
proposals	enhancing drugs	young athletes	elite sports
options	banned substances	junior high school	high school sports
answers		senior high school	

My Research Project

Identify Search Terms

To generate keywords for your searches, use one or more of the following strategies.

1. Review your research question, position statement, thesis statement, and working bibliography. Highlight important words and phrases, the names of important authors, and titles of important sources. Create a list of keywords and phrases.

2. Choose one of the words or phrases in your list of search terms and brainstorm about it. Create a list of terms that might be related in some way to the search term you've chosen. Don't worry about how well each new term might work. Instead, jot down ideas as quickly as you can. Then review your list and add the most promising words or phrases to your list of search terms.

3. Choose one of the words or phrases and freewrite about it. Write quickly, without worrying about grammar or mechanics. Then review your freewriting, highlight words and phrases that might serve as search terms, and add them to your list.

4. Try a looping activity by using one of the words or phrases from your freewriting activity as the starting point for a new freewriting session. Repeat the process several times, choosing a promising new word or phrase as a new starting point. At the end of your looping session, highlight promising words and phrases and add them to your list of search terms.

5. Use clustering to generate new search terms. Place a word or phrase from your list at the center of a piece of paper, in the middle of a word processing document, in a blank document in an image editor, or in a phone or tablet mind-mapping app such as iThoughtsHD or SimpleMind. Add related terms, and then add terms related to those terms. Add the most promising new words and phrases to your list of search terms.

6. Identify synonyms for words in your list of search terms by using one or more of the following strategies.

   - Open a word processor and use its built-in thesaurus. In Microsoft Word, you can find the thesaurus in the Review ribbon.
   - Visit a website such as **Thesaurus.com** or the Merriam Webster Online Thesaurus (**merriam-webster.com/thesaurus/**).

- Search the Web using the search term preceded by the word *synonym* or *define*.
- Consult a print thesaurus, such as *Roget's 21st Century Thesaurus* or *Webster's New World Pocket Thesaurus*.

7. Use sentence starters, such as the following, to generate additional search terms.
  - The word ___ reminds me of ___.
  - If I were focusing on ___, I would need to think about ___.
  - ___ couldn't happen without ___.
  - The most important aspect of ___ is ___.
  - The most important thing about ___ within my major is ___.

Plan Basic Searches

A basic search allows you to look for documents that contain a single word or phrase in the subject, title, or — text or, in the case of databases, in other parts of a database record (see p. 159 for more information about databases). Basic searches can return large sets of results. To find results that will be relevant to your subject, consider using additional keywords, exact phrases, and wildcards.

WORKING TOGETHER

Generate New Search Terms

Work together with your classmates to generate additional keywords and phrases relevant to your issue.

1 Describe your issue. Briefly explain what the issue involves, why you are interested in it, and what you think your role might be in the conversation you hope to join (p. 35).

2 Share your list of search terms. Ask your classmates to jot down ideas that occur to them as they read your list.

3 Brainstorm. Conduct a brief brainstorming session (see p. 20). Listen to your classmates and write down the words and phrases that come up during the session.

4 Ask questions. Conduct a brief discussion in which your classmates ask questions about the issue. Keep track of words and phrases that come up during the discussion.

Repeat these activities for each person in the group.

III Collecting Information

Adding Keywords   In most cases, using several keywords together will limit the number of results returned by your search. This strategy is especially helpful when searching the Web, which tends to produce thousands (sometimes millions) of hits for individual words or phrases (see Figure 10.1).

Searching for Exact Phrases   Sometimes the best way to locate information is to search for an exact phrase. To further refine your search, you might use the phrases *adolescent girls* and *competitive sports* (see Figure 10.2). This would eliminate sources in which the words *adolescent* and *girls* appear but are separated by other words. The basic search forms in many catalogs, databases, and Web search sites permit you to specify phrases by using quotation marks.

Using Wildcards   Sometimes you're not sure what form of a word is most likely to occur. Rather than conducting several searches for *compete*, *competes*, *competitive*, *competition*, and *competitions*, for example, you can combine keywords into a single wildcard search. Wildcards are symbols that take the place of letters or

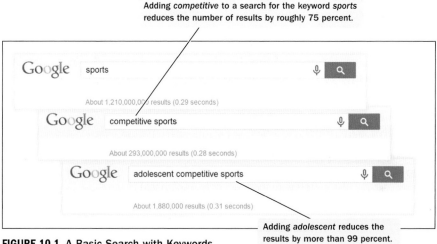

FIGURE 10.1 A Basic Search with Keywords

FIGURE 10.2 A Basic Search with Phrases

III Collecting Information

strings of letters. By standing in for multiple letters, they allow you to expand the scope of your search.

The most commonly used wildcard symbols are:

* usually takes the place of one or more characters, such as compet*

? usually takes the place of a single character, such as wom?n

Other wildcard symbols include !, +, #, and $. Consult the help section in a catalog or database or the advanced search page of a Web search engine to learn whether wildcard symbols are supported.

Plan Advanced Searches

In addition to simple searches, most library catalogs, databases, and Web search sites provide an advanced search page. These pages allow you to focus your searches in powerful ways using Boolean operators (which are used to search for all, some, or none of the words in a search box), special symbols (which are used primarily in Web searches), and search limits (such as publication date and document characteristics).

Focusing Searches with Boolean Operators   Boolean operators let you focus a search by specifying whether keywords or phrases can, must, or must not appear in the results. Some Boolean operators also allow you to search for keywords or phrases that appear next to, before or after, or within a certain distance from one another within a document. Table 10.1 lists commonly used Boolean operators and their functions.

TABLE 10.1 COMMONLY USED BOOLEAN OPERATORS

Boolean Operator	Function	Example
AND/&/+	Finds sources that include both terms (either keywords or phrases)	adolescent AND girls adolescent & girls +adolescent +girls
OR/l	Finds sources that include either term	sports OR athletics sports l athletics
NOT/–	Finds sources that include one term but not the other	girls NOT boys girls –boys
ADJ (adjacent)	Finds sources in which the keywords appear next to each other	competitive ADJ athletics
NEAR	Finds sources in which the keywords appear within a specified number of words from each other	adolescent NEAR athlete
BEFORE	Finds sources in which keywords appear in a particular order	competitive BEFORE athletics
Parentheses ( )	Parentheses are used to group keywords and Boolean operators	competitive AND (athletics OR sports) AND (girls NOT boys)

Many databases, library catalogs, and Web search sites include the use of Boolean search terms—typically AND, OR, and NOT or plus (+) and minus (–) signs—in their advanced search forms (see Figure 10.3) or in expert search forms (see Figure 10.4).

Limiting Searches   Advanced search forms allow you to limit your searches to documents that have particular characteristics, such as publication date and document type (see Figures 10.5 and 10.6). Search limits allow you to narrow your search in ways that are not available in simple searches. Although the specific limits that are available in an advanced search form vary across databases, library catalogs, and Web search sites, common limits include publication date (or, in the case of Web pages, the date on which a page was last updated), type of document, and the availability of full text (for databases). Many databases and library catalogs also allow you to search within a set of results. This allows you to narrow your results further by adding search terms and setting additional limits.

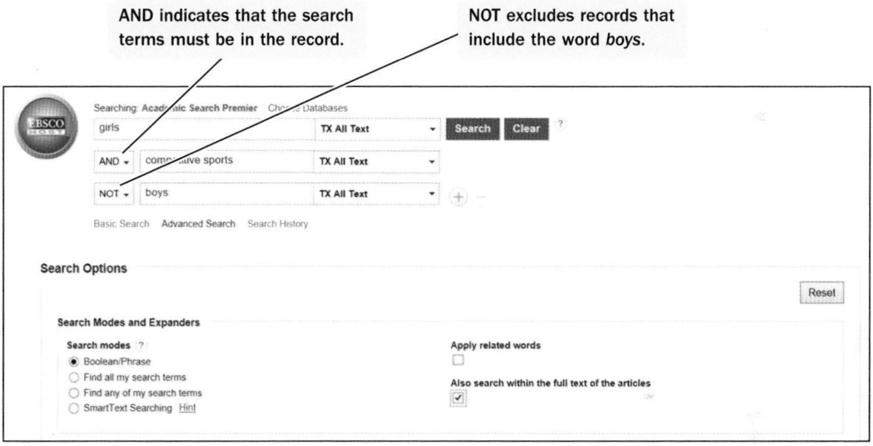

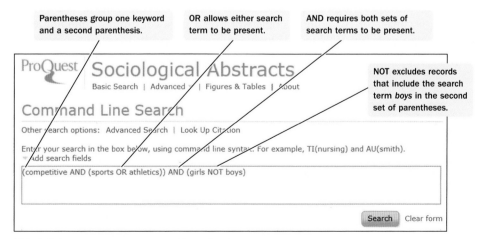

FIGURE 10.3 Advanced Search Form Using Boolean Operators

FIGURE 10.4 Expert Search Form Using Boolean Operators

III Collecting Information

The Limits section provides numerous options for customizing a search.

Limit by document type

Limit to documents available in full text

Limit to sources with references

Limit by publication type

FIGURE 10.5 Advanced Search Using Limits in a Database

III Collecting Information

ⓘ INFORMATION LITERACY   As you conduct advanced searches, avoid confusing publication date with what many Web search engines refer to as "modification date," the date on which a particular Web page was most recently updated. Adding an image or changing a single word on a page constitutes a modification. A page created in 1997 will be included in search results for recent sources if a spelling error was corrected last week. Similarly, some Web search engines report a "found on date," which differs from publication date as well. It can take a while for a search site to locate new pages—sometimes as little as an hour after the page is released and sometimes as long as two weeks. In addition, some pages and documents might have been created several years ago but have been found only recently because they have just been made public on a website. ▩

Using Special Operators in Web Searches   A number of leading websites, such as Google, Yahoo!, Ask, and Bing, offer special operators that allow you to fine-tune a Web search (see Figure 10.7). These special operators can be used in combination with keyword, phrase, wildcard, and Boolean searches. Table 10.2 lists several special operators in Web searches.

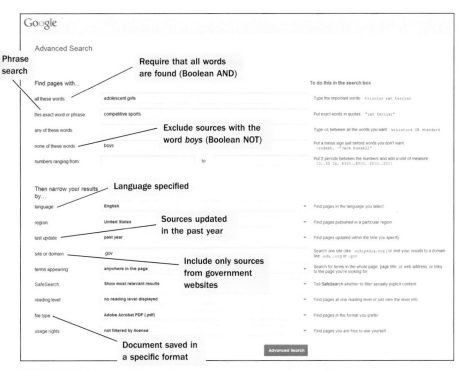

FIGURE 10.6 Advanced Search Using Limits on a Web Search Site

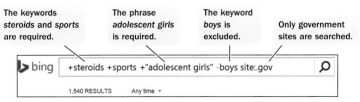

The keywords *steroids* and *sports* are required.

The phrase *adolescent girls* is required.

The keyword *boys* is excluded.

Only government sites are searched.

FIGURE 10.7 Searching with Special Operators

TABLE 10.2 SPECIAL OPERATORS

Function	Ask	Bing	Google	Yahoo!
Words in Body Text		inbody:steroid	intext:steroid	
Words in Page Title	intitle:steroid	intitle:steroid	intitle:steroid	intitle:steroid
Words in URL	inurl:steroids	inanchor: steroids	inurl:steroids	inurl:steroids
Search a Single Domain	site:www .theantidrug .com	site:www .theantidrug .com	site:www .theantidrug .com	site:www .theantidrug .com
Locate Pages Linking to a Page	inlink:www .theantidrug .com	inbody:www .theantidrug .com	link:www .theantidrug .com	link:www .theantidrug .com
Find Documents in a Specific Format	filetype:pdf	filetype:pdf	filetype:pdf	filetype:pdf

TUTORIAL

How do I conduct an advanced search in a database?

Use the advanced search in a database to conduct a Boolean search that includes limits. In this example, Brandon Tate conducted a search in the Academic Search Premier database.

1. Use Boolean operators to specify which terms must be in the source (AND), can be in the source (OR), or must not be in the source (NOT).

2. Enter your keywords and phrases. This search looks for articles about hydraulic fracturing and legislation in Colorado that do not involve discussions of lobbying.

3. Choose the database fields that should be searched. Here, the author field is chosen to exclude authors named Drajem, since he already has that source.

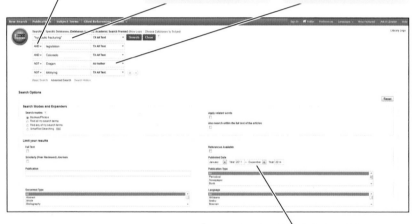

4. Set additional limits on your search, such as availability of full text, scholarly journals, and publication date range.

My Research Project

Plan Advanced Searches

If basic searches are likely to result in large sets of results, plan to conduct advanced searches. To get started, review your research plan or research proposal. Then, with your list of potential search terms in mind, consider the following questions.

1. Should I limit my searches to particular types of documents, such as scholarly journals or recent newspaper articles, magazine articles, and blog posts? Should I focus on scholarly books? Should I focus on trade and professional journals? Should I focus on Web discussion forums and e-mail discussion lists? Should I focus on images and video?

2. Should I limit my searches to sources published during a certain time period, such as the past two years or between 1960 and 1963?

3. How can I focus my searches by using Boolean search terms?

4. How can I focus my searches of the Web by using special search symbols?

10b

How can I locate sources using digital tools?

Writers can turn to four general sets of online resources to locate information about their subjects: library catalogs, databases, the Web, and media search sites. You can search these resources using basic and advanced searches.

Search Library Catalogs

Online catalogs provide information about the author(s), title, publication date, subject heading, and call number for each source in the library's collection. Typically, they also indicate the location of the source in the library and whether the source is available for checkout.

Library catalogs typically help you locate:

- books
- journals owned by the library (although not individual articles)
- newspapers and magazines owned by the library (although not individual articles)
- documents stored on microfilm or microfiche
- videotapes, audiotapes, and other multimedia items
- maps
- theses and dissertations completed by college or university graduate students

III Collecting Information

In addition to searching the library catalog at your college or university, you can also benefit from searching other catalogs available on the Web. The Library of Congress online catalog (catalog.loc.gov), for example, presents a comprehensive list of publications on a particular subject or by a particular author. Some sites, such as WorldCat (worldcat.org), allow you to locate or search multiple libraries. If you find a promising source that your library doesn't own, you can request it through interlibrary loan.

Use Search Features   Most library catalogs allow you to search or browse for sources by keyword, author(s), title, subject, and call number. The following examples illustrate common types of searches.

Search by Keyword   You can search for a specific word or phrase.

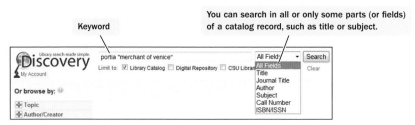

FIGURE 10.8 **Searching by Keyword in a Library Catalog** [Courtesy of Morgan Library, Colorado State University.]

Search by Author   If you search by author, you can find sources written by a particular person or organization. Featured writer Cori Schmidtbauer searched for sources written by John Brannigan, one of the writers she'd learned about as she explored her topic.

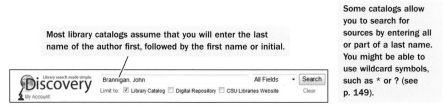

FIGURE 10.9 **Searching by Author** [Courtesy of Morgan Library, Colorado State University.]

Search by Title   If you know the exact title of a source or some of the words in the title, you can search by title to find sources.

Most online library catalogs do not include the articles *a, an,* and *the* at the beginning of titles. They typically move them to the end, as in *Twentieth Century: A Century of Chaos, The.* If you search for sources using a title, be sure to omit initial articles.

You can search for a complete or partial title. Partial titles produce a list of sources whose titles begin with the phrase or word you enter.

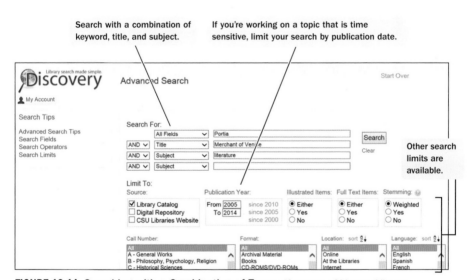

FIGURE 10.10 Searching by Title [Courtesy of Morgan Library, Colorado State University.]

Search with Multiple Strategies   Library catalogs can help you locate sources quickly, especially when you conduct basic searches, such as an author search by last name. If the last name is a common one such as Smith, Garcia, or Chen, however, your search might produce far more results than you would like. In this case, it might help to use the catalog's advanced search form to search with more than one type of strategy—such as author and keyword—at the same time.

Search with a combination of keyword, title, and subject.

If you're working on a topic that is time sensitive, limit your search by publication date.

III Collecting Information

FIGURE 10.11 Searching with a Combination of Terms [Courtesy of Morgan Library, Colorado State University.]

Browse by Subject Heading or Call Number   To locate sources related to a promising result, browse by either subject heading or call number (see Figure 10.12).

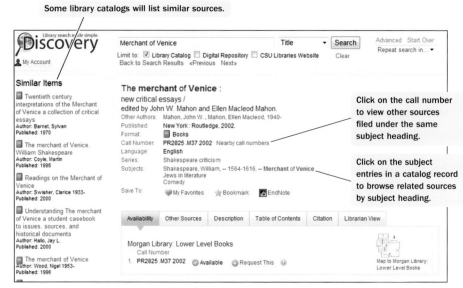

FIGURE 10.12 **Browsing by Library of Congress Subject Heading** [Courtesy of Morgan Library, Colorado State University.]

To browse directly by subject heading or call number, find out whether your library uses the Library of Congress or Dewey decimal classification system. Then conduct a call number or subject setting search in your library catalog (the specific options for doing so vary across library catalogs) and enter a main subject heading or call number.

Library of Congress Classification System

A   General Works

B   Philosophy, Psychology, Religion

C   Auxiliary Sciences of History

D   History: General and Old World

E   History: United States

F   History: United States Local and America

G   Geography, Anthropology, Recreation

H   Social Sciences

J   Political Science

K   Law

L   Education

M   Music and Books on Music

N   Fine Arts

P   Language and Literature

Q   Science

R   Medicine

S   Agriculture

T   Technology

U   Military Science

V   Naval Science

Z   Library Science and Information Resources

Dewey Decimal Classification System

000	Computers, Internet, and Systems	500	Science
100	Philosophy	600	Technology
200	Religion	700	Arts
300	Social Sciences, Sociology, and Anthropology	800	Literature, Rhetoric, and Criticism
400	Language	900	History

i **INFORMATION LITERACY** As you work with subject headings, keep in mind that they differ in important ways from keywords. Subject headings are categories librarians use to organize sources on particular topics. If you search with subject headings in a library catalog, you will find only those sources that have been assigned to that category. If the source is listed under another subject heading, you won't find it even if it contains the same words used in your subject heading search. In contrast, keyword searches will allow you to locate sources that contain the words you are using in your search, but they will not help you find sources that might be relevant to your subject but do not contain those words. In general, it's usually best to search library catalogs in multiple ways. ▓

My Research Project

Prepare to Search Library Catalogs

As you get ready to search library catalogs, return to your research plan or research proposal and make a list of names, keywords, and phrases. Examine your working bibliography to identify the authors, titles, and subjects of your best sources. Then answer the following questions.

1. What are the names of authors I can use to search by author?

2. What are the titles of works that have been referred to me or that I have found in works cited pages that I can use to search by title?

3. What words and phrases can I use to search by keyword?

4. What words and phrases can I use to search by subject?

5. Does it make sense to search by date? If so, what are the dates I should search within?

6. Would call numbers in the Library of Congress or Dewey decimal classification system be useful for me to browse? If so, what are these call numbers?

Search Databases

Databases operate much like library catalogs, although they focus on a different collection of sources. Whereas a catalog allows you to search for publications owned by the library, a database allows you to search for sources that have been

III Collecting Information

published on a particular subject or in a particular discipline regardless of whether the library owns the sources. Although some databases, such as ERIC, MedLine, and ScienceDirect, are available publicly via the Web (p. 162), most are available only through library computers or a library website.

Libraries subscribe to databases in a manner similar to subscribing to a magazine. Because libraries purchase subscriptions to databases, they typically restrict access to the databases to library patrons, such as students, staff, and faculty.

Databases supply publication information and brief descriptions of the information in a source; some — but not all — provide digital copies of the source. Databases that provide digital copies — sometimes referred to as "full-text" databases — cut out the middle step of needing to search for the source. If you are not sure your library will own the sources provided by a database, or if you'd simply like to locate them more quickly, consider using full-text databases, such as Academic Search Premier, ERIC, IEEE Xplore, LexisNexis Academic, and ScienceDirect.

Identify Relevant Databases   Databases tend to specialize in particular subject areas and types of sources. To identify databases that might be relevant to your issue, review your library's list of databases or consult a reference librarian. Ask yourself the following questions.

Am I focusing on an issue that is likely to have been addressed in recent news coverage?   If so, search *news and information databases* that focus on newspapers and weekly newsmagazines, such as the following.

- Alternative Press Index
- LexisNexis Academic
- ProQuest Newspapers

Am I focusing on a broad area of interest, such as business, education, or government?   If so, search *subject databases* that focus on more general issues, such as the following.

- Academic Search Premier
- Article First
- Catalog of U.S. Government Publications
- WorldCat

Am I focusing on an issue that is related to a particular profession or academic discipline?   If so, consult *bibliographies* that focus on that area. Many library websites categorize databases by profession or discipline. For example, if you are interested in an issue related to sociology, you might consult the following databases.

- Family and Society Studies Worldwide
- Social Science Abstracts
- Sociological Abstracts

Have I already identified sources about my issue? If you have already located promising sources, search *citation indexes* to identify additional ones that refer to your sources. Depending on your area, you might search the following databases.

- Arts & Humanities Citation Index
- Science Citation Index
- Social Sciences Citation Index

Is the full text of the source available? *Full-text databases* offer the complete source for viewing or download. These databases cut out the middle step of locating the specific periodical that published the article. Databases that offer some of or all of their sources in full text include the following.

- Academic Search Premier
- ERIC
- IEEE Xplore
- LexisNexis Academic
- ScienceDirect

Am I searching for images, video, or audio? If you are seeking nontextual sources, turn to *media databases* such as the following.

- ARTstor
- AccessScience
- Mountain West Digital Library

III Collecting Information

My Research Project

Record Searches

One of the most important research strategies you can use as you collect information is keeping track of your searches. This will save you time, should you need to search again later, and will help determine which keywords and phrases returned the most promising results.

In your research log, record the following information for each of your searches.

1. Resource that was searched
2. Search terms used (keywords, phrases, publication information)
3. Search strategies used (simple search, wildcard search, exact phrase search, Boolean search)
4. Date search was conducted
5. Number of results produced by the search
6. Relevance of the results
7. Notes about the search

Search the Web

Web search sites can help you sift through the vast amount of information available on the Web, including Web pages, blogs, social networking sites, magazine and journal articles, books, music, photos, and video. While Web search is among the easiest and quickest ways to locate information, keep in mind that Web-based sources have not been carefully selected by librarians and editors, as is typically the case with the sources found through library catalogs and databases. Instead, sources found on the Web can be uneven in quality, ranging from peer-reviewed articles in scholarly journals to blogs created by eighth graders.

To determine which search sites might be best suited to the needs of your research writing situation, consider their areas of emphasis, which range from general to such focused areas as blogs or social networking sites, and the tools they offer to support searching and working with results.

Use Web Search Engines   Web search engines keep track of Web pages and other forms of information on the Internet—including PDF files, PowerPoint files, Word files, blogs (p. 164), and newsgroup posts—by locating documents on websites and entering them in a searchable database. Leading Web search engines include:

- Ask: ask.com
- Bing: bing.com
- Duck Duck Go: duckduckgo.com
- Excite: excite.com
- Google: google.com
- Yahoo!:   search.yahoo.com

ⓘ **INFORMATION LITERACY**   Keep two cautions in mind as you use Web search engines. First, because most search engines index only a portion of the Web—sometimes as much as 50 percent and sometimes as little as 5 percent—you should use more than one search engine. If you don't find what you're looking for on one, it doesn't mean you won't find it on another. ▰

Use Meta Search Sites   On a meta search site, you can conduct a search on several Web search engines or Web directories at the same time. These sites typically search the major search engines and directories and then present a limited number of results on a single page. Leading meta search sites include:

- Dogpile: dogpile.com
- Ixquick: ixquick.com
- WebCrawler: webcrawler.com

Use News Search Sites   You can search for news on most major Web search sites and directories, such as Ask, Bing, Google, and Yahoo!, as well as the sites for news providers such as BBC, CNN, and Reuters. In addition, specialized news search sites allow you to conduct focused searches for current and archived news reports, while social news sites such as Digg and Stumbleupon allow you to view news stories and videos that have been recommended by other readers. Leading news search sites include:

- Ask News: news.ask.com
- Bing News: bing.com/news
- Digg: digg.com
- Google News: news.google.com
- Stumbleupon: stumbleupon.com
- World News: wn.com
- Yahoo! News: yahoo.com/news

Use Reference Search Sites   A reference site allows you to search for information that has been collected in encyclopedias, almanacs, atlases, dictionaries, and other reference resources. Some reference sites, such as Encyclopedia Britannica Online, offer limited access to information from their encyclopedias at no charge and complete access for a fee. Other sites, such as Information Please and Bartleby.com, allow unrestricted access to recently published reference works, including the *Columbia Encyclopedia*, *The Encyclopedia, of World History*, and *The World Factbook*.

Leading reference search sites include:

- Bartleby.com Reference: bartleby.com/reference
- Encyclopedia.com: encyclopedia.com
- Encyclopedia Britannica Online: britannica.com
- Information Please: infoplease.com
- Wikipedia: en.wikipedia.org

ⓘ **INFORMATION LITERACY**   Like other Wikis, the widely used reference site Wikipedia is collaboratively written by its readers. Because of its comprehensiveness, Wikipedia can serve as a useful starting point for research on a topic. However, because any reader can make changes to the site, it's best to double-check the information you find there. For more information about the drawbacks of relying on Wikis as authoritative sources of information, see p. 82. ▮

Use Government Document Sites   Most government agencies and institutions use the Web as the primary means of distributing their publications. USA.gov, for example, allows you to search the federal government's network of online resources, while the State and Local Government Directory provides access to a wide range of materials related to state and local government.

Leading government document sites include:

- Canadian Government Search Engines: recherche-search.gc.ca
- Government Printing Office: govinfo.gov

- GovSpot.com: govspot.com
- State and Local Government Directory: statelocalgov.net
- USA.gov: usa.gov

Use E-book Sites   E-books are available through a wide variety of sources, including Amazon (**amazon.com**), Barnes & Noble (**bn.com**), and Google Books (**books.google.com**), as well as several open-access publishers, such as Project Gutenberg (**gutenberg.org**). You can also locate (and often preview) e-books by visiting sites such as Apple iTunes and Google Play online stores. Some other e-book sites include:

- Internet Archive Community Books: archive.org/details/texts
- Kobo: kobo.com
- Online Books Page: onlinebooks.library.upenn.edu
- Wikibooks: wikibooks.org

Use Blog Search Sites   Blogs—short for Weblogs—consist of chronologically ordered entries on a website and most closely resemble entries in a diary or journal. Blog entries usually include a title and a body and can also incorporate images, audio, video, and other types of media.

Many entries provide links to other pages on the Web. Blogs have a number of purposes.

- Some blogs report on events and issues. The bloggers who provided daily—sometimes hourly—reports on the 2016 U.S. political conventions offered valuable, firsthand insights not found in the mainstream media. Similarly, the bloggers who reported on the Syrian refugee crisis offered a perspective on events that would not have been available otherwise.

- Some blogs alert readers to information elsewhere on the Web. These blogs cite recently published news reports and articles, the latest developments in a particular discipline, and new contributions to an ongoing debate—and provide commentary on that information.

- Some blogs serve as public-relations spaces for institutions and organizations, such as corporations, government agencies, and colleges. These blogs typically focus on services or activities associated with the institution or organization.

- Some blogs serve largely as a space for personal reflection and expression. A blogger might share his or her thoughts about daily life, current events, or other issues with friends and family.

Writers can use blogs as sources of information and commentary on an issue and as sources of firsthand accounts by people affected by an issue. If you find blogs by experts in the field, you can begin a discussion with people involved in or knowledgeable about your topic. To locate blogs that are relevant to your research question, use the following sites.

- Alltop: alltop.com
- BlogCatalog: blogcatalog.com
- WordPress: en.search.wordpress.com

Search Social Media Sites   Social media sites provide opportunities to identify people who share your interest in an issue. By searching these sites, you can identify individuals who might be knowledgeable about an issue or have been affected by it. You can search social networks using the following sites.

- Facebook Search: search.fb.com
- Google+ Search: plus.google.com
- LinkedIn Search: linkedin.com
- Reddit Search: reddit.com/search
- Social Mention: socialmention.com
- Tumblr Search: tumblr.com/tagged/tumblr-search
- Twitter Search: twitter.com/search-home

Search Media Sites

The Web is home not only to textual information, such as articles and books, but also to a growing collection of other types of media, such as photographs, podcasts, and streaming videos. You can search for media using established search sites, such as Ask, Google, and Yahoo!, as well as newer search sites that focus on specific media.

Use Image Search Sites and Directories   Image searches have long been among the search tools available to writers. Using Google's image search, for example, you can locate graphics by using keywords and phrases, and you can conduct advanced searches by specifying the size and kind of image you desire. The following search sites and directories allow you to locate images.

- Bing Image Search: bing.com/images
- Google Image Search: images.google.com
- PicFindr: picfindr.com
- Picsearch: picsearch.com
- Yahoo! Image Search: images.search.yahoo.com

Use Audio Search Sites   Thinking of the Web as the first place to visit for new music has become second nature for many of us. But the audio content available through the Web includes more than just music. You can also find radio broadcasts, recordings of speeches, recordings of natural phenomena, and other forms of sound. Sites such as FindSounds allow you to search for sounds and listen to them before downloading. Leading audio search sites include:

- FindSounds: findsounds.com
- Freesound: freesound.org

- Internet Archive: archive.org/details/audio
- Library of Congress American Memory: memory.loc.gov/ammem
- Wav Central: wavcentral.com

Use Video Search Sites   Through sites such as YouTube and Yahoo! Video, Web-based video has become one of the fastest-growing parts of the Internet. You can view everything from news reports on CNN.com to a video about the effects of a recent earthquake to documentaries about the Iraq War. Of course, much of the material will be of limited use in a writing project. With careful selection and evaluation, however, you might find video that will help you better understand and contribute to the discussion of your subject. The following are some leading video search sites.

- Bing Video Search: bing.com/videos/trending
- Blinkx: blinkx.com
- Google Video: google.com/videohp
- Yahoo! Video Search: video.search.yahoo.com
- YouTube: youtube.com

10c

How can I locate sources using print resources?

Contrary to recent claims, there is life (and information) beyond the World Wide Web. The print resources available in a library can help you locate a wealth of relevant material that you won't find online. If your writing project has a historical component, for example, bibliographies and indexes can point you toward sources that cannot be located using a database or a Web search site. By relying on the careful selections librarians make when adding to a collection, you will be able to find useful, credible sources that reflect your purpose and address your subject.

To locate information using print resources, discuss your search plan with a librarian, visit the library stacks, browse periodicals, and check reference works.

Discuss Your Search Plan with a Librarian

As you begin collecting information about your subject, use your search plan to capitalize on your library's print resources — and its librarians. Given the wide range of specialized print resources that are available, a few minutes of discussion with a librarian could save you a great deal of time or point you to key resources you might have overlooked.

Visit the Library Stacks

The library stacks—or shelves—house the library's collection of bound publications. By browsing the stacks and checking publications' works cited pages, you can locate related sources. Once you've decided that a source is relevant to your project, you can check it out or request it through interlibrary loan.

One advantage of the classification systems used by most libraries—typically the Library of Congress or the Dewey decimal classification system—is that they are subject based. Because books on similar subjects are shelved together, you can browse the stacks to look for sources on a topic. For example, if your research takes you to the stacks for books about alcohol abuse, you're likely to find books about drug abuse, treatment programs, and codependency nearby. When you find a publication that seems useful, check the works cited list for related works. The combination of browsing the stacks for sources and checking those sources' works cited lists can lead you to publications relevant to your subject.

You can usually take library books—and even some periodicals and media items—home with you to read or view at your own pace. In some cases, a publication you want might not be available because it has been checked out, reserved for a course, or placed in off-site storage. If a publication has been checked out, you might be able to recall it—that is, ask that it be returned to the library and held for you. If it has been placed on reserve, ask whether you can scan it or take notes about it. If it has been placed in off-site storage, you can usually request it at the circulation desk.

i **INFORMATION LITERACY** If you can't obtain a particular book, periodical, or media item from your library, use interlibrary loan to borrow it from another library. Most libraries allow you to request materials through the library catalog. And you might be able to check the status of your request or renew interlibrary loan materials in the catalog as well. To learn how to use interlibrary loan, consult your library's website or ask a librarian.

Browse Periodicals

Periodicals include newspapers, magazines, and academic and professional journals. A periodicals room—or journals room—contains recent issues that library visitors may browse. Many libraries also have a separate room for newspapers published in the last few weeks or months. To ensure everyone's access to recently published issues, most libraries don't allow you to check out periodicals published within the last year, and they usually don't allow newspapers to be checked out at all.

Older periodicals are sometimes placed in bound volumes in the stacks. Few libraries, however, keep back issues of newspapers in paper form. Instead, you can often find back issues of leading newspapers in full-text databases or in microform. *Microform* is a generic name for both microfilm, a strip of film containing greatly reduced images of printed pages, and microfiche, film roughly the size of

III Collecting Information

an index card containing the same kinds of miniaturized images. You view these images using a microform reader, a projection unit that looks something like a large computer monitor. Many microform readers allow you to print copies of the pages.

In addition to browsing periodicals, use databases to locate specific articles on your subject. They are more likely than print indexes and bibliographies to contain listings of recent publications. Once you've identified an article you want to review, you'll need to find the periodical in which it appears. Conduct a title search for the periodical in the same way you conduct a title search for a book. The library catalog will tell you the call number of the periodical and usually will give information about its location in the library. In addition, some libraries provide a printed list that identifies where periodicals are located. If you have difficulty finding a periodical or judging which publications are likely to be useful for your writing project, ask a librarian for assistance.

Check Reference Works

Reference rooms contain reliable print resources on a range of topics, from government to finance to philosophy to science. Although many of these reference books serve the same purposes as databases, others offer information not available in databases. Using reference books to locate print resources has several advantages over using databases.

- **Most databases have short memories.** Databases typically index sources only as far back as the mid-1980s and seldom index anything published before 1970. Depending on your subject, a database might not include some important sources. If you use a reference book, however, you might be able to locate print resources dating back a century or more.

- **Most databases focus on short works.** In contrast, many of the print resources in library reference rooms will refer you to books and longer publications as well as to articles in periodicals.

- **Many library reference resources are unavailable in digital form.** For instance, the *Encyclopedia of Creativity*, which offers more than two hundred articles, is available only in print form.

- **Entries in print indexes are easier to browse.** Despite efforts to aid browsing, databases support searching far better than they do browsing.

Some of the most important print resources you can consult in a reference room include bibliographies, indexes, biographies, general and specialized encyclopedias, handbooks, almanacs, and atlases.

Consult Bibliographies   Bibliographies list books, articles, and other publications that have been judged relevant to a topic. Some bibliographies provide only citations, while others include abstracts—brief descriptions—of listed sources. Complete bibliographies attempt to list all the sources published about a topic, while selective bibliographies attempt to list only the best sources on a topic. Some bibliographies limit their inclusion of sources by time period, often focusing on sources published during a given year.

You're likely to find several types of bibliographies in your library's reference room or stacks.

- **Trade bibliographies** allow you to locate books published about a particular topic. Leading trade bibliographies include *The Subject Guide to Books in Print, Books in Print,* and *Cumulative Book Index.*

- **General bibliographies** cover a wide range of topics, usually in selective lists. For sources on humanities topics, consult *The Humanities: A Selective Guide to Information Sources.* For sources on social science topics, see *Social Science Reference Sources: A Practical Guide.* For sources on science topics, go to bibliographies such as *Information Sources in Science and Technology, Guide to Information Sources in the Botanical Sciences,* and *Guide to Information Sources in the Physical Sciences.*

- **Specialized bibliographies** typically provide lists of sources — often annotated — about a specific topic. For example, *Bibliography of Modern American Philosophers* focuses on sources about important American philosophers.

Although most general and trade bibliographies can be found in the library reference room, specialized bibliographies are usually shelved in the library's stacks. To locate them, start by consulting a cumulative bibliography, such as *The Bibliographic Index: A Cumulative Bibliography of Bibliographies,* which identifies bibliographies on a wide range of topics and is updated annually. You might also search your library's catalog using keywords related to your subject plus the keyword *bibliography.* If you need help finding bibliographies that are relevant to your subject, ask a reference librarian.

Review Indexes Indexes provide citation information for sources found in a particular set of publications. Frequently, indexes also include abstracts — or brief descriptions — that can help you determine whether a source is worth locating and reviewing. The following types of indexes can be found in libraries.

- **Periodical indexes** list sources published in magazines, trade journals, scholarly journals, and newspapers. Some periodical indexes, such as *The Reader's Guide to Periodical Literature,* cover a wide range of general-interest publications. Others, such as *Art Index,* focus on periodicals that address a single subject. Still others focus on a small subset of periodicals or even an individual periodical: *The New York Times Index,* for example, lists articles published only in that newspaper and organizes entries by subject, geography, organization, and references to individuals.

- **Indexes of materials in books** can help you locate articles in edited volumes. Turn to resources such as the *Essay and General Literature Index,* which indexes nearly five thousand book-length collections of articles and essays in the arts, humanities, and social sciences. You might also find subject-specific indexes. *The Cumulative Bibliography of Asian Studies*, for example, covers articles in edited books about Asian studies.

- **Pamphlet indexes** list the pamphlets that libraries frequently collect. If your subject is likely to be addressed in pamphlets, ask a reference librarian whether your library has a pamphlet index. You can also consult the *Vertical File Index*, which lists roughly three thousand brief sources on ten to fifteen newsworthy topics each month.

- **Government documents indexes** list publications from federal, state, and local governments. The most useful indexes include *Monthly Catalog of United States Government Publications*, *CIS Index to Publications of the United States Congress*, *Congressional Record* (for daily proceedings of the House of Representatives and the Senate), *United States Reports* (for Supreme Court documents), and *Statistical Abstract of the United States* (for census data and other statistical records). These types of indexes might be found in either the reference room or a separate government documents collection in your library. Ask a reference librarian for help with these resources.

- **Citation indexes** allow you to determine which sources make reference to other publications, a useful strategy for finding sources that are engaged in the same conversation. For example, to learn which sources refer to an article published in a scientific journal, consult the *Science Citation Index*.

Check Biographies   Biographies cover key figures in a field, time period, or geographic region. *Who's Who in America*, for instance, provides brief biographies of important figures in the United States during a given year, while *Great Lives from History* takes a broader view, offering biographies of key figures in world history.

Browse Encyclopedias   General encyclopedias attempt to provide a little knowledge about a lot of subjects. The purpose of a general encyclopedia, such as the *New Encyclopaedia Britannica*, is to present enough information about a subject to get you started on a more detailed search. Specialized encyclopedias, such as *The MIT Encyclopedia of the Cognitive Sciences*, take a narrower focus, usually covering a field of study or a historical period. Articles in specialized encyclopedias are typically longer than articles in general encyclopedias and offer more detailed coverage of subjects.

Consult Handbooks   Like encyclopedias, handbooks can provide useful background information about a subject in a compact form. Unlike encyclopedias, most handbooks, such as *The Engineering Handbook* and the *International Handbook of Psychology*, cover a specific topic area. The entries in handbooks are also much shorter than the articles found in encyclopedias.

Review Almanacs   Almanacs contain lists, charts, and tables of information of various types. You might be familiar with *The Old Farmer's Almanac*, which is known for its accuracy in predicting weather over the course of a year. Information in almanacs can range from the average rainfall in Australia to the batting averages of the 1927 Yankees to the average income of Germans and Poles before World War II.

Scan Atlases   Atlases provide maps and related information about a region or country. Some atlases take a historical perspective, while others take a topical perspective.

My Research Project

Discuss Your Research Project with Others

Return to your research log and review what you've learned about your issue. Then ask whether you've taken advantage of the print resources available in your library reference room. If you're uncertain about how you might use these resources, discuss your project with a reference librarian. Given the wide range of specialized print resources that are available, a few minutes of discussion with a knowledgeable librarian could save you a great deal of time.

QUICK REFERENCE

Searching for Information

✔ Prepare to search by reviewing your progress to date, identifying search terms, and planning basic and advanced searches. (p. 145)

✔ Search library catalogs. (p. 155)

✔ Search databases. (p. 159)

✔ Search the Web. (p. 162)

✔ Search media sites. (p. 165)

✔ Discuss your search plan with a librarian. (p. 166)

✔ Use the library stacks to locate sources. (p. 167)

✔ Use the periodicals room to locate sources. (p. 167)

✔ Use the reference room to locate sources. (p. 168)

III Collecting Information

11

Collecting Information with Field Research

Key Questions

Published documents aren't the only source of information for a writing project. Nor are they always the best. Books, articles, websites, and television reports offer someone else's interpretation of an event or an issue. By relying on published sources, you are looking through the eyes of the authors who created those texts, rather than through your own.

You don't have to use published reports to find out how an event or issue has affected people—you can ask them yourself. You don't have to watch television coverage of an event—you can go experience it yourself. You don't have to rely on someone else's survey of public opinion—you can conduct your own. And you don't have to do field research by yourself—you can form a team and share the work.

11a

When should I use field research methods? ❓ WHAT'S MY PURPOSE?

Some research writers think of field research as the next-best thing to learning about an issue through a published source. If they can't find anything relevant in books, in articles, in newspapers, in blogs, or on Twitter, they think, then field research might be worth considering.

These writers misunderstand the value and power of field research. Far from being a good fallback position, field research is sometimes the best way to learn about an issue or collect information to support a position.

Consider using field research methods if you find yourself in one of the following situations.

- If published sources address your issue from a perspective that you don't find useful, field research can provide another way of approaching the issue. For example, most discussions of gun rights and gun control focus on constitutional arguments. If you want to consider the issue from another perspective, such as differences in how people from rural areas and urban or suburban areas understand the issue, you might find it useful to collect information through interviews, surveys, or correspondence.

- If you are interested in an issue that most people think of as settled, published sources are unlikely to include information, ideas, and arguments that might help you challenge the conventional wisdom about the issue. Field research, in contrast, can bring new voices, experiences, and ideas into the conversation.

- If the issue you are addressing is so current that little authoritative information is available, field research can provide needed information about it.

- If you come up with a new idea or argument that seems reasonable and obvious about an aspect of an issue not yet addressed by your sources, field research can provide a useful reality check, allowing you to explore your idea or argument through interviews, observation, surveys, or correspondence.

- If your argument can be strengthened by including evidence from primary sources, turn to field research. Including information from interviews, correspondence, or observation notes can bring a document to life, providing your readers with firsthand reports from people who know about or have been affected by an issue. Similarly, incorporating information into your document from a survey can allow your readers to see trends and differences among groups, relationships that might not otherwise be clear.

Thinking carefully about the role field research might play in your research project can help you decide whether and how to conduct it. Sometimes the decision to use a particular field research method is a natural extension of the kind of work you're doing. For example, although Alexis Alvarez was able to find plenty of information from other sources about the pressures that would lead adolescent female athletes to use performance-enhancing drugs, she decided to interview friends and family members who had played competitive sports because she knew that firsthand reports would strengthen her argument.

At other times, the decision to conduct an interview isn't so much the result of careful planning as it is the recognition of an available opportunity. Brandon Tate, who created a website about hydraulic fracturing, learned that one of his friends had recently volunteered for a local campaign against fracking. He followed his friend over the course of a day, observing his interactions and the work that he did. Brandon's observations provided him with a personal perspective about fracking that he wouldn't have been able to find through print or digital sources. Similarly, Nicholas Brothers had the opportunity to interview a professor who provided him with valuable insights about his issue, the growing use of private military corporations by the U.S. government.

Whether you rely primarily on field research or use it in combination with information from published sources, remember that field research methods can be powerful tools for exploring your issue and developing your position. As you conduct field research, keep in mind the strategies discussed in Chapter 8 for managing print and digital information. Those strategies will help you save and organize the information you collect so you can locate it quickly and easily.

11b

How can I conduct an interview?

Interviews — in which one person seeks information from another — can provide firsthand accounts of an event, authoritative interpretations of events and issues, and reactions to an event or issue from the people who have been affected by it. Most interviews follow a question-and-answer format, but some more closely resemble a free-flowing discussion. You can conduct interviews face to face, over the telephone, via e-mail, and even through an instant-messaging program.

Plan Your Interview

The most important things to consider as you plan your interview are whom to interview, what to ask, and how to conduct your interview.

Decide Whom to Interview   Your decisions about whom to interview should be based on the kind of information you want for your research project.

- If you're trying to better understand a specific aspect of a conversation, interview an expert in the field such as a professor, government official, or member of the business community.

- If you want to learn what people in general think about an issue, interview a number of people who are affected by the issue in different ways.
- If you're hoping to collect quotations from people who are authorities on a subject, interview someone who will be recognized as knowledgeable by your readers.

Once you've decided what sorts of people you want to interview, you'll need to identify and contact interview candidates. If you're working on a research project for a class, ask your instructor and classmates for suggestions. Then ask whether they can introduce you to the people they suggest. Before you call to set up an interview, make some preparations.

1. Write a script to help you remember what to say.
2. Prepare a list of dates and times that work for you.
3. Estimate how much time you'll need to complete the interview.
4. Be ready to suggest a location for the interview.
5. Leave your phone number or e-mail address so that your interview candidate can get in touch with you if a conflict arises.

Decide What You Should Ask   [FRAMING MY ARGUMENT]   Your interview questions should focus on the issue you want to address in your project. As you prepare your questions, keep the following principles in mind.

1. *Consider your research question, the role you are adopting, and the kind of information you want to collect.* Are you seeking background information, or do you want someone's opinion? An answer to the question, "How did this situation come about?" will be quite different from an answer to the question, "What do you think about this situation?"

2. *Ask questions that require more than a yes or no answer.* You'll learn much more from an answer to a question such as "What factors will affect your vote on referendum X?" than from an answer to "Will you vote for referendum X?"

3. *Prepare a limited number of main questions and many follow-up questions.* Good interviews seldom involve more than eight to ten main questions, but experienced interviewers know that each question can lead to several follow-up questions, such as "Why do you think this has happened?" or "How did your coworkers react to the new policy?"

4. *Be flexible.* Be prepared to tailor your follow-up questions to the interviewee's responses.

Decide How to Conduct Your Interview   You can conduct interviews face to face, over the telephone, and through a wide range of computer-based tools, such as e-mail, chat, and video communication programs. Each method has advantages and disadvantages.

III Collecting Information

- **Face-to-face interviews** conducted in person or through a computer-based video tool such as Skype or Google Voice allow you to carry out a nearly normal conversation with the person you are interviewing. You can rely on your experiences in other conversations to determine whether the interview is effective, whether the person you are interviewing is comfortable, and whether he or she understands your questions. Most interviewees will answer your questions directly, and most will elaborate by giving examples, suggestions about related resources, and so on. If you can see the person you interview, pay close attention to nonverbal cues, such as facial expressions, body positions, and eye contact. Nonverbal cues can help you understand whether your questions are clear, welcome, or surprising and can alert you to opportunities to ask useful follow-up questions.

- **Telephone interviews** also let you hold a fairly normal conversation, but it's important to ensure that you can carry out your side of the conversation in relative peace and without distractions. You won't have visual cues to help you connect with the person you are interviewing, so be sure to pay attention to pauses, tone of voice, and changes in speaking volume that might indicate surprise, discomfort, or confusion. As in face-to-face interviews, you'll receive fairly direct responses and elaboration to questions.

- **Written interviews** conducted by e-mail, chat, text messaging, or letter can be a good option if the person you'd like to interview is difficult to reach because of distance or a busy schedule. Written responses to interview questions are generally more precise than spoken responses. Written responses can be reviewed and revised by the person being interviewed to ensure that statements are clear and accurate, while spoken responses are usually more spontaneous.

Decide Whether to Share Questions in Advance   Sharing questions in advance can have benefits and drawbacks. It can allow the person you'll interview to reflect on your questions and prepare a response. If you are interested in seeing candid reactions to a question, however, or if you worry that seeing the questions might make the interviewee reluctant to go through with the interview, don't share them. Ultimately, the decision about whether to share questions in advance depends on your purpose.

Decide How to Record and Take Notes on Your Interview   Recording or saving a transcript of an interview, along with taking notes, provides you with a complete record of what was said, which helps you ensure the accuracy of quotations, paraphrases, and summaries.

- **Recordings** If you plan to record a face-to-face, telephone, or video-based interview, seek permission in advance or at the start of the interview. Remember that some people might be nervous about being recorded, and be prepared to explain how you'll use a recording. If you think someone might be nervous about being recorded, be sure that your initial questions will allow him or her to become comfortable about the interview process.

- **Transcripts** If you are conducting an interview via e-mail (or even via a series of text messages), you'll have a written record of all the responses to your questions. Similarly, you can save a transcript from most chat sessions and even Google Voice conversations, either by saving a file from the chat program or copying and pasting the transcript into a word processing file. Transcripts can be used to create accurate quotations, and they make it relatively easy to review responses to your questions.

- **Taking Notes** You should always take notes during an interview. Recordings and transcripts can be lost through everything from running out of file space on a recorder to computer crashes. More important, taking notes allows you to record your reactions to new information and ideas, to save your thoughts about how you might use all or part of an interview in your document, and to identify important parts of the interview for later review.

Conduct Your Interview

Consult the following checklist before you conduct your interview.

CHECKLIST FOR CONDUCTING INTERVIEWS

✔ **Arrive early and review your questions.** If you are conducting your interview over the phone or via computer, set time aside before the interview to review your questions and then contact the person you are interviewing at the agreed-upon time.

✔ **Introduce yourself and ask for permission to record the interview.** Explain why you are conducting the interview. Ask for permission to record or generate a transcript and ensure that you will be allowed to use quotes from the interview.

✔ **Set up and test your recording equipment or computer.** Ideally, use an audio or video recorder to make a complete record of face-to-face or phone interviews and use the built-in recording or transcript-generating features in online communication tools. At a later time, you can review what was said and create exact quotations from the recording or transcript.

✔ **Ask your questions clearly and be ready to respond with follow-up questions.** Allow the person you are interviewing a chance to answer your questions fully and without interruption. Don't insist on strictly following your list of interview questions; if discussion naturally flows in another useful direction, be prepared to shift your line of questioning.

CHECKLIST FOR CONDUCTING INTERVIEWS (*continued*)

✔ **Take notes, even if you are creating a recording or transcript.** A set of hand-written notes will serve as a backup if there are technical glitches and will help you remember ideas you had during the interview. You should write down key points made during the interview as well as any important ideas that come to mind.

✔ **Be alert for related sources mentioned in the interview.** If specific sources that might be relevant to your research writing project are mentioned during the interview, ask for copies of those sources or for the exact titles and where you might find them.

✔ **Leave your contact information when the interview is over.** Provide a way for the person you interviewed to reach you to change or add anything to his or her comments.

✔ **Send a thank-you note or an e-mail message.** Let the person that you interviewed know how much you appreciated the opportunity to learn from him or her.

Analyze Your Results

Treat your interview recording or transcript as you would any other source. Read it, listen to it, or view it critically. If you've taken notes during the interview, review them and record your reactions (see Figure 11.1).

- Look for new information, ideas, and arguments.
- Look for statements that confirm or contradict information from your other sources.
- Look for inconsistencies and contradictions within the interview as a whole.
- Ask whether the information, ideas, and arguments are relevant and credible.
- Ask whether you consider the person you interviewed as qualified as you'd expected when you planned the interview.
- Look for statements that might be useful in providing context about the issue.
- Look for statements that might help your readers better understand the issue or that would help them view the issue in a particular way.

Then ask whether you can use the information, ideas, and arguments from the interview in your project document. If not, ask whether it is useful for helping you understand the issue more fully or raises questions that you could investigate in other ways.

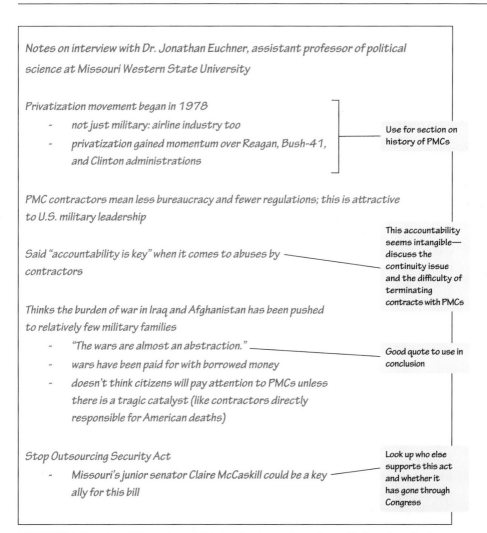

FIGURE 11.1 Annotated Notes from Nicholas Brothers's Interview with Jonathan Euchner

III Collecting Information

11c

How can I conduct an observation?

Like interviewing, observing a setting can provide you with valuable information you would not be able to find in other sources. Although some observations can involve a significant amount of time and effort, an observation need not be complicated to be useful.

Plan Your Observation

As you plan your observation, determine the following.

Decide What You Should Observe and How Often You Should Observe It   If, for example, you've decided to observe children in a day-care center, you'll quickly learn that there are not only many day-care providers in your community but also several different kinds of providers. Clearly, observing a large day-care center won't tell you much about what happens in a small center operated out of a home. In addition, there's no guarantee that what you'll see in one day-care center on any given day will be typical. Should you conduct multiple observations? Should you observe multiple types of day-care providers?

The answers to these questions will depend largely on what role the information you collect during your observations will play in your research writing project. If you want to learn more about the topic but don't plan to use anything you observe as a source of evidence in your project, then you might want to conduct a fairly limited observation. If you decide to use evidence from your observations throughout your project, then you will need to conduct multiple observations, possibly in more than one setting. In this case, as you prepare for each observation, review your notes from previous sessions so that you can focus on the most important aspects of what you've observed so far.

Decide What to Look For   The biggest limitation of observation is that you can see only one thing at a time. Experienced observers focus their observations on activities that are most relevant to their research projects. As a result, their observations are somewhat selective. Spreading yourself too thin will result in fairly "thin" results. Then again, narrowing in too quickly can mean that you miss important aspects of the setting. Your reasons for conducting an observation and what you hope to gain from it are probably your best guide as to what to focus on.

Decide Whether You Need Permission to Observe   Seeking permission to observe someone can be complicated. People have expectations about privacy, but people can (and often do) change their behavior when they know they are being observed. As you consider whether to ask for permission, imagine yourself in the position of someone who is being observed. If you are still uncertain, ask your instructor for advice.

If you decide to seek permission to conduct your observations, consider how best to approach the person you'll ask for permission. If you decide to send a letter or an e-mail message, be sure to include a clear description of your research writing project and explanations of why you believe observation will enhance your work on the project, how the observations will be used in your project, and how you will ensure the privacy of the individuals, groups, or organization you observe. If you decide to contact the person by telephone, jot down some notes before you call. In some cases, you might find it useful to use a permission form (see Figure 11.2).

Current School / Program Information

Name _____

Address _____

City _____ State _____

Zip Code _____

Phone _____

E-mail _____

I, the undersigned, hereby authorize [*observer name*] to observe [*the setting*] for the purposes of completing work on [*name of the research writing project*]. I understand that I may revoke this authorization, in writing, at any time.

Signature: _____

Date: _____

FIGURE 11.2 Sample Permission Form for Observation Sessions

Conduct Your Observation

You'll find a number of similarities between collecting information in an interview and collecting information during an observation. The checklist that follows will help you conduct your observation.

CHECKLIST FOR CONDUCTING OBSERVATIONS

✔ **Arrive early.** Give yourself time to get prepared.

✔ **Review your planning notes.** Remind yourself what you're looking for and how you will record your observations.

✔ **Introduce yourself.** If you have asked for permission to observe a setting (such as a class or a day-care center), introduce yourself before you begin your observation. Use your introduction as an opportunity to obtain signatures or consent forms if you need them.

✔ **Set up your recording equipment.** You'll certainly want to make sure you've got a notepad and pens or pencils. You might also have an audio or a video recorder, a laptop computer, or a smartphone or tablet. Test whatever you've brought with you to make sure it's working properly.

CHECKLIST FOR CONDUCTING OBSERVATIONS (*continued*)

✔ **Take notes.** As with interviews, take notes during your observation even if you're using an audio or a video recorder. Noting your impressions and ideas while conducting an observation can help you keep track of critical events. In addition, if your recorder doesn't work as expected, a set of notes can mean the difference between salvaging something from the observation and having to do it all over again. If you find yourself in a situation where you can't take notes—such as at a swimming lesson, when you're taking part in the lesson—try to write down your thoughts about what you've observed immediately after the session.

✔ **Leave contact information and send thank-you notes.** If you have asked someone for permission to observe the setting, give the person a way to contact you, and send a thank-you note after you have completed the observation.

Analyze Your Results

Treat your observation notes or recording as you would any other source. Ask whether you observed the setting thoroughly enough to feel confident about moving forward with an analysis. If so, do the following.

- Identify key features and patterns of behavior.
- Identify key individuals and describe their actions.
- Look for unusual and surprising patterns and actions.
- Ask what you've learned about the issue through observation.
- Look for patterns and actions that might be useful in providing context about the issue.
- Look for patterns and actions that, if described, might help your readers better understand the issue or lead them to view the issue in a particular way.

Then ask whether you are confident enough about the results of your analysis to use what you've learned in your project document. If not, ask whether it is useful for helping you understand the issue more fully or raises questions that you could investigate in other ways.

11d

How can I conduct a survey?

Surveys allow you to collect information about beliefs, attitudes, and behaviors from a group of people. Typically, surveys help you answer *what* or *who* questions, such as "Who will you vote for in the next election?" Surveys are less useful in obtaining the answers to *why* questions. In an interview, for instance, you can ask, "Why did you vote the way you did in the last election?" and expect to get a reasonably well-thought-out answer. In a survey, however, you're unlikely to collect lengthy, carefully written responses. Surveys are far more useful for collecting numerical information and indications of agreement or disagreement.

If you simply want opinions from a handful of people, you can gain that information more efficiently by interviewing or corresponding with them. The strength of surveys, in contrast, lies in sheer numbers. A well-designed survey administered to a sizable group of people can provide insights into an issue that often can't be obtained easily using other methods.

Plan Your Survey

As you plan your survey, determine the following.

Decide Whom to Survey   You must decide whom and how many people to survey. For instance, if you're interested in what students in a specific class think about an issue, survey all of them. Even if the class is fairly large (say, one hundred students), you probably won't have too much trouble tabulating the results of a brief survey. Keep in mind, however, that most surveys aren't given to everyone in a group. National polls, for instance, seldom survey more than one thousand people, yet they are used to assess the opinions of everyone in the country. So how will you select your representative sample? One way is to choose people from the group at random. You could open your school's directory and then pick, say, every twentieth name. Another option is to stratify your sample. For example, you could randomly select a specific number of first-year, second-year, third-year, and fourth-year students — and you could make sure that the number of men and women in each group is proportional to their enrollment at the school.

Decide What to Ask and How to Ask It with Integrity   Designing effective surveys can be challenging. Understanding the strengths and weaknesses of the kinds of questions that are frequently asked on surveys is a good way to get started. Figure 11.3 illustrates the main types of questions found on surveys. As you consider the types of questions you'll use, keep in mind the importance of asking questions that do not cue the people taking your survey to respond in a particular way. Consider, for example, how you might respond to the following questions.

- Do you support increasing income tax rates to reduce the federal debt?
- Do you support increasing income tax rates to ensure that future generations are not crushed under the burden of a spiraling federal debt?
- Do you support increasing income tax rates to enable the federal government to continue its irresponsible, uncontrolled spending on entitlements?

Determine Whether You Are Asking Your Questions Clearly   Test your survey items before administering your survey by asking your classmates or family members to read your questions. A question that seems perfectly clear to you

III Collecting Information

Election Survey

Thank you for completing this survey.

A 1. Did you vote in the last presidential election? ☐ yes ☐ no

2. I vote:

In every election	In most elections	In about half of the elections	Rarely	Never
☐	☐	☐	☐	☐

B 3. I have voted in the following types of elections (check all that apply):
   ☐ Regular local elections
   ☐ Special local elections
   ☐ Regular statewide elections
   ☐ National elections

C 4. Voting is a civic duty: ☐ true ☐ false

D 5. All eligible voters should participate in local, state, and national elections:

Strongly Agree	Agree	Not Sure	Disagree	Strongly Disagree
☐	☐	☐	☐	☐

6. Please rate the following reasons for voting on a 1-to-5 scale, in which 5 indicates very important and 1 indicates not at all important:

	1	2	3	4	5
To be a good citizen	☐	☐	☐	☐	☐
To have a say in how government affects my life	☐	☐	☐	☐	☐
To support a particular cause	☐	☐	☐	☐	☐
To vote against particular candidates	☐	☐	☐	☐	☐

E 7. Please rank the following types of elections from most important (4) to least important (1):
   _____ Presidential elections
   _____ Statewide elections
   _____ Local (city and county) elections
   _____ Student government elections

F 8. Please tell us what influenced your decision to vote or not vote in the last election.

FIGURE 11.3 Sample Survey

A Yes/no items divide respondents into two groups.

B Multiple-choice items indicate whether a respondent knows something or engages in specific behaviors. Because they seldom include every possible answer, be careful when including them.

C True/false items more often deal with attitudes or beliefs than with behaviors or events.

D Likert scales measure respondents' level of agreement with a statement, their assessment of something's importance, or how frequently they engage in a behavior.

E Ranking forces respondents to place items along a continuum.

F Short-answer items allow greater freedom of response but can be difficult to tabulate.

might confuse someone else. Rewrite the questions that confuse your "testers" and then test them again. Doing so will help you improve the clarity of your survey. Consider the evolution of the following question.

Original Question

What can be done about voter turnout among younger voters?

> Does "about voter turnout" mean increasing voter turnout, decreasing voter turnout, or encouraging younger voters to be better informed about candidates? Does the phrase "younger voters" mean 18-year-olds or 30-year-olds?

Revised Question

In your opinion, what can be done to increase turnout among 18- to 24-year-old voters?

Distribute Your Survey   Surveys are typically distributed via e-mail, the Web, or social media, although a number of research writers still conduct paper-based surveys. Online surveys are easier to distribute and offer more choices of tools for creating them (such as SurveyGizmo, SurveyMonkey, and Quibblo). Online survey tools also make tabulating results easier, allowing you to break down responses and create charts from survey data. The disadvantages include low response rates and the likelihood that the people who respond will do so because of a specific interest in the issue. In other words, you might find that most of your respondents have some sort of interest or bias that leads them to want to respond and are therefore not a representative sample of the group you hope to understand.

Paper-based surveys are most useful in situations where you can pass them out to a group, such as students in a class or people attending a meeting.

Surveying people over the phone tends to result in a low response rate and might be prohibited by local and state laws regarding telephone solicitations. Telephone surveys are seldom a productive tool for collecting responses.

Conduct Your Survey

The sheer number of surveys people are asked to complete these days has reduced the public's willingness to respond to them. In fact, a "good" response rate for a survey is 60 percent, and many professional pollsters find lower response rates acceptable.

Analyze Your Results

Once you've collected your surveys, you must tabulate your responses. It's usually best to tabulate survey responses using a spreadsheet program, which provides flexibility when you want to analyze your results. When you've tabulated your responses, look for trends and patterns. For example, ask whether age or experience seems to predict responses or whether groups respond differently to particular questions. Look as well for surprising results, such as unexpectedly high levels of agreement or disagreement with Likert-scale items or striking differences in the responses to short-answer questions.

As you conduct your analysis, keep in mind the need to ensure confidentiality for your respondents. Survey respondents usually do not expect their names to be revealed in reports about a survey or to find personally identifiable information in reports. As you review your responses, be on the lookout for information that might help someone identify a particular respondent. A respondent might reveal, for example, that she is the only Iraq War veteran in a particular writing class. If you gather this kind of information, do not include it in your report.

CHECKLIST FOR CONDUCTING SURVEYS

✔ **Keep it short.** Surveys are most effective when they are brief. Don't exceed one page.

✔ **Format and distribute your survey appropriately.** If your survey is on paper, make sure the text is readable, there is plenty of room to write, and the page isn't crowded with questions. If you are distributing your survey through e-mail, you can either insert the survey questions into the body of your e-mail message or attach the survey file. If you are distributing your survey on the Web, use the formatting options in your Web survey tool to test out various layouts for your survey questions.

✔ **Explain the purpose of your survey.** Explaining who you are and how you will use the results of the survey in your research writing project can help increase a respondent's willingness to complete and return your survey.

✔ **Treat survey respondents with respect.** People respond more favorably when they think you are treating them as individuals rather than simply as part of a mailing list. Address potential respondents by name in e-mail messages or cover letters. If you are mailing your survey, handwrite the name and address so that your survey doesn't arrive looking like junk mail.

✔ **Make it easy to return the survey.** If you are conducting your survey on the Web or via e-mail, be sure to provide directions for submitting or returning completed surveys. If you are distributing the survey to students in classes, provide a large envelope with your name and contact information into which the surveys can be placed.

11e

How can I engage in other forms of field research?

Other common forms of field research include engaging in correspondence and attending public events. In addition, you can often collect more information by working with others.

Engage in Correspondence

Correspondence includes any textual communication—such as letters and e-mail—as well as real-time communication using chat or text messaging. If you use chat or text messaging, be sure to save a transcript of the exchange. You can

TUTORIAL

How do I write a good survey question?

Developing a good survey question is challenging. The process is similar to writing an essay. The first drafts of survey questions serve to express your thoughts. Subsequent revisions help clarify questions for survey respondents. Keep your purpose in mind to be sure your question will elicit the information you need.

In this example, Brandon Tate devised a survey question to find out how fellow students view hydraulic fracturing—or *fracking*.

1 Write a first draft of the question.

Do you pay attention to television ads about fracking and why or why not?

2 Simplify the question.

Why do you pay attention to—or ignore—television ads about fracking?

3 Consider alternative ways of asking a question—including whether it should be a question.

What are your reasons for paying attention to—or ignoring—television ads about fracking?

4 Identify and then clarify keywords and phrases.

List five words to describe television ads about fracking.

5 Ask for feedback from potential respondents. Review and clarify keywords and phrases. Consider potential reactions to phrasing.

Please describe your reaction when you view a television ad about fracking.

correspond with experts in a particular area; people who have been affected by or are involved with an issue or event; staff at corporations, organizations, and government agencies; or even journalists who have written about a subject. In general, it's helpful to explain who you are, what you are writing about, and why you want to correspond.

Attend Public Events

Public events, such as lectures, conferences, and public meetings and hearings, often provide writers with useful information. You can record public events by taking notes or using a smartphone or digital recorder to capture them (if permitted). If you attend a public event in person or on the Web, find out whether a transcript of the proceedings will be available.

Collaborate with Others

Conducting field research can be time intensive. If you and your classmates are working on an assignment that involves fieldwork, consider forming collaborative teams to collect information. You can use one or more of the following strategies.

- If you are conducting an observation or attending a public event, you'll find that a single perspective might limit your ability to see what's happening. If another classmate is also conducting observations, you can help each other out. You might observe at the same time as your classmate so that together you can see more of what is taking place. Or you and your classmate might observe the same setting at different times, effectively doubling the amount of information you can obtain. The additional information will help you better understand the contexts being observed. If you decide to work with a classmate, consider creating an observation checklist so that each observer will know what to look for.

- If you are conducting an interview, share your interview questions with a classmate before conducting the interview. Have your classmate role-play the interviewee. Then ask him or her how you might improve your questions.

- If you are gathering information through correspondence, ask a classmate to review your letter or message before you send it and to offer suggestions for improving it. Your classmate can follow the guidelines for conducting an effective peer review (see p. 295).

- If you are conducting a survey, share drafts of your survey with a few classmates. Ask them to note any questions that seem unclear, irrelevant, or ineffective. If they identify any questions that could be improved, ask them why they found the questions problematic and whether they have any suggestions for revision.

III Collecting Information

My Research Project

Assess the Relevance of Field Research Methods

Think about whether the field research methods discussed in this chapter might contribute to your research project. If you decide to use observations, interviews, surveys, correspondence, or other forms of field research, seek advice from researchers who have used these methods or from your instructor or a librarian. Ask questions such as the following.

- How would field research methods help me accomplish my purpose for this project?
- How will my readers react to my use of evidence from field research methods?
- Is evidence from field research typically used in the type of document I plan to write?

In your research log, write down the responses you receive to these and related questions. Then decide whether using field research is a good choice for your project.

 QUICK REFERENCE

Collecting Information with Field Research

✔ Consider reasons for using field research. (p. 173)

✔ Plan and conduct interviews. (p. 174)

✔ Plan and conduct observations. (p. 179)

✔ Design, conduct, and analyze a survey. (p. 182)

✔ Use correspondence to collect information. (p. 186)

✔ Attend public events that are relevant to your issue. (p. 188)

✔ Enlist help in carrying out collaborative projects. (p. 188)

III Collecting Information

PART IV

Creating Your Document

After you have collected information, you'll have a better understanding of the scope of your issue. In the chapters that follow, you'll learn how to use your new knowledge to create a well-written, well-designed document.

12

Developing Your Thesis Statement

Key Questions

12a. How can I prepare to draft my thesis statement? 193
Review your position statement
Review your notes
Consider your purpose and role
Reflect on your readers

12b. How can I develop an effective thesis statement? 195
Identify important information, ideas, and arguments associated with your position
Focus on your role
Consider the type of document you plan to write
Draft alternatives
Choose your thesis statement
Refine your thesis statement

As you shift your attention away from collecting and working with sources and toward crafting your own contribution to the conversation about your issue, you'll begin the process of planning your argument. That process begins with reviewing your position statement, your notes, and your purpose in order to draft an effective thesis statement.

12a

How can I prepare to draft my thesis statement?

Your thesis statement provides a clear, focused expression of the main point you want to make. It is, in a nutshell, the most important idea or argument you want to convey to your readers. Your thesis statement should invite your readers to do one of three things: learn something new, change an attitude or belief, or take action. Featured writer Alexis Alvarez, for example, asked her readers to learn something new.

> Although competitive sports can provide young female athletes with many benefits, they can also have negative effects, the worst of which is increasing drug use.

In contrast, featured writer Brandon Tate asked readers to take action to support changes in the regulation of hydraulic fracturing.

> Coloradoans should develop a coordinated response to the growing use of hydraulic fracturing in or near watersheds that supply drinking water to the state.

Your efforts to develop a thesis statement will be influenced by what you've learned about your issue and by your writing situation. Before you begin drafting your thesis statement, review your current position statement, review your notes, and consider your writing situation.

Review Your Position Statement

As you have collected, skimmed, critically read, and evaluated sources, you've almost certainly developed — and perhaps written, reviewed, and revised — a statement defining your position on your issue (p. 58). Now, as you begin the process of deciding what you want to convey to your readers, it is time to reflect on that position. If you have already drafted a position statement, you can turn to it and ask whether it still represents the most important point you want to make about your issue. If you haven't drafted a position statement, do so now. You can use brainstorming, looping, and other idea-generation strategies to help formulate your position statement (p. 20).

Review Your Notes

With your position statement in mind, review your notes. As you do so:

- identify important information, ideas, and arguments that you've come across in your reading
- consider whether the information, ideas, and arguments you've identified in your notes will allow you to pursue your personal, academic, and professional interests
- review and elaborate on ideas and arguments that you've come up with as a result of your own thinking about the subject

As you carry out your review, reflect on your position statement. Ask how well it conveys the information, ideas, and arguments you would most like to address in your document. Ask how well it aligns with your personal and professional interests. If you find that it does not fully capture your understanding of the issue — that is, if it doesn't seem to reflect the main point you want to make about your issue — revise your position statement.

Consider Your Purpose and Role WHAT'S MY PURPOSE?

Reviewing your notes will help you deepen your understanding of your issue. That understanding, in turn, is likely to affect how you view your purpose and role as a writer and, by extension, the main point you want to make in your document. Use the following questions to guide how you think about your thesis statement.

- Have your purposes—the reasons you are working on this research writing project—changed since you started? If so, how do you view your purpose now?

- Has your role as a writer—for example, to inform or to solve a problem—changed since you started your research writing project? If so, how do you view your role now?

If your answers to any of these questions suggest that the main point you want to make has changed, revise your position statement.

Reflect on Your Readers

In the same way that you considered your purpose and role, ask whether focusing on a particular main point will help you address your readers' purposes, needs, and interests. If you find that your main point is not well aligned with your readers' concerns, revise your position statement.

12b

How can I develop an effective thesis statement?

To draft your thesis statement, consider what you learned through your reflections on your position statement, notes, and writing situation. Your work on your thesis statement will be affected by the information, ideas, and arguments you've encountered in your reading, the role or roles you are adopting in relation to your readers, and the type of document you plan to write.

Step 1: Identify Important Information, Ideas, and Arguments Associated with Your Position

Begin developing your thesis statement by identifying important information, ideas, and arguments related to your position. When you first explored a conversation (see Chapter 2), you asked questions to learn about your subject. Review those questions and examine them for important words and phrases. Then look through your notes to see how your sources address those questions or use those words and phrases. Consider the following example, which shows how a writer identified keywords and phrases in her research question, position statement, and notes.

Research Question about Effects of the War on Drugs in South America

How can we reduce the economic impact of the war on drugs on South American coca farmers?

Position Statement

The U.S. and South American governments should adopt the "zero cocaine, not zero coca" policy.

Notes on "Bolivia's Knot: No to Cocaine, but Yes to Coca," by Juan Forero

Newly elected Bolivian president, Evo Morales, is "an Aymara Indian who grew up in poverty in the highlands and became a coca grower" (para. 6). He plans to remove sanctions for growing coca even as he shows "zero tolerance toward trafficking" (para. 6). This is part of his "yes to coca, no to cocaine" campaign. Morales has been a long-time opponent of U.S. efforts to eradicate the coca crop, pointing to its lack of "mind-altering effects" and its use to "mitigate hunger and increase stamina" (para. 7). Morales plans to work with foreign governments to find a market for products made from coca, despite the fact that since 1961 the UN has blacklisted all products made from coca. Those products include soaps, shampoos, toothpaste, flour, and tea, "which is legal and popular in the Andes" (para. 7).

Review the words and phrases you've identified as important and keep them in mind as you begin to draft alternative thesis statements.

Step 2: Focus on Your Role   [FRAMING MY ARGUMENT]

In the same way that your role as a writer—the manner in which you'll relate to your readers—has an impact on your research question (p. 42), your role will shape your thesis statement. Asking your readers to learn something new, as you would be doing if you adopted the roles of observer (reflecting), reporter (informing), interpreter (analyzing), inquirer (developing new knowledge), or evaluator (evaluating), will lead to thesis statements that differ significantly from those that might emerge from roles such as problem solver (to define or solve problems) or advocate (to convince or persuade). Featured writer Nicholas Brothers, for example, adopted the dual roles of interpreter and advocate, first analyzing the U.S. military's growing reliance on private military contractors in the Iraq and Afghanistan wars and then arguing that readers should change their attitudes about—more specifically, to be skeptical of—their use.

> By relying heavily on private military corporations to carry out military operations, the U.S. Department of Defense is undermining its own counterinsurgency efforts in Iraq and Afghanistan.

Had Nicholas adopted the role of informer and simply reported on the growing use of private military contractors, his thesis statement might have resembled the following.

> As the U.S. has expanded its involvement in foreign wars, it has dramatically increased its reliance on private military corporations.

Table 12.1 provides a list of some of the most important roles you might adopt and offers examples of the kinds of thesis statements writers adopting a particular role might use. You can use the sentence starters in the table to generate your ideas for your thesis statement.

TABLE 12.1 THE RELATIONSHIP AMONG ROLES AND THESIS STATEMENTS		
Role	**Purpose**	**Sample Sentence Starters**
Reporter	To inform	Understanding _____ is essential if we are to _____.
		The best way to understand _____ is to view it as _____.
		Understanding _____ can only be achieved by _____.
Inquirer	To create and share new knowledge	_____ causes _____.
		The most important effects of _____ are _____.
		_____ can [cure/repair/prevent] _____.
Observer	To reflect	The most important lessons we can learn from _____ are _____.
		My reflections on _____ have helped me _____.
		_____ is important because _____.
Evaluator	To evaluate	In general, evaluations of _____ have shown us that it _____.
		The most important influences on _____ are _____.
		The best choices available for addressing _____ are _____.
		_____ has [these strengths and weaknesses].
Interpreter	To analyze	_____ causes _____ because _____.
		What are the effects of _____?
		The data suggest that _____ [is/is the result of] a _____.
		_____ is similar to _____ because _____.
		_____ differs from _____ because _____.
Problem Solver	To solve problems	_____ is a problem because _____.
		The solution to _____ is _____.
		We should adopt _____ as a solution because _____.
Advocate	To convince (change readers' beliefs or attitudes), persuade (cause readers to take action), or mediate (seek to establish common ground among readers)	The origins of this argument are found in _____.
		The status of this argument is _____.
		The best argument about _____ is _____.
		The writers and readers involved in conversation about _____ want to [see/avoid] _____.
		We should do _____ about _____.
		We should accomplish _____ by doing _____.
		We can find common ground about _____ by doing _____.

Step 3: Consider the Type of Document You Plan to Write

An effective thesis statement will reflect the type of document — or genre — you plan to write. Depending on the type of document, your readers will have different expectations about how you present your thesis statement. Readers of an academic essay within a particular discipline, such as philosophy or political science, are likely to expect a calm, clearly written statement of what you want them to learn, believe, or do. Readers of an informative newspaper article will expect you to identify, in a balanced and seemingly unbiased manner, what you want them to learn. Readers of an opinion column will expect you to be more assertive, and perhaps even more entertaining, about your position on an issue. Consider how the following thesis statements, all addressing problems with the recruitment of athletes at a college or university, reflect the type of document the writer plans to draft.

Argumentative Academic Essay
The University should ensure that its recruiting practices are fully in compliance with NCAA regulations.

A strong but formal assertion

Informative Newspaper Article
The University is taking steps to bring its recruiting practices in line with NCAA regulations.

A seemingly unbiased statement of fact

Opinion Column
The University's coaches need to get their act together before the NCAA slaps them with sanctions.

An informal tone

Step 4: Draft Alternatives

An effective thesis statement can invite your readers to learn something new, suggest that they change their attitudes or beliefs, or argue that they should take action of some kind. Consider how the following thesis statements reflect these three ways of focusing a position statement.

Position Statement
The U.S. and South American governments should adopt the "zero cocaine, not zero coca" policy.

Thesis Statement: Asking Readers to Learn Something New
The coca plant, which is used to create cocaine, has numerous economic and medicinal benefits.

Thesis Statement: Asking Readers to Change Their Attitudes or Beliefs
U.S. citizens, long accustomed to equating any form of the coca plant (which is used to manufacture cocaine) as undesirable, will be surprised by its many economic and medicinal benefits.

Thesis Statement: Asking Readers to Take Action
Given the proven economic and medicinal benefits of the coca plant, the United States should rethink its policy toward coca farming in South America.

My Research Project

Generate Draft Thesis Statements

Use the following table to generate draft thesis statements. To complete the activity, identify the role or roles that you are most likely to adopt. Then choose a column, such as "Change Their Attitudes or Beliefs," and generate draft thesis statements. You need not complete every cell in the table, and you can create more than one statement in each cell.

To generate statements, use freewriting or the sentence starters found in Table 12.1.

GOAL: ASKING READERS TO . . .				
Role	**Purpose**	**Learn Something New**	**Change Their Attitudes or Beliefs**	**Take Action of Some Kind**
Reporter	To inform			
Inquirer	To create and share new knowledge			
Observer	To reflect			
Evaluator	To evaluate			
Interpreter	To analyze			
Problem Solver	To solve problems			
Advocate	To convince, persuade, or mediate			

Step 5: Choose Your Thesis Statement

Review your thesis statements. Ask the following questions about each one.

- Will this thesis statement help me achieve my goals as a writer?
- Do the sources I've read so far give me confidence that I will be able to support the thesis statement?
- Will it address my readers' expectations?
- Will it be consistent with the genre I'm likely to choose?
- Will it sustain my interest in this project?

Of these questions, the most important may be the last. Be sure, however, that the thesis statement you choose will help you accomplish your goals, meet the expectations of your readers, and find support from your sources.

Step 6: Refine Your Thesis Statement

Once you've chosen a thesis statement, take time to refine it. As you refine your thesis statement, ask continually how doing so will frame your readers' attention. Consider how the following thesis statement might be refined by adding information, referring to shared assumptions, and narrowing its scope.

Draft Thesis Statement
The U.S. government should stop attempting to eradicate coca plants and instead focus on eliminating the manufacture and distribution of cocaine.

Add Information   You can frame your readers' understanding of the issue by incorporating relevant information into your statement.

Refined Thesis Statement
Given the failure of the "War on Drugs" to stem the flow of cocaine into the United States, the U.S. government should stop attempting to eradicate coca plants and instead focus on eliminating the manufacture and distribution of cocaine.

> Adding information about an area of weakness in the war on drugs directs readers' attention to the need to find an alternative approach.

Refined Thesis Statement
The U.S. government should stop attempting to eradicate coca plants, which have been central to the economic well-being of Bolivian farmers for centuries, and instead focus on eliminating the manufacture and distribution of cocaine.

Refer to Shared Assumptions and Common Knowledge   You can refine your thesis statement by calling attention to assumptions that have been made by the community of writers and readers who are addressing your issue, by referring to existing conditions relevant to your issue, or by using conditional words and phrases to set up a main point.

Refined Thesis Statement: Referring to Shared Assumption
Given our national commitment to economic opportunity and fairness for all, the U.S. government should stop attempting to eradicate coca plants and instead focus on eliminating the manufacture and distribution of cocaine.

> The writer calls attention to a widely shared national value.

Refined Thesis Statement: Referring to Common Knowledge
The U.S. government, recognizing the important role coca farming plays in Bolivia's economy, should stop attempting to eradicate coca plants and instead focus on eliminating the manufacture and distribution of cocaine.

> Calling attention to information many writers have referred to frames readers' understanding of the status of the issue.

Refined Thesis Statement: Referring to Existing Conditions

The U.S. government, <u>recognizing its failure to date to eradicate coca plants,</u> should focus on eliminating the manufacture and distribution/of cocaine.

> Referring to the current state of government efforts calls
> readers' attention to a more effective allocation of resources.

You can also use conditional words and phrases to narrow the focus of a thesis statement. You can find a list of these words and phrases on p. 49.

Refined Thesis Statement: Using Conditional Words and Phrases

<u>Although the war on drugs is well intended, it is clear given its lack of results</u> that we should stop attempting to eradicate coca plants and instead/focus on eliminating the manufacture and distribution of cocaine.

> Conditional words and phrases are used to acknowledge good
> intentions even as they set the stage for an alternative approach.

Narrow the Scope of Your Thesis Statement   You can narrow the scope of your thesis statement by looking for vague words and phrases and replacing them with more specific words or phrases.

Draft Thesis Statement

The U.S. government should <u>focus less on coca plants</u> and more on cocaine.

Refined

The U.S. government should <u>stop attempting to eradicate coca plants</u> and instead focus on eliminating the manufacture and distribution of cocaine.

Further Refined

The U.S. government should stop attempting to eradicate coca plants <u>by burning fields and leaving farmers and their families without a means to earn an income</u> and instead focus on eliminating the manufacture and distribution of cocaine, which affect Americans directly.

As you work to refine your thesis statement, keep in mind that it is—and will remain until the late stages of your work on your project—a work in progress. Stay alert to new ideas and information that might change your thinking about your position on your issue. Continue to think about how you might refine or even substantially revise your thesis statement so that you can better frame the issue for your readers.

Table 12.2 presents the featured writers' movements from research question to position statement to thesis statement. Note how each thesis statement answers its research question and directs readers' attention to one aspect of the conversation, encourages them to change their attitudes or beliefs, or urges them to take action of some kind.

IV Creating Your Document

TABLE 12.2 THE FEATURED WRITERS' MOVEMENT FROM RESEARCH QUESTION TO THESIS STATEMENT

Featured Writer	Research Question	Position Statement	Thesis Statement
Alexis Alvarez	What are the effects of competitive soccer on adolescent girls?	Steroid use by adolescent girls involved in competitive sports should be addressed by educating athletes, parents, and coaches about health consequences and emphasizing fair play.	Although competitive sports can provide young female athletes with many benefits, they can also have negative effects, the worst of which is increasing drug use.
Nicholas Brothers	What dangers are associated with U.S. reliance on private military corporations in its war on terror?	The overreliance of the United States on private military corporations is a danger to national and international security.	By relying heavily on private military corporations to carry out military operations, the U.S. Department of Defense is undermining its own counterinsurgency efforts in Iraq and Afghanistan.
Elizabeth Leontiev	How can we reduce the economic impact of the war on drugs on South American coca farmers?	The U.S. and South American governments should adopt the "zero coca," not zero coca" policy.	The "zero cocaine, not zero coca" policy will boost the Bolivian economy, allow native Andeans to maintain their cultural practices, and reduce cocaine trafficking into the United States.
Lauren Mack	What factors are causing damage to coral reefs?	A combination of human (anthropogenic) and natural factors are causing damage to coral reefs.	The importance of coral reefs to the global environment demands that we take action to protect them.
Cori Schmidtbauer	How does Portia's character in *The Merchant of Venice* fit in with Elizabethan ideas of women?	Portia appears to rebel against the expectations of Elizabethan culture.	By gaining the upper hand in traditionally male-dominated systems of exchange (notably marriage) and cross-dressing as a male lawyer to defend Antonio in court, Portia assaults the idea of the weak Renaissance woman from every angle. However, a fresh look at *The Merchant of Venice* reveals that Portia—in a strange way—may have reflected Renaissance culture just as much as she contradicted it.
Brandon Tate	What do we need to know about fracking in order to make responsible decisions about its use?	Fracking has many potential benefits as well as negative consequences, and it should be evaluated alongside other sources of energy.	Fracking encourages reliance on fossil fuels and should be less of a priority than finding sources of renewable energy.
Josh Woelfle	What recent advancements in cancer treatment have been the most promising?	While chemotherapy and radiation have been mainstays of cancer treatment, their side effects can be debilitating, and new forms of treatment are becoming very effective.	Cancer-fighting drugs that focus on growth-signaling enzymes and MDR proteins may soon overtake chemotherapy and radiation as standard cancer treatment.

My Research Project

Refine Your Thesis Statement

In your research log, complete the following activity to refine your thesis statement.

1. I have chosen the following thesis statement:

2. I can refine my thesis statement and frame my readers' understanding of the issue by

- adding the following relevant information:
- referring to the following shared assumptions:
- referring to the following common knowledge:
- referring to the following existing conditions:
- replacing the following vague words and phrases:
- using the following conditional words and phrases:

 QUICK REFERENCE

Developing Your Thesis Statement

☑ Review and reflect on your research question, position statement, notes, and writing situation. (p. 193)

☑ Begin to draft your thesis statement by identifying important information, ideas, and arguments. (p. 195)

☑ Consider your role, the type of document you are writing, and any disciplinary writing conventions. (p. 196)

☑ Generate potential thesis statements. (p. 198)

☑ Choose and refine your thesis statement. (p. 199)

13

Developing and Organizing Your Argument

Key Questions

13a. How can I develop my argument?   205
Choose reasons to support your main point
Select evidence to support your reasons
Decide how to appeal to your readers
Decide how to address opposing arguments
Check for logical fallacies

13b. How can I organize my argument?   215
Choose an organizing pattern
Review and arrange your evidence
Create an outline

Once you've determined your position on an issue and expressed it as a thesis statement, you've laid the foundation for developing your contribution to the conversation you've decided to join. Developing your argument involves a number of key stages: identifying reasons to accept the main point you've advanced in your thesis statement, selecting evidence to support your reasons, deciding how to appeal to your readers, and determining how best to address counterarguments. To improve the overall effectiveness of your argument, you should also assess the integrity of your reasoning and organize your evidence clearly and logically. Creating an outline will help you to do this, giving you a framework for arranging your evidence and using an appropriate organizing pattern.

13a

How can I develop my argument?

Developing an effective argument involves far more than knowing what you want others to understand or believe or how you want them to act. It requires the development of a strategy to explain and support the main point made in your thesis statement. That strategy should reflect not only your purpose and role but also your readers' needs, interests, values, beliefs, and knowledge of an issue. It should also take into account the conventions typically used in the type of document you plan to write. Most important, it should reflect a willingness to change your argument—from your thesis statement to your reasons and evidence—in response to new information, ideas, and arguments that you might encounter as you work on your research writing project.

Choose Reasons to Support Your Main Point

In longer documents, such as essays, reports, and websites, writers usually present several reasons for readers to accept or act on their thesis statements. The kinds of reasons they choose will vary according to the type of document they are writing. In informative articles in newspapers and magazines, for example, writers are likely to focus on the three or four most important aspects of the issue they want readers to understand. In blog posts that analyze an issue, in contrast, writers are likely to choose reasons that help readers understand the results of the analysis. In an argumentative essay, writers usually offer a series of claims that will lead readers to accept their argument or take action in response to it.

To choose reasons to support your main point, consider your readers' expectations.

- Readers of informative documents, such as reports, essays, and articles, expect you to help them understand something about an issue. As you plan an informative document, ask what you want to convey to your readers and what they are most likely to want to know about it.

- Readers of evaluative documents, such as movie and media reviews and progress reports, expect you to provide a reasonable judgment based on a fairly selected set of criteria. As you choose reasons to accept your evaluation, ask what readers will want to gain from reading your document and what you want them to understand about the results of your evaluation.

- Readers of argumentative documents, such as argumentative essays, opinion columns, and blog posts, will expect you to provide a set of reasons for accepting your argument. As you choose your reasons, consider what your readers will know about the issue, how they are likely to respond to your overall argument, and the likely counterarguments they might propose.

As you develop reasons to support your main point, remember that your overall goal is to help your readers pay attention to—and perhaps even take action in response to—your argument. To guide your efforts, ask questions such as the following, and respond to them by brainstorming, freewriting, looping, clustering, or mapping.

- **Costs** What costs are associated with not accepting and acting on your main point? Are there monetary costs? Will time and effort be lost or wasted? Will valuable resources be wasted? Will human potential be wasted? Will lives be lost?

- **Benefits** What will be gained by accepting and acting on your main point? Who or what will benefit if your main point is accepted and acted on? What form will these benefits take?

- **Alternatives, Choices, and Tradeoffs** In what ways are the potential costs or benefits associated with accepting or acting on your main point preferable to those associated with rejecting your main point or accepting an alternative point?

- **Parallels** Can you find similarities between the main point you are making about this issue in your thesis statement and claims made about other issues? Can you argue that, if your main point is accepted and acted on, the outcomes will be similar to those found for other issues?

- **Personal Experience** What does your personal experience tell you is likely to happen if your main point is accepted and acted on? What does it tell you might happen if it is rejected?

- **Values and Beliefs** In what ways is your main point consistent with your values and beliefs? With those of your readers? In what ways is it consistent with larger societal and cultural values and beliefs?

Examine the list of reasons you've generated to determine which ones best suit your purpose and will most likely appeal to your readers. Select the reasons that, individually and as a group, best support your main point. If you see inconsistency between the reasons you've chosen and your current thesis statement, consider revising your thesis statement (p. 290).

Decide How Your Reasons Support Your Main Point Effective arguments make connections (sometimes called *warrants*) between a main point (sometimes called an *overall claim*) and the reasons offered to support it. Sometimes readers accept a connection because they share the writer's values and beliefs or have similar experiences with and knowledge of an issue. In other cases, readers accept a connection because the writer explains it effectively. This explanation (sometimes called *backing*) provides readers with information and analysis that help them understand and accept the connection (see Figure 13.1).

As you consider your reasons, ask how clearly they connect to your main point as it is expressed in your thesis statement. Ask whether you should explain each connection or leave it unstated. Your answers will depend in part on the

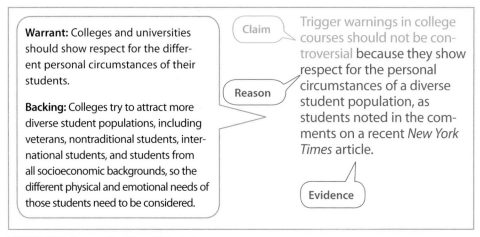

FIGURE 13.1 Supporting Your Main Point

extent to which your readers share your values, beliefs, experience, and knowledge of the issue. If your readers' backgrounds and knowledge differ from yours, connections that make sense to you might not be clear to them.

Select Evidence to Support Your Reasons

For every reason you offer to support your main point, you'll need evidence—such as details, facts, personal observations, and expert opinions—to back up your assertions and help your readers understand your ideas.

You can draw evidence from your sources in the form of quotations, paraphrases, summaries, numerical data, and visual images (p. 77). You can also gather evidence firsthand by conducting interviews, observations, and surveys, or by reflecting on your personal experience (pp. 174–86).

As you choose evidence to support your reasons, think about whether—and, if so, how—you will show the connections between reasons and evidence. These connections, often called *appeals* (p. 208), help readers understand why a reason is appropriate and valid (see Figure 13.2). Common appeals include

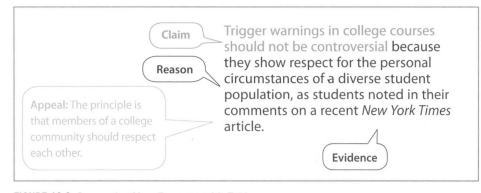

FIGURE 13.2 Supporting Your Reasons with Evidence

IV Creating Your Document

citing authorities on an issue; using emotion to sway readers; calling attention to shared principles, values, and beliefs; asking readers to trust the writer; and using logic.

As you select supporting evidence, consider the type of document—or genre—you plan to write. The types of evidence used in various genres can differ in important ways. Articles (p. 281) in magazines, in newspapers, and on websites, for example, are more likely to rely on interviews, observations, and illustrations as primary sources of evidence than are academic essays, whose writers tend to draw information from published sources found in a library or database. Multimodal essays (p. 277), in contrast, are likely to use not only textual information and images but also audio, video, and animation. Evidence also varies widely depending on your discipline or profession, with some relying heavily on textual evidence and others relying on data from original research.

My Research Project

Select Evidence to Support Your Reasons

Use the following prompts to help identify evidence to support your reasons.

1. List the reasons you are offering to support your main point.

2. Identify relevant evidence, and then list the evidence below each reason. You might need to review your sources to locate additional evidence or even obtain additional sources.

3. Determine whether you are relying too heavily on information from a single source.

4. Determine whether you are relying too heavily on one type of evidence.

5. Determine whether you've chosen evidence that is consistent with the type of document you plan to write.

6. Determine whether the evidence you've collected might lead you to revise the reasons you are offering to support your main point—or whether the thesis statement in which you express your main point should be revised.

Decide How to Appeal to Your Readers   [FRAMING MY ARGUMENT]

For thousands of years, writers have appealed to readers to accept their ideas as reasonable and valid. Much of the work of ancient Greek and Roman thinkers such as Aristotle and Cicero revolved around strategies for presenting an argument to an audience. Their work continues to serve as a foundation for how we think about conveying information, ideas, and arguments to readers.

In particular, the concept of an *appeal* to an audience plays a central role in thinking about how to develop an argument. Essentially, when you ask readers to accept your argument, you are appealing to them—you are asking them to consider what you have to say and, if they accept it as appropriate and valid, to believe or act in a certain way.

You can persuade your readers to accept your argument by appealing to authority, emotion, principles, values, beliefs, character, and logic. Your choice of these appeals should reflect your understanding of your research writing situation and your sense of which appeals might be most effective—individually or in combination—at helping you achieve your goals as a writer.

Appeals to authority ask readers to accept a reason because someone in a position of authority supports it. Evidence for this kind of appeal typically takes the form of quotations, paraphrases, or summaries of the ideas of experts on an issue, of political leaders, or of people who have been affected by an issue.

Appeals to emotion attempt to elicit an emotional response to an issue. The famous "win one for the Gipper" speech delivered by Pat O'Brien, who was playing the part of Notre Dame coach Knute Rockne in the 1940 film *Knute Rockne: All American*, is an example of an appeal to emotion. At halftime during a game against Army, with Notre Dame trailing, he said:

> Well, boys . . . I haven't a thing to say. Played a great game . . . all of you. Great game. I guess we just can't expect to win 'em all.
>
> I'm going to tell you something I've kept to myself for years. None of you ever knew George Gipp. It was long before your time. But you know what a tradition he is at Notre Dame. . . . And the last thing he said to me—"Rock," he said, "sometime, when the team is up against it—and the breaks are beating the boys—tell them to go out there with all they got and win just one for the Gipper. . . . I don't know where I'll be then, Rock," he said, "but I'll know about it—and I'll be happy."

Using emotional appeals to frame an argument—that is, to help readers view an issue in a particular way—is a tried-and-true strategy, especially in advertising, fund-raising, and personal communication. But use it carefully, if you use it at all. In some types of documents, such as scholarly articles and essays, emotional appeals are used infrequently, and readers of such documents are likely to ask why you would play on their emotions instead of making a logical appeal or appeals to authority.

Appeals to principles, values, and beliefs rely on the assumption that your readers value a given set of principles. Religious and ethical arguments are often based on appeals to principles, such as the need to respect God, to love one another, to trust in the innate goodness of individuals, to believe that all of us are created equal, or to believe that security should never be purchased at the price of individual liberty. The effectiveness of these appeals relies largely on the extent to which your readers share a given principle, value, or belief.

Appeals to character can be thought of as the "trust me" strategy. When politicians refer to their military experience, for example, they are saying, "Look at me. I'm a patriotic person who has served our country." When a celebrity endorses a product, he or she is saying, "You know and like me, so please believe me when I say that this product is worth purchasing." When scientists or philosophers present arguments, for example, they sometimes refer to their background and experience or perhaps to their previous publications. In doing so, they are implicitly telling their readers that they have proved to be accurate and truthful in the past and that readers can continue to trust them. As you consider this kind of appeal, reflect on your character, accomplishments, and experiences, and ask how they might persuade your readers to trust you.

Appeals to logic ask readers to work through a set of propositions to reach a considered conclusion. For example, you might argue that a suspect is guilty of murder because police found her fingerprints on a murder weapon, her DNA in blood under the murder victim's fingernails, and video of the murder from a surveillance camera. Your argument would rely on the logical presentation of evidence to convince a jury that the suspect was the murderer and persuade them to return a verdict of guilty. As you develop reasons to support your claim, consider using logical appeals such as deduction and induction.

Deduction is a form of logical reasoning that moves from general principles to a conclusion. It usually involves two propositions and a conclusion.

Proposition 1 (usually a general principle):	Stealing is wrong.
Proposition 2 (usually an observation):	John stole a candy bar from the store.
Conclusion (results of deductive analysis):	John's theft of the candy bar was wrong.

Deduction is often used in arguments about issues that have ethical and moral dimensions, such as birth control, welfare reform, and immigration policy.

Induction is a form of logical reasoning that moves from specific observations to general conclusions, often drawing on numerical data to reveal patterns. Medical researchers, for example, typically collect a large number of observations about the effectiveness and side effects of new medications and then analyze their observations to draw conclusions about the overall usefulness of the medications. Induction is based on probability; that is, it can tell you whether something seems likely to occur based on what has been observed. Three commonly used forms of induction are trend analysis (p. 71), causal analysis (p. 71), and data analysis (p. 72).

My Research Project

Decide How to Appeal to Your Readers

To develop an argumentative strategy, reflect on your purpose, your readers, and your main point. In your research log, record your responses to the following.

1. List each of your reasons.

2. Ask what sorts of appeals are best suited to each reason. Ask, for example, whether appeals to emotion, logic, or character are appropriate for a particular reason.

3. Sketch out promising appeals. Ask, for example, how you would appeal to authority, or how you would appeal to logic.

4. Ask how your readers are likely to respond to a given appeal.

5. Ask whether the kind of document you are writing lends itself to the use of particular appeals.

Decide How to Address Opposing Arguments

If you are writing to convince or persuade your readers, if you are offering an evaluation or analysis that might be challenged by your readers, or if you are proposing a solution to a problem, take the time to identify opposing arguments, or counterarguments. You might assume that calling attention to counterarguments will undermine your argument. Nothing is further from the truth. Identifying counterarguments provides opportunities to test and strengthen your reasons and evidence by comparing them with those put forth by other writers. Considering counterarguments also allows you to anticipate questions and concerns your readers are likely to bring to your document. And later, as you are writing your draft, your responses to these opposing arguments provide a basis for clearly explaining to your readers why your argument, evaluation, analysis, or solution is superior to others.

Remember that if reasonable alternatives to your argument didn't exist, there would be no need for a conversation about the issue in the first place. As a writer contributing to an ongoing conversation, you have a responsibility to indicate that you're aware of what has been said and who has said it. More important, you have a responsibility to consider carefully how your argument improves on the arguments made by other members of the conversation.

Identify Counterarguments   To identify counterarguments, review the sources you encountered as you learned about your issue. Identify the most compelling opposing viewpoints you found, and ask how the reasons and evidence offered to support them compare to yours. Then ask whether you can think of reasonable alternative positions that haven't been addressed in the sources you've consulted. Finally, talk with others about your issue and ask them what they think about it.

Address Counterarguments   To address counterarguments, consider the strengths and weaknesses of each claim in relation to your argument and in relation to the other opposing claims you might have identified. Then decide whether to concede, refute, or ignore each claim.

Concede Valid Claims   Show your readers that you are being fair—and establish common ground with readers who might otherwise be inclined to disagree with you—by acknowledging opposing points of view and accepting reasonable aspects of counterarguments. For example, if you are arguing that your state government should spend more to repair roads and bridges, acknowledge that this will probably mean reducing funding for other state programs or increasing state taxes.

You can qualify your concession by explaining that although part of a counterargument is sound, readers should consider the argument's weaknesses. You might note, for example, that reducing funding for some state programs could be offset by instituting fees for those who use those programs most.

Refute Widely Held Claims   A counterargument might be widely advocated or generally accepted yet still have significant weaknesses. If you identify widely held claims that have weaknesses such as cost, undesirable outcomes, or logical flaws, describe the counterargument, point out its flaws, and explain why your claim or reason is superior. For example, you might note that, although it is costly to maintain roads and bridges, allowing them to fall into disrepair will cost far more in the long run—in terms of funding, possible injury, or loss of life.

Ignore Competing Claims   Don't assume that addressing counterarguments means giving every competing claim equal time. Some counterarguments will be much stronger than others, and some will be so closely related to one another that you can dismiss them as a group. Once you've addressed valid and widely held competing claims, you can safely ignore the rest. Even though your sense of fairness might suggest that you should address every counterargument, doing so will result in a less effective (and potentially much longer) essay.

Later, as you draft your document, remember to present your discussion of counterarguments using a reasonable and polite tone. You will gain little, if anything, by insulting or belittling writers with whom you disagree, particularly when it's possible that some of your readers think a certain counterargument has merit. You will find it preferable—and generally more effective in terms of achieving your goals as a writer—to carefully and politely point out the limitations of a particular counterargument.

Check for Logical Fallacies

To ensure the integrity of your argument, acquaint yourself with common logical fallacies—errors in logic that have the potential to undermine readers' willingness to accept an argument. Then check that your argument does not fall victim to them.

WORKING TOGETHER

Identify and Consider Counterarguments

Working with a group of two or more classmates, carry out a "devil's advocate" exercise to identify and consider opposing claims. First, briefly describe your issue, main point, and reasons. Other members of the group should offer reasonable alternative arguments. One member of the group should serve as a recorder, taking careful notes on the exchange, listing opposing claims, reasons supporting those claims, and your response to the claims. Once the exchange (which might last between three and ten minutes) is completed, switch roles and repeat the activity for every other member of the group.

This activity can be carried out face to face or electronically. If you are working on the activity using a chat program or a threaded discussion forum, you can record your exchange for later review. Most chat programs allow you to create a transcript of a session, and threaded discussion forums will automatically record your exchange.

Check for Fallacies Based on Distraction

A **red herring** is an irrelevant or distracting point. The term originated with the practice of sweeping a red herring (a particularly aromatic type of fish) across the trail being followed by a pack of hunting dogs to throw them off the scent of their prey. The question *Why worry about the rising cost of tuition when the government is tapping our phones?* is a red herring. Government surveillance has nothing to do with increases in college tuition.

Ad hominem **attacks** attempt to discredit an idea or argument by suggesting that a person or group associated with it should not be trusted. If you hear someone say that a proposed wind farm should be rejected because its main supporter cheated on her taxes, you're listening to an *ad hominem* attack.

Irrelevant history suggests that something associated with an idea should disqualify it. You might hear, for instance, that an idea is bad because someone came up with it while they were drunk. Base your assessment of the idea on its strengths and weaknesses. Otherwise, you might as well say that an idea is undoubtedly sound because someone thought of it while he or she was sober.

Look for Fallacies Based on Questionable Assumptions

Sweeping generalizations, sometimes known as *hasty generalizations*, are based on stereotypes. Asserting that the rich are conservative voters, for example, assumes that everyone who is rich is just like everyone else who is rich.

Straw-man attacks oversimplify or distort another person's argument so it can be dismissed more easily. Just as a boxer can easily knock down a scarecrow, a writer who commits this fallacy might characterize an opposing position as more extreme than it actually is or might refute obviously flawed counterarguments while ignoring valid objections.

Citing inappropriate authorities can take several forms: citing as an authority someone who is not an expert on a subject, citing an authority who has a strong bias on an issue, suggesting that an individual voice represents consensus when that person's ideas are far from the mainstream, or treating paid celebrity endorsements as expert opinion.

Jumping on a bandwagon, also known as *argument from consensus*, implies that if enough people believe something, it must be true. This type of argument substitutes group thinking for careful analysis.

Search for Fallacies Based on Misrepresentation

Stacking the deck, often referred to as *cherry-picking* or *suppressing evidence*, is the act of presenting evidence for only one side of an argument when sufficient evidence exists for an alternative argument.

Base-rate fallacies are commonly found in arguments based on statistics. If you read that drinking coffee will triple your risk of developing cancer, you might be alarmed. However, if you knew that the risk rose from one in a billion to three in a billion, you might pour another cup.

Questionable analogies, also known as *false analogies*, make inappropriate comparisons. They are based on the assumption that if two things are similar in one way, they must be similar in others. For example, a writer might argue that global warming is like a fever, and that just as a fever usually runs its course on its own, so too will the climate recover without intervention.

Locate Fallacies Based on Careless Reasoning

Post hoc fallacies, formally known as *post hoc, ergo propter hoc* fallacies ("after this, therefore because of this"), argue that because one event happened before a second event, the first event must have caused the second event.

Slippery-slope arguments warn that a single step will inevitably lead to a bad situation. For instance, one of the most common arguments against decriminalizing marijuana is that it leads to the use of stronger narcotics.

Either/or arguments present two choices, one of which is usually characterized as extremely undesirable. In fact, there might be a third choice, or a fourth, or a fifth.

Non sequiturs are statements that do not follow logically from what has been said. For example, arguing that buying a particular type of car will lead to a successful love life is a non sequitur.

Circular reasoning, also known as *begging the question*, restates a point that has just been made as evidence for itself. Arguing that a decline in voter turnout is a result of fewer people voting is an example of circular reasoning.

As you build your argument, you might need to refine your thesis statement and perhaps even your main point. In fact, most writers refine their argument as they learn more about an issue and consider how best to contribute to a conversation. As you prepare to write a first draft, take another look at your main point, thesis statement, reasons, and evidence. Do they still make sense? Do they stack up well against competing arguments? Do they overlook anything obvious? Do you have enough evidence to meet the expectations of your intended readers? If you answer "no" to any of these questions, continue to develop and refine your argument.

13b

How can I organize my argument?

A well-organized document allows a reader to anticipate — or predict — what will come next. Choose an appropriate organizing pattern by reflecting on your writing situation, main point, thesis statement, reasons, evidence, counterarguments, and appeals. Then use labeling, grouping, clustering, and mapping to arrange your argument and formal and informal outlining strategies to organize your document.

Choose an Organizing Pattern WHAT'S MY PURPOSE?

Organizing patterns provide an overall principle for arranging your argument and your research writing project document. Common organizing patterns include the following.

Chronology The document's organization reflects the sequence in which events occur over time. For example, you might focus attention on a sequence of events in a recent election or during the course of a certain time span. If you are writing an academic essay or developing a multimedia presentation about a historical issue, you might find this organizing pattern useful.

Description The document provides a point-by-point description of the physical attributes of a subject. For example, you might focus on the typical architectural features of a suburb or use a spatial arrangement that mimics the movement of the human eye as it takes in an image (left to right, top to bottom, near to far, and so on). Description is best for documents that address physical spaces, objects, or people — things that we can see and observe — rather than theories or processes that are not visible.

Definition   The document lays out the distinguishing characteristics of a subject and then provides examples and reasoning to explain what differentiates it from similar subjects. For instance, an essay defining *pride* might begin by stating that it is an emotion and then move on to explain why that particular emotion is not as harmful as many people believe.

Cause/Effect   The document is organized according to factors that lead to (cause) an outcome (effect). For example, you might identify the reasons behind a recent strike by grocery store employees or the health risks that contribute to heart disease.

Process Explanation   The document outlines the steps involved in doing something or explains how something happens. You might, for example, help readers understand the stages of nuclear fission or teach them what steps to take in the event of a meltdown in a nearby power plant.

Pro/Con   Ideas and information are organized to show support for and opposition to an argument or a proposal. For example, a writer might organize an analysis of legislation calling for increased reliance on nuclear power by explaining why some groups support the legislation (pro) and others oppose it (con).

Multiple Perspectives   The document arranges information, ideas, and arguments according to a range of perspectives about a subject. Documents using this organizing pattern frequently provide an analysis supporting one perspective. For instance, a document addressing the use of tidal power as an alternative energy source might present the perspectives of utility company executives, environmentalists, oceanographers, legislators, and waterfront residents, ultimately favoring one group over the others.

Comparison/Contrast   The document identifies similarities and differences among the information, ideas, and arguments relevant to a subject. Documents that compare and contrast can be constructed in one of two ways. In the point-by-point approach, the writer presents each relevant point individually and then analyzes how that point operates in the two items being compared. In the whole-by-whole approach, the writer addresses the first item in its entirety, as a whole, and then moves on to the second item. For example, a document analyzing a policy initiative to decriminalize marijuana possession might compare current drug laws to alcohol prohibition or attempt to contrast medical and recreational uses of marijuana.

Strengths/Weaknesses   The document examines positive and negative aspects of a subject, such as increasing federal funding for health care by instituting a national lottery. Documents using this organizing pattern typically work toward a conclusion that one or two considerations outweigh the others.

Costs/Benefits   The tradeoffs associated with a subject, usually a choice or proposal of some sort, are considered in turn. For example, an evaluative essay might discuss why the expenses associated with implementing a particular educational initiative are justified (or not) by the potential for higher test scores.

Problem/Solution   Documents define a problem and discuss the appropriateness of one or more solutions. If multiple solutions are proposed, an argument is usually made for the superiority of one over the others. For instance, an informative article might explain the problem of "brain drain," in which highly educated and skilled workers move out of state, and then argue in support of a proposal to retain and attract more skilled workers.

Your choice of organizing pattern will reflect your purpose and the role or roles you adopt as a writer. If you're adopting the role of *reporter*, for example, you might select chronology, cause/effect, or comparison/contrast. If you're adopting the role of *evaluator* or *problem solver*, you're likely to choose from patterns such as strengths/weaknesses, pro/con, comparison/contrast, or multiple perspectives. If you're adopting the role of *advocate*, you might opt for an organizing pattern that is well suited to argumentation, such as pro/con or strengths/weaknesses.

Your choice of organizing pattern should also reflect the argument you are making in your document and the reasons, evidence, and appeals you use to make your argument. Keep in mind as well that a writer may use more than one organizing pattern in a document. For instance, a process explanation often works in tandem with chronology, since both present steps in a sequence. Similarly, a document presenting multiple perspectives might also adopt a strengths/weaknesses pattern to evaluate the merits of each perspective.

Review and Arrange Your Evidence

Once you have selected an organizing pattern, you can use strategies such as labeling, grouping, clustering, and mapping to determine how to arrange your argument. These strategies will also help you later as you develop an outline for your document.

Label Evidence   Labeling can help you understand at a glance how and where you will use evidence from your sources. For example, you might label notes or sources containing the evidence you want to use in your introduction with "Introduction," those that you plan to use to define a concept with the name of that concept, and so on. If you have taken digital notes or saved digital sources, as Brandon Tate did, you have a number of options (see Figure 13.3). Once you've labeled your notes and sources, you can organize them into groups or order them according to the outline you will create.

Group Evidence   Grouping involves categorizing the evidence you've obtained from your sources. Paper-based notes and copies of sources can be placed in related piles or file folders; sources and notes in word processing files or a smartphone can be saved in larger files or placed in folders; items in Bookmarks or Favorites lists can be sorted by category.

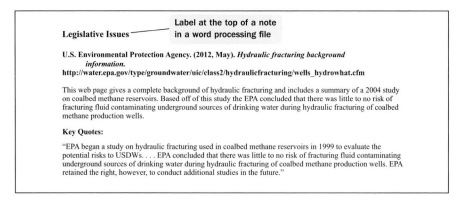

FIGURE 13.3 Labeling Digital Notes and Sources

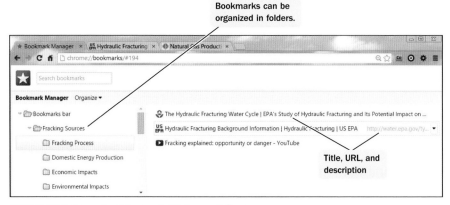

FIGURE 13.4 Grouping Electronic Notes and Sources

Use Clustering Clustering can be used to explore the relationships among your thesis statement, reasons, and evidence. Clustering involves arranging these elements of your argument visually on a sheet of paper or on a computer screen. By putting your thesis statement at the center of the cluster and your reasons and evidence around it, you can explore how reasons and evidence relate to your main point, and how your reasons relate to each other.

Clustering can be used at several points in a research writing project: as you begin to explore your topic, as you brainstorm to come up with ideas, as you explore relationships among the material you've collected, and now as you begin to arrange your argument.

Use Mapping You can use mapping to explore sequences of reasons and evidence. For example, you might use mapping to create a timeline or to show how an argument builds on one supporting point after another. This use of mapping

> ## My Research Project
> ### Arrange an Argument by Clustering
> Clustering can help you explore the relationships among your main point, thesis statement, reasons, and evidence. To create a cluster:
>
> 1. In the middle of a sheet of paper, or in the center of a digital document (word processing file or graphics file), write your main point or thesis statement.
> 2. Place your reasons around your main point or thesis statement.
> 3. List the evidence you'll present to support your reasons next to each reason.
> 4. Think about the relationships among your main point, reasons, and evidence, and draw lines and circles to show those relationships.
> 5. Annotate your cluster to indicate the nature of the relationships you've identified.

is particularly effective as you begin to think about organizing your project document, and it often relies on the organizing patterns discussed on pp. 215–17, such as chronology, cause/effect, comparison/contrast, cost/benefit, and problem/solution.

The tutorial on pp. 220–21 shows a map that Nicholas Brothers created to organize his thoughts regarding the argument in his research essay about U.S. reliance on private military corporations.

Create an Outline

An outline represents the sequence in which your reasons and evidence will appear in your document. As you develop an outline, you'll make decisions about the order in which you will present your reasons and the evidence you'll use to back them up. Later, as you draft, your outline can serve as a plan for creating your document.

Create an Informal Outline Informal outlines can take many forms: a brief list of words, a series of short phrases, or even a series of sentences. You can use informal outlines to remind yourself of key points to address in your document or of notes you should refer to when you begin drafting. Elizabeth Leontiev, who wrote a research essay about the impact of the U.S. war on drugs on South American coca farmers, created the informal outline shown in Figure 13.5. In her outline, each item represents a section she planned to include in her essay.

Nicholas Brothers wrote a "thumbnail outline," a type of informal outline, as he worked on his research essay about private military corporations. Nicholas identified the major sections he would include in his research essay and noted which sources he would use to provide background information and to support his argument (see Figure 13.6).

How can I map my argument?

You can map your argument by arranging your reasons and evidence to support your main point. In this example, Nicholas Brothers maps the reasons and evidence in his argumentative essay about U.S. reliance on private military corporations (PMCs) in its war on terror. Later, he will use this map as he develops his outline.

1 List your main point or thesis statement.

2 Review your notes to identify reasons that support your main point.

3 Based on the reasons you will use to help readers accept or act on your main point, choose an organizing pattern (pp. 215–17). Here, the writer chooses a cause/effect pattern to arrange his argument.

4 Use the organizing pattern to map your argument. Here, the writer maps the causes and effects of U.S. reliance on private military corporations.

5 List evidence near supporting points. Here, the writer includes references to sources in parentheses.

Thesis Statement: By relying heavily on PMCs to carry out military operations, the U.S. Department of Defense is undermining its own counterinsurgency efforts in Iraq and Afghanistan.

Carter administration begins privatization movement, using private contractors to provide U.S. government services. Movement gains strength through 1980s and 1990s (Euchner).

9/11 attacks give rise to U.S. War on Terror.

Rumsfeld Doctrine calls for highly mobile infantry supported by air strikes and private military contractors (Scahill).

U.S. invades Afghanistan and Iraq.

U.S. military is overextended (Chivers).

U.S. dramatically increases use of private military corporations in Iraq and Afghanistan (Singer, Schmitt).

Use of PMCs increases cost of War on Terror (Schwartz, CBO).

Higher salaries paid by PMCs leads to a "brain drain" of the U.S. military, in which highly qualified personnel leave the military to take jobs with PMCs (Pelton, quoted in Scahill).

Lack of accountability leads to PMC abuses and other problems (Capps, Scahill).

PMC abuses fuel insurgency movements (Schwartz).

Increased use of PMCs to fight insurgents.

IV Creating Your Document

1. *Introduction — what is coca? where is it grown?*

2. *Cultural and economic importance of coca crop*

3. *Evo Morales's plan: "zero cocaine, not zero coca"*
   - benefits of the Morales plan

4. *Brief history of other plans and their failures*
   - U.S. "war on drugs"
   - aerial fumigation / coca eradication
   - alternative cropping

5. *Conclusion supporting the Morales plan*

FIGURE 13.5 Elizabeth Leontiev's Informal Outline

Intro

Introduce private military corporations as integral to U.S. military operations. Present the many costs of PMCs to be examined.

Section 1

Explain the history of PMCs, from the Napoleonic era to today. Focus on the post-9/11 era and how privatization of the U.S. military has increased in the last ten years. Key sources: interview transcripts from Brothers and Euchner.

Section 2

Discuss the frequent use of PMCs in Iraq and Afghanistan, as well their diversified functions. Examine the distinction between PMCs and mercenaries. Key sources for background and argument: Scahill and Singer.

Section 3

Give examples of abuses and illegal acts by PMC contractors. Explain why contractors have not been convicted of crimes. Key sources for abuse evidence: Capps, Simpson, and Savage; key sources for lack of legal accountability: Singer, Yeoman, and Risen.

Section 4

Present the view that abuses by contractors undermine the image and goals of the U.S. military. Key sources: the Army Field Manual and the Congressional Research Service report.

Section 5

Discuss other "costs" of PMCs, in particular the amount of taxpayer money spent on them and the brain drain that occurs. Key sources: Stanger, Moshe, and Pelton.

Conclusion

Look at ways Americans can take civic action to end the overreliance on PMCs.

FIGURE 13.6 Nicholas Brothers's Thumbnail Outline

Create a Formal Outline A formal outline provides a complete and accurate list of the points you want to address in your document. Formal outlines use arabic numerals, letters, and roman numerals to indicate the hierarchy of information. An alternative approach, common in business and the sciences, uses numbering with decimal points:

```
I.
    A.
        1.
        2.
    B.
        1.
        2.
    II.
```

```
1.
    1.1
        1.1.1
        1.1.2
    1.2
        1.2.1
        1.2.2
    2.
```

Writers use formal outlines to identify the hierarchy of information, ideas, and arguments. You can create a formal outline to identify:

- your main point and/or thesis statement
- your reasons
- the sequence in which those reasons should be presented
- evidence for your reasons
- the notes and sources you should refer to as you work on your document

The most common types of formal outlines are topical outlines and sentence outlines.

Topical outlines present the topics and subtopics you plan to include in your research document as a series of words and phrases. Items at the same level of importance should be phrased in parallel grammatical form.

In her topical outline for her research essay on steroid use among adolescent girls, Alexis Alvarez includes her thesis statement, suggests the key points she wants to make in her document, maps out the support for her points, and uses a conventional system of numbers and letters (see Figure 13.7).

Sentence outlines use complete sentences to identify the points you want to cover (see Figure 13.8). Sentence outlines typically serve two purposes.

1. They begin the process of converting an outline into a draft of your document.
2. They help you assess the structure of a document that you have already written.

When you've created your outline, ask whether it can serve as a blueprint for the first draft of your document. Taking the time to create an effective outline now will reduce the time needed to write your first draft later.

IV Creating Your Document

Thesis statement: Although competitive sports can provide young female athletes with many benefits, they can also have negative effects, the worst of which is increasing drug use.

I. **Female Participation in Competitive Athletics**
   A. Short history and current trends
   B. Understanding the female athlete
II. **Positive Impact of Competitive Athletics**
   A. Physiological (Kane & Larkin)
      1. Reduced risk of obesity and heart disease
      2. Increased immune functioning and prevention of certain cancers
      3. Improved flexibility, strength, and aerobic power
   B. Psychological (Kane & Larkin)
      1. Improved self-esteem
      2. Enhanced mental health
      3. Effective in reducing symptoms of stress, anxiety, and depression
   C. Sociological
      1. Expansion of social boundaries
      2. Teaches responsibility, discipline, and determination
      3. Educational asset
III. **Negative Impact of Competitive Athletics**
   A. Physiological (Graham)
      1. Overtraining
      2. Eating disorders
      3. Exercise-induced amenorrhea and osteoporosis

FIGURE 13.7 Part of Alexis Alvarez's Topical Outline

Thesis statement: Although competitive sports can provide young female athletes with many benefits, they can also have negative effects, the worst of which is increasing drug use.

I. Society has been concerned with the use of performance-enhancing drugs among younger male athletes, but many don't know that these drugs are also used by younger female athletes.
   A. Women began participating in sports in the mid-19th century, although participation was not encouraged until recently. Millions of girls are involved in a wide range of physical activities and are participating in school-sponsored sports.
   B. In response to pressures of competitive sports, girls' steroid use has increased and younger and younger girls are taking steroids.
II. Sports can benefit a girl's growth and development physiologically as well as psychologically and sociologically.
   A. Participation in sports has a wide range of positive physiological effects on adolescent girls.
      1. Studies have shown that participation in sports can reduce the risk of obesity and heart disease.
      2. Studies have shown that participation in sports appears to increase immune functioning and prevent certain cancers.
      3. Participation in sports has also been linked to improved flexibility, strength, and aerobic power.

FIGURE 13.8 Part of Alexis Alvarez's Sentence Outline

My Research Project

Create and Review Your Outline

In your word processing program or in your research log, create an outline. If your word processing program has an outlining tool, use it to create a formal outline. In Microsoft Word, use Outline View (available in older versions of Word through the View Outline menu command) to view your document in outline mode. Use the Promote and Demote buttons on the outlining toolbar to set the levels for entries in your outline. Use the Collapse and Expand buttons to hide and show parts of your outline.

Review your outline by asking yourself the following questions.

1. Does my outline provide an effective organization for my document?

2. Have I covered all of my key points?

3. Have I addressed my key points in sufficient detail?

4. Do any sections seem out of order?

QUICK REFERENCE

Developing and Organizing Your Argument

 Identify reasons to accept your thesis statement. (p. 205)

✔ Select evidence to support your reasoning. (p. 207)

✔ Decide how to appeal to your readers. (p. 208)

✔ Consider and address opposing arguments. (p. 211)

✔ Check for logical fallacies. (p. 212)

✔ Choose an organizing pattern for your argument. (p. 215)

✔ Arrange your evidence. (p. 217)

✔ Create an outline. (p. 219)

IV Creating Your Document

14

Drafting

 Key Questions

If you're new to research writing, you might be surprised at how long it's taken to get to the chapter about writing your document. If you are an experienced research writer, you know that you've been writing it all along. Research writing isn't so much the act of putting words to paper or on-screen as it is the process of identifying and learning about an issue, reflecting on what you've learned, and contributing to the conversation about your issue.

14a

How can I help my readers follow my argument?

After all the work you've done learning about your issue and formulating your ideas about what you want to share with your readers, you still need to write an effective document—one that your readers will find easy to read and understand. To help your readers follow your argument, work from an outline, write effective paragraphs, use transitions and cues to move your readers through your document, and integrate information from sources effectively.

Work from an Outline

Your outline provides a framework you can use to draft your document. Your outline likely includes your plans for:

- the points you will include in your document
- the order in which you will make your points
- the evidence you will use to support each point

As you review your outline, check whether you have organized your points in a way that will allow you to achieve your purpose and whether you are addressing the needs, interests, values, and beliefs of your readers.

If you have listed information about the sources you will use to support your points, you can check whether you are:

- providing enough evidence to support your points
- relying too heavily on a limited number of sources
- relying too heavily on support from sources that favor one side of the conversation

If you created an informal outline, you can begin to flesh it out by translating key points in your outline into sentences or paragraphs. If you created a formal outline, you can turn major headings in the outline into headings or subheadings in your draft and then use the points under each heading as the basis for topic sentences for your paragraphs. If your outline is highly detailed, you can use minor points as the basis for supporting sentences within each paragraph.

Make sure that you use your notes and review the paraphrases, summaries, and quotations you wrote down. Take advantage of the time you spent thinking about which sources are most appropriate for a particular section of your document.

As you work on your draft, you might find it necessary to reorganize your ideas. Think of your outline as a flexible guide rather than a rigid blueprint.

TUTORIAL

How do I use an outline to draft my document?

Use your outline as the "skeleton" of the first draft of your document. In this example, Alexis Alvarez expands her outline into a rough draft.

1 Save your outline with a new name, such as Draft1.doc.

2 Turn major headings in your outline into headings and subheadings in your draft.

3 Convert lower-level entries into topic sentences for paragraphs.

4 Use lists of items as sentences in each paragraph.

5 Locate evidence to support your points. Quote, paraphrase, and summarize sources identified in your outline.

1. Benefits of Sports for Girls
  a. Physical Health Benefits
      i. Reduces risks of adult-onset coronary disease and some cancers (Kane & Larkin, 1997)
      ii. Enhances immune system, posture, strength, flexibility, and heart-lung endurance (Kane & Larkin, 1997; "Sports in America," 1994)
  b. Mental Health Benefits (Kane & Larkin, 1997; Orozco interview)
      i. Positive body image
      ii. Confidence and self-esteem
      iii. Sense of control
  c. Social Benefits (Orozco and Alvarez interviews)
2. Problems Caused by Sports for Girls
  a. Physical side effects

Girls and Sports: The Upside

According to Kane and Larkin (1997), adolescent girls who exercise regularly can lessen their risks for adult-onset coronary disease and certain cancers. Girls' involvement in sports and exercise also tends to improve immune functioning, posture, strength, flexibility, and heart-lung endurance (Kane & Larkin, 1997; "Sports in America," 1994).

In addition, competitive athletics can enhance mental health by offering adolescent girls positive feelings about body image; tangible experiences of competency, control, and success; improved self-esteem and self-confidence; and a way to reduce anxiety (Kane & Larkin, 1997). Juan Orozco, who has coached competitive soccer for nine years at the adolescent female level, confirmed that making a competitive sports team is a privilege that many girls work toward with determination and longing and that being picked to participate encourages these young athletes to believe in themselves and their abilities (personal interview, Sept. 22, 2004).

A final benefit is that sports expand social boundaries and teach many of the personal and social skills girls will need throughout their lives. According to Orozco, through competitive athletics girls learn a crucial lesson in how to

Create Paragraphs That Focus on a Central Idea

Writers use paragraphs to present and develop a central idea. Depending on the complexity of your argument and the type of document you are writing, a single paragraph might be all you need to present your reasoning and evidence—or it might play only a small role in conveying your thinking about an issue. You can create effective paragraphs by ensuring that they are focused, organized, and well developed. You can help readers follow your argument by using transitions that clearly convey the relationships among paragraphs.

Paragraphs often have a topic sentence in which the writer makes an assertion, offers an observation, or asks a question. The rest of the sentences in the paragraph elaborate on the topic. Consider the following paragraph, drawn from Nicholas Brothers's research essay.

> Given the potential costs in justice and national security, why hire contractors at all? Ironically, perhaps the most often-cited reason for using private contractors is that using these corporations saves the taxpayer money since the government can hire them on an as-need basis and does not have to pay for contractors' training, health care, or pensions. Professor Allison Stanger of Middlebury College challenges this notion in her 2009 book *One Nation Under Contract: The Outsourcing of American Power and the Future of Foreign Policy* when she points out that nearly all private contractors previously served in the military, meaning that many of them are receiving pension payments anyway. Stanger writes that "the federal government is effectively paying for the training and retirement of the contractors it hires, all appearances to the contrary, as well as paying double or triple the daily rate for their services." Therefore the Department of Defense would actually save taxpayers money by reversing the trend of privatization.

The central idea of the paragraph follows an initial question.

The third and fourth sentences use evidence from a source to show the real cost of hiring contractors.

The final sentence draws a conclusion that supports the essay's thesis statement.

Create Paragraphs That Use Appropriate Organizing Patterns

Effective paragraphs follow an organizing pattern, often the same one that the document as a whole follows, such as chronology, description, or costs/benefits (pp. 215–17). These common patterns help readers anticipate what you'll say. Readers who recognize a pattern, such as problem/solution, will find it easier to focus on your ideas and argument if they understand how you are organizing your paragraph. Note how the following paragraph, drawn from featured writer Alexis Alvarez's essay, uses the problem/solution organizing pattern.

> What can we do to help adolescent female athletes avoid illicit drug use? How can we help them avoid the pitfalls of competitive athletics? Parents, coaches, and the athletes themselves all play a crucial role in averting bad choices. First, parents and coaches need to be aware that performance-enhancing drugs are a problem. Some adults believe that steroid use is either

The paragraph begins by restating the problem.

The central idea of the paragraph is provided in the third sentence.

One part of the solution to the larger problem is provided in the fourth sentence.

minimal or nonexistent among teenagers, but one study concluded that "over half the teens who use steroids start before age 16, sometimes with the encouragement of their parents. . . . Seven percent said they first took 'juice' by age ten" (Dudley, 1994, p. 235).

> **The fifth sentence provides evidence from a source to illustrate the nature of the problem.**

Create Transitions within and between Paragraphs

Transitions help readers understand the relationships among sentences, paragraphs, and even sections of a document. Essentially, they smooth the way for readers, helping them understand how information, ideas, and arguments are related to one another. Transitions are most effective when they don't call attention to themselves, but instead move the reader's eye along to the next sentence, paragraph, or section. Consider the following examples of the steps involved in preparing fish.

No Transitions
Catch the fish. Clean the fish. Fillet the fish. Cook the fish. Eat the fish. Catch another fish.

Inconsistent Transitions
First, catch the fish. Secondly, clean the fish. When you've done that, fillet the fish. Next, cook the fish. Fifth, eat the fish. After all is said and done, catch another fish.

Consistent Transitions
First, catch the fish. Second, clean the fish. Third, fillet the fish. Fourth, cook the fish. Fifth, eat the fish. Finally, catch another fish.

Transitions frequently appear as words and phrases, such as those used in the previous example. They can also take the form of sentences and paragraphs. Transitional sentences, such as the following, often appear at the end or beginning of paragraphs and serve to link two paragraphs.

> . . . a series of tests. The results of the tests revealed a surprising trend.

> Incredibly, the outcome was far better than we could have hoped. After reviewing . . .

Transitional paragraphs, such as the following example, call attention to a major shift in focus within a document.

> In the next section, we explore the reasons behind this surprising development. We focus first on the event itself. Then we consider the reasons underlying the event. Our goal is to call attention to the unique set of relationships that made this development possible.

As you create transitions, pay attention to the order in which you introduce new information and ideas in your paragraphs. In general, it is best to begin a sentence with a reference to information and ideas that have already been introduced and then to introduce new information and ideas at the end of a sentence.

Common transitions and their functions are presented below.

To Help Readers Follow a Sequence	To Compare	To Signal a Concession
furthermore	similarly	I admit that
in addition	in the same manner	of course
moreover	like	granted
next	as in	it is true that
first/second/third	**To Elaborate or Provide Examples**	**To Introduce a Conclusion**
To Contrast	for example	as a result
however	for instance	as a consequence
on the other hand	such as	because of
nevertheless	in fact	therefore
nonetheless	indeed	thus
despite	to illustrate	for this reason
although/though		

Provide Cues to Keep Your Readers on Track

A document that is well organized and well designed allows a reader to antici-pate—or predict—what will come next, which helps readers understand your goals more easily and stay within the frame you've provided. The test is whether your readers can move smoothly through your document without wondering, "Where did that come from?" As you draft, check whether your document is organized and designed consistently and predictably. You might find the follow-ing techniques useful.

Provide Forecasts and Cross-References   A forecast is a type of transitional sentence that prepares your readers for a shift in your document, such as the boundary between one section and the next. Cross-references tell your readers that they can find related information in another section of the document or let them know that a particular issue will be addressed in greater detail elsewhere. On a website, forecasts and cross-references might take the form of small images, flags, or statements such as "Continue to next section" or "Follow this link for more information."

Use Headings and Subheadings   You can help your readers keep their place in your document by using headings and subheadings. Your formatting should dis-tinguish between headings (major sections) and subheadings (subsections).

Use a Menu   If you are writing a digital document such as a website, or a multi-modal essay, you can add a menu on the side, top, or bottom of your pages that readers can see as they work through your site. Brandon Tate provided a menu on every page of his site (see Figure 14.1).

Pay Attention to Design Principles As you draft your document, pay attention to the principles of effective design. Using a readable body font that is clearly different from the font used for headings and subheadings, for example, can improve readability significantly. Similarly, breaking out information using bulleted and numbered lists, providing descriptive page headers or footers, and integrating illustrations effectively into your text can greatly enhance readability. If you are drafting a digital document, keep in mind the uses of digital illustrations. You can read more about design in Chapters 16 and 18.

Integrate Information from Sources Effectively

Information from sources can be used to introduce an important concept, establish the strength of a writer's argument, and elaborate on the central ideas in your document. Writers frequently state a point, offer a reason to accept it, and support their reasoning with evidence from a source, typically in the form of quotations, paraphrases, and summaries. You can read more about integrating information from sources in Chapter 15.

Learn More
The Pros
Environmental Benefits
Economic Benefits
The Cons
Impact on Water
Impact on Air Quality
The Conclusion

About This Site
Bibliography
Author

FIGURE 14.1 Menu on Brandon Tate's Website *The menu helps readers understand the organization of the site and move to pages within it.*

14b

How can I write with style and engage my readers?

As you draft your document, consider how you'll keep your readers' attention — and be aware of how the construction of your sentences and paragraphs can affect their willingness to keep reading.

Use Details to Capture Your Readers' Attention

An effective paragraph does more than simply convey information — it provides details that bring an issue to life. Consider the differences between the following paragraphs.

Example 1: Minimal Details
Hydraulic fracturing has become a growing controversy in the United States of America. This is because many people believe that the environmental harms of this oil and gas drilling technique outweigh its benefits. Others, in contrast, argue that it has helped sustain our use of natural gas and petroleum.

Example 2: Extensive, Concrete Details

Hydraulic fracturing, also known as fracking, has become a growing controversy in the United States of America. This is because many people believe that its environmental harms outweigh any possible benefits it may offer. According to the U.S. Environmental Protection Agency [EPA] (2012), fracking is used to "maximize the extraction of underground resources." The horizontal drilling technique involves pumping water, chemicals, and specialized sand into shale formations deep down inside the earth at intense pressure (EPA, 2012). This creates fractures in the formations, allowing the bounded resources such as natural gas and petroleum to be released. Combined, these two fossil fuels generate roughly 75% of all energy consumed in the United States (U.S. Energy Information Administration [EIA], 2017).

Both examples, drawn from Brandon Tate's website on hydraulic fracturing, convey the same main point. The first example, however, does little more than state the facts. The second example provides details from sources published by the U.S. Environmental Protection Agency and the U.S. Energy Information Administration. The details drawn from these sources allow readers to gain a more complete, and more concrete, understanding of the issue.

Write Clearly and Concisely

Readers don't want to work any harder than necessary to follow the information, ideas, and arguments in a document. To keep your readers from setting your document aside, write clearly and concisely. Consider, for example, the following passages.

> Please join me, Mr. Watson. I have concluded that I am in a situation in which I require your assistance.

> Come here, Mr. Watson. I need you.

> Help!

The second passage, reputed to be the first words ever spoken on a telephone, was spoken by Alexander Graham Bell after he'd spilled acid on his pants. Had he spoken the first passage instead, he might have wasted crucial time while he waited a few extra seconds for his assistant to figure out what he was being asked to do. The simple exclamation of "Help!" might have been even more effective and would certainly have taken less time to utter. Then again, it might have been too vague for his assistant to figure out just how he needed to act and what sort of help was required.

In general, if two sentences provide the same information, the briefer sentence is usually easier to understand. In some cases, however, writing too little will leave your readers wondering what you are trying to get across.

The following techniques can help you write clearly and concisely.

- **Avoid unnecessary modifiers.** Unnecessary modifiers are words that provide little or no additional information to a reader, such as *fine, many, great, somewhat, quite, sort of, lots, really,* and *very.*

Example Sentence with Unnecessary Modifiers

The Volvo S90 serves as a <u>really</u> excellent example of a <u>very fine</u> performance sedan.

Revised Example

The Volvo S90 serves as an <u>excellent</u> example of a performance sedan.

- **Avoid unnecessary introductory phrases.** Avoid phrases such as *there are, there is, these have, these are, here are, here is, it has been reported that, it has been said that, it is evident that, it is obvious that,* and so on. Sentences beginning with *It goes without saying,* for example, allow you to emphasize a point, but you can often recast such sentences more concisely by simply stating the point.

  ### Example Sentence with Unnecessary Introductory Phrase

  <u>It goes without saying</u> that drinking water should be clean.

  ### Revised Example

  Drinking water should be clean.

- **Avoid stock phrases.** As you draft, express yourself clearly by avoiding the use of stock phrases, such as the following.

Stock Phrase	Alternative
as a matter of fact	in fact
at all times	always
at that point in time	then
at this point in time	now, currently
because of the fact that	because
by means of	by
due to the fact that	because
in order to	to
in spite of the fact that	although, though
in the event that	if

Write Actively (Most of the Time)

One of the easiest things you can do to engage your readers is to write in the *active voice*. A sentence written in active voice specifies an actor—a person or thing—who carries out an action.

Active Voice

Juan took an exam.

The tornado leveled the town.

Kevin Love scored the game-winning basket with .2 seconds remaining in overtime.

In contrast, a sentence written in *passive voice* indicates that something was done, but it does not necessarily specify who or what did it.

Passive Voice

The exam was taken by Juan.

The town was leveled.

The game-winning basket was scored with .2 seconds remaining in overtime.

In general, you'll want to emphasize the actor, because sentences written in active voice are easier to understand and provide more information — not only *what* was done, but also *who* did it. Passive voice, however, can be effective when active voice would require the inclusion of unnecessary information. For example, many scientific experiments are conducted by large teams of researchers. Few readers would want to know which members of the team carried out every task discussed in an article about the experiment. Rather than using active voice (for example, "Heather Landers, assisted by Sandy Chapman and Shaun Beaty, anesthetized the mice, and then Dave Johnson and Justin Switzer examined their eyes for lesions"), you can use passive voice ("The mice were anesthetized, and their eyes were examined for lesions"). In this case, the sentence written in passive voice is clearer, easier to understand, and free of unnecessary information.

Passive voice is also useful if you wish to emphasize the recipient of the action, rather than the person or thing carrying out the action. Police reports, for example, often use passive voice ("The suspect was apprehended at the corner of Oak and Main Streets").

Adopt a Consistent Point of View

Writers typically adopt a particular point of view as they write:

- first person: *I, we*
- second person: *you*
- third person: *she, he, it, one, they*, or nouns that describe a particular group or an individual, such as *doctors, teachers, engineer, lawyer, Mr. Smith*, or *Lee Chen*

When writers shift their point of view within a sentence, readers notice — and sometimes have to stop and ask themselves what just happened. Consider the following example.

Shift in Point of View

After the climbers reached the summit in record time, we burst into song.

The sentence begins with a third-person point of view (*the climbers*) and then shifts to first person (*we*). The sentence would be easier to understand if it were written in either first or third person.

Consistent Point of View

After the climbers reached the summit in record time, they burst into song.

After we reached the summit in record time, we burst into song.

To keep your readers engaged—or, more accurately, to avoid disrupting the smooth reading of your document—ensure that you adopt a consistent point of view.

Vary Your Sentence Structure

Understanding the types of sentences that you can write and the types of sentence structures you can use can help you create a document that will maintain your readers' interest. You can begin to accomplish this by understanding the four basic types of sentences.

Statements:	Dick runs quickly.
Questions:	How quickly did Dick run?
Commands:	Run, Dick, run.
Exclamations:	Way to go, Dick!

You can continue by understanding the four basic sentence structures, which are distinguished by the types and numbers of *clauses* they contain. A clause—a sequence of words containing a subject and a verb—can be either *independent* or *dependent*. (Sometimes these types of clauses are referred to as *main* and *subordinate*, respectively.) The primary difference between these types of clauses is that independent clauses can function on their own as a complete sentence, while dependent clauses cannot.

Simple (a single independent clause)
Jane runs quickly.

■ Independent clause
■ Dependent clause

Compound (two or more independent clauses)
Jane runs quickly, but she doesn't run as quickly as Dick.

Complex (an independent clause and a dependent clause)
Although Jane runs quickly, Dick is quicker.

Compound-Complex (two or more independent clauses and at least one dependent clause)
All things considered, the Dick and Jane readers were wildly successful, but they have faded into the comfortable oblivion of history.

Mixing sentence types and structures will help you produce an appealing rhythm in your writing. If you neglect to vary your sentences, on the other hand, your readers are likely to find your document monotonous and boring. To keep your readers' interest, vary your sentence type, structure, and length. Consider the following examples.

Similar Sentence Structure and Length

We decided to spend the morning at El Rastro. El Rastro is a Sunday morning flea market extraordinaire. We decided to take the subway to get there. A man stood quite close as we got on. I found this strange in an uncrowded subway station. Then I felt his hand in my left pocket. I also felt his hand on my back. It's a good thing that I'm ticklish. I instinctively shrugged away from his hands. Then I swore loudly and imaginatively at him. (It's inappropriate to swear on a Sunday in Spain. I wouldn't have done it under normal circumstances.) He had almost gotten away with my sunglasses. This would almost certainly have disappointed him. I know it would have inconvenienced me.

Each sentence uses the same sentence type (statements) and the same simple sentence structure. Sentence length ranges from seven to nine words.

Varied Sentence Structure and Length

We decided to spend the morning at El Rastro, a Sunday morning flea market extraordinaire. As we got on the subway to get to El Rastro, I noticed that a man was standing quite close to me—strange, since the subway wasn't crowded. Then I felt his hand in my left pocket and his hand on my back. (Fortunately, I'm ticklish.) "What the heck?" I thought, instinctively shrugging away and swearing at him (an inappropriate thing to do on a Sunday morning in Spain, but I was caught off guard). He had almost gotten away with my sunglasses, which would have disappointed him and inconvenienced me.

Sentence types include statements and questions. Sentence structures include simple, compound, and complex. Sentence length ranges from three to twenty-eight words.

Choose Your Words Carefully WHAT'S MY PURPOSE?

The reading process can be disrupted—and sometimes stopped altogether—by shifts in formality or the introduction of surprising or hard-to-understand words. As you draft your document, pay attention to level of formality and the extent to which specialized terms are used in the conversation about your issue. Pay attention as well to the variety and specificity of your words.

Formality Your reading of other documents that contribute to the conversation about your issue will give you insights into the level of formality you should strive for when you draft your document. Some written conversations, such as those conducted on blogs and Web discussion forums, are relatively informal and can even show evidence of lack of respect for the opinions of other participants in the discussion. Others, such as those conducted through scholarly journals in the sciences or the arts and humanities or through magazines such as the *Nation* or the *Atlantic Magazine,* adopt a formal, restrained tone. Still others, such as those conducted through many popular media outlets, are casual but respectful. As you read about your issue, note the level of formality and the manner in which writers refer to ideas and arguments in other sources.

Informal Writing

It was awesome to see how well the U.S. soccer team did in the last World Cup.

IV Creating Your Document

Formal Writing
The performance of the U.S. soccer team in the most recent World Cup was gratifying.

Specialized Language Specialized language, sometimes called *jargon*, can allow writers and readers to communicate effectively and efficiently—but only if both parties are familiar with the terms. If you are contributing to a conversation in which specialized language is used heavily, familiarize yourself with the terms your readers will expect you to use. For example, if you plan to write an article for a website that focuses on motorcycle touring, you can write more concisely and with greater accuracy if you use the proper terminology.

Ineffective Use of General Language
Braking that involves a mechanism that coordinates proportionally the amount of pressure applied to your front and rear brakes during turns that get progressively tighter can be hazardous if you fail to initiate the turn properly.

Effective Use of Specialized Language
Linked braking during decreasing-radius turns can be hazardous if you fail to initiate the turn properly.

In contrast, readers who are unfamiliar with specialized language will find it more difficult to understand your point. Most people in the United States, for example, have at least a passing familiarity with basketball, but many would find it difficult to understand the following statement.

Ineffective Use of Specialized Language for a General Audience
Box-and-one defenses are largely ineffective against well-executed pick-and-roll plays that result not in shots, but in skip passes, particularly if the pick-and-rolls are initiated on the baseline.

Variety Variety is not only the spice of life—it's also the key ingredient in an effective, engaging document. Even a well-conceptualized and thoroughly supported argument can fail to impress if it's presented in dull, monotonous language. Consider the differences between the following examples.

Lack of Varied Word Choice
The U.S. space program has benefited the United States in more ways than most U.S. government programs, largely because of the important technologies that have found their way into the U.S. economy.

Varied Word Choice
NASA has benefited the nation in more ways than most federal programs, largely because of the important technologies that have found their way into the U.S. economy.

Avoid Sexist Language

It is still technically correct to use male pronouns, such as *he*, *him*, and *his*, when the gender of a noun, such as *doctor* or *nurse*, is unspecified. Most readers, however, object to this assumption—or they are at least sensitive to it. Readers are even more likely to object if you make the mistake of referring to representatives of particular professions using gender-specific pronouns.

> When describing your symptoms to a doctor, be sure to tell him everything that's relevant. Similarly, when a nurse is taking your blood pressure, feel free to let her know how you feel.

By implying that all doctors are male and all nurses are female, the writer of this passage plays into common stereotypes. The result is that many readers will form a negative opinion of the writer.

To avoid sexist language, recast your sentences so that generic references, such as *a doctor*, are plural (*doctors*), as in the following example.

Sexist Language
A doctor who pursues an advanced specialization might need to spend as many as fifteen years of study before he can go into practice on his own.

Nonsexist Language
Doctors who pursue advanced specializations might need to spend as many as fifteen years of study before they can go into practice on their own.

Consult a Good Handbook

The strategies discussed in this chapter provide a good starting point for improving your style. Your decisions about style, however, are likely to touch on a far wider range of concerns than are addressed here. As you work to improve your writing, consult a good handbook. There you'll find detailed discussions and numerous examples of strategies you can use to polish your style.

14c

How can I use my introduction to frame my issue? [FRAMING MY ARGUMENT]

All readers expect documents to include some sort of introduction. Whether they are reading a home page on a website or an opening paragraph in a research report, readers want to learn quickly what a document is about.

As you begin to draft, consider strategies you might use to frame and introduce your main point. Many writers find that crafting an effective introduction is the most challenging part of drafting. If you run into difficulties, put your introduction aside and come back to it after you've made more progress on the rest of the document. There's no law that says you have to write the introduction first.

Call Attention to an Aspect of the Issue

Your introduction provides a framework within which your readers can understand and interpret your contribution to the conversation about your issue. By calling attention to a specific situation, by asking a particular question, or by

IV Creating Your Document

conveying a carefully chosen set of details, you can help your readers view the issue in a particular way. Consider, for example, the differences between two introductions to an essay about how buying habits changed among younger Americans following the Great Recession.

Introduction 1

In the face of an economic downturn, frugality was undergoing a revival in America. Young people were cutting up their credit cards, clipping coupons, and sticking to detailed budgets. In effect, they were adopting the very habits they mocked during the heady days of easy credit and weekend shopping sprees. Secondhand stores and thrift stores like Goodwill and the Salvation Army were drawing record numbers of customers, while once-stable retail giants such as Circuit City and the Sharper Image had gone out of business (*Wall Street Journal*). In fact, retail sales during the Christmas season were down 2.8% in 2008, the lowest since 1995 (CNN Money). The causes of this sea change in the spending habits of young Americans were complex and varied: high rates of unemployment, fewer jobs for recent college graduates, difficulty securing credit, and that elusive factor economists call "consumer confidence."

Introduction 2

The new frugal spending habits of American consumers between the ages of 18 and 34 were endangering the very individuals who were trying to save money. Plagued with rising unemployment, widespread hiring freezes, and difficulty securing credit, young Americans naturally turned to their spending habits as one area they could control. They cut down on how much money they spent in restaurants, bars, retail stores, and entertainment venues. As a result, usually robust Christmas sales were down an alarming 2.8% in 2008, the lowest since 1995 (CNN Money). Even once-stable retail giants such as Circuit City and the Sharper Image went out of business (*Wall Street Journal*). While the desire to hold on to their money is logical, all this coupon clipping, budgeting, and thrift-store shopping threatened the key to economic recovery, what economists call "consumer confidence." It was clear that if younger Americans hadn't loosened their grip on their wallets and injected some much-needed cash into the system, we would have faced far more dire economic consequences in the following years.

The first introduction frames the subject as an explanation of why younger Americans changed their buying habits. The second introduction frames the subject as a warning that those changing habits might have caused more harm than good. While both introductions draw on the same basic information about historic rates of spending, and while both will do a good job of introducing the essay, they point readers' attention to different aspects of the subject.

You can frame your discussion by calling attention to specific aspects of a topic, including:

- ■ The agent: a person, an organization, or a thing that is acting in a particular way
- ■ The action: what is being done by the actor
- ■ The goal: why the actor carried out the action
- ❑ The result: the outcome of the action

Introduction 2

The new frugal spending habits of American consumers between the ages of 18 and 34 were endangering the very individuals who were trying to save money. Plagued with rising unemployment, widespread hiring freezes, and difficulty securing credit, young Americans naturally turned to their spending habits as one area they could control. They cut down on how much money they spent in restaurants, bars, retail stores, and entertainment venues. As a result, usually robust Christmas sales were down an alarming 2.8% in 2008, the lowest since 1995 (CNNMoney. com). Even once-stable retail giants such as Circuit City and the Sharper Image went out of business (*Wall Street Journal*). While the desire to hold on to their money is logical, all this coupon clipping, budgeting, and thrift-store shopping threatened the key to economic recovery, what economists call "consumer confidence." It was clear that if younger Americans hadn't loosened their grip on their wallets and injected some much-needed cash into the system, we would have faced far more dire economic consequences in the following years.

Choose an Appropriate Strategy for Your Introduction

Your introduction offers the best opportunity to grab your readers' attention and shape their response to your ideas. You can frame your readers' understanding of your issue by choosing one of several introductory strategies.

State the Topic   Tell your readers what your issue is, what conversation you are focusing on, and what your document will tell them about it, as in the following introduction.

> Artists and their artwork do not exist in a vacuum. The images artists create help shape and in turn are shaped by the society and culture in which they are created. The artists and artworks in the Dutch Baroque period are no exception.

Establish the Context   In some cases, you'll want to give your readers background information about your subject or an overview of the conversation that has been taking place about it. Notice, for example, how Mark Hemingway sets up his article in *National Review Online* in response to media coverage of private military contractors.

> In the reams of media coverage surrounding the Blackwater incident last week one curious detail remains virtually unreported. The general theme of the coverage remains that private military contractors are somehow "above the law," but almost no media sources have referred to the fact that, as of last fall, contractors are subject to the same Uniform Code of Military Justice that governs U.S. soldiers.

State Your Thesis   If your research document presents an argument, evaluation, solution, or interpretation, use your introduction to get right to your main point. In other words, lead with a thesis statement, as in the following introduction.

> While the private tragedies of its central characters have public implications, William Shakespeare's *Julius Caesar* is more about personal struggles than political ambition. It is easy to see the play as one whose focus is the political action

of public events. The title character, after all, is at the height of political power. However, the interior lives of Julius Caesar, Marcus Brutus, and their wives offer a more engaging storyline. Shakespeare alternates between public and private scenes throughout the play to emphasize the conflict between duties of the Roman citizenry and the feelings and needs of the individual, but it is the "private mind and heart of the individual" that the reader is compelled to examine (Edwards 105).

Define a Problem   If your research has led you to propose a solution to a problem, you might begin your document by defining the problem. Alexis Alvarez used this strategy to introduce her essay.

> Almost daily, headlines and newscasters tell us about athletes' use of performance-enhancing drugs. Indeed, stories of such drug use seem to increase each year, with investigations of possible steroid use by college football players, by major league baseball players, and even by Olympic gold medalists. It is easy to gain the impression that many adult athletes, particularly males, may be using drugs in order to improve their performance and physical appearance. What may be surprising and even shocking to most of us, however, is that these drugs, especially anabolic steroids, are increasingly used by adolescent athletes and that girls are just as likely as boys to be users.

Read Alexis Alvarez's research essay on p. 375.

Make a Surprising Statement   Grab your readers' attention by telling them something they don't already know. It's even better if the information is shocking, unusual, or strange.

> What is the most common cause of hunger in the world? Is it drought? Locusts? Crop diseases? Nope. Most hunger in the world has absolutely nothing to do with food shortages. Most people who go to bed hungry, both in rich and in poor countries, do so in places where markets are filled with food that they cannot have.

Ask a Question   Asking a question invites your readers to become participants in the conversation. At the end of her introduction, Alexis Alvarez encouraged her readers to take an interest in the problem of steroid use by adolescent female athletes by asking a question.

> What role is competitive sports playing in this dangerous trend? Why are some girls feeling the need to ingest performance-enhancing drugs?

Tell a Story   Everyone loves a story, assuming it's told well and has a point. This writer began her newspaper article about the benefit of writing by hand with a story of a young boy who struggles to master the skill.

> Ask preschooler Zane Pike to write his name or the alphabet, then watch this 4-year-old's stubborn side kick in. He spurns practice at school and tosses aside workbooks at home. But Angie Pike, Zane's mom, persists, believing that handwriting is a building block to learning. She's right. Using advanced tools such as magnetic resonance imaging, researchers are finding that writing by hand is more than just a way to communicate. The practice helps with learning letters and shapes, can improve idea composition and expression, and may aid fine motor-skill development.

Provide a Historical Account   Historical accounts can help your readers understand the origins of a situation and how the situation has changed over time. A website focusing on relations between the People's Republic of China and Taiwan used this historical account.

> On February 21, 2000, the People's Republic of China (PRC) shocked the world with its release of the white paper "The One-China Principle and the Taiwan Issue." In this 18-page document, the Chinese government outlined its case that, in keeping with the "One China" principle to which the United States and Taiwan had allegedly agreed, Taiwan is the rightful property of the People's Republic of China, and revealed that it intended to use force if Taiwan did not move to reunite with the mainland.

Draw a Contrast   Drawing a contrast asks your readers to begin making a comparison. Elizabeth Leontiev began her essay by contrasting what the word *cocaine* means to U.S. citizens and South American coca farmers.

> To most Americans, the word *cocaine* evokes images of the illegal white powder and those who abuse it, yet the word has a completely different meaning to the coca farmers of South America.

Read Elizabeth Leontiev's research essay on p. 350.

Lead with a Quotation   A quotation allows your readers to learn about the issue from someone who knows it well or has been affected by it, as in the following introduction.

> "Without a few lucky breaks, we'd still be bagging groceries at Albertsons," says lead singer Rickie Jackson of the recent Grammy-winning band, Soft Affections.

Provide a Map   The most direct way of framing an issue and signaling the organization of your document is to provide a map, or preview, of your supporting points in your introduction.

> This report will cover three approaches to treating cancer of the bladder: chemotherapy, a combination of chemotherapy and radiation, and surgical removal of the organ.

IV Creating Your Document

14d

How can I use my conclusion to frame my issue?

Your conclusion provides an opportunity to reinforce your message. It offers one last chance to achieve your purpose as a writer and to share your final thoughts about the issue with your readers.

Reinforce Your Argument

At a minimum, your conclusion should summarize the reasons you've offered to support your thesis statement. You might also want to restate your thesis (in different words) to reinforce the main idea for readers. If you didn't include a thesis statement in your introduction, consider stating your main idea in your conclusion. Ending with a clear indication of what you want someone to think, believe, or do as a result of reading your document gives you one final opportunity to influence your readers.

Elizabeth Leontiev concluded her analysis of the impact of Evo Morales's vision for South American coca farmers like this.

> Through his bold program of "zero cocaine, not zero coca," Morales aims to improve the lives of Andean farmers and the economies of South American countries, while still remaining committed to controlling the illegal drug trade. Morales's example illustrates that it is time to work *with* coca farmers, rather than against them.

Select an Appropriate Strategy for Your Conclusion

Conclusions that simply summarize a document, like Elizabeth's, are common — and sometimes effective, especially when the writer has presented complex concepts. But a conclusion can do much more than simply restate your points. It can also give your readers an incentive to continue thinking about what they've read, to take action about the subject, or to read more about it.

As you draft, think about what you want to accomplish. You can choose from a range of strategies to write an effective conclusion.

Offer Additional Analysis   Extend your discussion of the issue by supplying additional insights. In a website about wind-generated electrical power, one writer concluded a discussion of wind power and the environment by linking wind power to the production of hydrogen gas.

> Another promising area — in terms of wind power's contribution to clean energy — is the role it can play in a "hydrogen economy." Because hydrogen gas, when burned, does not produce carbon dioxide (its only emission is water vapor), some legislators and environmentalists are looking to hydrogen as a replacement for fossil fuels. Generating hydrogen gas, however, requires power, and a number of plans to generate it rely on coal-powered plants. Wind-power advocates argue, instead, that wind turbines can supply the power needed to produce hydrogen gas. Recent government studies support this approach (National Renewable Energy Laboratory, 2016).

Speculate about the Future   Reflect on what might happen next. The author of an essay about the potential use of hydrogen as a fuel source, for example, might use this technique.

> It is certain, though, that at some point the fossil fuels that have sustained our society's electricity and run our motor vehicles for over a century will run out — or become so expensive that they'll no longer provide an economically viable source of energy. Whether that day comes in five years or fifty, we need to shift to a new energy source — one that is practical, economical, and environmentally friendly. Hydrogen has demonstrated great promise as a new candidate for fuel. To realize that promise, however, we must work to remove the barriers that currently prevent hydrogen's emergence as a mainstay of our future economy.

Close with a Quotation   Select a quotation that does one of the following:

- offers deeper insight into the points you've made in your document
- sums up the points you've made in your document
- points to the future of the issue
- suggests a solution to a problem
- illustrates what you would like to see happen
- makes a further observation about the issue
- presents a personalized viewpoint from someone who has experienced the issue you are addressing

Alexis Alvarez used a quotation from a personal interview to underscore her main point about the use of steroids among adolescent girls involved in competitive sports.

> In short, these athletes have not lost sight of the true objective of participating in sports—they know that their success is due to their efforts and not to the effects of a performance-enhancing drug. When asked what she would say to athletes considering steroid use, Melissa Alvarez said:
>
>> If you are training and doing your best, you should not have to use steroids. At the end of the day, it is just a game. You should never put your health at risk for anything, or anyone. It should be your top priority. (personal communication, September 26, 2004)

Close with a Story   Tell a story about the issue you've discussed in your document. The story might suggest a potential solution to the problem, offer hope about a desired outcome, or illustrate what might happen if a desired outcome isn't realized. This writer concluded his newspaper article by continuing a story he used in his introduction.

> So [Scott] struggles to get a foothold in the civilian workforce. His brother in Boston lost his roommate, and early last month Scott moved into the empty bedroom, with his parents paying Scott's share of the $2,000-a-month rent until the lease expires on Aug. 31. And if Scott does not have a job by then? "I'll do something temporary; I won't go back home," Scott said. "I'll be a bartender or get work through a temp agency. I hope I don't find myself in that position."

Close with a Question   Questions provide an effective means of inviting readers to consider the implications of the ideas explored in a document. After summarizing his position in his argumentative essay, Nicholas Brothers's included a compelling question in his closing paragraph.

> In the end, we as voters and taxpayers must ask ourselves, who do we want to carry out U.S. defense missions abroad: those accountable to the U.S. military, or those beholden to private corporations?

Read Nicholas Brothers's argumentative essay on p. 404.

Call Your Readers to Action   Make a recommendation or urge your readers to do something specific. For example, you might ask them to participate in solving a problem by donating time, money, or effort to a project. Or you might ask them to write to someone, such as a politician or corporate executive, about an issue. Calls to action ask readers to do more than simply accept what you've written; they ask readers to do something. Nicholas Brothers used this strategy in an earlier draft of his argumentative essay.

> On her website, Jan Schakowsky urges Americans to contact their representatives to cosponsor the legislation and become citizen cosponsors of the Stop Outsourcing Security Act themselves. Political action may be the most powerful remedy to our current state of apathy.

Link to Your Introduction   This technique is sometimes called a "bookends" approach because it positions your introduction and conclusion as related ends of your document. The basic idea is to turn your conclusion into an extension of your introduction.

- If your introduction used a quotation, end with a related quotation or respond to the quotation.
- If your introduction used a story, extend that story or retell it with a different ending.
- If your introduction asked a question, answer the question, restate the question, or ask a new question.
- If your introduction defined a problem, then you can provide a solution to the problem, restate the problem, or suggest that readers need to move on to a new problem.

QUICK REFERENCE

Drafting

- ✔ Use your outline to begin drafting your document. (p. 227)
- ✔ Draft focused, well-organized paragraphs. (p. 229)
- ✔ Include effective transitions, signals, and cross-references. (p. 230)
- ✔ Keep readers on track with the use of headings, menus, and effective design. (p. 231)
- ✔ Integrate information from sources clearly. (p. 232)
- ✔ Use details to engage your readers. (p. 232)
- ✔ Write with style by writing clearly and concisely, using active voice, adopting a consistent point of view, varying your sentence structure, choosing your words with care, avoiding sexist language, and consulting a handbook. (p. 233)
- ✔ Use your introduction to frame your issue. (p. 239)
- ✔ Use your conclusion to reinforce your argument. (p. 243)

IV Creating Your Document

15

Using Sources Effectively

> **Key Questions**
>

As you draft your document, remember the range of strategies you can use to support your points, convey your ideas, and illustrate positions taken by other authors. In this chapter, you'll learn how to integrate sources into your document and how to work with numerical information, images, audio, and video.

247

Much of the information in this chapter is based on MLA style, which is commonly used in the humanities. See Chapter 20 for more on MLA style and Chapters 21–23 for guidelines on APA, *Chicago*, and CSE styles.

15a

How can I use sources to accomplish my purposes as a writer?

Your sources can help you introduce ideas, contrast the ideas of other authors with your own, provide evidence for your points, align yourself with an authority, define concepts, illustrate processes, clarify statements, set a mood, provide an example, and qualify or amplify a point. You can present information from sources in several ways:

- as a quotation, paraphrase, or summary
- as numerical information
- as illustrations such as images, audio, video, and animations

As you draft your document, consider how your use of sources can lead your readers to view your issue in terms that are most favorable to your purposes. By selecting source information carefully, you can make your point more directly than you might want to using your own words. Calling opponents of a proposal "inflexible" and "pigheaded," for example, might signal your biases too strongly. Quoting someone who uses those terms, however, allows you to get the point across without undermining an otherwise even and balanced tone.

The following are some of the most effective ways to use information, ideas, and arguments from sources to contribute to a written conversation about an issue.

Introduce an Idea or Argument [FRAMING MY ARGUMENT]

You can use a quotation, paraphrase, or summary to introduce an idea or argument to your readers.

Note how the following quotation frames a public debate about education reform as a battle between reformers and an entrenched teachers union.

"The teachers union has balked at even the most reasonable proposals for school reform," said Mary Sweeney, press secretary for Save Our Schools, which has sponsored a referendum on the November ballot calling for funding for their voucher plan. "We believe the November election will send a wake-up call about the need to rethink their obstructionist behaviors."

If Sweeney and supporters of Referendum D are successful, the educational landscape in . . .

Phrases such as "balked at even the most reasonable proposals" and "their obstructionist behaviors" place the blame for the problem on the teachers union.

In contrast, note how the following quotation frames the debate as a question of how best to spend scarce education funds.

> "In the past decade, state and local funding of public education in real dollars has declined by 7.2 percent," said Jeffrey Allister, state chair of the governor's Special Commission on Education Reform. "Referendum D, if passed, would further erode that funding by shifting state dollars to private schools." As the state considers the merits of Referendum D, opponents of the measure have . . .

Phrases such as "funding of public education in real dollars has declined" and "further erode that funding" call attention to the financial challenges faced by schools.

Contrast Ideas or Arguments

When you want to indicate that disagreement exists on an issue, you can use source information to illustrate the nature and intensity of the disagreements. The following example uses partial quotations (p. 253) to highlight differences in proposed solutions to a problem.

> Solutions to the state's higher education funding shortfall range from traditional approaches, such as raising taxes, to more radical solutions, among them privatizing state colleges and universities. Advocates of increased taxes, such as Vincent Richards of the Higher Education Coalition, argue that declines in state funding of higher education "must be reversed immediately or we will find ourselves in a situation where we are closing rural community colleges and only the wealthiest among us will have access to the best education" (A4). Those in favor of privatizing higher education suggest, however, that free market approaches will ultimately bring about "a fairer situation in which the poor, many of whom have no interest in higher education, are no longer asked to subsidize higher and higher faculty salaries and larger football stadiums" (Pieters 23).

Base your choices about how to contrast ideas and arguments on the clarity and conciseness of your sources and on the effects you hope to achieve. If you want to express complex ideas as concisely as possible, you might use paraphrase and summary. If you want to convey the emotional qualities of an author's position on an issue, use quotations.

Provide Evidence for Your Argument

Arguments that consist of a series of unsupported assertions amount to little more than a request for a reader's trust. Even when the writer is eminently trustworthy, most readers find such arguments easy to dismiss. In contrast, providing evidence to support your assertions increases the likelihood that your readers will accept your argument. Note the differences between the following passages.

Unsupported Assertion
Given a choice between two products of comparable quality, reputation, and cost, American consumers are far more likely to purchase goods that use environmentally friendly packaging. Encouraging the use of such packaging is a good idea for America.

No evidence is provided to support the writer's assertion.

IV Creating Your Document

Supported Assertion

Given a choice between two products of comparable quality, reputation, and cost, American consumers are far more likely to purchase goods that use environmentally friendly packaging. A recent study by the High Plains Research Institute found that the shelf life of several biodegradable plastics not only exceeded the shelf life of the products they were used to package, but also cost less to produce (Chen and Lohann 33). In addition, a study by the Consumer Products Institute found that, when made aware that products were packaged in environmentally friendly materials, consumers were more likely to buy those products.

> Summaries of the results of two studies provide evidence for the assertion made in the first sentence.

Similarly, visual sources can lend support to an assertion. For example, an assertion about the unintended consequences of military action might be accompanied by a photograph of a war-torn street or a wounded child.

Align Your Argument with an Authority

Aligning an argument with an authority—such as a subject-matter expert, a scientist, a politician, or a religious figure—allows you to borrow someone else's credibility and status. Start by making an assertion and follow it with supporting information from a source, such as a quotation, paraphrase, or source summary.

> New developments in computers and robotics promise to bring about significant changes in both the workplace and daily life. "We are nearing the point where computers and robots will be able to see, move, and interact naturally, unlocking many new applications and empowering people even more," said Bill Gates, cofounder and former chairman of Microsoft Corporation (par. 3).

Define a Concept, Illustrate a Process, or Clarify a Statement

Writers commonly turn to information from sources when that information is clearer and more concise than what they might write themselves. You might define a concept by quoting or paraphrasing a dictionary or an encyclopedia, or use an illustration to help readers understand a complex process, such as the steps involved in cellular respiration. You might also use information from a source to clarify a statement.

> Some studies have found connections between weight loss and coffee intake. Unfortunately, drinking a couple of cups of coffee each day won't necessarily lead to weight loss. In fact, notes Mayo Clinic certified dietitian Katherine Zeratsky, it could lead to weight gain. "Some caffeinated beverages, such as specialty coffees, are high in calories and fat," states Zeratsky. "So instead of losing weight, you might actually gain weight if you drink too many of these" (197).

Set a Mood

You can also choose quotations and illustrations with an eye toward establishing an overall mood for your readers. The emotional impact of images of a celebration at a sporting event, an expression of grief at a funeral, or a calming mountain vista can lead your readers to react in specific ways to your document. Similarly, a striking quote, such as "The screams of pain coming out of that room will stay with me as long as I live," can evoke a specific mood among your readers.

Provide an Example

It's often better to *show* with an example than to *tell* with a general description. Examples provide concrete evidence in your document. Note how the writer of the following passage used an example from a well-known film to illustrate a point about her family's relationship with food.

> And the obsession with eating! My grandmother feeds us constantly. My dad and I always laugh at that scene in *Goodfellas* where the mobsters show up at two in the morning after killing someone, and one mobster's mother whips up a full pasta meal for them. We know that my grandmother would do the same thing: "Are you hungry? Here, sit, eat!" Grandma holds interventions over pasta. If she is unhappy with something someone in the family is doing, she invites everyone over for pasta and we hash it out together.

Amplify or Qualify a Point

You can use amplification to expand the scope of a point. Consider how information from a source is used in the following example to broaden a discussion of the dangers football players face when they add bulk.

> NFL offensive linemen who weigh less than 300 pounds are often described as "undersized," so it's no surprise that young football players are getting the message that bigger is better—and bulking up. A recent study of high school linemen in Iowa showed that 45% were overweight and 9% were severely obese, while only 18% of other young males were overweight; even more troubling, a study in Michigan revealed that among football players from ages 9 to 14, 45% could be considered overweight or obese (qtd. in Longman 28).

Qualifications, in contrast, allow you to narrow the scope of a statement, reducing the possibility that your readers might misunderstand your meaning. Note how the writer made it clear that deaths related to weight gain are a rare occurrence in football.

> While few high school football linemen suffer severe and immediate health consequences as a result of added weight, Skinner and her colleagues report that weight gain during adolescence "may lead to the development of ongoing obesity that becomes even more severe when they no longer have the physical activity to compensate for caloric intake" (926).

IV Creating Your Document

15b

How can I integrate sources into my draft?

You can integrate information, ideas, and arguments from sources into your draft by quoting, paraphrasing, summarizing, presenting numerical information, and using illustrations. As you do so, make a point of distinguishing your ideas and information from those found in your sources.

Identify Your Sources

You should identify the sources of information in your document for several reasons. First, doing so fulfills your ethical obligation to document your sources. Second, it allows you (and your readers) to recognize the boundaries between your ideas and those borrowed from sources. Third, it can help you strengthen your document by calling attention to the qualifications or experiences of the person whose ideas you are incorporating.

Use Attributions and In-Text Citations   Whenever you quote, paraphrase, or summarize, distinguish between your ideas and information obtained through your sources by using attributions—brief comments such as "according to" or "as the author points out"—to alert your readers that the point is not your own.

Writers who use the MLA or APA documentation format also provide citations—or acknowledgments of source information—within the text of their document to indicate where borrowed material ends. These citations, in turn, refer readers to a list of works cited or a list of references at the end of the document.

Note the following examples, which use attributions and in-text citations.

MLA Style

Pamela Coke argues, "Education reform is the best solution for fixing our public schools" (22).

> Attributions identify the author of the quotations.

"Education reform is the best solution for fixing our public schools" (Coke 22).

> MLA-style in-text citations include the author's name and exact page reference.

APA Style

Pamela Coke (2017) has argued, "Education reform is the best solution for fixing our public schools" (p. 22).

> APA-style in-text citations include the author's name, publication date, and exact page reference.

"Education reform is the best solution for fixing our public schools" (Coke, 2017, p. 22).

As you acknowledge material you've borrowed from sources, you'll want to vary the wording of your attributions. As you do, be aware of the way that the verbs in attributions can convey important shades of meaning—for example, the difference between writing that someone "alleged" something and someone "confirmed" something. The form your attributions take will depend on your use of citation style. MLA recommends present tense ("the author points out"), while APA recommends past tense ("the author pointed out") or present perfect tense ("the author has explained").

Some Common Attributions

according to	claimed	inquired	said
acknowledged	commented	interpreted	stated
affirmed	confirmed	mused	suggested
alleged	declared	noted	thought
asked	denied	observed	told
asserted	described	remarked	wondered
assumed	disputed	reported	wrote

You can learn more about in-text citations and the MLA, APA, *Chicago*, and CSE documentation systems in Part V.

Provide a Context   As you quote your sources, do more than simply place text between two quotation marks. Such "orphan quotations"—quotations dropped into a paragraph without any introduction—are confusing. Worse, paraphrases and summaries inserted without context can easily be mistaken for the writer's own work, leading to accusations of plagiarism.

To provide a clear context for your source information, establish why the quotation, paraphrase, or summary is reliable by identifying the source's credentials. In addition, indicate how it relates to your main idea and what it contributes to the point you are making. If you don't, readers will wonder why it's there.

> However, Wechsler et al. (2003) of the Harvard School of Public Health analyzed trends at schools using social norms marketing and revealed that the campaigns did not necessarily decrease student drinking; in some cases, schools even reported higher alcohol consumption, according to seven criteria that measured whether students drank, how much, and how often. As the researchers explained, "individual students' drinking behaviors align more closely to the drinking behaviors of their immediate social group rather than to the overall student population at a given school" (para. 31).

Attribution identifies the source as experts.

Writer follows APA style; parenthetical citation identifies the paragraph where the quotation was found.

Quote Strategically

A well-chosen quotation can have a powerful impact on your readers' perception of your argument and on the overall quality of your document. Quotations can also add a sense of immediacy by bringing in the voice of someone who has been affected by an issue or can lend a sense of authority to your argument by conveying the words of an expert.

Quotations can be parts of sentences (partial), whole sentences (complete), or long passages (block). When you choose one type of quotation over another, consider the length and complexity of the passage as well as the obligation to convey ideas and information fairly. As you integrate quotations into your document, remember that you might need to modify them to suit your purpose and fit the flow of your sentences. When you do, be careful to punctuate them properly.

Partial quotations   can be a single word, phrase, or most of a sentence. They are often used to convey a well-turned phrase or to complete a sentence using important words from a source, as in the following example.

> Nadine K. Maxwell, a guidance services coordinator in Fairfax, Virginia, says that students' chances of being admitted can be greater if they apply early, although this varies from school to school and year to year and "may depend upon the applicant pool at the school where they are applying" (32).

Quotation marks indicate the borrowed phrase.

Source information, including the number of the page containing the quotation, is clearly identified.

IV Creating Your Document

Complete quotations are typically one or more complete sentences and are most often used when the meaning of the passage cannot be conveyed adequately by a few well-chosen words, as in the following example.

> I smiled when I read Elizabeth Gilbert's memoir *Eat, Pray, Love*. She writes, "The Neapolitan women in particular are such a gang of tough-voiced, loud-mouthed, generous, nosy dames, all bossy and annoyed and right up in your face just trying to friggin' *help* you for chrissake, you dope — *why they gotta do everything around here?*" (78).

> Since the source of the quotation is identified in an attribution ("Elizabeth Gilbert's memoir . . ."), only the page number appears in the citation at the end of the sentence.

Block quotations are extended quotations (usually more than four typed lines) that are set off in a block from the rest of the text. In general, use a colon to introduce the quotation, indent the entire quotation half an inch from the left margin, and include source information according to the documentation system you are using (such as MLA, APA, *Chicago*, or CSE). Since the blocked text indicates that you are quoting directly, you do not include quotation marks.

In the article "In the Best Interest of America, Affirmative Action in Higher Education Is a Must," William H. Gray III states:

Quotation marks are not used to surround block quotations.

> High school achievement and test scores are considered to be very important criteria in the admissions process. . . . Nonetheless, high school grades and test scores are not the only factors considered by colleges and universities in the admissions process. Other factors that influence college admissions decisions include high school rank, being an athlete, alumni connections, extracurricular activities, special talents, and other personal characteristics of applicants. (par. 5)

In block quotations, the citation information is placed after the period.

A paragraph number is provided for an online source.

Modify Quotations Appropriately   You can modify quotations to fit your draft. It is acceptable, for example, to delete unnecessary words or to change the tense of a word in a partial quotation so that it fits your sentence. For example, if you wanted to change the tense of a verb in a partial quotation so that it fits the sentence, you would use brackets to indicate the change.

Original Quotation
"They treated us like family and refused to accept a tip."

Quotation Modified Using Brackets
It's a place where the staff treats you "like family and [refuses] to accept a tip," said travel writer Melissa Ancomi.

Brackets indicate a word that has been changed.

Keep in mind, however, that research writers have an obligation to quote sources accurately and fairly. You should indicate when you have added or deleted words, and you should not modify quotations in a way that distorts their meaning.

The most useful strategies you can use to modify quotations include using ellipsis marks (. . .) to indicate deleted words, using brackets [ ] to clarify meaning, and using "*sic*" to note errors in a source. You can learn more about modifying quotations using these strategies on pp. 87–89.

Punctuate Quotations Correctly   The rules for punctuating quotations are as follows.

- Use double quotation marks (" ") around partial or complete quotations. Do not use quotation marks for block quotations.
- Use single quotation marks (' ') to indicate quoted material within a quotation.

  > "The hotel manager told us to 'make ourselves at home.'"

- Place commas and periods inside quotation marks.
- Place question marks and exclamation points outside quotation marks if the punctuation pertains to the entire sentence rather than the quotation. In the following example, the original quotation is not a question, so the question mark should be placed after the quotation mark.

  > But what can be gained from following the committee's recommendation that the state should "avoid, without exceptions, any proposed tax hike"?

- Place question marks and exclamation points inside quotation marks if the punctuation pertains to the quotation itself.

  > Dawn Smith asked an important question: "Do college students understand the importance of avoiding running up credit card debt?"

- Place colons and semicolons outside quotation marks.

  > Many young consumers consider themselves "free at last"; all too often, however, they find that freedom has its costs.

- When citation information is provided after a quotation, place the punctuation mark (comma, period, semicolon, colon, or question mark) after the parenthetical citation.

  > "Preliminary reports have been consistent," Yates notes. "Without immediate changes to current practices, we will deplete known supplies by mid-century" (335).

- At the end of a block quotation, place the final punctuation before the parenthetical citation.
- Use three spaced periods (an ellipsis mark) to indicate an omission within a sentence.

  > According to critic Joe Robinson, Americans are overworked: "Ask Americans how things are really going and you'll hear stories of . . . fifty- and sixty-hour weeks with no letup in sight" (467).

- Place a period before the ellipsis mark to indicate an omission at the end of a sentence:

> The most recent information indicates, says Chen, that "we can expect a significant increase in costs by the end of the decade.... Those costs, however, should ramp up slowly" (35).

CHECKLIST FOR INTEGRATING QUOTATIONS INTO A DOCUMENT

✔ Identify the source of the quotation.

✔ Punctuate the quotation appropriately.

✔ Use ellipsis marks, brackets, and "*sic*" as necessary.

✔ Check each quotation against the source to be sure you aren't introducing errors or misrepresenting the source.

✔ Use transitions and attributions to integrate the quotation effectively into your document.

✔ Ensure that the source is cited in your works cited or reference list.

Paraphrase Information, Ideas, and Arguments

A paraphrase is a restatement, in your own words, of a passage from a source. Paraphrases can be used to illustrate or support a point you make in your document or to illustrate another author's argument about an issue. Writers choose to paraphrase rather than quote when a paraphrase would present the point more clearly or concisely than would a quotation from a source. Writers also choose to use paraphrases to add variety to a document—particularly when a large number of quotations have already been used—or when they find that the original passage would alter the tone or style of their document. For example, a writer of an article about a band that was purposefully pushing the boundaries of contemporary music might want to note that an important music reviewer had written, "I found this 'concert' to be a complete waste of my time." If the writer had already quoted more compelling statements from several other reviewers, however, the writer might use a paraphrase to indicate that the reviewer had found little in the band's most recent concert to recommend its music.

Before you integrate a paraphrase into your document, reread the source to check the accuracy and fairness of your paraphrase, and then revise the paraphrase so that it fits the context and tone of your document. Use author attributions to ensure a smooth transition from your ideas to the ideas in the source.

In the following example, note how Alexis Alvarez lets her readers know where her statement ends and where the support for her statement, in the form of a paraphrase, begins.

> Competitive sports also teach athletes how to cope with failure — Alexis's idea
> as well as success. In the best of situations, as Sieghart (2004)
> noted, athletes are able to assess their achievements realistically, — The source of the paraphrase is cited per APA style.
> letting neither winning nor losing consume their reality.

An attribution marks the transition from Alexis's idea to her source's ideas.

How do I integrate a quotation into my draft?

After you select a passage to quote, you'll need to acknowledge the source, punctuate the quotation properly, and provide a context for the information. This example uses MLA style; be sure to follow the guidelines for the documentation style you are using.

Original Passage

1 Locate the passage you want to quote and identify the text you want to include in the quotation.

One clear warning from both resilience theory and practical experience is that prevention is better than cure. The empirical evidence is unambiguous: the trajectory of reef condition is declining globally, because once a reef is degraded it usually stays that way (but see below). Interventions need to focus (a) on reversing interacting slow drivers, particularly overfishing, pollution, and greenhouse gas emissions, to avoid transgressing thresholds leading to phase-shifts, and (b) on promoting processes like coral recruitment and herbivory that maintain the coral-dominated states of healthy reefs.

2 Add quotation marks or, if the quotation is long, set the text in a block (p. 253). If you modify the passage, use ellipsis marks and brackets appropriately (p. 254).

Source: Hughes, Terry P., et al. "Rising to the Challenge of Sustaining Coral Reef Resilience." *Trends in Ecology and Evolution*, vol. 25, no. 11, November 2010, pp. 619–80.

"One clear warning . . . is that prevention is better than cure. . . . Interventions need to focus (a) on reversing interacting slow drivers . . . and (b) on promoting processes like coral recruitment and herbivory that maintain the coral-dominated states of healthy reefs."

3 Identify the source of the quotation and the location, such as the page number. Give the author's qualifications in an author tag if you haven't already done so for this source in your document.

In their article "Rising to the Challenge of Sustaining Coral Reef Resilience," Terry P. Hughes et al. note, "One clear warning . . . is that prevention is better than cure. . . . Interventions need to focus (a) on reversing interacting slow drivers . . . and (b) on promoting processes like coral recruitment and herbivory that maintain the coral-dominated states of healthy reefs" (638).

4 Avoid "orphan quotations" by providing a context for your quotation. Introduce the quotation and indicate how it relates to your argument.

It is not enough to try to rehabilitate damaged reefs. In their article "Rising to the Challenge of Sustaining Coral Reef Resilience," Terry P. Hughes et al. note, "One clear warning . . . is that prevention is better than cure. . . . Interventions need to focus (a) on reversing interacting slow drivers . . . and (b) on promoting processes like coral recruitment and herbivory that maintain the coral-dominated states of healthy reefs" (638). Sustaining coral reefs involves protecting existing coral in healthy reef environments.

> **CHECKLIST FOR INTEGRATING PARAPHRASES INTO A DOCUMENT**
>
> ✔ Identify the source of the paraphrased material.
>
> ✔ Compare the original passage with your paraphrase. Make sure that you have conveyed the meaning of the passage but that the wording and sentence structure differ from those in the original passage.
>
> ✔ Use transitions and attributions to integrate the paraphrase smoothly into your document.
>
> ✔ Ensure that the source is cited in your works cited or reference list.

Summarize

A summary is a concise statement, written in your own words, of information found in a source. When you integrate a summary into your draft, review the source to make sure your summary is an accurate and fair representation of the ideas in the original source. Be careful, as well, to identify the source and include a citation. You can summarize an entire source, parts of a particular source, or a group of sources to support your argument.

Summarize an Entire Source   Research writers frequently summarize an entire work. In some cases, the summary might occupy one or more paragraphs or be integrated into a discussion contained in one or more paragraphs. In other cases, the summary might be as brief as a single sentence.

Alexis Alvarez summarized a report issued by the Centers for Disease Control and Prevention in her research essay about steroid use by adolescent girls involved in competitive sports.

In May 2004, the Centers for Disease Control and Prevention (CDC) published its latest figures on self-reported drug use among young people in grades 9 through 12. The CDC study, "Youth Risk Behavior Surveillance—December 2003," found that 6.1% of its survey participants reported using steroids at least once, up from 2.2% in 1993. The report also showed that use of steroids appears to be increasing among younger girls: While only 3.3% of 12th-grade girls reported using steroids, 7.3% of 9th-grade girls reported using them. Moreover, girls might be starting to use steroids at a higher rate than boys. The CDC study indicated that 9th-grade girls had reported slightly higher rates of steroid use than boys (7.3% and 6.9% respectively), while 10th-, 11th-, and 12th-grade girls all reported lower use than boys.

The author, title, and publication date are identified in the text, so a parenthetical citation is not required for either MLA or APA style.

The main point of the report

Additional information from the report

In contrast, Alexis offered a much briefer, "nutshell" summary of one related source.

A 2003 article in *Drug Week* stated that girls who participate in sports more than eight hours a week are at considerable risk for taking many illicit drugs: The higher the level at which athletes compete, the higher their risk for substance abuse ("Sporting Activities").

Summarize Specific Ideas and Information from a Source   You can also use summaries to convey key information or ideas from a source. In his research essay, Nicholas Brothers summarized a section of a book about private military corporations.

> Yet a look at definitions in Singer's *Corporate Warriors* reveals that PMCs and traditional mercenaries differ in several key ways. Perhaps the most important difference is that a private military corporation is just that: a legal corporate entity[9] (as opposed to the illegal adventurer or ragtag squad evoked by the word "mercenary"). Another significant distinction is that PMCs offer a wide range of services . . . while mercenaries can rarely do more than engage in combat.

The summary is introduced with the author and specific source of the ideas.

Per *Chicago* style, a citation appears as a numbered footnote.

Summarize a Group of Sources   It's not unusual to read phrases such as "Numerous authors have argued . . ." or "The research in this area seems to indicate that. . . ." Such collective summaries allow you to establish a point briefly and with authority. They are effective particularly at the beginning of a document, when you are establishing a foundation for your argument, and can serve as a transitional device when you move from one major section of the document to another.

When you are summarizing a group of sources, separate the citations with a semicolon. MLA guidelines require including author and page information, as in the following example.

> Several critics have argued that the Hemingway code hero is not always male (Graulich 217; Sherman 78; Watters 33).

APA guidelines require including author and date information, as in the following example.

> The benefits of early detection of breast cancer have been well documented (Page, 2017; Richards, 2017; Vincent, 2016).

IV Creating Your Document

CHECKLIST FOR INTEGRATING SUMMARIES INTO A DOCUMENT

✔ Identify the source you are summarizing.

✔ Ensure that you have summarized the source in your own words. Make sure that you do not merely string together a series of close paraphrases of key passages.

✔ Use transitions and attributions to integrate the summary smoothly into your document.

✔ Ensure that the source is cited in your works cited or reference list.

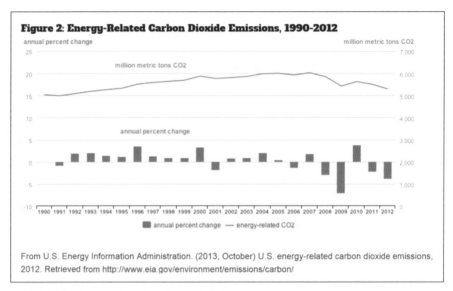

FIGURE 15.1 Chart on Brandon Tate's Website

Present Numerical Information

If it suits the issue you are addressing, you might use numerical information, such as statistics, in your document. You can present this information within sentences, or you might use tables, charts, or graphs, as Brandon Tate did on his website about hydraulic fracturing (see Figure 15.1). Keep in mind that you still need to accurately and fairly present the numerical information in your document and clearly identify the source of the information, just as you would for textual information. For more information about using tables, charts, and graphs, see pp. 270–73.

Use Images, Audio, Video, and Animations

Including images in your print document and images, audio, video, or animation files in your electronic document can enhance its effectiveness. Use caution, however, when using this kind of source material. Simply copying a photograph into your document might be a form of plagiarism. The same is true of audio, video, and animation files.

Lauren Mack carefully documented the sources of the images, audio clips, and video clips she used in her multimodal research essay. Since she was writing an academic essay—rather than a document intended for publication and wide distribution—she did not seek permission to use the images, audio, and video that she had found in other sources. (In contrast, the publisher of this book sought and received permission to publish those materials.)

 INFORMATION LITERACY   If you are creating a digital document, such as a Web page or a multimedia presentation, use the following approach to integrating digital illustrations.

- Make a link between your document and a document that contains an image, sound clip, or video clip—rather than simply copying the image and placing it in your document.
- If it isn't possible or appropriate to create a link to another document, you should contact the owner of the image, sound clip, or video clip for permission to use it.
- If you cannot contact the owner, review the fair use guidelines discussed on p. 132 for guidance about using the material.

As you've done for the other sources you cite in your document, make sure you fairly present images, audio, and video and identify their author or creator. ▥

15c

How should I document my sources?

You should cite your sources within the text of your document as well as provide complete publication information for each source you've used. Fully documenting your sources in this way can help you achieve your purpose as a writer, such as establishing your authority and persuading your readers. Documenting your sources also helps you avoid plagiarism, gives credit to others who have written about an issue, and creates a record of their work that your readers can follow and build on.

Documenting sources involves choosing a documentation system, identifying sources in the text of your document, and providing a works cited or reference list at the end of your document. Documentation systems commonly used in academic disciplines include those developed by the Modern Language Association (MLA), the American Psychological Association (APA), the University of Chicago Press (*Chicago*), and the Council of Science Editors (CSE).

Your choice of documentation system will be guided by the discipline or field within which you are writing and by any requirements associated with your research writing project. If your project has been assigned to you, ask the person who assigned it or someone who has written a similar document which documentation system you should use. If you are working on a project for a writing class, your instructor will most likely tell you which documentation system to follow.

Your choice will also be guided by the genre you have chosen for your document. For example, while academic essays and articles appearing in scholarly journals typically use a documentation system such as MLA or APA, newspaper and magazine articles often do not; instead, they identify sources in the main text of the document rather than in a works cited or reference list. If you write a digital document that cites other online sources, you might simply link to those sources.

You can read about how to use the MLA, APA, *Chicago*, and CSE documentation systems in Chapters 19–23.

IV Creating Your Document

15d

How can I ensure I've avoided unintentional plagiarism?

Because plagiarized material will often differ in style, tone, and word choice from the rest of your document, your readers are likely to notice these differences and wonder whether you've plagiarized the material—or, if not, why you've written a document that has so many stylistic inconsistencies. If your readers react negatively, it's unlikely that your document will be successful.

You can avoid unintentional plagiarism by quoting, paraphrasing, and summarizing accurately and appropriately; distinguishing between your ideas and ideas in your sources; and checking for unattributed sources in your document.

Quote, Paraphrase, and Summarize Accurately and Appropriately

Unintentional plagiarism usually occurs when a writer takes poor notes and then uses the information from those notes in a document. As you draft, do the following.

- Look for notes that differ from your usual style of writing. More often than not, if a note doesn't sound like your own writing, it isn't.
- Place quotation marks around any direct quotations, use ellipsis marks and brackets appropriately (see pp. 253–56), and identify the source and the page or paragraph number of the quotation.
- Make sure that paraphrases differ significantly in word choice and sentence structure from the passage being paraphrased, and identify the source and page or paragraph number from which you took the paraphrase.
- Make sure that summaries are not just a series of passages or close paraphrases copied from the source.

Distinguish between Your Ideas and Ideas in Your Sources

Failing to distinguish between your ideas and ideas drawn from your sources can lead readers to think other writers' ideas are yours. Examine how the writer of the following passage might have failed to distinguish his ideas from those of Joel Levine and Lawrence May, authors of a source used in the essay.

> **Failing to Credit Ideas to a Source**
> According to Joel Levine and Lawrence May, authors of *Getting In*, entrance exams are an extremely important part of a student's college application and carry a great deal of weight. In fact, a college entrance examination is one of the two most significant factors in getting into college. The other, unsurprisingly, is high school grades.

Because the second and third sentences fail to identify Levine and May as the source of the information about the second important factor affecting admissions decisions—high school grades—the passage implies that the writer of the research essay is the source of that information.

In contrast, the writer actually included the following passage in the essay.

Giving Credit to the Source

According to Joel Levine and Lawrence May, authors of *Getting In*, entrance exams are an extremely important part of a student's college application and carry a great deal of weight. In fact, they claim that a college entrance examination is "one of the two most significant factors" in getting into college (the other, unsurprisingly, being high school grades) (116).

> The attribution, "they claim," credits Levine and May as the source of the information.

> Quotation marks are used to indicate a partial quotation.

To distinguish between your ideas and those obtained through your sources, use attributions—words or phrases that alert your readers to the source of the ideas or information you are using. As you take notes and draft your document, use the name of an author or the title of the source you're drawing from each time you introduce ideas from a source (see p. 252).

Check for Unattributed Sources in Your Document

You should include a complete citation for each source you refer to in your document. The citation should appear in the text of the document (as an in-text citation, footnote, or endnote) or in a works cited list, reference list, or bibliography.

In the following MLA-style examples, the writer includes parenthetical citations that refer readers to a list of works cited at the end of the document. Note that MLA style allows for a combination of attributions and parenthetical information to refer to sources.

Reid Vincent argues, "We must explore emerging energy technologies before we reach a peak oil crisis" (322).

"We must explore emerging energy technologies before we reach a peak oil crisis" (Vincent 322).

> MLA-style in-text citations include the author's name and exact page reference.

> **QUICK REFERENCE**

Using Sources Effectively

☑ Use source information to accomplish your purpose. (p. 248)

☑ Integrate quotations appropriately. (p. 251)

☑ Integrate paraphrases appropriately. (p. 256)

☑ Integrate summaries appropriately. (p. 258)

☑ Integrate numerical information appropriately. (p. 260)

☑ Integrate images, audio, video, and animations appropriately. (p. 260)

☑ Choose a documentation system. (p. 261)

☑ Provide in-text references and a works cited or reference list. (p. 261)

☑ Check for unintentional plagiarism by checking your quotations, paraphrases, and summaries; checking for unattributed sources; and confirming that you distinguish between your work and information, ideas, and arguments from your sources. (p. 262)

16

Designing
Documents

Key Questions

Many writers think of designing a document as something that comes at the end of the writing process, after drafting, revising, and editing have been completed. In fact, design can be a powerful tool during the planning and drafting stages, and there are many composing programs and strategies worth considering. By incorporating design as you plan and work on your draft, you can create a document whose appearance helps you achieve your purpose, address your readers effectively, and take advantage of the context in which it will be read.

16a

What role does design play in my document?

Your decisions about the design of your document, from choosing appropriate fonts to presenting information in charts and tables to selecting compelling illustrations, can have powerful effects on how you shape and present your ideas and how your readers understand and react to your document. Understanding design principles and elements, as well as the design conventions of documents typically assigned in college courses, can help you craft a unique and substantial contribution to a conversation.

Understand Design Principles [FRAMING MY ARGUMENT]

Before you begin formatting text and inserting illustrations, consider how the document design principles of *balance, emphasis, placement, repetition,* and *consistency* can help you accomplish your goals as a writer.

Balance   Balance is the vertical and horizontal alignment of elements on your pages (see Figure 16.1). Symmetrical designs create a sense of rest and stability and tend to lead the reader's eye to focus on a particular part of a document. In contrast, asymmetrical—or unbalanced—designs suggest movement and guide the reader's eye across the page.

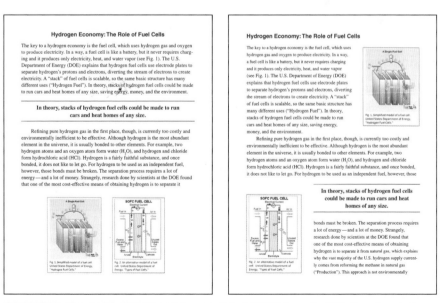

FIGURE 16.1 Symmetrical (*left*) and Asymmetrical (*right*) Layouts [U.S. Department of Energy.]

Emphasis   Emphasis is the placement and formatting of elements, such as headings and subheadings, so they catch your readers' attention. You can emphasize an element in a document by using a color or font that distinguishes it from other elements, by placing a border around it and adding a shaded background, or by using an illustration, such as a photograph, drawing, or graph.

Placement   Placement is the location of elements on your pages. Placing elements next to or near each other suggests that they are related. Illustrations, for example, are usually placed near the passages in which they are mentioned.

Repetition   Repetition is the use of elements, such as headers and footers, navigation menus, and page numbers, across the pages in your document. As readers move from page to page, they tend to expect navigation elements, such as page numbers, to appear in the same place. In addition, repeated elements, such as a logo or Web navigation menu, help establish a sense of identity across the pages in your document.

Consistency   Consistency is the extent to which you format and place text and illustrations in the same way throughout your document. Treating each design element—such as illustrations, headings, and footnotes—consistently will help your readers recognize the different roles played by the elements in your document and, by extension, help them locate the information they seek. A consistent design can also convey a sense of competence and professionalism to your readers, increasing their confidence in the quality and credibility of your document.

You should also keep two other principles in mind: *moderation* and *simplicity*. An overly complex design can work against the effectiveness of a document by obscuring important ideas and information. Using design elements moderately to create simple yet effective designs is the best approach.

Design for a Purpose   ❓ WHAT'S MY PURPOSE?

A well-designed document presents your information, ideas, and arguments in a manner that helps you accomplish your purpose.

You might use design to achieve any of the following goals.

- **Setting a Tone**   One of the most powerful tools writers have for accomplishing their purpose is establishing an emotional context for their readers. Drawing on the design principles of balance and placement, you can set a tone by using a particular color scheme, such as bright, cheerful hues, or by selecting photographs or drawings with a strong emotional impact.

- **Helping Readers Understand a Point**   You might use the design principles of emphasis and placement to introduce your points and help readers understand them. Headings or pull quotes can call your readers' attention to important ideas and information. To introduce a main point, you might use a contrasting font or color to signal the importance of the information. To highlight a definition or an example, you might use borders or place

FIGURE 16.2 Using Images to Create an Emotional Impact *How is the photograph likely to influence the reader's response to the headline?* [Adam Rogers/Wired; © Condé Nast. Ariana Cubillos/AP Images.]

the passage in a pull quote. You can also help readers understand a point by using illustrations.

- **Convincing Readers to Accept a Point** The key to convincing readers is providing them with appropriate, relevant evidence. Drawing on the principles of emphasis and placement, you can use illustrations, marginal glosses, pull quotes, and bulleted lists to call attention to that evidence.

- **Clarifying Complex Concepts** Sometimes a picture really is worth a thousand words. Rather than attempting to explain a complex concept using text alone, use an illustration. A well-chosen, well-placed photograph, flow chart, diagram, or table can define a complex concept such as photosynthesis in far less space, and in many cases far more effectively, than a long passage of text. You can also clarify the key elements of a complex concept with bulleted and numbered lists.

Design for Your Readers

A well-designed document helps readers understand the organization of the document, locate information and ideas, and recognize the function of parts of the document. It is also easy on your readers' eyes: Readers working with a well-designed document will not have to strain to read the text or discern illustrations.

Use document design to do the following.

IV Creating Your Document

Help Readers Understand the Organization of a Document You can use headings and subheadings to signal the content of each part of the document, as we do in this book. If you use headings, keep in mind the design principles of emphasis and consistency: Format your headings in a consistent manner that helps them stand out from other parts of the document.

Help Readers Locate Information and Ideas Many longer print documents use tables of contents and indexes to help readers locate information and ideas. Websites (see p. 285) and multimodal essays (see p. 277) typically provide a mix of menus and navigation headers and footers to help readers move around. You can distinguish these navigation aids from the surrounding text by using bordered or shaded boxes or contrasting fonts or colors.

Help Readers Recognize the Function of Parts of a Document If you include passages that differ from the main text of your document, such as sidebars and For More Information sections, help readers understand their function by designing them to stand out visually. Using emphasis, for example, you might format a sidebar in an article with a shaded or colored box. Similarly, you might format a list of related readings or Web links in a contrasting font or color.

Design to Address Genre Conventions

Genres are characterized not only by distinctive writing styles, types of evidence, and organizing patterns, but also by distinctive types of design. An article in a magazine such as *Time* or *Rolling Stone*, for example, is characterized by the use of columns, headings and subheadings, pull quotes, and illustrations, while an academic essay is characterized by wide margins, double-spaced lines, and comparatively restrained use of color and illustrations. Your readers will expect your document to be similar in design to other examples of that genre. This doesn't mean that you can't depart from those conventions should the need arise, but it does mean that you should take their expectations into account as you design your document.

IV Creating Your Document

16b

What design elements can I use?

Understanding the range of design elements at your disposal will enable you to decide which of these options to use as you design your document. These elements include fonts, line spacing, and alignment; page layout strategies; color, shading, borders, and rules; and illustrations.

Use Fonts, Line Spacing, and Alignment

Fonts, line spacing, and alignment choices are the most common design decisions made by writers. They are also among the most important, since poor choices can make a document difficult to read. The following examples provide an overview of the key features of fonts and the uses of fonts, line spacing, and alignment.

Use Page Layout Elements

Page layout is the placement of text, illustrations, and other objects on a page or screen. Successful page layout draws on a number of design elements, including white space, margins, columns, headers and footers, page numbers, headings, lists, captions, marginal glosses and pull quotes, and sidebars. Figure 16.5 on p. 271 illustrates these design elements.

Use Color, Shading, Borders, and Rules

Color, shading, borders, and rules (horizontal or vertical lines) can make your document, more attractive, call attention to important information, help readers understand the organization of your document, help readers recognize the function of specific passages of text, and signal transitions between sections (see Figure 16.6 on p. 272). As you use these design elements, exercise restraint. Avoid using more than three colors on a page unless you are using a photograph or work of art. Be cautious, as well, about using multiple styles of rules or borders in a document.

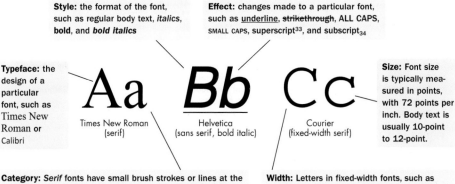

Style: the format of the font, such as regular body text, *italics*, **bold**, and ***bold italics***

Effect: changes made to a particular font, such as <u>underline</u>, ~~strikethrough~~, ALL CAPS, SMALL CAPS, superscript[33], and subscript[34]

Typeface: the design of a particular font, such as Times New Roman or Calibri

Times New Roman (serif)

Helvetica (sans serif, bold italic)

Courier (fixed-width serif)

Size: Font size is typically measured in points, with 72 points per inch. Body text is usually 10-point to 12-point.

Category: *Serif* fonts have small brush strokes or lines at the end of each stroke, are considered easier to read, and are often used for body text. *Sans-serif* fonts lack serifs and are often used for headings and subheadings. Other categories include *decorative* (*Limehouse Roman*, **Mambo Bold**) and *symbol* (Wingding: ✌📄■♻📖🎗👁🎵).

Width: Letters in fixed-width fonts, such as Courier, have the same width; these fonts are useful for displaying columns of numbers. Letters in variable-width fonts, such as Times New Roman and Helvetica, have different widths; these fonts are better suited to body text and headings.

FIGURE 16.3 Font Basics

Line spacing refers to the amount of space between lines of text. Larger line spacing appears easier to read, so you'll often find increased line spacing used in introductory paragraphs, executive summaries (which provide an overview of a longer document), and sidebars (see p. 271). When text is crammed together vertically, it is difficult to read and add comments. Keep this in mind if you are creating a document such as an essay on which someone else might write comments.

Alignment refers to the horizontal arrangement of text and illustrations (such as photos and drawings). You can select four types of alignment.

- **Left alignment** has a straight left margin and a "ragged right" margin; it is typically the easiest to read.
- **Right alignment** has a straight right margin and a ragged left margin.
- **Centered alignment** is seldom used for body text but can make headings stand out.
- **Justified alignment** has straight alignment on both the left and right margins. It adds a polished look and can be effective in documents that use columns—but it also produces irregular word spacing and hyphenation, which can slow the reading process.

On the Subject of Trigger Warnings

A teaching assistant responds to what feels like a crisis on campus.

By Siobhan Crowley

A college president at a Midwestern school recently took issue with the idea of "triggers" and "safe zones." He remarked vividly that his school "is not a daycare. [It] is a university." While I can appreciate the snarkiness of his comments, and the frustration with yet another roadblock to effectively teaching students, I have to disagree with his stance that there is anything infantile about dealing with triggering experiences. The trauma involved can be very real, and I think student concerns need to be met with serious reflection. I have concerns, however, over whether they can be met with equally serious action, if not for the reasons that a certain president mentions.

Let's start with the easy part of the argument: If a student has experiences that impede their ability to approach certain subject matter, then allowances absolutely need to be made. Alternative assignments might be created, for instance, or a student might be excused from multiple class session. Final tests might be adapted for the one or two students who have come privately to express their inability to address certain topics.

From there, however, the question gets more difficult. Let's say you study literature. Or sociology. And you can't read certain selections because the idea of imperialism or slavery is a trigger for you. So you don't study *Huckleberry Finn* or *Othello* for you. Marx or chunks of Weber. And then you go out into the world to use your degree and you have these glaring blind spots. You won't have been prepared adequately in the field you said you studied. Let's say you want to be a teacher (as many TAs in English go on to do). Are you going to *not* teach *Romeo and Juliet* because someone in your family committed suicide? Or not teach *Huck Finn* because you can't address the issue of race? That means to be a criminal neglect to students who need to learn this material, if only so that they can address *exactly these issues*. Will your papers ever be accepted in a sociological journal if you skip obvious references to canon theorists?

I appreciate the validity of trigger-warnings and other accommodation as a theory, but I think that they can only apply to non-major courses. Someone majoring in math certainly doesn't need to know *Othello* (though they might benefit from reading so). But someone who majors in English really ought to. Not even *Othello* specifically, but you just can't get away from race or sexual violence, or suicide, or any triggering issue in

> I would hate for students to miss an opportunity to work through their trauma in my classroom, where I can mediate discussions to ensure that comments are not hurtful.

Great literature is great because it tackles these painful topics.

literature because these are the very meat of what authors are trying to address.

The other concern, of course, is that great literature is great *because* it tackles these painful topics. *Beloved* and *Sula* were difficult books to read, but there is power in tapping into that artistic expression of pain. Power that I worry my students will need when they leave school behind and enter a culture that does not make the allowances that college professors can make. A world full of triggering episodes.

I would hate for students to miss an opportunity to work through their trauma in my classroom, where I can mediate discussions to ensure that comments are not hurtful. Particularly if that student makes me aware of their fears and I can work with them in conjunction with a university counselor. There is so much to be gained from the study of literature, including the ability to address and mediate the very triggering issues that students wants to avoid. It makes me sad to think that students will blindly turn away from that power and that opportunity. Even for the very best of reasons.

Fonts are a complete set of type of a particular size and typeface. As you choose fonts, consider the following.
- **Select fonts that are easy to read.** For body text, avoid decorative fonts and italics.
- **Select fonts that complement each other.** A serif body font, such as Times New Roman or Garamond, works well with a sans-serif heading font, such as Arial, Helvetica, or Calibri.
- **Exercise restraint.** Generally, use no more than four different fonts in a document.

FIGURE 16.4 Using Fonts, Line Spacing, and Alignment [Photo: David Crockett/Getty Images]

Use Illustrations   [FRAMING MY ARGUMENT]

Illustrations—charts, graphs, tables, photographs and other images, animations, audio clips, and video clips—can expand on or demonstrate points made in the text of your document. They can also reduce the text needed to make a point, help readers better understand your points, and increase the visual appeal of your document.

White space— literally, empty space—frames and separates elements on a page.

Columns generally appear in newspaper and magazine articles—and, to a growing extent, in articles published on the Web. Essays, on the other hand, are typically formatted in a single column. Columns can improve the readability of a document by limiting the eyes' physical movement across the page and by framing other elements.

Margins are the white space between the edge of the page or screen (top, bottom, right, and left) and the text or graphics in your document.

Headings and subheadings identify sections and subsections, serve as transitions, and allow readers to locate information more easily.

Marginal glosses are brief notes in a margin that explain or expand on text in the body of the document.

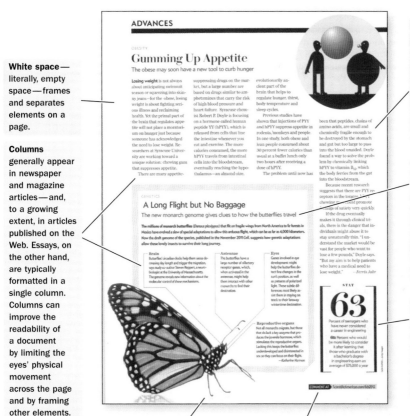

Captions and callouts describe or explain an illustration, such as a photograph or chart.

Headers, footers, and page numbers appear at the top or bottom of the page, set apart from the main text. They help readers find their way through a document; they provide information, such as the title of the document, its publication date, and its author; and they frame a page visually.

Pull quotes (not shown) highlight a passage of text—frequently a quotation—through the use of borders, white space, distinctive fonts, and contrasting colors.

Numbered and bulleted lists (not shown) display brief passages of related information using numbers or symbols (usually round "bullets"). The surrounding white space draws the eye to the list, highlighting the information for your readers, while the brief content in each entry can make concepts or processes easier to understand.

Sidebars (not shown) are brief discussions of information related to, but not a central part of, your document. Sidebars simplify the task of integrating related or supporting information into the body of the article by setting that information off in a clearly defined area.

IV Creating Your Document

FIGURE 16.5 Using Page Layout Elements [Reproduced with permission. Copyright © Scientific American 2012, a division of Nature America, Inc. All rights reserved. Photo: Don Farrall/Getty Images. Thomas Fuchs Illustration.]

Signal the organization of a document. In a longer print document, headers, footers, headings, and sub-headings might be formatted with a particular color to help readers recognize which section they are reading. On a website, pages in each section could share the same background or heading color.

Be consistent. Use the same colors for top-level headings throughout your document, another color for lower-level headings, and so on. Use the same borders and shading for sidebars. Use rules consistently in pull quotes, headers, and footers. Don't mix and match.

Signal the function of text. A colored or shaded background, as well as colored type, can be used to differentiate captions and pull quotes from body text. Rules can also separate columns of text on a page or screen.

THE WELL-BEING BALANCING ACT
Pleasure and purpose work together

EVEN THE MOST ardent strivers will agree that a life of purpose that is devoid of pleasures is, frankly, no fun. Happy people know that allowing yourself to enjoy easy momentary indulgences that are personally rewarding—taking a long, leisurely bath, vegging out with your daughter's copy of *The Hunger Games*, or occasionally skipping your Saturday workout in favor of catching the soccer match on TV—is a crucial aspect of living a satisfying life. Still, if you're primarily focused on activities that feel good in the moment, you may miss out on the benefits of developing a clear purpose. Purpose is what drives us to take risks and make changes—even in the face of hardship and when sacrificing short-term happiness.

Working to uncover how happy people balance pleasure and purpose, Colorado State's Steger and his colleagues have shown that the act of trying to comprehend and navigate our world generally causes us to deviate from happiness. After all, this mission is fraught with tension, uncertainty, complexity, short bursts of intrigue and excitement, and conflicts between the desire to feel good and the desire to make progress toward what we care about most. Yet overall, people who are the happiest tend to be superior at sacrificing short-term pleasures when there is a good opportunity to make progress toward what they aspire to become in life.

If you want to envision a happy person's stance, imagine one foot rooted in the present with mindful appreciation of what one has—and the other foot reaching toward the future for yet-to-be-uncovered sources of meaning. Indeed,

research by neuroscientist Richard Davidson of the University of Wisconsin at Madison has revealed that making advances toward achievement of our goals not only causes us to feel more engaged, it actually helps us tolerate any negative feelings that arise during the journey.

Nobody would pretend that finding purpose is easy or that it can be done in a simple exercise, but thinking about which activities you found most rewarding and meaningful in the past week, what you're good at and often recognized for, what you crave more time for can help. Also, notice whether your answers reflect something you feel that you ought to say as opposed to what you truly love. For example, being a parent doesn't necessarily mean that spending time with your children is the most energizing, meaningful part of your life—and it's important to accept that. Lying to yourself is one of the biggest barriers to creating purpose. The happiest people have a knack for being honest about what does and does not energize them—and in addition to building in time for sensory pleasures each day, they are able to integrate the activities they most care about into a life of purpose and satisfaction. **PT**

TODD B. KASHDAN is a psychologist at George Mason University and the author of *Mindfulness, Acceptance, and Positive Psychology*. **ROBERT BISWAS-DIENER** is the author of *The Courage Quotient*. Together they are coauthoring a book on a new approach to well-being in the business world.

HAPPINESS BY THE NUMBERS

.62 | 40 | 85 | 20

Distance from home, in miles, at which point people's tweets begin declining in expressed happiness (about the distance expected for a short work commute).

The percentage of our capacity for happiness that is within our power to change, according to University of California, Riverside researcher Sonja Lyubomirsky.

Number of residents out of every 100 who report feeling positive emotions in Panama and Paraguay, the most positive countries in the world.

The percentage of the U.S. population wealthy enough that their feelings of happiness are not affected by fluctuations in Americans' income equality.

Sources: The University of Vermont, *The How of Happiness*, Gallup, *Psychological Science*

THERAPISTS: *Interested in receiving Continuing Ed credit for reading this article? Visit* **NBCC.org**

July/August 2013 **Psychology Today** 59

Call attention to important information. Color, borders, and shading can subtly yet clearly emphasize an illustration, such as a table or chart, or an important passage of text, by distinguishing it from the surrounding body text.

FIGURE 16.6 Using Color, Shading, Borders, and Rules [*Psychology Today* © Copyright 2013. www.Psychologytoday.com.]

- **Photographs and other images,** such as drawings, paintings, and sketches, are frequently used to set a mood, emphasize a point, or demonstrate a point more fully than is possible with text alone.

- **Charts, graphs, and tables** represent information visually. They are used to make a point more succinctly than is possible with text alone or to present complex information in a compact and more accessible form. They frequently rely on numerical information.

- **Digital media,** including audio, video, and animations, can bring sound and movement to your document.

As you work with illustrations, keep the following guidelines in mind.

- **Use an illustration for a purpose.** Illustrations are best used when they serve a clear function in your document. Avoid including illustrations simply because you think they might make your document "look better."

- **Place illustrations near the text they illustrate.** In general, place illustrations as close as possible to the point where they are mentioned in the text. If they are not explicitly mentioned (as is often the case with photographs), place them at a point where they will seem most relevant to the information and ideas being discussed.

- **Include a title or caption that identifies or explains the illustration.** The documentation style you are using, such as MLA or APA, will usually offer advice on the placement and format of titles and captions. In general, documentation systems suggest that you distinguish between tables and figures (which include other illustrations), number tables and figures in the order in which they appear in the document, and use compound numbering of tables and figures in longer documents (for example, the second table in Chapter 5 would be labeled "Table 5.2"). Consult the documentation system you are using for specific guidelines on illustrations.

16c

How can I design my document?

Although essays are perhaps the most commonly used assignments in writing courses, you might have the opportunity to decide which genre you'll use to make your contribution to a conversation. Or you might be asked to adapt the contents of an academic essay for presentation in another genre, such as a brochure or Web page. As you consider your choices, you'll find a wide array of documents that you can use to reach your readers. In this chapter, you'll find discussions of how to design some of the most important print and digital genres.

Design an Academic Essay

Some writers might be surprised to see *design* and *academic essay* used in the same sentence. They're aware, of course, that they should use wide margins, readable fonts, and double-spaced lines, and they generally understand that they should do this to help readers—typically an instructor—read and respond to their work. Beyond these elements, however, they think of design as having little or no role in their essays.

They're wrong. Thoughtful design can help you achieve your goals, address your readers' expectations, and adapt to the context in which your essay will be written and read.

Ask How Design Can Help You Achieve Your Goals   Traditionally, essay assignments have focused on the written expression of ideas and arguments. As a result, writers have tended to use images sparingly, if at all, and to make limited use of design elements such as color, shading, borders, and rules in their academic essays. Writers have also tended to avoid the use of tables and charts, perhaps thinking that these kinds of design elements would be more appropriate for genres such as reports and professional articles.

Yet these design elements can help you present complex information and ideas more clearly, distinguish between items considered in an evaluation, illustrate the aspects of a particular problem, or frame your argument by calling readers' attention to particular information and ideas. As you draft your essay, consider how the wide range of design elements discussed on pp. 268–73 might help you accomplish your goals as a writer. As you consider your options, keep in mind your instructor's preferences regarding the use of these elements. If you are uncertain, ask for guidance.

Consider Reader Expectations   Readers approach an essay with a set of writing and design conventions in mind. They expect you to make a main point, to support your point with reasons and evidence, and to identify the sources you've drawn on in your essay. They also expect you to follow generally accepted design conventions, such as the guidelines provided by the documentation systems published by groups such as the MLA and APA (see Part V). You'll frequently find guidance on how to format an academic essay in your assignment. You can also consult your instructor if you have any questions.

As you design your essay, consider not only what your readers expect, but also how you can build on those expectations to accomplish your goals as a writer. You can use design elements such as fonts, color, shading, borders, and rules to help readers anticipate and more easily follow the organization of your essay. You can use tables, charts, and figures to let your readers view, understand, and carry out their own analysis of the information you include in your essay. If you are distributing your essay in digital format, you can help readers access related information, such as video clips, audio clips, animations, and related data sets, via links—or you can embed these materials directly in your essay. You can read more about how these design elements can help you in these areas on pp. 268–73.

View an Essay   The following pages are from an essay written by college freshman Gaele Lopez for his composition class. They reflect his awareness of his instructor's expectations about line spacing, margins, documentation system, page numbers, and inclusion of a title page.

You can view other essays formatted in MLA, APA, *Chicago*, and CSE styles in Part V.

CHECKLIST FOR DESIGNING ACADEMIC ESSAYS

Consider the following design conventions associated with academic essays.

✔ Cover page or essay header, depending on your instructor's preferences or documentation style formatting requirements

✔ Readable body font (example: 12-point Times New Roman)

✔ Double-spaced lines

✔ Wide margins, one inch or larger

✔ Consistent use of assigned documentation system

✔ Headers and footers in a readable font distinct from body font

✔ If used, headings and subheadings formatted in fonts and colors that distinguish them from the body text and show relative importance of heading levels

✔ If used, illustrations labeled and placed either within the text and close to relevant passages or in an appendix, according to your instructor's preferences

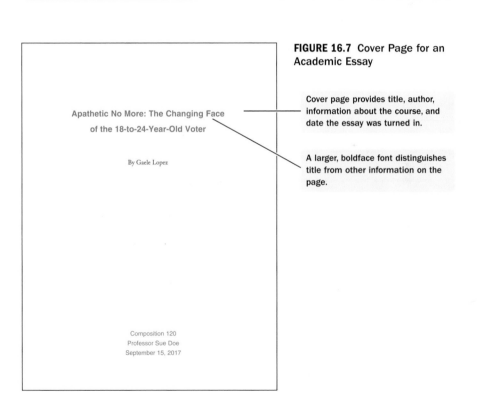

FIGURE 16.7 Cover Page for an Academic Essay

Cover page provides title, author, information about the course, and date the essay was turned in.

A larger, boldface font distinguishes title from other information on the page.

IV Creating Your Document

FIGURE 16.8 First Page of an Academic Essay

A header with writer's last name and page number is repeated at the top of each page.

Title is repeated on first page of essay in a larger, colored, sans-serif font that distinguishes it from the body text.

Body text is set in a serif font, which is more readable than most sans-serif fonts.

All body text is formatted consistently.

One-inch margins and double-spaced lines provide space for the teacher to write comments.

A graph appears near its mention in the text, supporting claims made there.

Lopez 2

Apathetic No More: The Changing Face of the 18-to-24-Year-Old Voter

Ever since 1972, when 18-year-olds gained the right to vote, voter turnout among America's youth has been significantly lower than that of older Americans. Following an initial turnout of 52 percent of younger registered voters in 1972, the percentage declined to an all-time low of only 32 percent in the 1996 presidential election, nearly 30 points below the turnout of voters over the age of 30 (see Figure 1). By the late 1990s, calls for voter reform – even to the point of suggesting that the vote be limited to those over 30, a suggestion once made by Winston Churchill – became all too common. When the 2000 presidential elections showed virtually no change in voting rates, commentators weighed in with criticisms that, at best, portrayed the youngest members of our society as apathetic when it came to politics and, at worst, as a bunch of freeloading slackers.

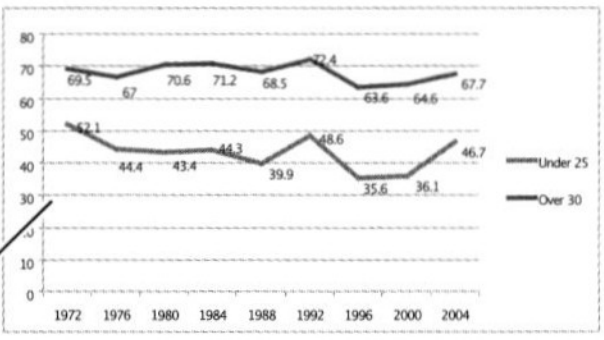

Figure 1. Voter Turnout by Age Group in Presidential Elections (Source: Lopez, Kirby, and Sagoff, 12)

Fortunately, times change. In 2004, turnout among younger voters increased to nearly 47 percent, and by the 2008 elections it seemed likely that turnout might be higher than that recorded in 1972, when anger and frustration over the Vietnam war resulted in the largest turnout to date among younger voters.

FIGURE 16.9 Interior Page of an Academic Essay

Lopez 3

In the 2008 primaries, turnouts among younger voters doubled, tripled, and in some case quadrupled the turnouts recorded in any previous primary (Pew Charitable Trust, par. 2). Analysts – even some of those who had suggested raising the voting age – quickly began to investigate why younger voters were turning out in such unprecedented numbers, what impact their votes would have on the upcoming presidential election, and what this change in behavior would have on future elections.

Factors Contributing to the Change in Voting Behaviors

Why the sudden change? Or is it as sudden as it seems? Analysts Mark Hugo Lopez, Emily Kirby, and Jared Sagoff, writing after the 2004 presidential elections, pointed to "the confluence of extensive voter outreach efforts, a close election, and high levels of interest in the 2004 campaign" as factors that drove turnout among younger voters to "levels not seen since 1992" (1). They cautioned, however, that it was unclear whether the 2004 results were indicators of a significant change or simply an aberration.

It would appear, based on patterns seen in the 2006 mid-term elections and in the 2008 presidential primaries, that there really is evidence of a change. In its report on record turnout in the 2008 primaries and caucuses, the Pew Charitable Trust notes,

The research showed that college students are deeply concerned about issues, involved personally as volunteers and ready to consider voting. But they want political leaders to be positive, to address real problems and to call on all Americans to be constructively involved (par. 5).

As we look toward the fall 2008 elections, it seems clear that young voters will not only play an important role in the election, but might in fact play the deciding role. Voters such as Reid Vincent,

A heading, formatted in blue and using a sans-serif font that differs from the serif body font, calls attention to a shift in Gaele's argument.

Block quotation is set off by indenting the margins on both sides. Quotation marks are not needed for block quotations.

FIGURE 16.10 Works Cited Page of an Academic Essay

Reference page is titled "Works Cited" per MLA style.

MLA format is used to cite sources. Entries are double-spaced and have a hanging indent.

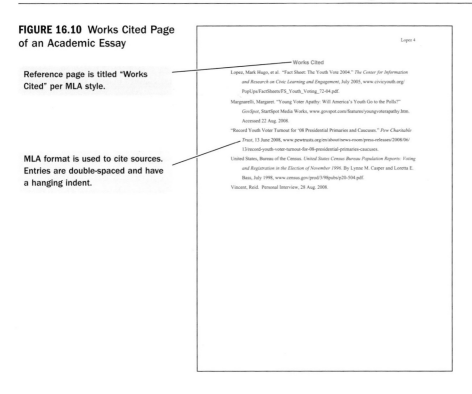

Design a Multimodal Essay

Multimodal essays are characterized by their essayistic form and their use of multiple types of illustrations. As essays, they present information in a linear sequence, one idea after another. As multimodal documents, they combine text with images, animation, sound, and/or video to establish a line of argument and support the writer's points.

Consider Your Purpose and Role   Multimodal essays require careful selection and organization of sources not only for their content, but also for the manner in which they appeal to readers. Depending on your argument, you might find that an embedded video clip is likely to be more effective than an audio clip or image. In each case, your purpose and role as well as your understanding of your readers' needs, interests, values, beliefs, experiences, and knowledge of the issue will affect your decisions about content and design.

Consider Reader Expectations about Design   Multimodal essays have emerged quite recently as a distinct genre. Your readers are likely to expect only that you'll provide a linear document that contains one or more types of embedded media; uses fonts, colors, borders, and lines consistently and effectively; and is designed to be viewed on a computer screen or tablet. If you develop an extended essay, such as the multimodal essay created by Lauren Mack, your readers are also likely to expect you to provide navigation aids such as tables of contents and page links that will allow them to move easily to different parts of the essay.

IV Creating Your Document

Choose Your Composing Tools Multimodal essays vary widely not only in form but also in the software used to create them. You can create multimedia essays using a word processing program such as Microsoft Word or Apple Pages, a multimedia presentation program such as PowerPoint or KeyNote, website development programs such as Dreamweaver, or Web-based tools such as Wix.com, Wordpress.com, and Google Sites (**sites.google.com**). As you choose your design tools, consider how their distinctive features will help you accomplish your goals as a writer. A word processing program might be a better choice than a multimedia presentation program, for example, if you plan to rely more heavily on text than on images and video. In contrast, a program such as PowerPoint offers more options for including multimedia elements than most word processing or Web development programs.

i **INFORMATION LITERACY** Microsoft PowerPoint and other multimedia presentation programs, such as Apple Keynote, Google Slides, or OpenOffice Impress, offer a set of tools that are well suited to integrating multimedia sources with text. The Insert Toolbar in PowerPoint, for example, allows you to add images, audio, video, and other media sources along with tables, text boxes, and links. To get started, create a new presentation and click on the Insert menu in the command ribbon.

FIGURE 16.11 PowerPoint's Insert Toolbar

Why Should We Care about the Environment?

We should care because we feel a connection with other living things. As we learn more about this sense of connectedness, we come to realize how important it is that we view the earth not as a set of resources to be exploited but rather as a community.

Yet we so often treat the earth as something that only we inhabit. To some extent, this reflects an unfortunate notion that intelligence can be measured only in human terms. This has proven to be a significant obstacle to efforts to find a way to preserve

FIGURE 16.12 *Text, a video, and images are used on a multimedia presentation slide.*

An image draws the reader's eye and sets the tone for the presentation.

The title and author are presented in readable fonts that stand out against the background.

FIGURE 16.13a Pages from a Multimodal Essay

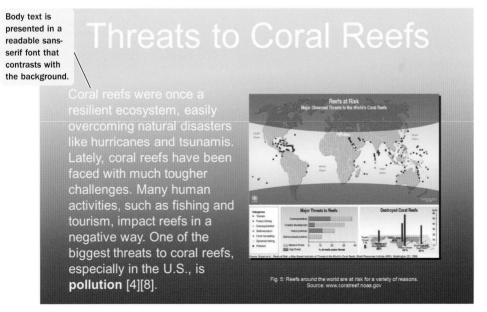

Body text is presented in a readable sans-serif font that contrasts with the background.

FIGURE 16.13b

Importance to Humans

Coral reefs have an estimated worth of **$30 billion** worldwide [9]. Should coral reefs disappear, it is likely that there would be a significant backlash in the fishing industry since a large portion of marine life that we eat such as snapper, grouper, scallop, and many more are found in those habitats [2].

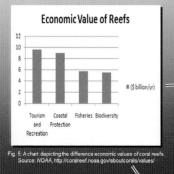

Economic Value of Reefs

■ ($ billion/yr)

Tourism and Recreation Coastal Protection Fisheries Biodiversity

Fig. 5: A chart depicting the difference economic values of coral reefs.
Source: *NOAA*, http://coralreef.noaa.gov/aboutcorals/values/

Those in the fishing industry aren't the only ones making a living off these beautiful ecosystems. In addition to providing food, they also boost their local economies by providing jobs in ecotourism through scuba diving, snorkeling, and recreational fishing [9][1].

Images illustrate key ideas in the text.

Coral reefs also have a reputation for saving us in more ways than one. Not only do reef structures protect our shoreline communities from maritime destruction, but scientists have also discovered that reefs hold a huge potential for medical advancements with compounds found only in coral reef environments [1].

FIGURE 16.13c

Source information and credits are provided for images.

Page headings are formatted consistently throughout the presentation.

Pollution Problems

Pollution has led to events such as global climate change and rising ocean temperatures, making it one of the major factors contributing to the loss of coral reef ecosystems [14].

Some reef problems associated with pollution include:

✳ Bleaching

✳ Ocean Acidification

✳ Marine Debris

A bulleted list previews upcoming points in the presentation.

FIGURE 16.13d

Using a multimedia presentation program to create a multimedia essay invites you to think of the program not as a set of bulleted slides, but as a group of pages that can be filled with various types of media. If you look at each page as a blank canvas, you can see how you might design an essay containing pages that look like those you might find in a magazine or on the Web. ▪

View a Multimodal Essay   The examples on pp. 279–80 are drawn from the multimodal essay written by Lauren Mack. Lauren developed her essay using PowerPoint. Note her use of text, illustrations, color, headings and subheadings, and menus to clearly convey her argument about the impact of climate change on coral reefs.

CHECKLIST FOR CREATING MULTIMODAL ESSAYS

✔ Use your experiences writing academic essays as a foundation for your work on a multimodal essay.

✔ Reflect on your purpose and role, the expectations of your readers, and the context in which your essay will be written and read.

✔ Choose your composing tools, keeping in mind their appropriateness for your writing situation and their tendency to drive design decisions in particular directions.

✔ Develop an appropriate and consistent design for your document, paying particular attention to issues such as the following:

- Consistent use of fonts, colors, shading, borders, and rules
- Readable heading and subheading fonts (example: 16-point Times New Roman or Verdana)
- Readable body font designed for onscreen reading (example: 11-point Calibri or Georgia)
- Placement of titles, text, and illustrations, with illustrations labeled and located near relevant text passages
- If used, transitions between pages (dissolves, page flips) quick and not distracting
- If used, background images and sounds chosen to enhance rather than obscure the elements on each page

✔ Create navigation tools such as next and previous buttons, links, menus, and tables of contents.

IV Creating Your Document

Design an Article

Articles appear in a wide range of publications, including newspapers, magazines, scholarly and professional journals, and websites, among others. Articles rely heavily on information obtained from sources such as books, websites, government reports, interviews, surveys, and observation. Article writers should consider several factors that affect design: the overall design of the publication in which they hope to place their article, the audience the publication addresses, the subjects typically written about in the publication, and the style and tone used in other articles in the publication.

Consider Your Purpose and Role   Articles are written for a wide range of purposes, from informing to evaluating to entertaining to persuading or convincing. As you consider potential design choices, keep your purpose and role in mind. If you are informing your readers about a complex concept, for example, you might use a diagram or chart to convey information in a way that would be difficult to do through words alone. If you are trying to persuade your readers to take action, you might select a color scheme that sets a particular mood or insert an image that evokes a strong emotional response.

Consider Reader Expectations about Design   Because most articles are written for a specific publication, writers typically have a clear picture of their readers (age, income, education, hobbies, and so forth) and can develop a line of argument that directly addresses their needs and interests. An article about an election, for example, might report on turnout among younger voters, offer a profile of a recently elected senator from the Midwest, or describe the activities of an organization such as the League of Women Voters.

Depending on the publication you are targeting, your article might use headings and subheadings, columns, sidebars, pull quotes, and a wide array of illustrations. To gain an understanding of your readers' expectations about the design of your article, scan other articles in the publication. Take note of the range of design choices in the articles. Then read a few of the articles more closely to gain insights into the choices the writers made as they wrote and designed their articles.

My Research Project

Analyze a Target Publication

Analyzing a publication involves asking questions about its readers, the subject its articles address, its writing conventions, and its design. To locate a print publication, visit your library's periodicals room (p. 167) or consult a reference librarian. You can also search for information about the publication on the Web (p. 162) or in databases (p. 159). To locate information about a digital publication, such as *Slate*, visit its website, conduct database searches, or consult a reference librarian.

In your research log, record your answers to the following questions about the publication to which you will submit your article.

Readers

Examine the publication as a whole to learn what you can about its readers.

- Can you find a "letters to the editor" section? If so, reading the letters and any responses from the editors might give you insights into who reads the publication and why they read it.

- If there are advertisements in the publication, do they tell you anything about the readers? Who advertises in the publication? What products or services do they offer or what issues or problems do they address?

- What can you learn about the readers from the range of subjects or issues addressed in articles and other parts of the publication?
- Can you find any information about the publisher? Can you tell whether it is a commercial enterprise, a government agency, a nonprofit organization, a scholarly or professional organization, or an individual? Does the publication have a mission statement? Does it describe its purpose or goals, the audience it hopes to reach, or its origins? If so, what does it tell you about the target audience?

Subjects

Look at recently published articles in the publication. You can often find them in tables of contents, indexes, and archives. Depending on the publication, you might also be able to search a full-text database (p. 159) or search the Web for archived articles.

- What issues and subjects are addressed in articles?
- How long are the articles? What are the shortest? What are the longest? Where do they fall on average?
- What do you think is the purpose of the publication? Is its goal to inform, to advocate, to address problems? Or does it address a range of purposes?

Writing Conventions

Study the articles in the publication to learn about its writing conventions.

- How would you characterize the style and tone of the articles? Is it generally formal, informal, or somewhere in between? Are contractions (*can't, won't, isn't*) used? Are individuals identified by their full names and titles (Dr. Shaun Beaty)?
- How are sources identified? Do the articles use an in-text citation system, such as MLA, APA, *Chicago*, or CSE (see Part V)? Do they use footnotes or endnotes? Do they link directly to the source? Do they informally identify the source?
- What do the authors of articles seem to assume about their readers? Do they use specialized language (or jargon)? Do they expect you to know a great deal about the subject? Do you think the authors expect you to be an expert in the field to understand their articles?

Design

To gain an understanding of your readers' expectations about the design of your article, scan articles in the publication, read a few carefully, and take notes.

- Would you characterize the articles as heavy on text? Or are images, tables, charts, figures, and other illustrations used? If the article is published in a digital format, does it include audio or video clips? Does it include other digital illustrations, such as animations or apps that a reader could work with?
- How is color used in the article, if at all? Does the article make use of borders, rules, and shading?
- Does the article use headings and subheadings? If so, how are they formatted? What kinds of fonts are used? Is there much variety in the fonts?
- How is the article laid out? Does it use columns? Sidebars? Block quotes?

View an Article The articles that follow were published in the *DePaulia*, the student newspaper at DePaul University. Paired with photos, the articles make use of font formatting and visual elements to set a mood, call attention to key points, and convey information.

Images in the masthead call attention to articles elsewhere in the newspaper.

The masthead (title) at the top of the front page contrasts with the text and the headlines for individual articles.

Bylines are set in a bold font to differentiate them from main body text.

Captioned photos add visual interest and information.

The newspaper article is formatted in columns.

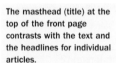

FIGURE 16.14 Front Page of a Student Newspaper [*The DePaulia*/depauliaonline.com.]

CHECKLIST FOR DESIGNING ARTICLES

With the results of your publication analysis in mind, consider the following design conventions.

✔ Column layout appropriate for target publication and target audience

✔ Line spacing typically single-space

✔ Readable body font (example: 10- or 11-point Century Schoolbook)

✔ Color, borders, shading, and rules used appropriately

✔ Heading and subheadings formatted in fonts and colors that distinguish them from body text and show the relative importance of heading levels

✔ Illustrations labeled and placed near relevant passages

Design a Website

Websites consist of linked pages, typically organized through a home page and navigational devices such as menus, tables of contents, indexes, and site maps. The main pages of websites usually provide broad overviews of the topic, and related pages add detailed information.

Consider Your Purpose and Role   Websites are able to engage readers in ways that print documents cannot: They can link directly to related sites, allow visitors to access video and audio files, and support communication among the site's readers and writers. This wealth of design and navigation options, however, carries significant design challenges for writers. As you consider your purpose in developing a website, you must reflect not only on what you hope to accomplish—informing or persuading readers, for example—but also on design elements that can help you achieve your purpose. Key considerations include helping readers move easily through your site, formatting text to highlight important information and ideas, and selecting effective digital illustrations.

Consider Reader Expectations about Design   Given the wide range of individuals with access to the Web, writers must anticipate the needs of a much more diverse group of readers than is the case with documents distributed in print. Designers of websites, as a result, typically attempt to provide their readers with a significant amount of guidance about the purpose, content, and organization of their sites on the pages readers usually visit first. This guidance can include site menus, tables of contents, links to pages that provide information about the site, and links to pages that provide contact information (see Figures 16.15–16.17).

Over the past decade, the appearance of many websites has grown similar to that of magazines, with a heavy use of images and other illustrations. Writers typically design a website with many of the same considerations they apply to the pages in a magazine article, choosing a unified color scheme, formatting headings and subheadings consistently across pages, and using borders, shading, and rules in a manner similar to that of many print publications. They must also

IV Creating Your Document

address, however, the placement and appearance of navigation menus and digital illustrations, such as audio and video clips, animations, and embedded programs and downloadable files.

View Pages from a Website

A side menu provides links to pages on the site.

A list of sources referenced on the site is available. Information about the author is provided.

A large heading identifies the issue addressed by the site.

Search allows readers to locate information on the site.

Body text is formatted in a serif font that is easy to read.

A bulleted list calls attention to important information.

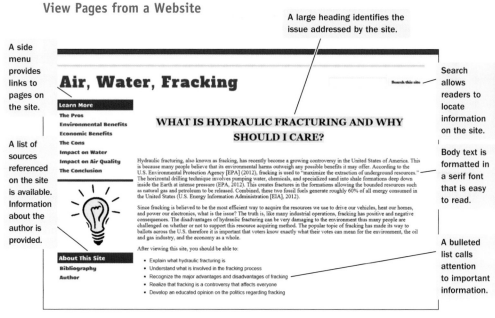

FIGURE 16.15 Website Home Page

A link to the site main page is provided on all pages.

Headings use a larger font and a contrasting color.

The side menu appears in the same place on every page.

A title appears above a chart.

A chart illustrates a key point raised in the body text.

Source information is provided. The font uses a contrasting color.

FIGURE 16.16 Website Content Page
[U.S. Energy Information Administration.]

Extra space after each paragraph helps differentiate one from another.

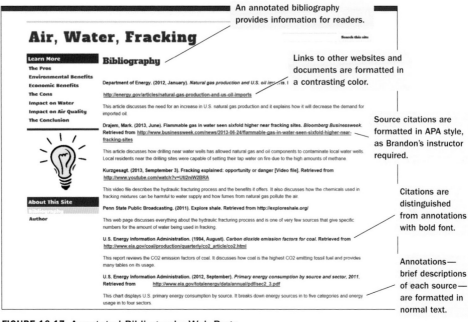

FIGURE 16.17 Annotated Bibliography Web Page

CHECKLIST FOR DESIGNING WEBSITES

✔ Organizational structure consistent with the purpose of the site and the needs and expectations of readers

✔ Home page provides links to main pages on the site

✔ Home page and main pages offer navigation tools appropriate for readers of the site

✔ Overall design consistent across the site (placement of titles, text, and navigation tools; use of fonts, colors, rules, and illustrations)

✔ Information presented in brief, readable chunks, using bulleted and numbered lists whenever possible

✔ Readable body font in font family designed for onscreen reading (examples: 11-point Verdana or Georgia)

✔ Headings and subheadings formatted in fonts and colors that distinguish them from body text and show relative importance of heading levels

✔ Labels, captions, and pop-up flags used to help readers understand links and images

✔ Color used to set a mood, highlight information, and help readers understand the function of text and illustrations on the site

✔ Illustrations placed near the passages to which they refer

✔ Images kept as small (in kilobytes) as possible, while being clear and easy to see

✔ Contact information and other relevant information included and easy to locate

QUICK REFERENCE

Designing Documents

✔ Understand the design principles of balance, emphasis, placement, repetition, and consistency. (p. 265)

✔ Design to achieve your purposes. (p. 266)

✔ Design to address your readers' needs, interests, values, and beliefs. (p. 267)

✔ Design to address genre conventions. (p. 268)

✔ Use design elements—such as fonts, line spacing, alignment, page layout, color, shading, borders, rules, and illustrations—appropriately to increase the readability and effectiveness of your document. (p. 268)

✔ Consider purpose, role, and reader expectations to design academic essays, multimodal essays, articles, and websites. (p. 273)

17

Revising and Editing

> **Key Questions**

17a. What should I focus on as I revise my document? 290
Consider your writing situation
Consider your argument and ideas
Consider your use and integration of sources
Consider the structure and organization of your document
Consider genre and design

17b. What strategies should I use to revise? 292
Save multiple drafts
Highlight your main point, reasons, and evidence
Challenge your assumptions
Scan, outline, and map your document
Ask for feedback

17c. What should I focus on as I edit my document? 297
Focus on accuracy
Focus on economy
Focus on consistency
Focus on style
Focus on spelling, grammar, and punctuation

17d. What strategies should I use to edit? 298
Read carefully
Mark and search your document
Use spelling, grammar, and style tools with caution
Ask for feedback

When writers revise and edit, they evaluate the effectiveness of their drafts and, if necessary, work to improve them. Although the two processes are related, they focus on different aspects of a document. Revising involves assessing how well a document responds to a specific writing situation, presents a main point and reasons to accept that point, and uses evidence. Editing includes evaluating and improving the expression—at the sentence and word levels—of the information, ideas, and arguments in the document.

289

17a

What should I focus on as I revise my document?

Revising involves rethinking and reenvisioning your document. It focuses on such big-picture issues as whether the document you've drafted is appropriate for your writing situation; whether your argument is sound and well supported; whether you've organized and presented your information, ideas, and arguments clearly and effectively; and whether you've made appropriate decisions about genre and design.

Consider Your Writing Situation ❓ WHAT'S MY PURPOSE?

As you revise, ask whether your document helps you achieve your purpose. If your goal is to inform readers about a particular subject, ask whether you've provided appropriate information, whether you've given enough information, and whether that information is presented clearly. If your purpose is to convince or persuade your readers in some way, ask whether you have chosen appropriate reasons and evidence and presented your argument as effectively as you can.

Review as well your readers' needs, interests, values, beliefs, and knowledge of the issue. Imagine how your readers will react to your document by asking questions such as these.

- Will my readers trust what I have to say? How can I establish my credibility?
- Will my readers have other ideas about how to address this issue? How can I convince them that they should believe what I say?
- Will my readers find my evidence appropriate and accurate? Is my selection of evidence consistent with their values and beliefs?

Finally, identify your requirements, limitations, and opportunities. Ask yourself whether you've met the specific requirements of the assignment, such as length and number of sources. Evaluate your efforts to work around limitations, such as lack of access to information. Think about whether you've taken full advantage of your opportunities and any new ones that have come your way.

Consider Your Argument and Ideas [FRAMING MY ARGUMENT]

As you revise, ask how well you are conveying your argument and ideas to your readers. First, check the clarity of your thesis statement. Is it phrased in a way that is compatible with the needs, interests, values, and beliefs of your readers? Second, ask whether the argument and ideas in your document help your readers understand and accept your thesis statement. As you make this assessment, keep in mind the role or roles you've decided to adopt—such as informing your readers, interpreting or analyzing, or advocating for a particular position.

Consider Your Use and Integration of Sources

Think about how you've used source information in your document. First, review the amount of support you've provided for your points and the appropriateness of that support for your purpose and readers. Then, if you are arguing about an issue, determine whether you've identified and addressed reasonable opposing viewpoints.

It's also important that you integrate your sources effectively into your document and acknowledge them according to the documentation system you are following. Ensure that you have cited all your sources and that you've clearly distinguished between your ideas and those of other writers. Review your works cited or reference list for completeness and accuracy. Remember that improper documentation can reduce your document's effectiveness and your credibility.

Consider the Structure and Organization of Your Document

Your readers should be able to locate information and ideas easily. As you read your introduction, ask whether it clearly and concisely conveys your main point and whether it helps your readers anticipate the structure and organization of your document. Reflect on the appropriateness of your organizing pattern (p. 215) for your purpose and readers. If you've used headings and subheadings, evaluate their effectiveness.

Make sure your document is easy to read. Check for effective paragraphing and paragraph structure. If you have a number of small paragraphs, you might combine paragraphs with similar ideas. If you have a number of long paragraphs, break them up and add transitions. Finally, ask whether your conclusion leaves your readers with something to think about. The most effective conclusions typically provide more than a summary of your document.

Consider Genre and Design

Consider both the genre—or type—of document that you are writing (p. 268) and your use of design principles and elements (see Chapter 16). Ask whether the choices you've made about the content and style of your document are consistent with your readers' expectations about that type of document. Be sure to consider, for example, issues such as level of formality, accepted sources of evidence, and organization.

Take a careful look, as well, at how you've designed your document. Does it resemble what your readers will expect? For example, if you're writing an academic essay, have you double-spaced your lines, used a readable font, and set wide margins? If you are creating a website, have you made it easy for your readers to find their way around? Have you used design principles and elements to achieve your purpose and address the needs and interests of your readers?

IV Creating Your Document

17b

What strategies should I use to revise?

You can draw on several strategies to review and improve your document. These strategies range from saving multiple drafts of your document to assessing its argument and organization to obtaining feedback from others.

Save Multiple Drafts

You might not be happy with every revision you make. To avoid wishing that you hadn't made extensive revisions to a draft of your document, save a new copy of your draft before every major revising session. Name your drafts by number — as in Draft1.docx, Draft2.docx, and so on — or by date, as in Draft-April6.docx and Draft-April10.docx. Or come up with a naming system that works for you. What's important is that you save multiple versions of your drafts in case you don't like the changes you've made.

Highlight Your Main Point, Reasons, and Evidence

As you revise, ensure that your main point (usually expressed as a thesis statement), reasons, and evidence are fully developed. An effective way to do this is to identify and examine each element in your draft, both individually and as a group of related points. If you are working with a printed document, use a highlighter, colored pens or pencils, or sticky notes. If you are working in a word processing program, use the highlighting tools to mark the text. You might use different colors to highlight your main point, supporting points, and evidence. If you are focusing solely on the evidence in your document, use different colors to highlight evidence from different sources (to help you check whether you are relying too heavily on a single source) or to differentiate the types of evidence you are using (such as quotations, paraphrases, summaries, and numerical data).

Challenge Your Assumptions

It's easy to agree with an argument that you've developed. Challenge your main idea, reasons, and evidence by using one of the following strategies. Keep track of your challenges by using the Comment tool in your word processor.

- **Put yourself in the place of your readers.** As you read, pretend that you are one of your readers. Try to imagine a single reader — or, if you're ambitious, a group of readers. Ask questions they might ask. Imagine concerns they might bring to their reading of your document. A reader interested in solving a problem might ask, for example, whether a proposed solution is cost effective, is more appropriate than alternative solutions, or has unacceptable side effects. As you revise, take these questions and concerns into account.

- **Play devil's advocate.** A devil's advocate raises reasonable objections to ideas and arguments. As you review your document, identify your key claims and pose reasonable objections to them. Make note of these potential objections and take them into account as you revise.

- **Play the "so what?" game.** As you read your document, ask why readers would care about what you are saying. By asking "so what?" questions, you can gain a better understanding of what your readers are likely to care about and how they might respond to your arguments and ideas. Make note of your responses to these questions and consider them as you revise.

Scan, Outline, and Map Your Document

ⓘ INFORMATION LITERACY Use the following strategies to review the structure and organization of your document.

- **Scan headings and subheadings.** If you have used headings and subheadings, they can help you track the overall flow of your argument and ideas. Ask whether the organization they reveal is appropriate for your writing situation and your role as a writer.

- **Scan the first sentence of each paragraph.** A quick reading of the first sentence in each paragraph can reveal points at which your argument shifts. As you note these shifts, think about whether they are appropriate and effective.

- **Outline your document.** Create a topical or sentence outline of your document (p. 219) to assess its structure and organization. This strategy, sometimes called a *reverse outline*, helps you identify the sequence of your points and amount of space you've devoted to each aspect of your document. If you are viewing your document in a word processor, use the Styles tool to assign levels to headings in your document and then view it in outline view.

- **Map your document.** On paper, in a word processing program, or in a graphics program, draw a visual map of your document. Show relationships among your ideas by using lines, arrows, circles, and (in a word processing or drawing program) text boxes. Like an outline, a map can help you identify the organization of your points and the amount of evidence you've used to support them. ▮

As you review the organization and structure of your document, reflect on whether it is appropriate given your purpose, readers, argument, and available information.

Ask for Feedback

After spending long hours on a project, you may find it difficult to identify problems your readers might have with your draft. You might read the same paragraph eight times, failing to notice that the evidence you are using to support a point actually contradicts it. Or you might not notice that your document's

IV Creating Your Document

TUTORIAL

How do I strengthen my argument during revision?

By this point in your research writing process, you are probably quite comfortable with your argument. But what would a reader with fresh eyes think? Imagine that you are a reader encountering this essay for the first time, and then respond as the author. The following comments are drawn from a review of a draft written by featured writer Nicholas Brothers.

	Reader's Comments	**Author's Responses**
① Look for confusing or unclear points. As you read the essay, do any questions form in your mind? Write down your questions, then—wearing your author's hat again—consider how your essay can address them more fully.	—You mention mercenaries, but it's not clear how they're different from contractors. —You say that contractors are under different rules than members of the military, but it's not clear why.	—Must distinguish the two roles more clearly; maybe provide a historical look at the differences and do a direct comparison —Need to sort out the reasons behind the different codes of justice and make these more clear
② Play devil's advocate. Identify your key claims and pose reasonable objections to them. Consider how you could address them in your essay.	—You claim that contractors have abused their power, but haven't there been cases of soldiers committing crimes?	—Need to include this point—and talk about accountability of military vs. contractors
③ Play the "so what?" game. As a reader, consider why you should care about this topic. Then respond to help readers identify the significance of your issue.	—What if I'm not interested in private military corporations? Why should I pay attention?	—Talk about the "brain drain" on our armed forces—good soldiers going to PMCs rather than continuing to serve in the military —Address national security threats made worse by PMCs

---

CHECKLIST FOR REVISING

✔ **Review your research writing situation.** Ask whether your document helps you achieve your purposes; addresses your readers' needs, interests, values, and beliefs; meets your requirements; effectively works around limitations; and takes advantage of opportunities. (p. 290)

✔ **Evaluate your argument and ideas.** Ask whether your document provides a clear and appropriate thesis statement and whether your argument and ideas support your thesis statement and are consistent with your roles. (p. 290)

✔ **Assess your use and integration of sources.** Ask whether you have offered adequate support for your points, considered reasonable opposing viewpoints, integrated and acknowledged your sources, and distinguished between your work and that of other writers. (p. 291)

✔ **Examine the structure and organization of your document.** Ask whether the introduction is clear and concise, conveys your main point accurately, and helps your readers anticipate the structure of your document. Also think about whether the organizational structure is easy to follow, paragraphs are easy to read, and transitions are effective. Ask whether the conclusion provides more than a summary of the document. (p. 291)

✔ **Evaluate genre and design.** Ask whether the genre you've created helps you accomplish your purpose. Check that you've followed the style and design conventions associated with the type of document you've created. (p. 291)

✔ **Use effective revision strategies.** Create multiple drafts to preserve earlier work; review your document to assess its argument and organization; get feedback from other writers. (p. 292)

---

organization could confuse your readers. You can ask for feedback on your draft from a friend, relative, colleague, or writing center tutor. It's generally a good idea to ask for help from someone who will be frank as well as supportive and to be specific about the kinds of comments you're looking for. Hearing "It's just fine" from a reviewer will not help you revise.

IV Creating Your Document

WORKING TOGETHER

Use Peer Review to Improve Your Document

One of the biggest challenges writers face is reading a draft of their own work as a reader rather than as the writer. Because you know what you're trying to say, you find it easy to understand your draft. To determine how you should revise your draft, ask a friend or classmate to read your essay and consider the questions below.

Purpose

1 What do you see as the purpose of the document? Did you learn anything new? Did it change your understanding of or attitudes toward the issue? Did it make you want to take action on the issue?

2 Is the design of the document appropriate for its purpose? How could it be improved?

Readers

3 Did you find the document interesting, persuasive, or otherwise useful? Why or why not?

4 Do the information, ideas, and arguments included in the document seem to take into account readers' needs, interests, values, beliefs, knowledge, and experience? How could this be improved?

5 Does the document seem fair? Did you detect any bias or agenda in the way information, ideas, and arguments were presented?

6 Did you find the reasons and evidence in the document convincing? What could I change to improve my argument?

7 Did you find the appeals appropriate? Effective? How could they be improved?

8 Did you notice any logical fallacies or other problems in reasoning?

Source

9 Does the document make sense? Can anything be added, clarified, or rearranged to help you understand the issue better? Do you think any of the details are unnecessary?

10 Do the sources strike you as reliable and appropriate? Does any of the information included in the document seem questionable?

Context

11 Is the subject sufficiently narrow and focused? Is the thesis statement clear?

12 Would any of the information be better presented in visual form?

13 Is the physical appearance of the document appropriate? Did you find the font easy to read? Did you find it easy to make comments?

For each of the points listed above, ask your reviewers to provide concrete advice about what you should do to improve your draft. It can help if you ask them to adopt the role of an editor—someone who is working with you to improve your draft.

17c

What should I focus on as I edit my document?

Before you begin to edit, remember that editing involves assessing the effectiveness, accuracy, and appropriateness of the words and sentences in a document, not its overall structure or ideas. If you're uncertain about whether you've organized your document as effectively as possible or whether you've provided enough support for your argument, deal with those issues first. In the same way that you wouldn't start painting a house until you've finished building the walls, hold off on editing until you're confident that you're finished revising.

Focus on Accuracy

You'll risk damaging your credibility if you provide inaccurate information in your document. To reduce this risk, do the following.

- **Check your facts and figures.** Your readers might think you're deliberately misleading them if you fail to provide accurate information. As you edit, return to your original sources or your notes to check any facts and figures.

- **Check every quotation.** Return to your original sources or consult your notes to ensure that you have quoted each source exactly. Make sure that you have noted any changes to a quotation with ellipsis marks or brackets (p. 254), and make sure that those changes haven't altered the original meaning of the passage. Make sure you have cited the source in the text and in a works cited or reference list.

- **Check the spelling of every name.** Don't rely on spelling checkers, which provide the correct spelling for only the most common or prominent names.

Focus on Economy

Editing for economy involves reducing the number of words needed to express an idea or convey information to your readers. Removing unnecessary modifiers and wordy introductory or stock phrases can make your writing more concise and to the point (p. 233). Editing for economy generally makes it easier for your readers to understand your meaning. However, you should use care when you edit for economy; your readers still need to understand the point you are trying to make.

Focus on Consistency

Editing your document for consistency helps you present information in a uniform way. Use the following techniques to edit for consistency.

- **Treat concepts consistently.** Review your document for consistent treatment of concepts, information, ideas, definitions, and anecdotes.

IV Creating Your Document

- **Use numbers consistently.** Check the documentation system you are using for its guidelines on the treatment of numbers. You might find that you should spell out the numbers zero through ten and use arabic numerals for numbers larger than ten.

- **Treat your sources consistently.** Avoid referring to some sources using first names and to others using honorifics, such as *Dr.*, *Mr.*, or *Ms.* Also check that you have cited your sources appropriately for the documentation style you are using, such as MLA or APA. Review each reference for consistent presentation of names, page numbers, and publication dates.

- **Format your document consistently.** Avoid any inconsistencies in your use of fonts, headings and subheadings, and tables and figures.

Focus on Style

Your readers will judge you—and what you have to say—not only on what you say but also on how you say it. Edit for matters of style by choosing the right words, using active and passive voice appropriately, adopting a consistent point of view, rewriting complex sentences, varying your sentence length and structure, providing transitions, and avoiding sexist language (see Chapter 14).

Focus on Spelling, Grammar, and Punctuation

Poor spelling doesn't necessarily affect your ability to get your point across— in most cases readers will understand even an atrociously spelled document—but it does affect what your readers think of you. Ignore enough spelling errors in your document and you'll erode their confidence in your ability to present information or make an argument. The same goes for grammar and punctuation. If you haven't made sure that subjects and verbs agree and that sentences end with the appropriate punctuation, a reader might not trust that you have presented your facts correctly.

17d

What strategies should I use to edit?

Thorough editing involves making several passes through your document to ensure that you've addressed accuracy, economy, and consistency; style; and spelling, grammar, and punctuation. The following tips can make that process both easier and more productive.

Read Carefully

As you've worked on your document, you've become quite familiar with it. As a result, it can be easy to read what you meant to write instead of what you actually wrote. The following strategies can help you read with fresh eyes.

- **Set your document aside before you edit.** If time permits, allow a day or two to pass before you begin editing your document. Taking time off between revising and editing can help you see your writing with new eyes.

- **Pause between sentences for a quick check.** Avoid getting caught up in the flow of your document—where the meaning takes precedence over the structure and expression of your sentences—by stopping after each sentence. Slowing down can help you identify problems with your text.

- **Read aloud.** Reading your document aloud can help you find problems that might not be apparent when it's read silently.

- **Read in reverse order.** To check for problems with individual sentences, start at the end of your document and read the last sentence first, then work backward through the document. To check for problems at the word level, read each word starting with the last one in the document. Disrupting the normal flow of your document can alert you to problems that might not stand out when it's read normally.

Mark and Search Your Document

INFORMATION LITERACY Use the following marking and searching strategies to edit for accuracy, consistency, and use of sexist language.

Mark Your Document As you read, use a highlighting pen or the highlighter tool in your word processor to mark errors or information that should be double-checked. Consider using different colors to highlight specific types of problems, such as sexist language or inconsistent use of formal titles.

Use the Find and Replace Tools Use your word processor to edit concepts, names, numbers, and titles for consistency and accuracy. Once you've identified a word or phrase that you'd like to check or change, you can search for it throughout your document. If you are referring to sources using a parenthetical style, such as MLA or APA, use the Find tool to search for an opening parenthesis. If you discover that you've consistently misspelled a word or name, use the Replace tool to correct it throughout your document.

Use the Split Window Tool Some word processors allow you to split your window so that you can view different parts of your document at the same time. Use this tool to ensure that you are referring to a concept in the same way throughout your document or to check for consistent use of fonts, headings, subheadings, illustrations, and tables. ▧

Use Spelling, Grammar, and Style Tools with Caution

INFORMATION LITERACY Most word processors provide tools to check spelling, grammar, punctuation, and style. Used with an awareness of their limitations, these tools can significantly reduce the effort required to edit a document.

Spelling checkers have two primary limitations. First, they can't identify words that are spelled correctly but misused—such as *to/two/too*, *their/they're/there*, and *advice/advise*. Second, spelling checkers are ineffective when they run into a word they don't recognize, such as proper names, technical and scientific terms, and unusual words. To compound this problem, spelling checkers often suggest replacement words. If you take the advice, you'll end up with a document full of incorrect words and misspelled names.

The main limitation of grammar, punctuation, and style checkers is inaccurate advice. Although much of the advice they offer is sound, a significant proportion is not. If you are confident about your knowledge of grammar, punctuation, and style, you can use the grammar and style-checking tools in your word processor to identify potential problem areas in your document. You'll find that these tools can point out problems you might have overlooked, such as a subject-verb disagreement that occurred when you revised a sentence. However, if you don't have a strong knowledge of grammar, punctuation, and style, you can easily be misled by inaccurate advice.

If you have any doubts about advice from your spelling checker, consult an up-to-date dictionary. If you have concerns about the suggestions you receive from your grammar, punctuation, and style checker, consult a good handbook. ▮

Ask for Feedback

One of the biggest challenges writers face is reading a draft of their own work as a reader rather than as the writer. Because you know what you're trying to say, you'll find it easy to understand your draft. And because you've read and reread your document so many times, you're likely to overlook errors in spelling, punctuation, and grammar. After you've edited your document, ask a friend, relative, or classmate to proofread it and to make note of any problems.

CHECKLIST FOR EDITING

✔ Ensure your document is accurate. Check facts and figures, quotations, and spelling of names. (p. 297)

✔ Strive for economy. Remove unnecessary modifiers, eliminate unnecessary introductory phrases, and avoid use of stock phrases. (p. 297)

✔ Ensure that your document is consistent. Use concepts, numbers, and source information consistently. Check your document for consistent use of formatting and design. (p. 297)

✔ Use appropriate tone and style. Use appropriate words, rewrite overly complex sentences, and vary sentence length and structure. (p. 298)

✔ Check for correct spelling, grammar, and punctuation. Use your word processor's spelling, grammar, punctuation, and style tools; consult a handbook and dictionary; and ask someone to proofread your draft. (p. 298)

QUICK REFERENCE

Revising and Editing

✔ Focus on the big picture when you revise by keeping your writing situation in mind. (p. 290)

✔ Revise more effectively by saving multiple drafts; highlighting; challenging your assumptions; scanning, outlining, and mapping your document; and asking for feedback. (p. 292)

✔ Focus on accuracy, economy, consistency, style, spelling, grammar, and punctuation when you edit. (p. 297)

✔ Take advantage of editing strategies. (p. 298)

IV Creating Your Document

18

Presenting
Your Work

Key Questions

Writers are frequently asked to present their work to others. In some cases, a presentation accompanies a formal written document, such as a report or a proposal. In other cases, it takes the place of a written document. Traditionally, presentations have involved some form of oral presentation to an audience — anything from a casual talk to a formal address. It is now common, however, to find writers presenting their work in the form of a recorded talk, a set of multimedia slides, or a print or digital portfolio. In this chapter, you'll find discussions of strategies for presenting your work in face-to-face and online settings.

18a

How can I make an oral presentation?

Writers are often asked to make a presentation, lead a discussion, or share their thoughts through speaking rather than writing. The ability to present your ideas through an oral presentation is an important skill that you'll use not only in your courses but also throughout your professional and personal life.

Making an effective oral presentation involves much more than simply taking what you've written and reading it aloud. When you're physically present to share your ideas, your ability to connect personally with your audience is affected by your choice of words, your physical appearance, your ability to maintain eye contact, your use of gestures and other forms of nonverbal communication, and variation in your tone of voice. In addition, your connection with your audience is affected by their ability to follow your line of argument. As you design your presentation, remember that most people find it more difficult to understand complex information, ideas, and arguments when they hear them than when they read (or reread) them. As a result, you should focus on how you can help your listeners follow your line of argument and see you as a credible presenter.

Consider Your Purpose and Audience  **WHAT'S MY PURPOSE?**

The most important thing to remember about designing an oral presentation is engaging your audience and keeping them interested in your ideas. As you plan your presentation, ask what you want to accomplish, what your audience expects to hear, and how you can balance your purpose with their needs and interests. The answers to these questions will shape everything in your speech, from language choices to visual aids.

Narrow Your Scope

How much does your audience know about your topic? With their knowledge and expertise in mind, focus on a few key points and decide how much detail you'll need to provide to help them follow your line of argument. If you have already drafted a written document, use it as the basis for your presentation, but don't try to cover every point and every piece of supporting evidence you've included in your document.

Draw on your thesis statement (p. 199), reasons and evidence (p. 205), and conclusions to create a brief overview of your presentation that you can use in your introductory remarks. This "preview statement" will help your audience gain an understanding of your line of argument and the organization right from the start.

Create a Bare-Bones Outline   [**FRAMING MY ARGUMENT**]

Once you've developed a focus for your presentation and determined its main point and general organization, you can create an outline. It's a good idea to begin with a basic outline that includes the following:

IV Creating Your Document

- an opening line that captures the attention of your audience
- a statement of your main point, typically in the form of a thesis statement
- a sentence establishing your credibility and purpose; your audience should understand that you care about and understand the issue, either through personal experience or through research, and that they can trust what you have to say
- two to four key points
- evidence to support your key points
- transition statements to guide your audience through your talk
- a conclusion that reinforces your audience's understanding of the main ideas they should take away from your talk
- a closing line or an invitation to ask questions that makes it clear to your audience that you have finished your presentation

WORKING TOGETHER

Develop Guidelines for Group Work

Group presentations are a common occurrence in college classrooms and the workplace. Unfortunately, many writers can look back at a group project and find something they didn't like about the experience. They might have had to do far more than their fair share on a project. At the last minute, they might have been left in the lurch by someone who failed to deliver a critical part of the project. Whatever the reason, many writers often prefer to work alone. Yet group work can be productive and satisfying, and most experienced writers can point to a wide range of situations in which working with other writers significantly improved their work on a writing project.

To get ready to work with other writers, reflect on your experiences with group work. Then, working with the members of your group, develop a set of guidelines that would improve the quality of group work. To carry out this activity, follow these steps.

1 Individually, spend five minutes brainstorming (p. 20) or freewriting (p. 21) about your experiences with collaborative work. List both positive and negative experiences.

2 As a group, discuss your experiences. Each person should note the advantages and disadvantages of collaborative work.

3 As a group, identify the most significant challenges to working together effectively.

4 As a group, create a list of guidelines that would address these challenges.

Once you've completed the activity, share your guidelines with other groups in the class. As a class, create a list of guidelines for collaborative work in your course.

Think about Language

In an oral presentation, you'll use spoken language to connect personally with your audience. Through your choice of words, phrases, metaphors, imagery, and turns of speech, you'll engage your listeners in your argument and ideas. Your choices about how to address your audience should be made with the goal of engaging them in your issue. For example, you might talk about how your issue affects "us" and ask them to consider what "we" should do to address it.

As you consider your language choices, keep in mind that spoken language is usually more casual than written language. If you adopt the formal tone of an academic essay, you might sound stiff and unnatural. Keep in mind, as well, the power of repetition in oral presentations. You'll help your audience follow your line of argument by stating important points more than once and in different ways. Finally, consider the role of emotional appeals in your presentation (p. 209). To connect personally with your audience and to engage your audience with your issue, you should explore the use of vivid descriptions, surprising statistics, and humor. Don't rely heavily on emotional appeals, however. To maintain your credibility, you'll want to balance emotional appeals with logic by presenting sound reasoning and support for your argument (p. 205).

Prepare Speaker's Notes

Although many speakers write their presentations word for word, this strategy usually does not produce outstanding results. It's better to develop a set of speaker's notes to prompt yourself as you present your points. Using notes, instead of a word-for-word speech, will force you to speak directly to your listeners. Many seasoned speakers use note cards for their speaker's notes, as they are easy to hold in one hand and are not as distracting as fluttering paper. As you prepare your notes, make sure that they are easy to read, so that you can view your next point with a quick glance. Your speaker's notes should include the following information:

- your opening line, written out in full, in case your mind goes blank due to nervousness
- your preview statement
- any statements that you need to give word for word, such as carefully worded observations about a controversial point or clear descriptions of a complex concept
- your supporting points and reminders of important evidence, including direct quotes, statistics, and names of important people
- transition sentences from one part of the presentation to the next
- memory prompts for parts of your presentation that you've found yourself forgetting as you practice
- reminders to use a visual aid, such as a chart

IV Creating Your Document

Engage with Your Audience

When you give an oral presentation, *how* you say something is almost as important in getting your message across as *what* you say. Important parts of your delivery include the following.

- **Maintain eye contact with your audience.** Eye contact communicates that you know your topic and that you care about making sure the audience understands your argument.

- **Vary the pitch of your voice.** Speaking in a monotone is the fastest way to put your audience to sleep. When you mention a startling statistic, raise your pitch. To demonstrate weight and importance, go to a lower register in your voice. Practice using this vocal variety to make sure that it sounds natural.

- **Speak loudly.** You might feel like you're yelling, but the audience will let you know (by looking surprised) if you are too loud. Speakers rarely are.

- **Articulate every word clearly.** Consonants are often dropped in casual conversation, so you should pay attention to making them clearer than you would in normal speaking.

- **Slow down.** Most presenters speak much too quickly. Slow down your normal rate of speaking to make sure that the audience has time to process your words. As you practice, note where you tend to speed up and add a comment—such as "Slow Down!"—to your speaker's notes.

View Speaker's Notes

Figures 18.1 through 18.3 show speaker's notes from Alexis Alvarez's oral presentation on the use of steroids by adolescent girls involved in sports.

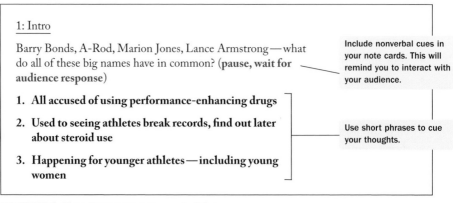

FIGURE 18.1 Note Card with a Nonverbal Cue

2: Establish Credibility & Preview

- My background as an athlete
- Explain why I care about the topic

SLOW DOWN!

Preview:

(1) First, I am going to talk about the positive impact that competitive athletics can have on young women.

(2) Then, I'll go over some of the negative consequences of competitive athletics on these young women, including steroid use.

(3) Finally, I want to talk about what parents and coaches can do to help create a positive athletic experience for these young women.

Use brief reminders about nonverbal communication. Format your nonverbal cues in a different color so you don't accidentally speak them out loud.

Write your preview statement word for word in your notes.

FIGURE 18.2 Note Card with a Preview Statement

3: Positive Impact of Competitive Athletics on Young Women

- President's Council on Physical Fitness and Exercise—ways sports impact young athletes

For the body:

- Less risk of heart disease and certain cancers as adults
- Improves:
  - Immune system
  - Posture
  - Strength
  - Flexibility
  - Endurance

Internal Transition: Also improves mental health

Include your source citations. Refer to your sources to establish your credibility.

Use internal transition cues to provide time for you to switch to your next note card as your audience thinks about the point.

FIGURE 18.3 Note Card with a Transition Cue and a Source Citation

IV Creating Your Document

CHECKLIST FOR DESIGNING ORAL PRESENTATIONS

✔ Determine the presentation's purpose.
✔ Narrow your presentation's scope to between two and four key points.
✔ Write a preview statement.
✔ Choose supporting evidence for your key points.

CHECKLIST FOR DESIGNING ORAL PRESENTATIONS (*continued*)

✔ Create a basic outline of your presentation.

✔ Prepare speaker's notes that you can read easily and quickly.

✔ Consider how the size and physical arrangement of the room will affect your ability to interact with your audience.

✔ Practice your presentation and ask for feedback from your practice audience.

✔ Arrive early to ensure adequate time for setup.

✔ During the presentation, observe and respond to your audience.

✔ Vary the pitch of your voice, speak loudly, and clearly articulate your words.

18b

How can I give a multimedia presentation?

Multimedia presentations allow you to illustrate points using more than spoken words alone, enabling your audience to follow your argument more easily and to understand complex ideas better. During these presentations, slides containing text or graphics are projected on a screen and, in some cases, audio, video, or animations are played. Multimedia presentations can also include links to the Web and embedded applications, such as spreadsheets. Some multimedia presentations are created for delivery via the Web, allowing a larger audience to access the presentation. Web-based multimedia presentations can be designed so that the speaker either appears in a smaller video window next to the presentation slides or provides a voice-over for each slide.

With multimedia presentation programs such as Apple Keynote, Google Slides, Microsoft PowerPoint, Microsoft Sway, and OpenOffice Impress, writers can create well-designed presentations. More specialized programs are also available for particular types of presentations. Prezi (**prezi.com**), for example, allows you to create "zooming" presentations that can be useful for creative purposes such as digital storytelling. Emaze (**emaze.com**), in contrast, offers a Web-based tool that stands out because of its innovative templates.

Consider Your Purpose ❓ WHAT'S MY PURPOSE?

A strong multimedia presentation highlights your points without stealing the show. When used with moderation and created according to good design principles, multimedia elements can add credibility to a presentation, aid your ability to make your argument, and help your audience better understand complex ideas. A presentation on recent changes in education policy, for example, might include video clips in which students, teachers, parents, and community members discuss the effects of those policies or the reasons leading to their development. A presentation on social networking might include links to social networking sites, a chart illustrating the growth in use of such sites over the past decade, or screenshots showing a range of purposes for which such sites are used.

Consider Audience Expectations about Design

Poorly designed multimedia presentations sometimes seem as numerous as grains of sand on a Caribbean beach. Audiences in settings ranging from business meetings to conferences to lecture halls have been subjected to them, and perhaps you have been too. If so, you'll be aware of the benefits of keeping in mind the following design guidelines.

- Keep text to a minimum. A general rule is six words per bullet point, six bullet points per slide, and no more than six slides in a row of all text.
- Use readable fonts, such as 44-point Corbel for headings and 28-point Calibri for body text.
- To enhance the readability of slides, use either a light background with dark text or a dark background with light text.
- Choose a color scheme that reflects the purpose and tone of your line of argument. Use bright colors, for example, for a lighthearted topic. Use neutral colors for a serious presentation.
- Use audio, video, and animation with moderation. Generally, clips should run no longer than one minute each.
- Be consistent in your choice of fonts, colors, and page layout.
- Avoid the use of slow or overly complex transitions between slides.
- Avoid the use of distracting sound effects on slides or during slide transitions.

CHECKLIST FOR DESIGNING MULTIMEDIA PRESENTATIONS

✔ Create an outline of your presentation, focusing on the line of argument you want to present to your audience.

✔ Identify points that would benefit from multimedia illustrations.

✔ Follow effective design principles regarding color scheme, fonts, and page layout.

✔ Use multimedia elements in moderation.

✔ To ensure that your slides are readable and well designed, preview your presentation on a screen similar in size to what you will be using during your talk.

✔ Face your audience as you make your presentation.

✔ Use multimedia elements to advance your line of argument, pointing out important information and illustrations on slides.

✔ Create a backup plan in case technology fails. Consider using handouts as a backup.

View a Multimedia Presentation

Figures 18.4 through 18.7 show slides from a multimedia presentation designed by Elizabeth Leontiev.

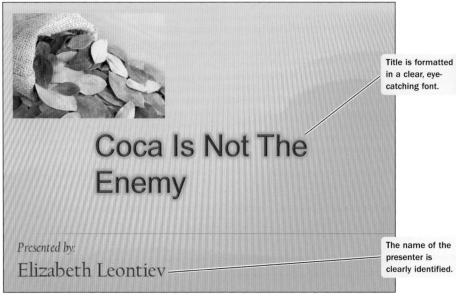

FIGURE 18.4 Title Slide [Ildi Papp/Shutterstock.]

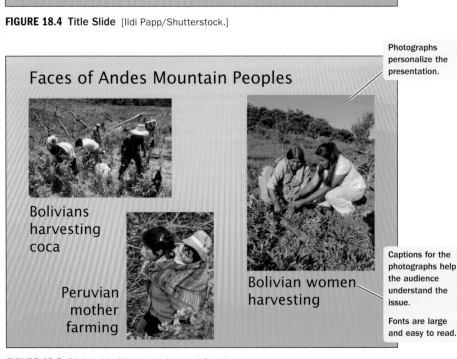

FIGURE 18.5 Slide with Photographs and Captions [*Top left:* AP Photo/Scott Dalton; *bottom left:* Gabor Kovacs Photography/Shutterstock; *right:* Sean Sprague/AGE Fotostock.]

FIGURE 18.6 Slide Supporting the Writer's Presentation [*Left:* Gayvonronskaya-Yang/Shutterstock; *right:* Joerg Reuther/imageBROKER/AGE Fotostock.]

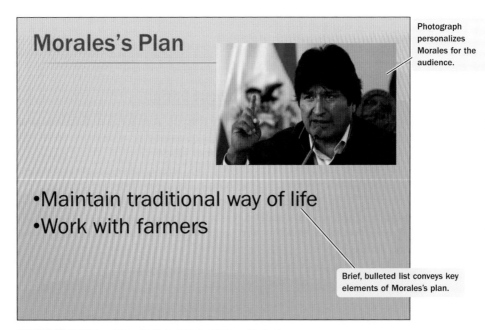

FIGURE 18.7 Slide with a Bulleted List [AP/Juan Karita.]

IV Creating Your Document

18c

How can I create a poster presentation?

Poster presentations are often given at conferences, workshops, or symposiums for particular disciplines and professions. Most poster exhibitions involve numerous presenters, typically in a large room or hallway, and audience members who look for posters that interest them.

Consider Your Purpose and Audience **?** WHAT'S MY PURPOSE?

Your audience will usually have some background knowledge in the discipline or area that your presentation addresses. For example, if you are giving a poster presentation at a microbiology conference, it is safe to assume that the individuals who stop to talk with you will have at least a basic understanding of the central terminology and research methods used in the discipline. You should expect that most members of your audience will spend about five minutes talking with you about a poster. Be prepared, as a result, to provide a brief overview of your project, its key findings, and their significance. You might find it useful to create speaker's notes that you can view between discussions to remind yourself of the key points you want to make.

Be prepared, as well, for likely questions and challenges. The individuals who stop to talk with you will usually have a strong interest in your issue and will want to know what you've learned about it.

Consider Audience Expectations about Design

Posters typically include a large, explanatory title; an abstract that describes your study and its findings; a list of key research questions or a description of the problem or issue that you've addressed; a brief description of your methods; a summary of results; and a list of conclusions and implications. It's best to organize your poster left to right and top to bottom, as most of the people who view your poster will begin reading in the upper left corner. Your poster should be clearly organized and able to stand on its own—that is, your poster should have just enough information to allow someone to gain an understanding of your project and findings.

As you plan your presentation, consider the following design guidelines.

- Limit your use of text by using bulleted and numbered lists, tables, charts, graphs, images, photographs, and diagrams to present information.
- Format your poster so that all text and illustrations can be read from four feet away.

- Use a limited number of complementary fonts.
- Use empty space (sometimes called "white space") to reduce clutter and help your audience identify important information.
- Choose a color scheme that is consistent with your purpose.
- Use color to create interest and capture audience attention.

View a Poster

Figure 18.8 shows a poster developed by Nicholas Brothers about private military corporations.

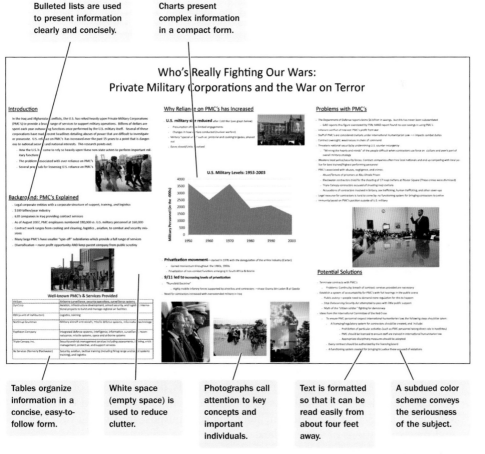

Bulleted lists are used to present information clearly and concisely.

Charts present complex information in a compact form.

Tables organize information in a concise, easy-to-follow form.

White space (empty space) is used to reduce clutter.

Photographs call attention to key concepts and important individuals.

Text is formatted so that it can be read easily from about four feet away.

A subdued color scheme conveys the seriousness of the subject.

FIGURE 18.8 Poster for a Presentation [*Left center:* AP Photo/Karen Tam; *top center:* Bettmann/Getty Images; *center center:* U.S. Department of State; *right center:* Tim Sloan/Getty Images; *bottom left:* Mark Wilson/Getty Images; *bottom center:* Jewel Samad/Getty Images; *bottom right:* Bernd Obermann/Getty Images.]

CHECKLIST FOR DESIGNING POSTER PRESENTATIONS

✔ Narrow your focus. Determine what absolutely needs to be included for a knowledgeable audience to understand your issue.

✔ Prepare a list of likely questions and your responses.

✔ Practice your presentation with a professor, an advisor, a friend, or a family member.

✔ Check for guidelines on poster size (many conferences have specific requirements).

✔ Plan for the physical setup of your poster. Will you need some sort of stand, or are you mounting your material on a board that stands on its own?

✔ Consider how to transport your poster to the site.

✔ During your presentation, remember that most questions are posed out of curiosity, not to catch you off guard. Be polite and professional, and avoid becoming defensive.

✔ Be prepared to share a handout about your project or even a complete written document.

18d

How can I develop a portfolio?

Portfolios are collections of written documents, reflections on the development of those documents, and related materials such as sources, notes, outlines, and brainstorming documents. They are typically, but not always, distributed via the Web. Widely used digital portfolio tools (typically referred to as e-Portfolios) include the e-Portfolio tools integrated into learning management systems such as Blackboard, Brightspace, Canvas, and Moodle. Some writers use programs such as PowerPoint or Dreamweaver to create portfolios that can be presented on a flash drive or some other form of off-line storage. Still others use free Web tools such as Google Sites (**sites.google.com**), Wix (**wix.com**), and WordPress (**wordpress.com**) to create websites to present their portfolios.

Most of these tools allow you to add documents, develop a table of contents, and choose a design template. As you create a portfolio, you should consider a number of issues that affect design, including your purpose for sharing your work and the expectations of your readers.

Consider Your Writing Situation ❓ **WHAT'S MY PURPOSE?**

Portfolios are sometimes created to showcase a writer's work, as might happen when you are seeking a job or wish to share your work with friends and family.

Portfolios are also created in response to class assignments and institutional assessment plans. Some colleges and universities, for example, ask students to create portfolios so that they can measure the overall writing ability of their students.

Readers are likely to expect your portfolio to communicate clearly its purpose and content and make it easy to locate and view the documents you've provided. They are also likely to expect you to make it easy to get in touch with you. A well-designed portfolio should provide, as a result, something like a table of contents and your contact information. In an e-Portfolio, this might consist of a navigation menu or a set of links on the main page. In a print portfolio, this information might appear on the first or second page.

Select Your Materials

A writing portfolio typically includes some or all of the following materials.

- Your contact information (e-mail address, phone number, and/or mailing address)
- An introduction to the portfolio that addresses its purpose and contents
- A reflection on the documents in the portfolio, on your growth as a writer, and on your goals as a writer. This often takes the form of a letter, statement, or brief essay. In an e-Portfolio, you could also share your reflections through video or audio clips.
- Final drafts of documents
- Rough drafts of documents, often with comments from instructors or other writers
- Sources used in a particular writing project, along with any notes or source evaluations
- Planning notes, freewriting and other forms of idea generation, and maps or outlines
- Your comments on the work of other writers
- Grades and comments from instructors

Choose a Publishing Tool

As with other types of documents, your choice of tools for composing and publishing your portfolio will affect not only how you present your materials but also your understanding of what is possible to present. If you create a print portfolio, you can collect and bind your work, place all of your work in a folder, or simply clip it together and share it with a reader. If some of your work turns out to be difficult to include in a print portfolio, as might be the case with note cards or pages in a journal, you might photograph or scan it, print it, and include it with the rest of your work. If you create an e-Portfolio, you have many other options. You can distribute an e-Portfolio as:

- a single word processing or PDF file
- a collection of word processing or PDF documents
- a PowerPoint or Keynote presentation
- a website or blog
- a collection of work in an e-Portfolio tool

Each of these tools offers possibilities quite different from what you can accomplish with a print portfolio. Even more important, the possibilities associated with each of these tools — and the experiences they can offer your readers — differ in striking ways from each other. Some tools will allow you to use video and audio clips while others will give you more control over the kind of navigation menus and links you can create. Some programs, such as PowerPoint and Keynote, will make it relatively easy to use page transitions and animations or to switch easily from one color scheme to another. Your decisions about the tool you use to create your portfolio, as a result, should reflect your purpose and an awareness of what a particular tool allows you to do.

Design Your Portfolio

As you design your portfolio, keep the principles of simplicity and consistency in mind. You should develop a consistent look and feel for your portfolio, focusing in particular on issues such as color and font scheme, page layout, and navigation tools. It is likely, of course, that the individual documents in your portfolio will have their own distinctive designs. Readers will expect this, and if the design of these documents is essential to their effect, you should not redesign them. However, if you are working with a set of essays in which your design decisions are less important than what you've written, you might consider reformatting them so that they follow the design you've chosen for the portfolio as a whole.

You should also spend some time thinking about how your readers will work with your portfolio. If you are creating a print portfolio, you might use a table of contents to help readers see how your portfolio is organized. You might also attach colored tabs to pages to help them find the start of each document. If you are creating an e-Portfolio, you might think about the type of navigation tools you might provide, such as tables of contents and menus, and you might consider the use of hyperlinks to help readers move from one part of the e-Portfolio to another.

Your design decisions should help your readers work easily and quickly with the materials you've included in your portfolio. In general, simple, uncluttered designs that use readable fonts and consistent colors will allow your readers to work through your portfolio without distraction.

CHECKLIST FOR DEVELOPING PORTFOLIOS

✔ Reflect on your writing situation, paying particular attention to the purposes of the portfolio, your readers' expectations, and the context in which your portfolio will be read.

✔ Select materials for your portfolio.

✔ Choose a tool to compose and publish your portfolio.

✔ Choose an organizing pattern for your portfolio.

✔ Develop a simple, consistent design for your portfolio. Pay particular attention to:

- font scheme
- color scheme
- page layout
- navigation tools

✔ Create an introduction that calls attention to particular aspects of your portfolio.

✔ Reflect on the materials presented in your portfolio, calling attention to key issues and offering evidence to support your conclusions.

QUICK REFERENCE

Presenting Your Work

✔ Make an oral presentation. (p. 303)

✔ Give a multimedia presentation. (p. 308)

✔ Create a poster presentation. (p. 312)

✔ Develop a portfolio. (p. 314)

IV Creating Your Document

PART V

Documenting Sources

As you complete your work on your research writing project, you can turn your attention fully to the task of citing and documenting your sources. This section discusses reasons to document your sources and describes four major documentation systems: MLA, APA, *Chicago*, and CSE.

19

Understanding
Documentation Syste.

Key Questions

19a. **What is a documentation system and which one should I use?** 321

19b. **How should I document my sources?** 322

Research writers document their sources to avoid plagiarism, give credit to others who have written about an issue, and create a record of their work that other members of the community can follow and build on. By documenting your sources, you show that you are aware that other writers have contributed to the conversation about your issue and that you respect them enough to acknowledge their contributions — as you hope they would do in return.

Documenting your sources can help you achieve your purpose as a writer, such as convincing or persuading your readers. If readers find that you haven't documented your sources, they'll suspect that you're careless or decide that you're dishonest. In either case, they won't trust what you have to say.

19a

What is a documentation system and which one should I use?

Many professional organizations and publications have developed their own rules for formatting documents and citing sources. As a result, writers in many disciplines know how to cite their sources clearly and consistently, and their readers know what to expect. For example, imagine that a psychologist is writing an article for the *Journal of Counseling Psychology*. The journal requires that writers use the documentation system created by the American Psychological Association (APA). Given the high level of competition for space in the journal, the writer knows that even if the article is substantive and compelling, it will not be accepted for publication if it does not use APA style appropriately. After ensuring the article is clearly written and well argued, the writer double-checks the article to ensure it follows the formatting and source citation guidelines specified by the APA.

Several of the documentation systems most commonly used in the various academic disciplines are covered in this book.

- **MLA** This style, from the Modern Language Association, is used primarily in the humanities — English, philosophy, linguistics, world languages, and so on. See Chapter 20.

- **APA** This style, from the American Psychological Association, is used mainly in the social sciences — psychology, sociology, anthropology, political science, economics, education, and so on. See Chapter 21.

- *Chicago* Developed by the University of Chicago Press, this style is used primarily in history, journalism, and the humanities. See Chapter 22.

- **CSE** This style, from the Council of Science Editors, is used mainly in the physical and life sciences — chemistry, geology, biology, botany, and so on — and in mathematics. See Chapter 23.

Your choice of documentation system will be guided by the discipline or field within which you are writing and by any requirements associated with your research writing project. If your project has been assigned to you, and a style hasn't been specified, ask your instructor or the person who assigned it which documentation system you should use.

If you don't have access to advice about which documentation system is best for your project, consider the discipline in which you are writing. In engineering and business, for example, a wide range of documentation styles are used, with most of them specific to scholarly journals or specializations within the discipline. Consider genre as well. The manner in which sources are cited can vary widely from one type of document to another. For example, while academic essays and articles appearing in scholarly journals typically use a documentation system such as MLA, APA, *Chicago*, or CSE, newspaper and magazine articles often do not and rely instead on identification of sources in the main text of the document rather than in a works cited or reference list.

19b

How should I document my sources?

How you document sources will depend on your writing situation. Most often, you will:

1. provide a reference to your source within the text
2. provide a complete set of citations, or formal acknowledgments, for your sources in a works cited or reference list

The specific format of your in-text citations will depend on the documentation system you use. If you use MLA or APA style, you'll cite—or formally acknowledge—information in the text using parentheses and add a list of sources to the end of your document. If you use the *Chicago* notes style, you'll acknowledge your sources in footnotes or endnotes and supply a bibliography at the end of your document. If you use the CSE citation-sequence style, you will number the citations in your text and list your sources in the order in which they are referenced. If you write a digital document that cites other online sources, you might simply link to your sources.

i **INFORMATION LITERACY** Many digital resources—such as library catalogs, websites, and databases—provide citations for a given source. Use caution when relying on these citation generators, which may not exactly match the style of the documentation system you are using. ▥

Table 19.1 presents examples of in-text citations and works cited or reference list entries for each of these major documentation styles. As Table 19.1 shows, although each style differs from the others, especially in the handling of in-text citations, they share a number of similarities.

With the exception of Web style, publication information is usually provided in a works cited list, reference list, or bibliography. These lists appear at the end of the document and include the following information:

- author(s) and/or editor(s)
- title
- publication date
- publisher and city of publication (for books)
- periodical name, volume, issue, and page numbers (for articles)
- for digital sources, the URL and access date or a digital object identifier (DOI)

Each documentation system creates an association between citations in the text of a document and the works cited or reference list page.

My Research Project

Review Your Working Bibliography

Start by reviewing the source citations in your working bibliography. Make sure that you've used the appropriate documentation system and entered sufficient source information to fully document your sources.

TABLE 19.1 EXAMPLES OF IN-TEXT CITATIONS AND BIBLIOGRAPHIC ENTRIES FOR MAJOR DOCUMENTATION STYLES

Style	In-Text Citation	Works Cited or Reference List Entry
MLA Style	Over the past few years, the Bolivian government has not seen much economic growth (Gordon 16).	Gordon, Gretchen. "The United States, Bolivia, and the Political Economy of Coca." *Multinational Monitor*, vol. 27, no. 1, Jan./Feb. 2006, www.multinationalmonitor.org/mm2006/012006/gordon.html.
APA Style	Over the past few years, the Bolivian government has not seen much economic growth (Gordon, 2006, p. 16).	Gordon, G. (2006). The United States, Bolivia, and the political economy of coca. *Multinational Monitor, 27*(1), 15–20. Retrieved from http://www.multinationalmonitor.org/mm2006/012006/gordon.html
Chicago **Style: Notes System**	Over the past few years, the Bolivian government has not seen much economic growth.[3] 3. Gretchen Gordon, "The United States, Bolivia, and the Political Economy of Coca," *Multinational Monitor* 27, no. 1 (2006): 16.	Gordon, Gretchen. "The United States, Bolivia, and the Political Economy of Coca." *Multinational Monitor* 27, no. 1 (2006): 15–20. http://www.multinationalmonitor.org/mm2006/012006/gordon.html. *Note: The citation is placed in a footnote or endnote, and again in the bibliography.*
CSE Style: Citation-Sequence System	Over the past few years, the Bolivian government has not seen much economic growth.[3]	3. Gordon G. The United States, Bolivia, and the political economy of coca. Multinational Monitor. 2006,27(1):15–20. http://www.multinationalmonitor.org/mm2006/012006/gordon.html. *Note: Numbered citations are placed in the reference list in the order in which they appear in the text.*
Web Style	Gordon notes that, over the past few years, the Bolivian government has not seen much economic growth.	Many Web documents will link directly to a cited work, as shown here. Or they may use a style such as MLA, APA, *Chicago*, or CSE.

QUICK REFERENCE

Understanding Documentation Systems

☑ Choose an appropriate documentation system. (p. 321)

☑ Document your sources in your text and, depending on the documentation system, create a works cited list, reference list, or bibliography. (p. 322)

☑ Review your sources for accuracy and completeness. (p. 323)

V Documenting Sources

20

Using MLA Style

 Key Questions

20a. How do I cite sources within the text of my document? 328

20b. How do I prepare the list of works cited? 331

Modern Language Association (MLA) style, used primarily in the humanities, emphasizes the authors of a source and the pages on which information is located in the source. Writers who use the MLA documentation system cite, or formally acknowledge, source information within their text using parentheses, and they provide a list of sources in a works cited list at the end of their document.

For more information about MLA style, consult the *MLA Handbook*, Eighth Edition. Information about the *MLA Handbook* can also be found at **mla.org**.

To see featured writer Elizabeth Leontiev's research essay formatted in MLA style, turn to p. 350.

CITATION TUTORIALS FOR COMMON WORKS CITED ENTRIES

CITATIONS WITHIN YOUR TEXT

ENTRIES IN YOUR WORKS CITED LIST

Books, Conference Proceedings, and Dissertations

Sources in Journals, Magazines, and Newspapers

Reference Works

20a

How do I cite sources within the text of my document?

MLA style uses parentheses for in-text citations to acknowledge the use of another author's words, facts, and ideas. When you refer to a source within your text, place the author's last name and specific page number(s)—if the source is paginated—within parentheses. Your reader then can go to the works cited list at the end of your document and find a full citation there.

1. Basic Format for Direct Quotation   Often you will want to name the author of a source within your sentence rather than in a parenthetical citation. By doing so, you create a context for the material (words, facts, or ideas) that you are including and indicate where the information from the author begins. When you are using a direct quotation from a source and have named the author in your sentence, place only the page number in parentheses after the quotation. The period follows the parentheses.

> Vargas reports that "each year, unintentional drownings kill more than 830 children younger than 14 and cause, on average, 3,600 injuries" (23).

When you have not mentioned the author in your sentence, you must place the author's name and the page number in parentheses after the quotation. Again, the period follows the parentheses.

> After car accidents, "drowning is the second-leading cause of unintentional deaths" among toddlers (Vargas 23).

When you are using a block (or extended) quotation, the parenthetical citation comes after the final punctuation and a single space.

If you continue to refer to a single source for several sentences in a row within one paragraph — and without intervening references to another source — you may reserve your reference until the end of the paragraph. However, be sure to include all relevant page numbers.

2. Basic Format for a Summary or Paraphrase   When you are summarizing or paraphrasing information gained from a source, you are still required to cite the source. If you name the author in your sentence, place only the page number in parentheses after the paraphrase or summary. Punctuation marks follow the parentheses. When you have not mentioned the author in your sentence, you must place the author's name and the page number in parentheses after the quotation.

> Vargas points out that drowning doesn't happen in the manner you might expect; children slip under the water quietly, making very little noise to alert unsuspecting parents or guardians (23).

3. Entire Source   If you are referring to an entire source rather than to a specific page or pages, you will not need a parenthetical citation.

> The explorations of race in ZZ Packer's *Drinking Coffee Elsewhere* can be linked thematically to the treatment of immigrants in Lahiri's work.

4. Corporate, Group, or Government Author   Cite the corporation, group, or government agency as you would an individual author. You may use abbreviations for the source in subsequent references if you add the abbreviation in parentheses at the first mention of the name.

> The Brown University Office of Financial Aid (BUOFA) has adopted a policy that first-year students will not be expected to work as part of their financial aid package (12). BUOFA will award these students a onetime grant to help compensate for the income lost by not working (14).

5. Unknown Author   If you are citing a source that has no known author, such as the book *Through Palestine with the 20th Machine Gun Squadron*, use a brief version of the title in the parenthetical citation.

> The members of the squadron rode horses while the cooks were issued bicycles, requiring the cooks to exert quite a lot of effort pedaling through the desert sand (*Through Palestine* 17).

6. Two or More Works by the Same Author   For references to authors with more than one work in your works cited list, insert a short version of the title between author and page number, separating the author and the title with a comma.

> (Ishiguro, *Unconsoled* 146)

> (Ishiguro, *Remains* 77)

7. Two or More Authors with the Same Last Name   Include the first initial and last name in the parenthetical citations.

> (G. Martin 354)

> (F. Martin 169)

8. Two Authors   Include the last name of each author in your citation.

> As Gostin and Gostin explain, "Interventions that do not pose a truly significant burden on individual liberty . . . go a long way towards safeguarding the health and well-being of the populace" (214).

9. Three or More Authors   Use only the last name of the first author and the abbreviation "et al." (Latin for "and others"). Note that there is no comma between the author's name and "et al."

> (Barnes et al. 44)

10. Literary Work   Along with the page number(s), give other identifying information, such as a chapter, scene, or line number, that will help readers find the passage.

> The sense of social claustrophobia is never as palpable in *The Age of Innocence* as when Newland realizes that all of New York society has conspired to cover up what it believes to be an affair between him and Madame Olenska (Wharton 339; ch. 33).

11. Work in an Edited Collection or Anthology   Cite the author of the work, not the editor of the anthology. (See also entry 30 on p. 335.)

> In "Beneath the Deep, Slow Motion," Leo says, "The Chinese call anger a weary bird with no place to roost" (Barkley 163).

MLA

V Documenting Sources

12. Sacred Text   Give the name of the edition you are using along with the chapter and verse (or their equivalent). (See also entry 34 on p. 336.)

> He should consider that "Where no counsel is, the people fall: but in the multitude of counselors there is safety" (*King James Bible*, Prov. 11.14).

> In the Qur'an, sinners are said to be blind to their sins ("The Cow" 2.7).

13. Two or More Works Cited Together   Use a semicolon to separate entries.

> Forethought is key in survival, whether it involves remembering extra water on a safari trail or gathering food for a long winter in ancient times (Estes and Otte 2; Wither and Hosking 4).

14. Source Quoted in Another Source   Ideally, you will be able to find the primary, or original, source for material used in your research project document. If you quote or paraphrase a secondary source—a source that contains information about a primary source—use the abbreviation "qtd. in" (for "quoted in") when you cite the source.

> MIT professor Richard Lundgren has stated, "Global warming is small and magnified by the alarmists with deeply compromised political pressure, data fudging, and out and out guesswork" (qtd. in de Garmo A13).

15. Source without Page Numbers   Give a section, paragraph, or screen number, if used, in the parenthetical citation.

> Teters believes the mascots dehumanize Native Americans, allowing spectators to dismiss the Native Americans' true culture as well as their hardships (Saraceno, par. 20).

If no page numbers are provided, list only the author's name in parentheses.

> Although his work has been influenced by many graphic artists, it remains essentially text based (Fitzgerald).

20b

How do I prepare the list of works cited?

MLA-style research documents include a reference list titled "Works Cited," which begins on a new page at the end of the document. If you wish to acknowledge sources that you read but did not cite in your text, you may include them in a second list titled "Works Consulted." In longer documents, a list of works cited may be given at the end of each chapter or section. In digital documents that use links, such as a website, the list of works cited is often a separate page to which other pages are linked. To see a works cited list in MLA style, go to p. 354.

The list is alphabetized by author. If the author's name is unknown, alphabetize the entry using the title of the source. To cite more than one work by the same author, alphabetize the group under the author's last name, with each entry listed alphabetically by title (see entry 21 on p. 334).

All entries in the list are double-spaced, with no extra space between entries. Entries are formatted with a hanging indent: The first line of an entry is flush with the left margin and subsequent lines are indented one-half inch. Unless otherwise noted (as after the author and title), use commas to separate items within each entry. Titles of longer works, such as books, journals, or websites, are italicized. Titles of short works, such as articles or chapters, are enclosed in quotation marks. MLA generally indicates the "container" of the source — the larger object, if any, in which the source can be found. Some sources may have multiple levels of containers, such as a periodical article that is accessed via a database. Occasionally, sources may be identified by a descriptive label (editorial, map, letter, photograph, and so on).

Since sources today can often be found in both print and digital form — for instance, you can easily access a *New Yorker* article in the print magazine or on the magazine's website — the source types that follow include model citations for both media. The section on digital sources (see p. 346) features source types that are native to digital formats, such as blogs or social-media platforms.

Books, Conference Proceedings, and Dissertations

16. One Author List the author's last name first, followed by a comma and the first name. Italicize the book title and subtitle, if any. List the publisher (abbreviating "University Press" as "UP"); then insert a comma and the publication year. End with a period.

Kolbert, Elizabeth. *The Sixth Extinction: An Unnatural History*. Henry Holt, 2014.

Cite an online book as you would a print book, providing the website and DOI (digital object identifier, a unique number assigned to specific content). If a DOI is not available, provide a stable URL.

Swinnen, Johan F. M., and Scott Rozelle. *From Marx and Mao to the Market: The Economics and Politics of Agricultural Transition*. Oxford UP, 2006. *Oxford Scholarship Online,* doi:10.1093/0199288917.001.0001.

Piketty, Thomas. *Capital in the Twenty-First Century*. Translated by Arthur Goldhammer, Harvard UP, 2014. *Google Books,* books.google.com/books?isbn=0674369556.

Cite an e-book as you would a print book; then provide the name of the e-reader.

Doerr, Anthony. *All the Light We Cannot See*. Charles Scribner and Sons, 2014. Nook.

TUTORIAL

How do I cite books using MLA style?

When citing a book, use the information from the title page and the copyright page (on the reverse side of the title page), not from the book's cover or a library catalog. Consult pp. 334–37 for additional models for citing books.

THE
PARTHENON
ENIGMA

Joan Breton Connelly

THIS IS A BORZOI BOOK
PUBLISHED BY ALFRED A. KNOPF

Copyright © 2014 by Joan Breton Connelly

All rights reserved. Published in the United States by Alfred A. Knopf, a division of Random House LLC, New York, and in Canada by Random House of Canada Limited, Toronto, Penguin Random House Companies.

www.aaknopf.com

Knopf, Borzoi Books, and the colophon are registered trademarks of Random House LLC.

Library of Congress Cataloging-in-Publication Data
Connelly, Joan Breton, [date]
The Parthenon enigma / Joan Breton Connelly.
pages cm
ISBN 978-0-307-59338-2 (hardback); ISBN 978-0-385-35050-1 (eBook)
1. Parthenon (Athens, Greece) 2. Symbolism in architecture—Greece —Athens. 3. Athens (Greece)—Buildings, structures, etc. I. Title.
NA281.c66   2014
726'.120809385—dc23   2013024771

Jacket photograph by Andreas Constantinou
Jacket design by Carol Devine Carson
Endpaper art by George Marshall Peters

v3.1_r1

A ⎯⎯⎯ **B** ⎯⎯⎯ **C** ⎯ **D**
Connelly, Joan Breton. *The Parthenon Enigma*. Alfred A. Knopf, 2014.

A **The author.** Give the last name first, followed by a comma, the first name, and the middle name or initial (if given). Omit titles such as *MD*, *PhD*, or *Sir*; include suffixes after the name and a comma (O'Driscoll, Gerald P., Jr.). End with a period.

B **The title.** Give full title; include subtitle (if any), preceded by a colon. Italicize title and subtitle; capitalize all major words. End with a period.

C **The publisher.** Give the name of the publisher as listed on the title page of the book. Use the full version of the publisher's name (HarperCollins Publishers, Penguin Books). Do not include the words *Company* or *Inc.* Use *UP* for *University Press* (Oxford UP). Follow with a comma.

D **The year of publication.** If more than one copyright date is given, use the most recent one. End with a period.

17. Two Authors List both authors in the same order as on the title page, last name first for only the first author listed. Use commas to separate the authors' names.

Brynjolfsson, Erik, and Andrew McAfee. *The Second Machine Age: Work, Progress, and Prosperity in a Time of Brilliant Technologies.* W. W. Norton, 2014.

18. Three or More Authors Provide the first author's name (last name first), followed by a comma, and then add the abbreviation "et al." (Latin for "and others").

Cunningham, Stewart, et al. *Media Economics.* Palgrave Macmillan, 2015.

19. Corporate or Group Author Write out the full name of the corporation or group, and cite the name as you would an author. If this name is also the name of the publisher, you may omit it in the author position.

Human Rights Watch. *World Report of 2015: Events of 2014.* Seven Stories Press, 2015.

20. Unknown Author When no author is listed on the title or copyright page, begin the entry with the title of the work. Alphabetize the entry by the first word of the title other than *A, An,* or *The.*

The Book of Nature. Kunth Verlag, 2010.

21. Two or More Books by the Same Author Use the author's name in the first entry. Thereafter, use three hyphens followed by a period in place of the author's name. List the entries alphabetically by title.

Pollan, Michael. *Cooked: A Natural History of Transformation.* Penguin Books, 2013.

---. *Food Rules: An Eater's Manual.* Penguin Books, 2009.

22. Editor(s) Cite the name of the editor(s) as you would an author, followed by "editor" or "editors."

Olson, Gregory Allen, editor. *Landmark Speeches on the Vietnam War.* Texas A&M UP, 2010.

23. Author(s) with an Editor or Translator List the author(s) first and then the title. Include the label "Edited by" or "Translated by" and the name of the editor or translator, first name first.

Eco, Umberto. *History of Beauty.* Translated by Alastair McEwen, Rizzoli, 2010.

24. Book in a Language Other Than English You may give a translation of the book's title in brackets.

Márquez, Gabriel García. *Del amor y otros demonios* [*Of Love and Other Demons*]. Vintage Books, 2010.

25. Edition Other Than the First Include the number of the edition and the abbreviation "ed." after the title.

Lavenda, Robert, et al. *Core Concepts in Cultural Anthropology.* 6th ed., Oxford
UP, 2016.

26. Multivolume Work Include the total number of volumes and the abbreviation "vols." after the date.

Chapman, Roger, and James Ciment, editors. *Culture Wars in America: An Encyclopedia
of Issues, Viewpoints, and Voices.* 2nd ed., M.E. Sharpe, 2014. 3 vols.

If you have used only one of the volumes in your document, include the volume number after the title.

Di Berardino, Angelo, et al. *Encyclopedia of Ancient Christianity.* Vol. 2,
InterVarsity Press, 2014. 3 vols.

27. Book in a Series If a series name and/or number appears on the title page, include it at the end of the citation, after the date.

Trindade, Luís, editor. *Narratives in Motion: Journalism and Modernist
Events in 1920s Portugal.* Berghahn, 2016. Remapping Cultural History 15.

28. Republished Book Indicate the original date of publication after the title.

Melville, Herman. *Bartleby, the Scrivener: A Story of Wall-Street.* 1853. Book
Jungle, 2010.

29. Book with a Title within the Title

Stuckey, Sterling. *African Culture and Melville's Art: The Creative Process in
Benito Cereno and* Moby-Dick. Oxford UP, 2009.

30. Work in an Edited Collection or Anthology Give the author and then the title in quotation marks. Follow with the title of the collection in italics, the label "edited by," and the names of the editor(s) (first name first), the publication information, and the inclusive page numbers for the selection or chapter.

Sayrafiezadeh, Saïd. "Paranoia." *New American Stories,* edited by Ben Marcus,
Vintage Books, 2015, pp. 3-29.

If you are using multiple selections from the same anthology, include the anthology itself in your list of works cited and cross-reference it in the citations for individual works.

Eisenberg, Deborah. *"Some Other, Better Otto."* Marcus, pp. 94-136.

Marcus, Ben, editor. *New American Stories.* Vintage Books, 2015.

Sayrafiezadeh, Saïd. "Paranoia." Marcus, pp. 3-29.

31. Foreword, Introduction, Preface, or Afterword   Begin with the author of the part you are citing and the name of that part. Add the title of the work; "by" or "edited by" and the work's author or editor (first name first); and publication information. Then give the inclusive page numbers for the part.

Burns, Ken. Foreword. *David's Inferno: My Journey through the Dark Wood of Depression,* by David Blistein, Hatherleigh Press, 2013, pp. xi-xii.

If the author of the foreword or other part is also the author of the work, use only the last name after "by."

Olson, Gregory Allen. Introduction. *Landmark Speeches on the Vietnam War,* by Olson, Texas A&M UP, 2010, pp. 1-12.

If the foreword or other part has a title, include the title in quotation marks between the author and the name of the part.

Walker, Alice. "Learning to Dance." Preface. *Hard Times Require Furious Dancing,* by Walker, New World Library, 2010, pp. xv-xvi.

32. Published Proceedings of a Conference   Provide information as you would for a book, adding information about the sponsors, date, and location of the conference after the title.

Meisner, Marx S., et al., editors. *Communication for the Commons: Revisiting Participation and Environment.* Proceedings of Twelfth Biennial Conference on Communication and the Environment, 6-11 June 2015, Swedish U of Agricultural Sciences. International Environmental Communication Association, 2015.

33. Screenplay   Provide information as you would for a book.

Cholodenko, Lisa, and Stuart Blumberg. *The Kids Are All Right: The Shooting Script.* Newmarket Press, 2011.

34. Sacred Text   Include the title of the version as it appears on the title page. If the title does not identify the version, place that information directly after the title.

The Oxford Annotated Bible with the Apocrypha. Edited by Herbert G. May and Bruce M. Metzger, Revised Standard Version, Oxford UP, 1965.

The Qur'an: Translation. Translated by Abdullah Yusuf Ali, Tahrike Tarsile Qur'an, 2001.

35. Graphic Narrative or Illustrated Work List the primary author/illustrator in the first position. If the author is also the illustrator, simply list him or her in the first position.

Gaiman, Neil. *The Sandman: Overture.* Illustrated by J. H. William III, DC Comics, 2015.

Kerascoët, illustrator. *Beautiful Darkness.* By Fabien Vehlmann, Drawn and
    Quarterly, 2014.

Smith, Lane. *Abe Lincoln's Dream.* Roaring Brook Press, 2012.

36. Dissertation or Thesis Cite as you would a book, with the title in italics, but include an appropriate label such as "Dissertation" or "Thesis" after the title. Add the school and the year the dissertation was accepted.

Hitotsubashi, N. S. *The Life and Times of Beowulf: Monsters and Heroes in the
    Named Lands of the North.* Dissertation, Wheaton College, 2013.

Sources in Journals, Magazines, and Newspapers

37. Article in a Journal Enclose the article title in quotation marks. After the journal title, list the volume number, issue number, season and year of publication, and inclusive page numbers.

Matchie, Thomas. "Law versus Love in *The Round House.*" *Midwest Quarterly,*
    vol. 56, no. 4, Summer 2015, pp. 353-64.

For an electronic journal, provide the print information, if given, and end with the URL.

Amao, Olumuyiwa Babatunde, and Ufo Okeke-Uzodike. "Nigeria, Afrocentrism,
    and Conflict Resolution: After Five Decades — How Far, How Well?" *African
    Studies Quarterly,* vol. 15, no. 4, Sept. 2015, pp. 1-23, asq.africa.ufl.edu/
    files/Volume-15-Issue-4-OLUMUYIWA-BABATUNDE-AMAO.pdf.

If the article is assigned a DOI, cite the source as you would a print article, then give the DOI. For an article from a database, cite the database name before the DOI.

Coles, Kimberly Anne. "The Matter of Belief in John Donne's Holy Sonnets."
    Renaissance Quarterly, vol. 68, no. 3, Fall 2015, pp. 899-931. *JSTOR,*
    doi:10.1086/683855.

38. Article in a Monthly or Bimonthly Magazine After the author's name and title of the article, list the title of the magazine, the date (use abbreviations for all months except May, June, and July), and inclusive pages.

McArdle, Megan. "The Freeloaders: How a Generation of File-Sharers Is Ruining
    the Future of Entertainment." *The Atlantic,* May 2010, pp. 34-35.

MLA

V Documenting Sources

How do I cite articles from periodicals using MLA style?

Born to Take the Highway:
Women, the Automobile, and
Rock 'n' Roll

Chris Lezotte

Periodicals include journals, magazines, and newspapers. This tutorial gives an example of a citation for a print journal article. Models for citing articles from magazines and newspapers are on pp. 337–41.

If you need to cite a periodical article you accessed electronically, follow the guidelines below and see also p. 339.

A **B**

Lezotte, Chris. "Born to Take the Highway: Women, the Automobile, and Rock

C **D** **E**

'n' Roll." *The Journal of American Culture*, vol. 36, no. 3, Sept. 2013,

F

pp. 161-76.

A **The author.** Give last name first, followed by a comma, first name, and middle initial (if given). Omit titles such as *MD*, *PhD*, or *Sir*; include suffixes after the name and a comma (O'Driscoll, Gerald P., Jr.). End with a period.

B **The article title.** Give the full title; include the subtitle (if any), preceded by a colon. Enclose the title and subtitle in quotation marks, and capitalize all major words. Place a period inside the closing quotation mark.

C **The periodical title.** Italicize the periodical title, including any initial *The*; capitalize all major words.

D **The volume number and issue number.** For journals, include the volume number, preceded by "vol." If the journal uses issue numbers, put a comma after the volume number, followed by "no." and the number of the issue.

E **The date of publication.** For journals and monthly magazines, give the month or season, followed by the year. For weekly magazines and newspapers, give the day, month, and year (in that order). Abbreviate the names of all months except May, June, and July.

F **Inclusive page number(s).** For numbers 100 and above, give only the last two digits and any other preceding digits if different from the first number (22-28, 402-10, 1437-45, 592-603). If an article continues on nonconsecutive pages, include the first page number followed by a plus sign. Include section letters for newspapers, if relevant. End with a period.

How do I cite articles obtained from databases using MLA style?

Libraries subscribe to services such as LexisNexis, InfoTrac, and EBSCOhost that provide access to databases of digital texts. The databases provide publication information, abstracts, and complete text of documents in a specific subject, discipline, or profession. (See also Chapter 10.)

Mackey, Allison. "Troubling Humanitarian Consumption: Reframing Relationality

in African Child Soldier Narratives." *Research in African Literatures,* vol. 44,

no. 4, Winter 2013, pp. 99-122. *JSTOR,* doi:10.2979/reseafrilite.44.4.82.

A   **The author.** Give the last name first, followed by a comma, the first name, and the middle initial (if given). Omit titles such as *MD*, *PhD*, or *Sir*; include suffixes after the name and a comma (O'Driscoll, Gerald P., Jr.). End with a period.

B   **The article title.** Give the title and subtitle (if any), preceded by a colon. Enclose the full title in quotation marks, and capitalize all major words. Place a period inside the closing quotation mark.

C   **The periodical title.** Italicize the periodical title. Capitalize all major words.

D   **The volume number and issue number, if appropriate.** Use the abbreviations "vol." and "no." to indicate the volume number and issue number.

E   **The date of publication.** For journals and monthly magazines, give the month or season, followed by the year. For weekly magazines and newspapers, give the day, month, and year, in that order. Abbreviate the names of all months except May, June, and July.

F   **Inclusive page number(s).** For numbers 100 and above, give only the last two digits and any other preceding digits if different from the first number (22-28, 402-10, 1437-45, 592-603). Include section letters for newspapers, if relevant.

G   **The name of the database.** Italicize the name of the database, followed by a comma.

H   **The DOI or URL.** Many sources from databases include a stable identifier called a permalink (a stable URL that is not likely to change) or a DOI (digital object identifier). Use that identifier in your works cited entry. If a source does not have a permalink or a DOI, include a URL.

39. Article in a Weekly or Biweekly Magazine   Give the exact date of publication, inverted.

Greider, William. "The Federal Reserve at 100 and Why It Needs a Total Overhaul."
    The Nation, 3 Mar. 2014, pp. 12-19.

Cite online articles the same way that you would a print article, and then give the URL.

Leonard, Andrew. "The Surveillance State High School." *Salon*, 27 Nov. 2012,
    www.salon.com/2012/11/27/the_surveillance_state_high_school/.

40. Article in a Newspaper   If the newspaper is not a national newspaper (such as *The Wall Street Journal*, *The Christian Science Monitor*, or *The Chronicle of Higher Education*) or the city of publication is not part of its title, give the name of the city in square brackets [Cincinnati] after the title. List the date in inverted order followed by the page numbers (use the section letter before the page number if the newspaper uses letters to designate sections). If the article does not appear on consecutive pages, write only the first page number and a plus sign (+), with no space between.

Sherry, Allison. "Volunteers' Personal Touch Turns High-Tech Data into Votes." *The
    Denver Post*, 30 Oct. 2012, pp. 1A+.

For newspaper articles found online, cite as you would a print article and give the URL.

Humphrey, Tom. "Politics Outweigh School Vouchers." *Knoxville News Sentinel*,
    24 Jan. 2016, www.knoxnews.com/opinion/columnists/tom-humphrey/
    tomhumphrey-politics-outweigh-arguments-about-school-vouchers-29c77b33
    -9963-0ef8-e053-0100007fcba4-366300461.html.

41. Unsigned Article in a Newspaper or Magazine   Begin with the title of the article. Alphabetize by the first word other than *A, An,* or *The*.

"FDA Sends e-Cigarette Companies a Warning." *The Detroit News*, 10 Sept. 2010,
    p. A22.

42. Article That Skips Pages   Give only the first page number and a plus sign (+), with no space between.

Mahler, Jonathan. "The Second Coming." *The New York Times Magazine*,
    15 Aug. 2010, pp. 30+.

43. Article with a Quotation in the Title   Enclose the quotation in single quotation marks within the article title, which is enclosed in double quotation marks.

Díaz, Isabel González. "Enriching the 'Rags-to-Riches' Myth." *The Black Scholar*,
    vol. 43, no. 1-2, Spring 2013, pp. 43-51.

44. Editorial in a Newspaper   Include the word "Editorial" after the URL or page number(s).

"City's Blight Fight Making Difference." *The Columbus Dispatch*, 17 Nov. 2015,
     www.dispatch.com/content/stories/editorials/2015/11/17/1-citys-blight
     -fight-making-difference.html. Editorial.

"Fixing Immigration, in Principle." *The New York Times*, 31 Jan. 2014, p. A20. Editorial.

45. Letter to the Editor   Include the word "Letter" after the URL or page number(s).

Hasl, Rudy. "Jefferson's Mammoth." *Smithsonian*, June 2010, p. 6. Letter.

46. Review   Start with the author and title of the review; then add the words "Review of" followed by the title of the work under review. Insert a comma and "by," "edited by" (for an edited book), or "directed by" (for a play or film) and the name of the author or director. Continue with publication information for the review. Use this citation format for all reviews, including those for books, films, and video games.

Walton, James. "Noble, Embattled Souls." Review of *The Bone Clocks* and *Slade House*,
     by David Mitchell, *The New York Review of Books*, 3 Dec. 2015, pp. 55-58.

Cite online reviews as you would a print review, then give the URL.

Savage, Phil. *"Fallout 4* Review." Review of *Fallout 4*, by Bethesda Game Studios, *PC
     Gamer*, Future Publishing, 8 Nov. 2015, www.pcgamer.com/fallout-4-review/.

47. Published Interview   Begin with the person interviewed. If the published interview has a title, give it in quotation marks. Next, write the words "Interview by," followed by the name of the interviewer. Then supply the publication information.

Kelley, Kitty. "The Secret Sharer." Interview by Deborah Solomon, *The New York
     Times Magazine*, 11 Apr. 2010, p. MM18.

Cite an online interview as you would a print interview, then give the URL.

Jaffrey, Madhur. "Madhur Jaffrey on How Indian Cuisine Won Western Taste
     Buds." Interview by Shadrach Kabango, *Q*, CBC Radio, 29 Oct. 2015,
     www.cbc.ca/1.3292918.

48. Article in a Special Issue   After the author and the title of the article (in quotation marks), include the title of the special issue (in italics), then write the words "special issue of" before the regular title of the periodical.

Redd, Steven B., and Alex Mitz. "Policy Perspectives on National Security and
     Foreign Policy Decision Making." *2013 Public Policy Yearbook*, special issue of
     Policy Studies Journal, vol. 41, no. S1, April 2013, pp. S11-S37.

Reference Works

49. Encyclopedia, Dictionary, Thesaurus, Handbook, or Almanac Cite as you would a book (see p. 333).

50. Entry in Encyclopedia, Dictionary, Thesaurus, Handbook, or Almanac (including a Wiki) Unless the entry is signed, begin your citation with the title of the entry in quotation marks, followed by a period. Give the title of the reference work (beginning with the first word other than *A*, *An*, or *The*), italicized, and the edition (if available) and year of publication. If a reference work is not well known (perhaps because it includes highly specialized information), provide the editor's name as well as all bibliographic information. If there is no date of publication, include your date of access.

"Ball's in Your Court, The." *American Heritage Dictionary of Idioms.* 2nd ed.,
    Houghton Mifflin Harcourt, 2013.

Cite an online entry as you would a print entry, then give the URL.

"House Music." *Wikipedia*, 16 Nov. 2015, en.wikipedia.org/wiki/House_music.

51. Map or Chart Generally, treat a map or chart as you would a book without authors, listing its title (italicized) and publication information. For a map in an atlas or other volume, give the map title (in quotation marks) followed by publication information for the atlas and page numbers for the map. If the creator of the map or chart is listed, use his or her name as you would an author's name.

"Greenland." *Atlas of the World.* 19th ed., Oxford UP, 2012, p. 154.

For a map or chart found online, cite as you would a print source, then give the URL.

"Map of Sudan." *Global Citizen*, Citizens for Global Solutions, 2011,
    globalsolutions.org/blog/bashir#.VthzNMfi_FI.

52. Government Publications In most cases, cite the government agency as the author. If there is a named author, editor, or compiler, provide that name after the title. Do not abbreviate "Congress," "Senate," "House," "Resolution," or "Report."

Canada, Minister of Aboriginal Affairs and Northern Development. *2015-16 Report
    on Plans and Priorities.* Minister of Public Works and Government Services
    Canada, 2015.

United States, Department of Agriculture, Food and Nutrition Service, Child
    Nutrition Programs. *Eligibility Manual for School Meals: Determining and
    Verifying Eligibility.* National School Lunch Program, July 2015, www.fns
    .usda.gov/sites/default/files/cn/SP40_CACFP18_SFSP20-2015a1.pdf.

When documenting a bill, report, or resolution of the United States Congress, include the number and session of Congress from which it emerged.

53. Brochure or Pamphlet   Format the entry as you would for a book (see p. 333).

Safety Planning Information for Neighbors of FPL's St. Lucie Nuclear Power Plant.
     Florida Power and Light, 2013.

Field Sources

54. Personal Interview   Place the name of the person interviewed first, words to indicate how the interview was conducted ("Personal interview," "Telephone interview," or "E-mail interview"), and the date. (Note that MLA style is to hyphenate "e-mail.")

Parlon, Charisse. Personal interview, 4 Feb. 2017.

55. Unpublished Letter   If written to you, give the writer's name, the words "Letter to the author" (no quotation marks or italics), and the date the letter was written.

Boyd, Edward. Letter to the author, 11 Aug. 2017.

If the letter was written to someone else, give that name rather than "the author."

56. Lecture or Public Address   Give the speaker's name and the title of the lecture (if there is one). If the lecture was part of a meeting or convention, identify that event. Conclude with the event information, including venue, city, and date. End with the appropriate label ("Lecture," "Address," "Panel discussion," "Reading").

Joseph, Branden. "1962." Dept. of Art History, U of Chicago, Cochrane Art
     Center, Chicago, 11 Mar. 2016. Lecture.

Smith, Anna Deavere. "On the Road: A Search for American Character." National
     Endowment for the Humanities, John F. Kennedy Center for the Performing
     Arts, Washington, D.C., 6 Apr. 2015. Address.

For lectures and public addresses found on the Web, provide the URL after the date. Then, end with the appropriate label ("Lecture," "Panel Discussion," "Reading").

Khosla, Raj. "Precision Agriculture and Global Food Security." US Department of
     State: Diplomacy in Action, 26 Mar. 2013, www.state.gov/e/stas/series/
     212172.htm. Address.

Media Sources

57. Film or Video   Generally begin with the title of the film (italicized). Always supply the name of the director, the distributor, and the year of original release. You may also insert other relevant information, such as the names of performers or screenplay writers, before the distributor.

Birdman or (The Unexpected Virtue of Ignorance). Directed by Alejandro González
    Iñárritu, performances by Michael Keaton, Emma Stone, Zach Galifianakis,
    Edward Norton, and Naomi Watts, Fox Searchlight, 2014.

If you wish to emphasize an individual's role in the film or movie, such as the director or screenplay writer, you may list that name first.

Olivier, Laurence, director and performer. *Hamlet*. Paramount, 1948.

For media other than film (such as videotape and DVD), cite it as for a film, unless you are discussing supplementary material found on the DVD, in which case your entry should refer to the DVD.

"Sweeney's London." Produced by Eric Young. *Sweeney Todd: The Demon Barber of
    Fleet Street*, directed by Tim Burton, DreamWorks, 2007, disc 2.

For videos found on the Web, give the URL after the publication information.

"The Ancient Art of the Atlatl." *Russell Cave National Monument*, directed by Antoine
    Fletcher, narrated by Brenton Bellomy, National Park Service, 12 Feb. 2014,
    www.nps.gov/media/video/view.htm?id=C92C0D0A-1DD8-B71C-07CBC6E8970CD73F.

58. Television or Radio Program   If the program has named episodes or segments, list those in quotation marks. Then include the title of the program or series (italicized), the producer, and the date that the program first aired. If there are relevant persons to name (such as an author, a director, a host, a narrator, or an actor), include that information after the title of the program or series. If the material you're citing is an interview, include the word "Interview" and, if relevant, the name of the interviewer.

"Federal Role in Support of Autism." *Washington Journal*, narrated by Robb
    Harleston, C-SPAN, 1 Dec. 2012.

Tempkin, Ann, and Anne Umland. Interview by Charlie Rose. *Charlie Rose: The
    Week*, PBS, 9 Oct. 2015.

If you accessed the program on the Web, include the URL after the date of publication.

"Take a Giant Step." *Prairie Home Companion*, narrated by Garrison Keillor,
    American Public Media, 27 Feb. 2016, prairiehome.publicradio.org/listen/
    full/?name=phc/2016/02/27/phc_20160227_128.63.

59. Sound Recording or Audio Clip Begin with the name of the person whose work you want to highlight: the composer, the conductor, or the performer. Next list the title, followed by names of other artists (composer, conductor, performers), with an indication of their roles. The recording information includes the manufacturer and the date.

Bizet, Georges. *Carmen*. Performances by Jennifer Larmore, Thomas Moser, Angela
  Gheorghiu, and Samuel Ramey, Bavarian State Orchestra and Chorus,
  conducted by Giuseppe Sinopoli, Warner, 1996.

If you wish to cite a particular track on the recording, give its performer and title (in quotation marks) and then proceed with the information about the recording. For live recordings, include the date of the performance between the title and the recording information. For recordings found online, include the URL after the publication date.

Adele. "Hello." *25*. XL, 2015.

For audio clips accessed on the Web, add the URL after the publication information.

Goldbarth, Albert. "Fourteen Pages." *The Poetry Foundation*, 15 Apr. 2016,
  www.poetryfoundation.org/features/audio/detail/89129.

60. Musical Score Give the composer, title, and date. Italicize the title unless it identifies the composition by form ("symphony," "suite"), number ("op. 39," "K. 231"), or key ("E-flat").

Beethoven, Ludwig van. Symphony no. 5 in C minor, op. 67. 1807.

If you are referring to a published score, provide publication data as you would for a book. Insert the date of composition between the title and the publication information.

Minchin, Tim. *Roald Dahl's Matilda — the Musical*. 2012. Wise-Music Sales, 2013.

61. Work of Art, Photograph, or Other Image Give the name of the artist, the title of the work (italicized), and the date of composition; the name of the collection, museum, or owner; and the city. If you are citing artwork reproduced in a book, add the publication information for the book at the end. If you are citing a photograph, add the label "Photograph" after the city.

Bradford, Mark. *Let's Walk to the Middle of the Ocean*. 2015, Museum of Modern
  Art, New York.

Feinstein, Harold. *Hangin' Out, Sharing a Public Bench, NYC*. 1948, Panopticon
  Gallery, Boston. Photograph.

For online visuals, including charts or graphs, include the website (italicized), and the URL.

"Brazilian Waxing and Waning: The Economy." *The Economist*, 1 Dec. 2015,
    www.economist.com/blogs/graphicdetail/2015/12/economic-backgrounder.

Hura, Sohrab. *Old Man Lighting a Fire*. 2015, *Magnum Photos*, www.magnumphotos
    .com/C.aspx?VP3=SearchResult&ALID=2K1HRG681B.

62. Advertisement   Provide the name of the product, service, or organization
being advertised, followed by the title of the publication in which the ad appeared.
Include the word "Advertisement" after the publication information. For advertisements found online, include the URL before "Advertisement."

AT&T. *National Geographic*, Dec. 2015, p. 14. Advertisement.

Toyota. *The Root*. Slate Group, 28 Nov. 2015, www.theroot.com. Advertisement.

63. Cartoon   Treat a cartoon like an article in a newspaper or magazine. Give
the cartoonist's name, the title of the cartoon if there is one (in quotation marks),
the publication information for the source, and the word "Cartoon."

Zyglis, Adam. "City of Light." *Buffalo News*, 8 Nov. 2015, adamzyglis.buffalonews
    .com/2015/11/08/city-of-light/. Cartoon.

64. Live Performance   Generally, begin with the performance title (italicized).
Then give the author and director; major performers; and theater, city, and date.

The Draft. By Peter Snoad, directed by Diego Arciniegas, Hibernian Hall, Boston,
    10 Sept. 2015.

Other Digital Sources

65. Entire Website   For a website with no author, provide the name of the site
in italics, followed by the sponsor or publisher, the copyright date or the most
recent update date (in reverse order), and the URL. A date of access is not
required for Web sources if a copyright or recent update date is provided.

The Newton Project. U of Sussex, 2016, www.newtonproject.sussex.ac.uk/prism
    .php?id=1.

66. Academic Course or Department Home Page   For a course page, give the
name of the instructor, the course title in italics, the department, the institution,
the year, and the URL. For a department page, give the department name, a
description such as "Department home page," the institution, the copyright date
or the most recent update date, and the URL.

Masiello, Regina. *355:101: Expository Writing*. Rutgers School of Arts and
    Sciences, 2016, wp.rutgers.edu/courses/55-355101.

Film Studies. Department home page. Wayne State University, College of Liberal
    Arts and Sciences, 2016, clas.wayne.edu/FilmStudies/.

67. Short Work from a Website Provide the name of the author; the title of the work in quotation marks; the title of the website, italicized; the date of publication, in reverse order; and the URL.

Enzinna, Wes. "Syria's Unknown Revolution." *Pulitzer Center on Crisis Reporting*, 24
　　Nov. 2015, pulitzercenter.org/projects/middle-east-syria-enzinna-war-rojava.

If there is no author given, begin the citation with the title of the work and proceed with the rest of the publication information. If the title of the website does not indicate the sponsoring organization, list the sponsor before the URL. If there is no date of publication, give the date of access after the URL.

"Social and Historical Context: Vitality." *Arapesh Grammar and Digital Language*
　　Archive Project, Institute for Advanced Technology in the Humanities, www
　　.arapesh.org/socio_historical_context_vitality.php. Accessed 22 Mar. 2016.

68. Message Posted to a Newsgroup, E-mail List, or Online Discussion Forum
Cite the name of the person who posted the message and the title (from the subject line, in quotation marks); if the posting has no title, add the phrase "Online posting." Then add the name of the website (italicized), the sponsor or publisher, the date of the message, and the URL.

Robin, Griffith. "Write for the Reading Teacher." *Developing Digital Literacies*,
　　NCTE, 23 Oct. 2015, ncte.connectedcommunity.org/communities/
　　community-home/digestviewer/viewthread?GroupId=1693&MID=24520&tab
　　=digestviewer&CommunityKey=628d2ad6-8277-4042-a376-2b370ddceabf.

69. Blog To cite an entry or a comment on a blog, give the author of the entry or comment (if available), the title of the entry or comment in quotation marks, the title of the blog (italicized), the sponsor or publisher (if different from the author), the copyright date or the date of the most recent update, and the URL. If the blog entry or comment has no date, give the date of access at the end of the citation.

Cimons, Marlene. "Why Cities Could Be the Key to Solving the Climate Crisis."
　　Thinkprogress.org, Center for American Progress Action Fund, 10 Dec. 2015,
　　thinkprogress.org/climate/2015/12/10/3730938/cities-key-to-climate-crisis/.

70. E-mail Message Start with the sender of the message. Then give the subject line, in quotation marks, followed by a period. Identify the recipient of the message and provide the date of the message. (Note that MLA style is to hyphenate "e-mail.")

Martin, Adrianna. "Re: Questions about the District Budget." Received by the
　　author, 19 Jan. 2017.

Pabon, Xavier. "Brainstorming for Essay." Received by Brayden Perry, 24 Apr.
　　2016.

TUTORIAL

How do I cite works from websites using MLA style?

You will likely need to scan the website to find some of the citation information you need. For some sites, all of the details may not be available; find as many as you can. If you cannot find a publication date, provide the date you accessed the website. Remember that the information you provide should allow readers to retrace your steps to locate the sources. Consult pp. 346–49 for additional models for citing Web sources.

┌──────────A──────────┐ ┌──────────────────B──────────────────┐

Alawa, Laila, and Wardah Khalid. "The Problem with Petitions — for Muslim School

┌──────────────────┐ ┌──────────────C──────────────┐

Holidays and Otherwise." *Altmuslim: Global Perspectives on Muslim Life,*

┌──────────────────┐ ┌────D────┐ ┌──────────E──────────┐

Politics, and Culture, Patheos, 29 Jan. 2014, www.patheos.com/blogs/

altmuslim/2014/01/the-problem-with-petitions-for-muslim-school-holidays

┌──────────────────┐

-and-otherwise/.

A **The author of the work.** Give the last name first, followed by a comma, the first name, and the middle initial (if given). Omit titles such as *MD*, *PhD*, or *Sir*; include suffixes after the name and a comma (O'Driscoll, Gerald P., Jr.). Insert a period. If no author is given, begin with the title.

B **The title of the work.** Give the full title; include the subtitle (if any), preceded by a colon. Enclose the title and subtitle in quotation marks, and capitalize all major words. Place a period inside the closing quotation mark. If you are citing an entire website, begin with the title of the website.

C **The title of the website.** Give the title of the entire site, italicized. If there is no clear title and it is a personal home page, use "Home page" without italicizing it. If the sponsoring organization is different from the website title, list that information next. Follow with a comma.

D **The date of publication or most recent update.** Use the day-month-year format; abbreviate all months except May, June, and July. End with a comma. If no publication information is given, provide the date of access at the end of the entry. After the URL, insert the word "Accessed" and the date you accessed the work.

E **The URL.** Give the URL for the work and end with a period.

71. Facebook Post or Comment Follow the general format for citing a short work on a website.

Bedford English. "Stacey Cochran explores Reflective Writing in the classroom and
as a writer." *Facebook*, 15 Feb. 2016, www.facebook.com/BedfordEnglish/
posts/10153415001259607.

72. Twitter Post (Tweet) Provide the entire tweet in place of the title, and include the time after the date.

Curiosity Rover. "Can you see me waving? How to spot #Mars in the night sky."
Twitter, 5 Nov. 2015, 11:00 a.m., twitter.com/marscuriosity/status/
672859022911889408.

73. Computer Software, App, or Video Game Cite computer software as you would a book.

Words with Friends. Version 5.84. Zynga, 2013.

Firaxis Games. *Sid Meier's Civilization Revolution*. Take-Two Interactive, 2008.

74. Other Sources For other digital sources, adapt the guidelines to the medium. The examples below are for a podcast of a radio program and a historical document available in an online archive.

McDougall, Christopher. "How Did Endurance Help Early Humans Survive?" *TED
Radio Hour*, National Public Radio, 20 Nov. 2015, www.npr.org/2015/11/
20/455904655/how-did-endurance-help-early-humans-survive.

Constitution of the United States. 1787. *The Charters of Freedom*, US National
Archives and Records Administration, www.archives.gov/exhibits/charters/.

MLA-Style Research Essay

Elizabeth Leontiev

Professor Lynda Haas

WR 39C

10 June 2013

The heading includes writer's name, instructor's name, course, and date.

Title is centered, and essay is double-spaced with one-inch margins.

Coca Is Not the Enemy

To most Americans, the word *cocaine* evokes images of the illegal white powder and those who abuse it, yet the word has a different meaning to the coca farmers of South America. *Erythroxylum coca*, or the tropical coca plant, has been grown in the mountainous regions of Colombia, Bolivia, and Peru since 3000 BC. The coca plant has been valued for centuries by indigenous South American cultures for its ability to alleviate pain and combat fatigue and hunger (Forero, "Bolivia's Knot"). Just as many Americans drink coffee every day, natives of the Andes Mountains chew coca leaves and drink coca tea for a mild stimulant effect. Easy to grow, not addictive, and offering many medicinal benefits, coca is part of the everyday lives of the people in this region.

Elizabeth's introduction provides important context.

Aside from its medicinal and cultural value, coca is also important to Andean farmers economically, as a result of a long history of illegal drug trafficking. Dried coca leaves mixed with lime paste or alkaline ashes produce cocaine — a highly addictive substance that delivers euphoric sensations accompanied by hallucinations (Gibson). Supplying the coca for the illegal drug trade accounts for a tremendous portion of the Bolivian, Peruvian, and Colombian economies. In Bolivia, for example, it has been estimated that coca makes up anywhere from one-third to three-quarters of the country's total exports (Kurtz-Phelan 108). In 1990 the Bolivian president even asserted that 70% of the Bolivian gross domestic product was due to the coca trade (Kurtz-Phelan 108).

MLA-style in-text citations include author and page number.

Despite such statistics, for most farmers in the region growing coca is about making a living and supporting their families, not becoming wealthy or furthering the use of cocaine. More than half of Bolivians live in poverty, with a large portion earning less than $2 a day (U.S. Foreign Affairs, Defense, and Trade Div. 2). In the words of one coca farmer, "'The U.S. says 'Coca is cocaine, coca is cocaine,' but it isn't,' says Argote. 'Coca is the tree of the poor'" (qtd. in Schultz and Gordon). Can we reduce cocaine trafficking without eliminating coca? Evo Morales, the current president of Bolivia, believes the answer is "yes" and has advocated a "zero cocaine, not zero coca" policy in

Elizabeth cites an indirect source: words quoted in another source.

his country. This policy would allow native Andeans to maintain their cultural practices, boost South American economies, and channel coca into a new market, away from cocaine traffickers. For all of these reasons, the Morales plan should become a model for other coca-growing countries.

Morales gained recognition for his "zero cocaine, not zero coca" program during his 2005 presidential campaign. His policy aims to legalize the coca crop but not the cocaine that is produced from that crop. He also expressed a desire to get the United Nations to rescind its 1961 convention declaring coca an illegal narcotic. In December 2005, Morales won the election with over 50% of the vote, and made history as the first indigenous Bolivian president (Forero, "Coca").

Morales's plan promotes the best interests of the Andean farmers and offers multiple economic and social benefits. First, South American countries would be able to export non-narcotic coca-based products, such as soaps, toothpaste, tea, alcohol, and candies (Logan). Products like these are already being produced for local use in Bolivia, and manufacturers would like to seek an international market for them. These new coca products would stimulate the Bolivian economy and put money in the pockets of coca growers to support their families, rather than in the pockets of the drug lords. Second, if the market for legal coca were to increase, farmers would be able to make a legal living from a crop that has long been a mainstay of their culture. With legal coca products, the indigenous people of the Andes would not have to sacrifice their way of life. Finally, an increase in the demand for legal coca products might also result in less cocaine being trafficked illegally around the world, since more of the raw material for cocaine will be used for new legal coca products.

In order to understand the benefits of Morales's plan, we must first investigate the failures of the alternatives. The United States has been waging various "wars on drugs" for decades, spending up to $1 billion trying to control cocaine trafficking from South America (Forero, "Bolivia's Knot"). In the 1990s the United States shifted its efforts from fighting the trafficking of cocaine to eliminating the source of the drug — the coca plants growing in Bolivia, Colombia, and Peru. Coca eradication has taken two main forms. In Bolivia, bands of soldiers move through the countryside using machetes to hack away coca plants (see Fig. 1). This process is slow and dangerous, and there have been reports of human rights abuses and extreme violence against the peasant farmers who grow coca (Gordon 16). In nearby Colombia, the United States funded aerial fumigation programs to

---

A brief title distinguishes two sources by the same author.

Elizabeth addresses counter-arguments and provides support for her assertion.

A reference to a photograph is included in the essay.

poison the coca fields; native farmers complain that the herbicide used in the fumigation is causing health problems and environmental pollution ("US Weighs Cost"). By destroying coca plants in Colombia, the United States has "left 500 million people poorer" (Padgett 8). It is unclear whether fumigation results in any benefit, since farmers respond by moving farther and farther into the jungle and replanting their crops there (Otis). Such dense areas are harder to see and therefore harder to fumigate effectively.

FIG. 1. Manual eradication of a coca field in Chapare, Bolivia. United Nations Office on Drugs and Crime. [United Nations Office on Drugs and Crime.]

> Caption includes figure number and source information.

Another U.S. effort encouraged farmers to replace coca with other crops, like coffee, bananas, and pineapples. Alternative crop programs seem like a good idea because they will get rid of the coca farms, but they have their own drawbacks. First, as coca grower Leonida Zurita-Vargas noted in her 2003 *New York Times* opinion column, transporting heavy fruits like pineapples from the mountainous coca-growing regions is expensive and difficult. Second, growers are seldom willing to give up coca farming because they can make more money by selling coca than any other crop. Even with government incentives for alternative cropping, coca remains more profitable, a big inducement for poor farmers who can barely support their families and send their children to school. The *Houston Chronicle* reports that even in areas where farmers have planted alternative crops, the farmers are being lured back to the coca plant by larger profits (Otis). One coca farmer asserted that by growing coca, he could "make ten times what he would make by growing pineapples or yucca" (Harman). Ultimately,

> The in-text citation provides just the author's name, since the online source did not include page numbers.

alternative cropping means less coca production overall, which will drive up coca prices and encourage more farmers to abandon their alternative crops and return to coca.

After decades of legislation and various eradication programs, cocaine trafficking remains a major problem. The most recent data show that coca cultivation throughout the region remains steady (see Fig. 2). Contrary to dire predictions, there has been no major spike in Bolivian coca production since Morales was elected at the end of 2005. Furthermore, critics argue that cocaine is no less available in the United States than before eradication began, and street prices remain low (Forero, "Colombia's Coca"). Instead of curbing cocaine trafficking, America's war on drugs has turned out to be a war against the peasants of Colombia, Bolivia, and Peru.

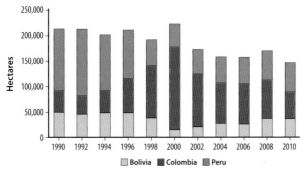

FIG. 2. Coca cultivation in the Andean region, 1990–2010. United Nations Office on Drugs and Crime. [Data from 1900–2008 Coca cultivation in the Andrean region by UNODC, UN Office on Drugs and Crime.]

Throughout the years, the various wars on drugs have failed to produce effective results for the United States. The programs of alternative cropping and eradication did not succeed due to the legislators' inability to see life through the eyes of the coca farmers — something Evo Morales is able to do. In 2006, Morales addressed the UN General Assembly and waved a coca leaf in the air: "[This] is a green coca leaf, it is not the white of cocaine. [T]his coca leaf represents Andean culture; it is a coca leaf that represents the environment and the hope of our peoples." Through his bold program of "zero cocaine, not zero coca," Morales aims to improve the lives of Andean farmers and the economies of South American countries, while still remaining committed to controlling the illegal drug trade. Morales's example illustrates that it is time to work *with* coca farmers, rather than against them.

The conclusion reinforces Elizabeth's thesis statement.

MLA

V Documenting Sources

Leontiev 5

Works Cited

Forero, Juan. "Bolivia's Knot: No to Cocaine, but Yes to Coca." *The New York Times*, 12 Feb. 2006, www.nytimes.com/2006/02/12/international/americas/12bolivia.html.

---. "Coca Advocate Wins Election for President in Bolivia." *The New York Times*, 19 Dec. 2005, www.nytimes.com/2005/12/19/world/americas/coca-advocate-wins-election-for-president-in-bolivia.html.

---. "Colombia's Coca Survives U.S. Plan to Uproot It." *The New York Times,* 19 Aug. 2006, www.nytimes.com/2006/08/19/world/americas/19coca.html.

Gibson, Arthur C. "Freud's Magical Drug." *The Mildred E. Mathias Botanical Garden*, UCLA, www.botgard.ucla.edu/html/botanytext-books/economicbotany/Erythroxylum/index.html. Accessed 22 Apr. 2007.

Gordon, Gretchen. "The United States, Bolivia, and the Political Economy of Coca." *Multinational Monitor,* vol. 27, no. 1, Jan./Feb. 2006, www.multinationalmonitor.org/mm2006/012006/gordon.html.

Harman, Danna. "In Bolivia, a Setback for US Anti-Coca Drive." *The Christian Science Monitor*, 22 Dec. 2005, www.csmonitor.com/2005/1222/p04s02-woam.html.

Kurtz-Phelan, Daniel. "'Coca Is Everything Here': Hard Truths about Bolivia's Drug War." *World Policy Journal*, vol. 22, no. 3, Fall 2005, pp. 103-12. *JSTOR*, www.jstor.org/stable/40209981.

Logan, Sam. "De-Vilifying the Coca Leaf." *International Relations and Security Network*, ETH Zurich, 9 Mar. 2007, www.isn.ethz.ch/Digital-Library/Articles/Detail//?ots591=4888caa0-b3db-1461-98b9-e20e7b9c13d4&lng=en&id=53001.

Otis, John. "Officials Urge Farmers to Try Alternative to Coca Crop." *Houston Chronicle*, 14 July 2000, www.chron.com/news/article/Officials-urge-farmers-to-try-alternative-to-coca-crop.

Padgett, Tim. "Taking the Side of the Coca Farmer: A Maverick Politician Stirs a Continent and Puts Washington's Drug War at Risk." *Time*, 5 Aug. 2002, p. 8.

Ribando, Clare M. *Bolivia: Political and Economic Developments and Relations with the United States*. CRS Report for Congress, Congressional Research Service, 26 Jan. 2007, www.fas.org/sgp/crs/row/RL32580.pdf.

Schultz, Jim, and Gretchen Gordon. "'Coca Is the Tree of the Poor': Indigenous People Leap Forward in Bolivia." *IMDiversity*, 5 Jan. 2013, imdiversity.com/villages/hispanic/coca-is-the-tree-of-the-poor-indigenous-people-leap-forward-in-bolivia/.

"US Weighs Cost of Plan Colombia." *BBC News*, 5 July 2005, news.bbc.co.uk/2/hi/americas/4627185.stm.

Zurita-Vargas, Leonida. "Coca Culture." *The New York Times*, 15 Oct. 2003, www.nytimes.com/2003/10/15/opinion/coca-culture.html.

Heading is centered.

Three hyphens indicate that a source was written by the same author as the previous source.

List is double-spaced and alphabetized by authors' last names.

Titles of publications are italicized.

Name of database followed by permalink for source.

Source without an author

MLA

V Documenting Sources

21

Using APA Style

 Key Questions

21a. How do I cite sources within the text of my document? 357

21b. How do I prepare the reference list? 360

American Psychological Association (APA) style, used primarily in the social sciences and in some of the natural sciences, emphasizes the author(s) and publication date of a source. Writers who use the APA documentation system cite, or formally acknowledge, information within their text using parentheses and provide a list of sources, called a reference list, at the end of their document. For more information about APA style, consult the *Publication Manual of the American Psychological Association,* Sixth Edition, and the *APA Style Guide to Electronic References.* Information about these publications can be found on the APA website at **apa.org.** To see Alexis Alvarez's research essay formatted in APA style, turn to p. 375.

CITATION TUTORIALS FOR COMMON REFERENCE LIST ENTRIES

CITATIONS WITHIN YOUR TEXT

21a

How do I cite sources within the text of my document?

APA uses an author-date form of in-text citation to acknowledge the use of another writer's words, facts, or ideas. When you refer to a source, insert a parenthetical note that gives the author's last name and the year of the publication, separated by a comma. Even when your reference list includes the day or month of publication, the in-text citation should include only the year. For a quotation, the citation in parentheses also includes the page(s) on which the quotation can be found, if the source has page numbers. Note that APA style requires using the past tense or present perfect tense to introduce the material you are citing: *Renfrew argued* or *Renfrew has argued*.

1. Basic Format for Direct Quotation   When you are using a direct quotation from a source and have named the author in your sentence, place the publication date in parentheses directly after the author's last name. Include the page number (with "p." for *page*) in parentheses after the quotation.

> Yousafzai (2013) wrote that the door to her all-girls school in Swat "was like a magical entrance to our own special world" (p. 2).

If you are using a direct quotation from a source and have not mentioned the author's name in your sentence, place the author's last name, the publication date, and the page number in parentheses.

> (Yousafzai, 2013, p. 86).

V Documenting Sources

2. Basic Format for Summary or Paraphrase   When you are summarizing or paraphrasing, place the author's last name and the date either in the sentence or in parentheses at the end of the sentence. Include a page or chapter reference if it would help readers find the original material in a longer work.

> Baker (2011) questions how advances in artificial intelligence might undermine the value of human intelligence and knowledge in some realms (p. 15).

> As the Watson experiment demonstrates, even the physical appearance of artificial intelligence devices is shaped by human preconceptions — and fears — of technology (Baker, 2011, p. 112).

3. Two Authors   List the last names of both authors in every mention in the text. If you mention the authors' names in a sentence, use the word "and" to separate the last names, as shown in the first example. If you place the authors' names in the parenthetical citation, use an ampersand (&) to separate the last names, as shown in the second example.

> Drlica and Perlin (2011) wrote that "although many infections tend to occur in persons having weakened immune systems, MRSA can infect anyone" (p. 3).

> Everyone is susceptible to MRSA, not just those who are already weak or ill (Drlica & Perlin, 2011, p. 3).

4. Three, Four, or Five Authors   In parentheses, name all the authors the first time you cite the source, using an ampersand (&) before the last author's name. In subsequent references to the source, use the last name of the first author followed by the abbreviation "et al." (Latin for "and others").

> Visual illusions serve an important scientific purpose in illustrating the brain's processes (Macknik, Martinez-Conde, & Blakeselee, 2010).

> Neuroscientists have found much value in studying magic and how it subverts the brain's expectations of visual input (Macknik et al., 2010).

5. More Than Five Authors   In all references to the source, give the first author's last name followed by "et al."

> Coles et al. (2011) demonstrated the correlation between prenatal alcohol exposure, smaller brain size, and diminished memory function.

6. Corporate or Group Author   In general, cite the full name of the corporation or group the first time it is mentioned in your text. If you add an abbreviation for the group in square brackets the first time you cite the source, you can use the abbreviation in subsequent citations.

> Reactions to the idea of global climate change vary widely and are subject to many influences, including personal beliefs and cultural values (American

Psychological Association [APA], 2010, p. 6). Similarly, the psychosocial effects of the signs of climate change, such as fear and anxiety over dwindling natural resources or unusual weather patterns, are functions of individual and cultural contexts (APA, 2010, p. 7).

7. Unknown Author Sources with unknown authors are listed by title in the list of references. In your in-text citation, shorten the title as much as possible without introducing confusion. Add quotation marks to article titles, and italicize book titles.

The debate over evolution and creationism continues in the wake of recent scientific discoveries ("Fossil," 2015).

If a source identifies its author as "Anonymous," use that word to cite the author of the source.

The rise in coastal water levels has been referred to as a national crisis (Anonymous, 2016).

8. Two or More Works List the sources in alphabetical order and separate them with semicolons. If you are referring to two or more sources by the same author, order those sources chronologically.

While the rush of adrenaline experienced during combat can be lifesaving at the time, adrenaline levels in combat veterans can remain high even after their return home, resulting in an array of stress-related health problems (Friedman & Sloane, 2008; Hoge, 2010).

9. Source Quoted in Another Source Ideally, you will be able to find the primary, or original, source for material used in your research writing project document. If you quote or paraphrase a secondary source—a source that contains information about a primary source—mention the primary source and indicate that it was cited in the secondary source. Include the secondary source in your reference list.

In discussing the need for child protection in Romania, Tabacaru (2011) argued, "If conditions are not in place for foster care, they will all go to institutions" (as quoted in Nelson, Fox, & Zeanah, 2014, p. 61).

10. Source with No Page Numbers Many Web sources lack stable page numbers. If the source has numbered paragraphs, include the paragraph number using the abbreviation "para." If the paragraphs are not numbered, include the section heading and indicate which paragraph in that section you are referring to.

Tomasulo (2011) suggested that "there is a pattern to who and how we love" based on an attraction to traits that are familiar to us (para. 10).

V Documenting Sources

11. Two or More Authors with the Same Last Name Use the authors' initials in each citation.

> While C. Smith (2015) has noted an increase in early childhood psychiatric disorders, L. W. Smith (2017) suggested that many of these diagnoses in very young children might be inaccurate.

12. E-mail and Other Personal Communication Give the first initial(s) and last name of the person with whom you corresponded, the words "personal communication," and the date. Don't include personal communication in your reference list.

> (A. L. Chan, personal communication, October 9, 2013)

13. Document from a Website To cite a quotation from a website, give the paragraph number, if indicated, and include the source in your reference list.

> Lehrer (2011) noted that the era of the "lone genius" may be ending, replaced instead by collaborative thinking and research (para. 13).

21b

How do I prepare the reference list?

The reference list contains publication information for all sources that you have cited within your document, with one main exception. Personal communications— such as correspondence, e-mail messages, and interviews—are cited only in the text of the document.

Begin the list on a new page at the end of the document and center the title "References" at the top. Organize the list alphabetically by author; if the source is an organization, alphabetize the source by the name of the organization. All entries should be double-spaced with no extra space between entries. Entries are formatted with a hanging indent: The first line of an entry is flush with the left margin and subsequent lines are indented one-half inch or five spaces. In longer documents, a reference list could be given at the end of each chapter or section. In digital documents that use links, such as websites, the reference list is often a separate page to which other pages are linked. For an example of a reference list in APA style, see p. 383.

Books, Conference Proceedings, and Dissertations

14. One Author Capitalize the first word, proper nouns, and the first word following a colon in titles.

Skloot, R. (2010). *The immortal life of Henrietta Lacks*. New York, NY: Crown.

TUTORIAL

How do I cite books using APA style?

When citing a book, use the information from the title page and the copyright page (on the back side of the title page), not from the book's cover or a library catalog. Consult pp. 360–65 for additional models.

Lanier, J. (2013). *Who owns the future?* New York, NY: Simon & Schuster.

A **The author.** Give the last name first, followed by a comma and initials for first and, if any, middle names. Separate initials with a space (Leakey, R. E.). Separate the names of multiple authors with commas; use an ampersand (&) before the final author's name.

B **The year of publication.** Put the most recent copyright year in parentheses, and end with a period (outside the parentheses).

C **The title and, if any, the subtitle.** Give the full title; include the subtitle (if any), preceded by a colon. Italicize the title and subtitle, capitalizing only the first word of the title, the first word of the subtitle, and any proper nouns or proper adjectives. End with a period.

D **The place of publication.** If more than one city is given, use the first one listed. Use an abbreviation for U.S. states and territories; spell out city and country names for locations outside the United States (Cambridge, England). For Canadian cities, also include the province. Insert a colon.

E **The publisher.** Give the publisher's name. Omit words such as *Inc.* and *Co.* Include and do not abbreviate such terms as *University*, *Books*, and *Press*. End with a period.

V Documenting Sources

APA recommends citing an e-book only if the print version is difficult or impossible to find. Cite an e-book as you would a print book, but identify the file format or e-reader type for the book in brackets following the title. If the book was found on the Web and it has a DOI (digital object identifier, a unique number assigned to specific content), provide the DOI at the end of the citation, preceded by "http://dx.doi.org/". Do not end the DOI with a period. If no DOI is available, provide the URL preceded by "Retrieved from."

Clark, Greg. (2015). *The making of a world city: London 1991 to 2021*. John
    Wiley & Sons. Wiley Online Library, http://dx.doi.org/10.1002/9781118609705

Emerson, L. (2016). *The forgotten tribe: Scientists as writers* [ePub]. Fort Collins, CO:
    The WAC Clearinghouse. Retrieved from http://wac.colostate.edu/books/emerson/

15. Two or More Authors   List the authors in the same order as the title page does, each with last name first. Use commas to separate authors and use an ampersand (&) before the final author's name. List every author up to seven; for a work with more than seven authors, give the first six names followed by a comma, three ellipsis dots, and the final author's name. (Do not use an ampersand.)

Watkins, D., & Brook, Y. (2016). *Equal is unfair: America's misguided fight against
    income inequality*. New York, NY: St. Martin's Press.

16. Corporate or Group Author   Write out the full name of a corporate or group author. If the corporation is also the publisher, use "Author" for the publisher's name.

Linguistic Society of America. (2016). *Annual report: The state of linguistics in
    higher education*. Washington, DC: Author.

17. Unknown Author   When there is no author listed on the title or copyright page, begin the entry with the title of the work. Alphabetize the entry by the first significant word of the title (not including *A, An*, or *The*).

Going within to get out. (2013). Bloomington, IN: Balboa.

18. Two or More Works by the Same Author(s)   Give the author's name in each entry and list the works in chronological order.

Duhigg, C. (2012). *The power of habit: Why we do what we do in life and
    business*. New York, NY: Random House.

Duhigg, C. (2016). *Smarter, faster, better: The secrets of being productive in life
    and business*. New York, NY: Random House.

19. Translated Book   List the author first, followed by the year of publication, the title, and the translator (in parentheses, identified by the abbreviation "Trans."). Place the original date of the work's publication at the end of the entry.

Oz, A. (2013). *Between friends* (S. Silverston, Trans.). New York, NY: Houghton
    Mifflin Harcourt.

20. Book in a Series   After the book title, provide the name of the series, followed by "Series" in square brackets.

Fidell, E. R. (2016). *Military justice.* Very short introductions 227 [Series]. Oxford, England: Oxford University Press.

21. Republication   Provide the most recent date of publication. Identify the original publication date in parentheses following the publisher information.

Freud, S. (2010). *The interpretation of dreams* (J. Strachey, Ed. & Trans.). New York, NY: Basic Books. (Original work published 1955)

22. Book in an Edition Other Than the First   Note the edition ("2nd ed.," "Rev. ed.") after the title.

Spatt, B. (2016). *Writing from sources* (9th ed.). Boston, MA: Bedford/ St. Martin's.

23. Multivolume Work   Include the number of volumes in parentheses after the title.

Delbanco, N., & Cheuse, A. (Eds.). (2010). *Literature: Craft and voice* (Vols. 1–3). Boston, MA: McGraw–Hill.

If you have used only one volume in a multivolume work, identify that volume by number and by title.

Delbanco, N., & Cheuse, A. (Eds.). (2010). *Literature: Craft and voice: Vol. 1. Fiction.* Boston, MA: McGraw–Hill.

24. Editor   Include "Ed." or "Eds." in parentheses.

Bryson, B. (Ed.). (2010). *Seeing further: The story of science, discovery, and the genius of the Royal Society.* New York, NY: Morrow.

25. Author with an Editor   Include the editor's name and the abbreviation "Ed." in parentheses after the title.

Mencken, H. L. (2010). *Mencken: Prejudices, first, second, and third* (M. E. Rodgers, Ed.). New York, NY: Library of America.

26. Anthology   To cite an entire anthology of essays or collection of articles, list the editor or editors first, followed by the abbreviation "Ed." or "Eds." in parentheses.

Van Wormer, K. S., & Thyer, B. A. (Eds.). (2010). *Evidence-based practice in the field of substance abuse: A book of readings.* Thousand Oaks, CA: Sage.

V Documenting Sources

27. Chapter in an Edited Book or Selection in an Anthology Begin the entry with the author, the publication date, and the title of the chapter or selection (not italicized). Follow this with the names of the editors (initials first) and the abbreviation "Ed." or "Eds." in parentheses, the title of the anthology or collection (italicized), inclusive page numbers for the chapter or selection (in parentheses, with abbreviation "pp."), and place and publisher.

Sargeant, S. (2016). Psychology and models of health. In A. Tom & P. Greasley (Eds.), *Psychology for nursing* (pp. 21–34). London, England: Polity Press.

28. Foreword, Introduction, Preface, or Afterword Treat as you would a chapter in a book.

Joli, F. (2016). Foreword. In J. Arena, *Legends of disco: Forty stars discuss their careers* (pp. 1–2). Jefferson, NC: McFarland.

29. Published Proceedings of a Conference Cite information as you would for a book.

Mayor, J., & Gomez, P. (Eds.). (2014). *Computational models of cognitive processes: Proceedings of the 13th Neural Computation and Psychology Workshop*. Singapore: World Scientific Publishing.

30. Paper Published in the Proceedings of a Conference Treat a conference paper as you would a selection from an edited collection.

Jacobs, G. M., & Toh-Heng, H. L. (2013). Small steps towards student-centered learning. In P. Mandal (Ed.), *Proceedings of the international conference on managing the Asian century* (pp. 55–64). Singapore: Springer.

31. Sacred Text Treat as you would a book (see p. 361).

The Holy Bible: King James version. (2010). Quatercentenary Ed. Oxford, England: Oxford University Press.

32. Published Dissertation or Thesis If a published dissertation or thesis is available through a commercial database, give the author, date, title, and a description in parentheses ("Doctoral dissertation" or "Master's thesis"). Then give the database name in italics, followed by any UMI or order number in parentheses.

Selberg, S. (2013). *Seeing the person within: Visual culture and Alzheimer's disease* (Doctoral dissertation, New York University). Available from *ProQuest Dissertations and Theses* database. (UMI No. 3553975).

If the material is accessed from an institutional database or other website, provide the URL.

Kim, J. (2012). *Promoting sustainable communities through Infill: The effect of Infill housing on neighborhood income diversity* (Doctoral thesis, University of Florida). Retrieved from http://ufdc.ufl.edu/UFE0044904/00001

33. Unpublished Dissertation or Thesis   Format as you would a book, replacing the publisher information with the phrase "Unpublished doctoral dissertation" or "Unpublished master's thesis," followed by information about the college or university.

McQueen, J. Y. (2013). *On the road of phonological treatment: Paths of learning* (Unpublished honors thesis). Indiana University, Bloomington.

Sources in Journals, Magazines, and Newspapers

34. Article in a Journal Paginated by Volume   Most journals continue page numbers throughout an entire annual volume, beginning again at page 1 only in the first volume of the next year. After the author and publication year, provide the article title, the journal title, the volume number (italicized), and the inclusive page numbers.

Pope, N. D., & Kang, B. (2010). Residential relocation in later life: A comparison of proactive and reactive moves. *Journal of Housing for the Elderly, 24,* 193–207.

If a DOI is available, include it at the end of the citation and precede it by "http://dx.doi.org/". Do not end the DOI with a period. You do not need to provide a retrieval date or database name.

Schwander, T., Vuilleumier, S., Dubman, J., & Crespi, B. J. (2010). Positive feedback in the transition from sexual reproduction to parthenogenesis. *Proceedings of the Royal Society Biology, 277,* 1435–1442. http://dx.doi .org/10.1098/rspb.2009.2113

If the article is obtained online, but no DOI is provided, give the exact URL for the article (or for the home page of the journal, if access requires a subscription).

Stieb, J. A. (2011). Understanding engineering professionalism: A reflection on the rights of engineers. *Science and Engineering Ethics, 17*(1), 149–169. Retrieved from http://springerlink.com/content/r58q044521917785/

If the article comes from a database but no DOI is provided, give the URL of the home page of the journal.

Robertson, L. A. (2010). The spiritual competency scale. *Counseling and Values, 55*(1), 6–24. Retrieved from http://www.counseling.org

TUTORIAL

How do I cite articles from periodicals using APA style?

The Politics of Poverty:
Definitions and Explanations

DENNIS RAPHAEL

Periodicals include journals, magazines, and newspapers. This tutorial gives an example of a citation for a print journal article. Models for citing articles from magazines and newspapers are on pp. 365–69. If you need to cite a periodical article you accessed electronically, follow the guidelines below and see p. 367.

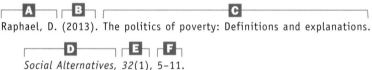

Raphael, D. (2013). The politics of poverty: Definitions and explanations.

Social Alternatives, 32(1), 5–11.

A   **The author.** Give the last name first, followed by a comma and initials for first and, if any, middle names. Separate the names of multiple authors with commas; use an ampersand (&) before the final author's name.

B   **The year of publication.** Put the year in parentheses and end with a period (outside the parentheses). For magazines and newspapers, include the month and, if relevant, the day (2010, April 13).

C   **The article title.** Give the full title; include the subtitle (if any), preceded by a colon. Do not underline, italicize, or put the title in quotation marks. Capitalize only the first word of the title, the first word of the subtitle, and any proper nouns or proper adjectives. End with a period.

D   **The periodical title.** Italicize the periodical title, and capitalize all major words. Insert a comma.

E   **The volume and issue number, if relevant.** For journals, include the volume number, italicized. If each issue starts with page 1, include the issue number in parentheses, not italicized. Insert a comma.

F   **Inclusive page number(s).** Give all numbers in full (248–254, not 248–54). For newspapers, include the abbreviation "p." for page and section letters, if relevant (p. B12). End with a period.

TUTORIAL

How do I cite digital periodical articles using APA style?

Many periodical articles can be accessed online, either through a journal or magazine's website or through a database (see Chapter 10). Provide the print publication information and then the Web information.

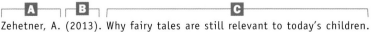

Zehetner, A. (2013). Why fairy tales are still relevant to today's children.

Journal of Paediatrics & Child Health, 49, 161–162.

http://dx.doi.org/10.1111/jpc.12080

A **The author.** Give the last name first, followed by a comma and initials. Separate the names of multiple authors with commas; use an ampersand (&) before the final author's name.

B **The date of publication.** Put the year in parentheses and end with a period (outside the parentheses). For magazines and newspapers, include the month and, if relevant, the day (2010, April 13).

C **The article title.** Give the full title; include the subtitle (if any), preceded by a colon. Do not underline, italicize, or put the title or subtitle in quotation marks. Capitalize only the first word of the title, the first word of the subtitle, and any proper nouns or proper adjectives. End with a period.

D **The periodical title.** Italicize the periodical title, and capitalize all major words. Insert a comma.

E **The volume number and issue number.** For journals, include the volume number, italicized. If each issue starts with page 1, include the issue number in parentheses, not italicized. Insert a comma.

F **Inclusive page numbers(s).** Give all numbers in full (317–327, not 317–27). For newspapers, include the abbreviation "p." for page and section letters, if relevant (p. B12). End with a period.

G **The DOI or URL.** Give the unique digital object identifier (DOI) number, preceded by "http://dx.doi.org/" and with no punctuation at the end. You do not need to provide a retrieval date or database name. If there is no DOI, include the words "Retrieved from" and the URL of the publication's home page.

35. Article in a Journal Paginated by Issue Some journals begin at page 1 for every issue. Include the issue number (in parentheses, not italicized) after the volume number.

Carlozzi, N. E., Horner, M. D., Kose, S., Yamanaka, K., Mishory, A., Mu, Q., . . .
George, M. S. (2010). Personality and reaction time after sleep deprivation.
Current Psychology, 29(1), 24–33.

36. Article in an Online Journal or Periodical If the article is obtained online or through a database, publication information is followed by the DOI or URL. Since the article was published online, it may not have page numbers.

Carillo, Ellen C. (2016). Engaging sources through reading-writing connections
across the disciplines. *Across the Disciplines, 13*(1). Retrieved from http://
wac.colostate.edu/atd/articles/carillo2016.cfm

37. Article in a Magazine The author's name and the publication date are followed by the title of the article, the magazine title (italicized), and the volume number, if any (also italicized). Include all page numbers.

Foer, F. (2016, October 2). Triumph of the oligarchs. *New York,* 17–19.

If the article is obtained online or through a database, publication information is followed by the DOI or URL. Since the article was published online, it is unlikely to have page numbers.

Colby, T. (2014, February 27). The failure of integration on Madison Avenue —
and what it says about race in America. *Slate.* Retrieved from http://www
.slate.com

38. Article in a Newspaper List the author's name and the complete date (year first). Next give the article title, followed by the name of the newspaper (italicized). Include all page numbers, preceded by "p." or "pp."

Filipov, D. (2010, October 1). Diehards say texting tough to kick. *The Boston
Globe,* p. B8.

39. Unsigned Article in a Newspaper Begin with the article title, and alphabetize in the reference list by the first word in the title other than *A, An,* or *The.* Use "p." or "pp." before page numbers.

RNA-only genes: The origin of species? (2012, April 28). *The Economist,
388*(8592), p. 40.

40. Letter to the Editor Include the words "Letter to the editor" in square brackets after the title of the letter, if any.

Gonzalez Hernandez, L. (2012, November 23). Stores should close on holidays
[Letter to the editor]. *Newsday,* p. A24.

41. Review After the title of the review, include the words "Review of the book ..." or "Review of the film ..." and so on in brackets, followed by the title of the work reviewed.

Lane, A. (2014, December 15). Swinging seventies [Review of the film *Inherent Vice*, 2014]. *The New Yorker*, p. 76.

When the review is untitled, follow the date with the bracketed information.

Turan, K. (2010, November 26). [Review of the film *The King's Speech*, 2010]. *Los Angeles Times*, p. D1.

42. Published Interview Cite a published interview like a journal article (see p. 365).

Massondo, A. (2010, July). Yellow-card journalism [Interview by C. Barron]. *Harper's, 321*(1921), 17–18.

43. Two or More Works by the Same Author in the Same Year List the works alphabetically and include lowercase letters (*a*, *b*, etc.) after the dates.

Iglehart, J. K. (2010a). The ACA's new weapons against health care fraud. *The New England Journal of Medicine, 363*, 1589–1591.

Iglehart, J. K. (2010b). Health reform, primary care, and graduate medical education. *The New England Journal of Medicine, 363*, 584–590.

Reference Works

44. Encyclopedia, Dictionary, Thesaurus, Handbook, or Almanac Cite a reference work, such as an encyclopedia or dictionary, as you would a book (p. 361).

Priest, S. H. (Ed.). (2016). *Encyclopedia of science and technology communication* (Vols. 1–2). Thousand Oaks, CA: Sage.

45. Entry in Encyclopedia, Dictionary, Thesaurus, Handbook, or Almanac Begin your citation with the name of the author or, if the entry is unsigned, the title of the entry. Proceed with the date, the entry title (if not already given), the title of the reference work, the edition number, and the pages.

Human genome project. (2016). In S. H. Priest (Ed.), *Encyclopedia of science and technology communication* (Vol. 1, pp. 374–379). Thousand Oaks, CA: Sage.

If the entry came from an online source, give the URL for the home page or index page.

Cultural anthropology. (2017). In *Encyclopaedia Britannica*. Retrieved from http://www.britannica.com

V Documenting Sources

46. Government Publication   Give the name of the department (or office, agency, or committee) that issued the report as the author. If the document has a report or special file number, place that in parentheses after the title.

U.S. Department of Health and Human Services. (2010). Ending the tobacco
epidemic: A tobacco control strategic action plan for the U.S. Department of
Health and Human Services. Washington, DC: Government Printing Office.

47. Brochure or Pamphlet   Format the entry as you would a book (p. 361).

Alcoholics Anonymous. (2011). *The A.A. member — medications and other drugs.*
New York, NY: Alcoholics Anonymous World Services.

Field Sources

48. Personal Interview   Treat unpublished interviews as personal communications and include them in your text only (p. 360). Do not cite personal interviews in your reference list.

49. Letter   Cite a personal letter only in the text (p. 360), not in the reference list.

50. Lecture or Public Address   Cite a lecture or public address the same way you would cite an unpublished paper presented at a conference.

Lander, E. (2010, April 19). Secrets of the human genome. Lecture presented at
Princeton University, Princeton, NJ.

Media Sources

51. Film or Video   List the director and producer (if available), the date of release, the title followed by "Motion picture" in square brackets, the country where the film was made, and the studio or distributor.

Aronofsky, D. (Director). (2010). *Black swan* [Motion picture]. United States: Fox
Searchlight.

For videos found on the Web, include the words "Video file" in square brackets after the title and give the URL after the publication information. If there is no author name, list the screen name provided.

GeckoGeekFr. (2010, January 6). How to make a traditional origami crane [Video
file]. Retrieved from http://www.youtube.com/watch?v=jUZaOWibCcs

52. Television or Radio Program   Cite as you would a chapter in a book. For a television program, list the director (if available), the broadcast date, and the title followed by "Television broadcast" or "Television series episode," in square brackets. Then add information on the series, location, and station.

Jennings, T. (Writer, Producer, & Director), & Bomse, S. (Writer). (2010, August 25). Law and disorder [Television series episode]. In D. Fanning (Executive producer), *Frontline*. Boston, MA: WGBH.

For a radio program, the title should be followed by "Radio broadcast" or "Radio series episode," in square brackets.

Young, R. (Host). (2011, January 21). Center focuses on treating Alzheimer's by comforting residents, not medicating them [Radio series episode]. In K. McKenna (Senior producer), *Here and now*. Boston, MA: WBUR.

If you accessed the program on the Web, include the URL.

Keillor, G. (Producer & Narrator). (2016, February 27). Take a giant step [Radio series episode]. In *A Prairie Home Companion*. St. Paul, MN: American Public Media. Retrieved from https://www.prairiehome.org/shows/51408

53. Sound Recording, Audio Clip, or Podcast   Name the author of the song, the date, the song title followed by "On" and the recording title in italics, the medium (in square brackets), and the production data.

Adele. (2015). Hello. On *25* [MP3]. London, England: XL Recordings.

For audio clips or podcasts accessed on the Web, add the URL after the publication information.

Jones-Walker, C. (2010, May 21). *Learning and becoming: The construction of identity in urban classrooms* [Audio podcast]. Retrieved from Swarthmore College website: http://media.swarthmore.edu/faculty_lectures/?p=182

54. Work of Art, Photograph, or Other Image   Cite as you would a recording. Include the artist and publication date, if known. If the artist is unknown, begin with the title of the work. If the date is unknown, use "n.d." for "no date." Indicate the medium in square brackets. Identify the city and gallery or publisher.

Vermeer, J. (1665). *Girl with a pearl earring* [Oil painting]. The Hague: Mauritshuis.

If the source is found online, include the URL.

Jet Propulsion Laboratory. (2014). Opportunity's *southward view of "McClure-Beverlin Escarpment" on Mars* [Photograph]. NASA. Retrieved from http://photojournal.jpl.nasa.gov/jpeg/PIA17943.jpg

Other Digital Sources

55. Nonperiodical Web Document   For a stand-alone Web source, such as a report, an online brochure, or a blog, cite as much of the following information as possible: author, publication date, document title, description of the material

TUTORIAL

How do I cite works from websites using APA style?

You will likely need to scan the website to find some of the citation information you need. For some sites, all of the details may not be available; find as many as you can. Remember that the citation you provide should allow readers to retrace your steps to locate the source. Consult pp. 371–74 for additional models for citing Web sources.

A **B** **C**

Moyer, H. (2014, February 10). A witness to environmental justice over twenty

D **E**

years [Article]. In *Compass: Pointing the way to a clean energy future.*

F

Retrieved from http://sierraclub.typepad.com/compass/2014/02

/a-witness-to-environmental-justice-over-20-years.html

A **The author of the work.** Give the last name first, followed by a comma and initials. Separate the names of multiple authors with commas; use an ampersand (&) before the final author's name. If the source has no author, list the title first and follow it with the date.

B **The date of publication.** Put the year in parentheses and include the month, if available. If there is no date, use "n.d." in parentheses, and include a retrieval date before the URL. End with a period (outside the parentheses).

C **The title of the work.** Give the full title, italicized; include the subtitle (if any), preceded by a colon. Capitalize only the first word of the title, the first word of the subtitle, and any proper nouns or proper adjectives. Do not use italics for articles and other short works within a larger work on the website. Do use italics if the work is a stand-alone report or other full-length document.

D **A description of the work.** Include a description of the work (such as "Report" or "Blog post") in brackets.

E **The title of the larger work.** If the work you are citing is part of a larger work on the website, provide the name of the larger work in italics, preceded by "In." Capitalize only the first word of the title, the first word of the subtitle, and any proper nouns or proper adjectives.

F **Retrieval information.** Include a retrieval date only if the material lacks a set publication date. If the website name (such as "Sierra Club") is not clear from the URL, include it with the retrieval information, without italics or quotation marks, capitalizing the first letter of all major words. (Since this article has a set publication date and the URL contains the website name, neither the retrieval date nor the site name is necessary.) End with the URL.

in brackets, and URL. Include a retrieval date before the URL only when the original publication date is unknown. Include the site name in the retrieval statement if the site name is not part of the URL.

Mayo Clinic. (2016, June 9). *Quit smoking* [Web page]. Retrieved from http://
    www.mayoclinic.com/health/quit-smoking/MY00433

For a chapter or section within a Web document, identify the section title, followed by a description in brackets, as well as the main document.

Davis, J. L. (2015). Coping with anxiety [Article]. In *Anxiety and panic disorders
    guide.* Retrieved from http://www.webmd.com/anxiety-panic/guide/coping
    -with-anxiety

American Psychological Association. (n.d.). *Topics in psychology* [Web page].
    Retrieved March 12, 2017, from http://www.apa.org/topics/index.aspx

56. E-mail Message or Real-Time Communication   Because e-mail messages are difficult or impossible for your readers to retrieve, APA does not recommend including them in your reference list. You should treat them as personal communications and cite them parenthetically in your text (see entry 12 on p. 360).

57. Article Posted on a Wiki   Include a description in brackets after the article or entry title. Include a retrieval date only if the material does not include a specific publication date.

Sensory deprivation [Wiki entry]. (2017, February 27). Retrieved from http://
    en.wikipedia.org/wiki/Sensory_deprivation

58. Message Posted to a Newsgroup, E-mail List, or Online Discussion Forum   List the author, the posting date, the message title, and a description of the message in brackets. Then add the retrieval information, including the name of the list or forum.

Nelms, J. (2016, January 14). Re: Evaluating writing faculty [Online discussion list
    post]. Retrieved from https://lists.asu.edu/cgi-bin/wa?A1=ind1601&L=WPA-L#50

59. Blog   To cite an entry on a blog, give the author (or screen name), the date the material was posted, the title of the entry, a description of the entry in brackets ("Blog post" or "Blog comment"), and the URL.

Gudmundsen, J. (2014, February 18). Toy Fair 2014: The way your kids play is
    about to change [Blog post]. Retrieved from http://www.commonsensemedia
    .org/blog/toy-fair-2014-the-way-your-kids-play-is-about-to-change

V Documenting Sources

Jane. (2010, November 10). Re: For caregivers, it's OK to feel good and bad [Blog comment]. Retrieved from http://www.mayoclinic.com/health /alzheimers-caregivers/MY01563_comments#post

60. Twitter Post (Tweet) Include the author's real name, if known, followed by the screen name in brackets. If the real name is not known, provide only the screen name without brackets. Provide the date, the complete text of the tweet, followed by "Tweet" in brackets, and the retrieval URL.

Applebaum, Y. (2016, March 29). I can say as a historian, with a fair amount of confidence, that scholars will certainly mine social media in the future — they already are [Tweet]. Retrieved from https://twitter.com/YAppelbaum /status/714822912172285952

61. Facebook Page, Post, or Status Update Include the author or organization name, followed by the date, title, or text of the update. Then include the description of the entry in brackets ("Facebook page," "Facebook note," or "Facebook status update") and the retrieval URL.

NSA — National Security Agency. (2014, February 27). This article suggests that instead of focusing on cybersecurity, companies need to move to "cyber resilience." Do you agree? http://ow.ly/tyZUL [Facebook status update]. Retrieved from https://www.facebook.com/NSACareers

62. File Obtained Online Cite as you would a nonperiodical Web document (see p. 371). Identify the medium in square brackets after the title.

Jessedee. (n.d.). 5 Presentation lessons from *The King's Speech* [PowerPoint slides]. Retrieved March 9, 2017, from http://www.slideshare.net/jessedee /presentation-lessons-from-the-kings-speech-6551851

63. Computer Software Sometimes a person is named as having rights to the program, software, or language: In that case, list that person as the author. Otherwise, begin the entry with the name of the program and identify the source in square brackets after the name as "Computer software." Treat the organization that produces the software as the publisher. If you're referring to a specific version that isn't included in the name, put this information in parentheses immediately after the title.

Microsoft Office 365 [Computer software]. Redmond, WA: Microsoft.

Other Sources

64. General Advice about Other Sources For citing other types of sources, APA suggests that you use as a guide a source type listed in their manual that most closely resembles the type of source you want to cite.

APA-Style Research Essay

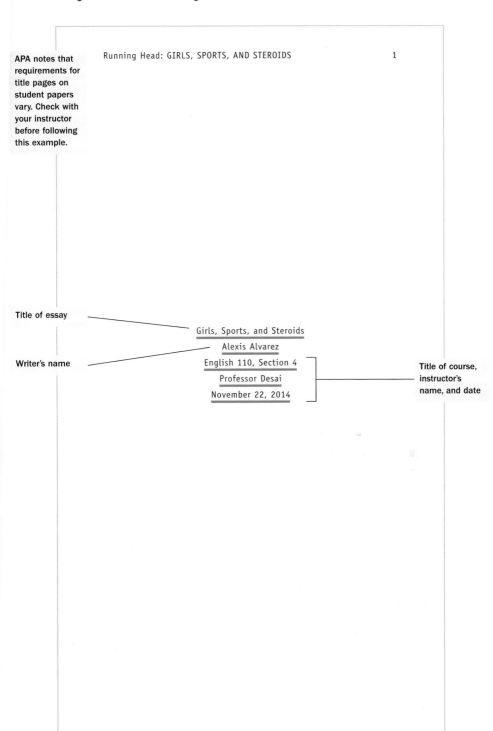

APA notes that requirements for title pages on student papers vary. Check with your instructor before following this example.

Running Head: GIRLS, SPORTS, AND STEROIDS   1

Title of essay

Writer's name

Girls, Sports, and Steroids
Alexis Alvarez
English 110, Section 4
Professor Desai
November 22, 2014

Title of course, instructor's name, and date

Title of essay repeated

Girls, Sports, and Steroids

Almost daily, headlines and newscasters tell us about athletes' use of performance-enhancing drugs. Indeed, stories of such drug use seem to increase each year, with investigations of possible steroid use by college football players, by major league baseball players, and even by Olympic gold medalists. It is easy to gain the impression that many adult athletes, particularly males, may be using drugs in order to improve their performance and physical appearance. What may be surprising and even shocking to most of us, however, is that these drugs, especially anabolic steroids, are increasingly used by adolescent athletes and that girls are just as likely as boys to be users.

> **Alexis's statement is likely to surprise readers, drawing them into the essay.**

In May 2004, the Centers for Disease Control and Prevention (CDC) published its latest figures on self-reported drug use among young people in grades 9 through 12. The CDC study, "Youth Risk Behavior Surveillance — December 2003," found that 6.1% of its survey participants reported using steroids at least once, up from 2.2% in 1993. The report also showed that use of steroids appears to be increasing among younger girls: While only 3.3% of 12th-grade girls reported using steroids, 7.3% of 9th-grade girls reported using them. Moreover, girls might be starting to use steroids at a higher rate than boys. The CDC study indicated that 9th-grade girls had reported slightly higher rates of steroid use than boys (7.3% and 6.9%, respectively), while 10th-, 11th-, and 12th-grade girls all reported lower use than boys. Other studies support the conclusion that steroid use is both widespread and rising quickly among adolescent girls. According to Mundell (2004), experts estimate that as many as a million high school students have used steroids — and that a significant percentage of that group are girls. Moreover, since the late 1990s, studies have shown that steroid use is increasing among adolescent girls. In 1998, *Teacher Magazine* reported that steroid use among high school girls had increased 300% since 1991, from 0.4% of all high school girls to 1.4% ("Girls and Steroids," 1998). And Manning (2002) wrote, "A 1999 Youth Risk Behavior Surveillance study by the Centers for Disease Control and the 2001 Monitoring the Future survey both show steady growth in steroid use by 8th- to 12th-graders" ("Kids, steroids don't mix," para. 2).

> **Effective use of statistical evidence shows growth of the problem over time.**

> **Source of paraphrased information is acknowledged using APA's parenthetical reference system.**

> **A source that does not have an author is identified by shortened title and publication year.**

> **Section heading and paragraph number are given for location of material quoted from an online source.**

What role are competitive sports playing in this dangerous trend? Why are some girls feeling the need to ingest performance-enhancing drugs? Although competitive sports can provide young female athletes with many benefits, they can also have negative effects, the worst of which is increasing drug use. Let's look first at the positives.

> **Thesis states Alexis's main point.**

Girls and Sports: The Upside

Millions of girls are now involved in a variety of sports activities, and girls' participation in school athletics and community-based programs continues to increase. As the President's Council on Physical Fitness and Sports (1997) has pointed out, when girls participate in competitive sports, their lives can be affected in a number of positive and interrelated ways. Physical and psychological health, a positive sense of identity, good relationships with friends and family, and improved performance in school all work together to influence a girl's complete growth and development.

According to the President's Council (1997), adolescent girls who exercise regularly can lessen their risks for adult-onset coronary disease and certain cancers. Girls' involvement in sports and exercise also tends to improve immune functioning, posture, strength, flexibility, and heart-lung endurance (Dudley, 1994; President's Council, 1997).

In addition, competitive athletics can enhance mental health by offering adolescent girls positive feelings about body image; tangible experiences of competency, control, and success; improved self-esteem and self-confidence; and a way to reduce anxiety (President's Council, 1997). Juan Orozco, who has coached adolescent females in competitive soccer for nine years, confirmed that making a competitive sports team is a privilege that many girls work toward with determination and longing and that being picked to participate encourages these young athletes to believe in themselves and their abilities (personal communication, September 22, 2014).

A final benefit is that sports expand social boundaries and teach many of the personal and social skills girls will need throughout their lives. According to Orozco, through competitive athletics girls learn a crucial lesson in how to interact with, get along with, and depend on athletes from different social and economic groups. In short, they learn to adapt to and enjoy each other's differences. Melissa Alvarez, a 17-year-old athlete who has participated in high school basketball and club soccer, draws a similar conclusion. In an interview, she stated that sports "give you something to work for as an individual and as a team. You learn self-discipline and dedication, which are essential skills to have in life" (personal communication, September 26, 2007). Competitive sports also teach athletes how to cope with failure as well as success. In the best of situations, as Sieghart (2004) noted, athletes are able to assess their achievements realistically, letting neither winning nor losing consume their reality.

Marginal annotations:

Headings, boldface and centered throughout, help readers follow the essay's organization.

Shortened name of the council; it was introduced by its full name the first time it was cited.

Title of essay, shortened if necessary, followed by page number on the right

Two sources are cited in one parenthetical citation.

Personal communication — an interview — is cited in the text of the document but not in the reference list.

An author tag alerts readers that information is taken from a source.

V Documenting Sources

Girls and Sports: The Downside

In spite of the many positive effects of competitive athletics, sports can have a negative impact on girls' bodies and minds, and some girls falter under the pressure to succeed. Overtraining, eating disorders, and exercise-induced amenorrhea (which may result in osteoporosis) are some of the most common negative physical side effects that young female athletes experience; negative psychological and social side effects include increased stress and anxiety and a loss of self-confidence. Let's look at each of these effects.

Negative Physical Side Effects

Overtraining occurs when your body can no longer adapt to increasing workloads — instead of building up, it breaks down. When a young girl overtrains, her body's balance between training and recovery is lost. Because the athlete's body can't recover, her performance stays flat and she cannot improve. Overtraining also makes a young female athlete prone to a variety of physical and psychological ills, such as unusual fatigue, irritability, feelings of apathy, and menstrual irregularities (Graham, 1999).

Another negative effect is amenorrhea, which refers to an atypical inability to menstruate. Graham (1999) pointed out, "In some sports as many as 50% of the athletes who are competitive may suffer from what's known as exercise-induced or athletic amenorrhea" (p. 26). Furthermore, research has shown that when a woman does not menstruate regularly, she loses bone density and becomes more prone to stress fractures (cracks in bones, especially hands and feet) and osteoporosis later in life. Amenorrhea can be caused by inadequate nutrition as well as by overtraining, both of which cause the athlete to burn more calories than she eats. As a result, her body shuts down its reproductive function to conserve energy (Graham, 1999).

The tendency to develop an eating disorder, such as anorexia or bulimia, is a third possible effect. Although young women may develop eating disorders for a variety of reasons, Graham (1999) noted, "Disordered eating is high among female athletes competing in sports where leanness and/or a specific weight are considered important for either performance or appearance" (p. 74). Being slim and trim may be the goal of many adolescent female athletes, but when they seek that goal by means of an eating disorder, they hinder their athletic performance. A calorie deficit actually decreases immune function, reduces aerobic capacity, decreases muscle mass and strength, and causes low energy and fatigue (Graham, 1999).

Page number identifies the location of material quoted from a print source.

GIRLS, SPORTS, AND STEROIDS   5

Negative Psychological and Social Effects

Just as a girl's body and mind often benefit from sports, so too are body and mind linked when it comes to those aspects of sports that are not positive. Often, negative physical effects occur because female athletes feel the need to win at any cost and the pressure to attain an unrealistic ideal. They may resort to extremes such as overtraining in order to have the "ideal" body or be the "best of the best." When they can't meet these expectations, some girl athletes lose self-confidence and become overly stressed and anxious. In fact, they may see their failures as a serious threat to their self-esteem (Davies & Armstrong, 1989).

Pressures at home, at school, among friends, and from coaches can be daunting as well because young athletes tend to worry about the actions and reactions of the people who make up their social circles (Brown & Branta, 1988). In addition, learning to balance the demands of sports, school, family, and fun can be incredibly fatiguing. Juan Orozco recalled that some of the girls he coached were involved in three sports at a time and still had to keep their grades up in order to participate (personal communication, September 22, 2014). Add to these demands the pressure from parents, and real problems can occur. Gary Anderson, a girls' basketball coach for more than two decades, has seen it all: parents who are overly dramatic, teams that serve primarily as stages for a few superstar athletes, and girls who seem "factory-installed with a sense of entitlement simply because they know their way around a ball and a pair of high-tops" (Dexheimer, 2004, para. 15). All of these situations and pressures affect young female athletes and can result in their making some regrettable, if not devastating, choices.

Girls' Reactions: Burnout and Steroids

What happens when these young women decide the pressure is too much? What measures will they take to lighten their load? Some of these athletes simply burn out. They stop participating in competitive athletics because the pressure and anxiety make them physically ill. They no longer enjoy competitive sports, but consider them a torment to be endured. In fact, according to Davies and Armstrong (1989), it is not unusual for promising 12-year-olds to abandon the game entirely by the age of 16 and move on to less distressing pastimes. Melissa Alvarez had one such experience while playing high school basketball. The coach put so much pressure on her that her stomach began to ache during games and during practice. The more the coach yelled, the worse she played, but when the coach

---

Subheadings are set in boldface and aligned flush left to differentiate them from higher-level headings.

A partial quotation is integrated into the sentence.

GIRLS, SPORTS, AND STEROIDS   6

was absent, her performance improved dramatically and her stomach
problems disappeared. Eventually, Melissa quit the basketball team
because the game had become a burden instead of something she
enjoyed (M. Alvarez, personal communication, September 26, 2014).

An alternative much more dangerous than burnout, however, is
the use of performance-enhancing drugs such as anabolic steroids. A
2003 article in *Drug Week* stated that girls who participate in sports
more than eight hours a week are at considerable risk for taking
many illicit drugs: The higher the level at which athletes compete,
the higher their risk for substance abuse ("Sporting Activities").

Teenage girls take steroids for some of the same reasons that
professional athletes do — to increase stamina and strength and
to acquire a lean, muscular body. However, girls also take steroids
to compete for athletic scholarships ("Girls and Steroids," 1998).
According to Charles Yesalis, a professor of sports science and senior
author of a Penn State report, a lot of young women see steroid use
as an investment in their future; athletes can take the hormones
for a few months in high school, qualify for a college scholarship,
and then stop taking the drugs before sophisticated lab tests can
spot them (Faigenbaum, Zaichkowsky, Gardner, & Micheli, 1998).
What teenagers don't realize, though, is that even a few months of
steroid use can permanently damage the heart, trigger liver failure,
stunt physical growth, and put a woman's childbearing ability at
risk. Steroids cause muscles to outgrow and injure the tendons and
ligaments that attach them to the bone (Faigenbaum et al., 1998).
As Farnaz Khadem, spokeswoman for the World Anti-Doping Agency
has emphasized, "A lot of these young people have no idea of what
this is doing to their bodies. This is a real health danger" (DeNoon,
2004).

Although health is the most important concern in the issue
of steroid use, it is not the only one. Possessing or selling steroids
without a prescription is a crime, so those who are involved in such
activities may also endure criminal penalties (Gorman, 1998). Young
women who use steroids are resorting to illegal actions and may
eventually be labeled as "criminals," a label that will follow them
for the rest of their lives. Doors to coaching jobs, teaching careers,
and many other occupations may be shut permanently if one has a
criminal past.

How Girl Athletes Can Avoid Steroid Use

What can we do to help adolescent female athletes avoid illicit
drug use? How can we help them avoid the pitfalls of competitive

Since the
publication year
is given in the
sentence, it is
not included in
the citation.

In APA style, the
first parenthetical reference to
a source with
three to five
authors lists
all authors . . .

. . . subsequent
references to the
source use "et
al." in place of
all but the first
author.

athletics? Parents, coaches, and the athletes themselves all play a crucial role in averting bad choices. First, parents and coaches need to be aware that performance-enhancing drugs are a problem. Some adults believe that steroid use is either minimal or nonexistent among teenagers, but one study concluded that "over half the teens who use steroids start before age 16, sometimes with the encouragement of their parents. . . . Seven percent said they first took 'juice' by age ten" (Dudley, 1994, p. 235).

Parents need to take the time to know their children and know what their children are doing. Coaches must know their players well enough to be able to identify a child in trouble. When asked what parents and coaches could do to help girl athletes remain healthy and not use drugs or overwork themselves, Juan Orozco offered the following advice:

> An athlete should be happy in her activity of choice, and her parents should encourage her desires to do well. Parents should be involved in her life and let her know that her efforts are valued highly, but they also need to be on the lookout for danger signs — such as unusual weight loss or moodiness. As a coach, I need to know the personalities of my players and get them to trust me, not only as their coach but as their friend — someone they can talk to if they have a problem. (personal communication, September 22, 2014)

It is also important for parents and coaches to teach the athletes how to develop a healthy lifestyle and not focus only on winning. If an athlete seems to take her sport too seriously, parents might negotiate with her, encouraging her to balance sports with other endeavors. Some parents and coaches push kids too hard, teaching them to win at any cost. In fact, a number of researchers believe that some parents and coaches are actually purchasing expensive black-market steroids for their young athletes (Costello). As University of Massachusetts researcher Avery Faigenbaum has put it, "I don't know a lot of ten-year-olds who have a couple of hundred dollars — to spend on drugs or anything else" (Costello, "Too Late?" para. 4).

Athletes, too, must take responsibility for their own lives. Adolescent girls should try to resist undue pressures imposed by parents, coaches, and society. They must learn about the damage steroids can cause and understand that pursuing an "ideal" body type is not only unrealistic but also unhealthy (Yiannakis & Melnick, 2001). Most of all, young female athletes need to know that they

An ellipsis indicates that words from the source were not included in the quotation.

Extended quotation is set off in block style without quotation marks.

are more important than the competition. No scholarship or medal is worth liver failure or losing the ability to bear children.

The vast majority of excellent athletes do not overtrain, become bulimic, or wind up using steroids. Clearly, they have learned to avoid the pitfalls of competitive athletics. They believe in themselves and their abilities and know how to balance sports and other activities. They have learned how to sacrifice and work hard, but not at the expense of their integrity or health. In short, these athletes have not lost sight of the true objective of participating in sports — they know that their success is due to their efforts and not to the effects of a performance-enhancing drug. When asked what she would say to athletes considering steroid use, Melissa Alvarez said:

> If you are training and doing your best, you should not have to use steroids. At the end of the day, it is just a game. You should never put your health at risk for anything, or anyone. It should be your top priority. (personal communication, September 26, 2014)

In the essay's conclusion, Alexis uses a quotation to reinforce her main point.

GIRLS, SPORTS, AND STEROIDS   9

References

Brown, E. W., & Branta, C. F. (Eds.). (1988). *Competitive sports for children and youth: An overview of issues and research.* Champaign, IL: Human Kinetics.

Centers for Disease Control and Prevention. (2004, May 21). Youth risk behavior surveillance — December 2003. *Morbidity and Mortality Weekly Report 53* (Report No. SS-2). Retrieved from http://www.cdc.gov/mmwr/PDF/SS/SS5302.pdf

Costello, B. (2004, July 4). Too late? Survey suggests millions of kids could be juicing. *New York Post.* Retrieved from http://www.nypost.com

Davies, D., & Armstrong, M. (1989). *Psychological factors in competitive sport.* New York, NY: Falmer Press.

DeNoon, D. (2004, August 4). *Steroid use: Hitting closer to home.* Retrieved from http://webmd.com/fitness-exercise /features/steroid-use-hitting-closer-to-home

Dexheimer, E. (2004, May 13). Nothing to lose: The Colorado Impact teaches girls about life — then hoops. *Denver Westword.* Retrieved from http://www.westword.com

Dudley, W. (Ed.). (1994). *Sports in America: Opposing viewpoints.* San Diego, CA: Greenhaven Press.

Faigenbaum, A. D., Zaichkowsky, L. D., Gardner, D. E., & Micheli, L. J. (1998). Anabolic steroid use by male and female middle school students. *Pediatrics, 101*(5), e6. http://dx.doi .org/10.1542/peds.101.5.e6

Family Education Staff (n.d.). *Teen steroid use.* Retrieved from http:// life.familyeducation.com/athletic-training/drugs-and-alcohol /58291.html?page=1&detoured=1

Girls and steroids. (1998). *Teacher Magazine 9*(5), 11. Retrieved from http://www.teachermagazine.org

Gorman, C. (1998, August 10). Girls on steroids. *Time 152*(6), 93. Retrieved from http://www.time.com

Graham, J. (1999). *The athletic woman's sourcebook.* New York, NY: Avon Books.

Manning, A. (2002, July 9). Kids, steroids don't mix. *USA Today.* Retrieved from http://www.usatoday.com

Mundell, E. J. (2004, May 12). Schools struggle to control steroid use. *HealthDay.* Retrieved from http://www.healthday.com

President's Council on Physical Fitness and Sports. (1997, May). *Physical activity and sport in the lives of girls: Physical and mental health dimensions from an interdisciplinary approach.* Retrieved from University of Minnesota, Tucker Center for

Sources alphabetized by author's name or, if no author, by title

First line of each entry starts at left margin, additional lines indented one-half inch, or five spaces

Online news-paper article

Book with two authors

Source URL given

Edited book

Online article with a DOI

Nonperiodical Web document

Online articles without DOIs

Book with one author

Online news-paper article

List of references on a separate page, heading centered

Edited book

Online govern-ment report

Source titles only capital-ize first words, words following a colon or ques-tion mark, and proper nouns

Titles of books and journals italicized

Nonperiodical website

URL of publication's home page

V Documenting Sources

GIRLS, SPORTS, AND STEROIDS   10

Research on Girls and Women in Sport website: http://cehd.umn
.edu/tuckercenter/projects/PresidentsCouncil/pcpfs_report.pdf

Sieghart, M. A. (2004, August 27). Competitive sport is harsh and
unforgiving: That's why it's good for children. *The Times* of
London. Retrieved from http://www.the-times.co.uk

Sporting activities impact illegal drug use among male and female
teenagers. (2003, September 26). *Drug Week*, pp. 16–17.

Yiannakis, A., & Melnick, M. J. (Eds.). (2001). *Contemporary issues in
sociology of sport*. Champaign, IL: Human Kinetics.

Online news-
paper article

Book editors
identified with
(Ed.) or (Eds.)

Magazine article
without a named
author

22

Using *Chicago* Style

The documentation style described in *The Chicago Manual of Style: The Essential Guide for Writers, Editors, and Publishers*, Sixteenth Edition, is used in the humanities and in some of the social sciences. The *Manual* recommends two systems: an author-date system similar to the APA system (see Chapter 21) and a notes system. This chapter describes and provides models for the notes system.

In the notes system, researchers acknowledge their sources in footnotes or endnotes. Footnotes appear at the bottom of a printed page, whereas endnotes appear at the end of the document. Although a bibliography can be omitted when using the notes system (since all relevant publication information is provided in the notes), the *Manual* encourages authors to provide a bibliography or list of works cited in documents when more than a few sources are cited. For more information about this system, consult *The Chicago Manual of Style*. Information about the manual can also be found at **chicagomanualofstyle.org**.

To see Nicholas Brothers's research essay formatted in the *Chicago* style notes system, turn to p. 404.

22a

How do I cite sources within the text of my document?

Chicago uses footnotes or endnotes. Notes can also be used to expand on points made in the text—that is, notes can contain both citation information and commentary on the text. For digital documents such as websites that consist of multiple "pages" of text, footnotes can take the form of links to notes at the end of a "page" or to pop-up windows that display the notes.

The first time you refer to a source in a note, provide complete publication information for the source. In subsequent references, you need to cite only the author's last name, a shortened version of the title, and the page numbers (if the source has page numbers) to which you refer. Separate the elements with commas and end with a period. *Chicago* style italicizes titles of books and periodicals.

The following examples illustrate the most common ways of citing sources within the text of your document using *Chicago*'s notes system.

1. Numbering   Notes should be numbered consecutively throughout your work, beginning with 1.

2. Placement of the Note Numbers in the Text   Place the number for a note at the end of the sentence containing the reference after punctuation and outside any parentheses. If you are citing the source of material that comes before an em dash (or two hyphens) used to separate parts of a sentence, the note number should precede the dash. Note numbers are set as superscripts.

> Lee and Calandra suggest that the poor organization of online historical documents may impair students' ability to conduct research without guidance.[1]

> Tomlinson points out that the erosion of Fiji's culture was accelerated by both British and Indian immigration[2] — though the two immigrant groups inhabited very different roles and social classes.

3. Placement of Notes   You may choose between footnotes, which appear at the bottom of the page containing corresponding note numbers, and endnotes, which appear at the end of the document in a section titled "Notes." Longer works, such as books, typically use endnotes. The choice depends on the expectations of your readers and your preferences. Regardless of placement, notes are numbered consecutively throughout the document. If you use a bibliography, it follows the last page of text or the last page of endnotes. Model notes for various types of sources appear in section 22b below.

4. Including Page Numbers in a Note Use page numbers whenever you refer to a specific page of a source rather than to the source as a whole. The use of page numbers is required for quotations.

> 4. Rinker Buck, *The Oregon Trail: A New American Journey* (New York: Simon & Schuster, 2016), 92.

5. Cross-Referencing Notes If you are referring to a source identified in a previous note, you can refer to that note instead of repeating the information.

> 5. See note 3 above.

6. Citing the Same Source in Multiple Notes If you refer to the same source in two or more notes, provide a full citation in the first note. In subsequent notes, provide the author's last name, a brief version of the title, and the page number. If you are referring to the same source cited in the previous note, you can use the Latin abbreviation "ibid." (for *ibidem*, or "in the same place").

> 1. Anna Scternshis, *When Sonia Met Boris: An Oral History of Jewish Life under Stalin* (New York: Oxford University Press, 2017), 17.
>
> 2. Ibid., 54.
>
> 6. Scternshis, *When Sonia Met Boris*, 131.

7. Citing a Source Quoted in Another Source

> 7. José María Arguedas, *Obras Completa* (Lima: Editorial Horizonte, 1983), 1:129, quoted in Alberto Flores Galindo et al., *In Search of an Inca: Identity and Utopia in the Andes* (New York: Cambridge University Press, 2010), 199.

22b

How do I format notes and prepare the bibliography?

The Chicago Manual of Style provides guidelines for formatting notes and entries in a bibliography of works that are relevant to but not necessarily cited within your document. In print documents and linear documents that are distributed electronically (such as a word processing file or a newsgroup post), the bibliography appears at the end of the document. In longer documents, a bibliography could be given at the end of each chapter or section. In digital documents that use links, such as a website, the bibliography is often a separate page to which other pages are linked. To see a bibliography in *Chicago* style, go to p. 413.

For notes, include the number of the note, indented and not superscripted, followed by these elements:

- author's name (first name first)
- title (followed by the title of the complete work if the source is an article, chapter, or other short work contained in a larger work)
- publisher (for a book) or publication title (for a journal, magazine, or newspaper)
- date
- page(s) being cited

For entries in the bibliography, include these elements:

- author's name (last name first)
- title (followed by the title of the complete work if the source is an article, chapter, or other short work contained in a larger work)
- publisher (for a book) or publication title (for a journal, magazine, or newspaper)
- date
- page(s) (if the source is a shorter work included in a complete work)

Keep in mind that well-known reference works, such as encyclopedias, and all types of personal communication—personal interviews, letters, surveys, e-mail messages, online discussion groups—are cited in a note only. They are not usually included in the bibliography.

Note: For each type of source, a pair of examples is presented in this section—a model note followed by a model bibliographic entry.

Books, Conference Proceedings, and Dissertations

8. One Author   Use the basic format described on p. 390. When citing a book, use the information from the title page and the copyright page (on the reverse side of the title page), not from the book's cover or a library catalog.

8. Doris Kearns Goodwin, *The Bully Pulpit: Theodore Roosevelt, William Howard Taft, and the Golden Age of Journalism* (New York: Simon & Schuster, 2013), 498.

Goodwin, Doris Kearns. *The Bully Pulpit: Theodore Roosevelt, William Howard Taft, and the Golden Age of Journalism*. New York: Simon & Schuster, 2013.

If the book is found in a digital format, identify the book type (such as "ePub," "PDF e-book," or "Kindle e-book") at the end of the citation. If a DOI (digital object identifier, a unique number assigned to specific content) is provided, include it. If the book was found on the Web and a DOI is not available, provide the URL.

9. Craig Adam, *Forensic Evidence in Court: Evaluation and Scientific Opinion* (Winchester, UK: Wiley, 2016), doi:10.1002/9781119054443.

Adam, Craig. *Forensic Evidence in Court: Evaluation and Scientific Opinion*. John Wiley & Sons, 2016. Wiley Online Library, PDF e-book. doi:10.1002/9781119054443.

TUTORIAL

How do I cite books using Chicago *style?*

PLATO AT THE GOOGLEPLEX

Copyright © 2014 by Rebecca Goldstein

All rights reserved. Published in the United States by Pantheon Books,
a division of Random House LLC, New York, and in Canada by Random
House of Canada Limited, Toronto. Penguin Random House companies.

Pantheon Books and colophon are registered trademarks of
Random House LLC.

Owing to limitations of space, permissions to reprint from previously
published material are listed following the bibliographical note.

Library of Congress Cataloging-in-Publication Data
Goldstein, Rebecca, [date]
Plato at the Googleplex : why philosophy won't go away / Rebecca Goldstein.
pages cm
Includes bibliographical references.
HC ISBN 978-0-307-37809-4 EBK ISBN 978-0-307-90887-2
1. Plato—Influence. 2. Philosophy—History—21st century.
3. Imaginary conversations. I. Title.
B395.G4455 2014 184—dc23 2013029660

www.pantheonbooks.com

Jacket design by Pablo Delcán
Printed in the United States of America
First Edition
2 4 6 8 9 7 5 3 1

When citing a book, use information from the title page and the copyright page (on the back side of the title page), not from the cover or a library catalog. This tutorial gives an example of a *Chicago*-style footnote or endnote. An example of the bibliography entry for this source is at the bottom of the page. Consult pp. 389–95 for additional models for citing books.

Note

╭──────────── **A** ────────────╮ ╭──────────────── **B** ────────────────╮
1. Rebecca Newberger Goldstein, *Plato at the Googleplex: Why Philosophy*

╰──────────╮ ╭──────── **C** ────────╮ ╭─**D**─╮
Won't Go Away (New York: Pantheon, 2014), 234-36.

A   **The author.** In the note, give the first name first. Follow the last name with a comma. Separate the names of multiple authors with commas; use the word "and" before the final author's name.

B   **The title.** Give the full title; include the subtitle (if any), preceded by a colon. Italicize the title and subtitle, capitalizing all major words.

C   **Publication information.** Enclose the city, publisher, and date in parentheses. If more than one city is given, use the first one listed. For a city that may be unfamiliar to your readers or confused with another city, add an abbreviation of the state, country, or province (Cambridge, MA, or Waterloo, ON). Insert a colon. Give the publisher's name. Omit words such as *Inc.* and *Co.* Include and do not abbreviate such terms as *Books* and *Press.* Insert a comma. Give the year of publication, using the most recent copyright year. Close the parentheses and insert a comma.

D   **Inclusive page number(s).** Give the specific page or pages on which you found the information. For numbers 100 and above, give only the last two digits and any other preceding digits if different from the first number (22–28, 402–10, 1437–45, 599–603).

Bibliography Entry

In the bibliography, give the author's last name first, and separate the elements with periods. Do not enclose the publication information in parentheses.

Goldstein, Rebecca Newberger. *Plato at the Googleplex: Why Philosophy Won't Go Away*. New York: Pantheon, 2014.

9. Two or Three Authors   List the authors in the order in which they appear on the title page. In a note, list the first name for each author first. In the bibliography, list the first author's last name first and list the first names for each other author first.

9. Neil Steinberg and Sara Bader, *Out of the Wreck I Rise: A Literary Companion to Recovery* (Chicago: University of Chicago Press, 2016), 247.

Steinberg, Neil, and Sara Bader. *Out of the Wreck I Rise: A Literary Companion to Recovery*. Chicago: University of Chicago Press, 2016.

10. Four or More Authors   In a note, give only the first author's name followed by "et al." (Latin for "and others"). In the bibliography, list all the authors that appear on the title page.

10. Harry Markopolos et al., *No One Would Listen: A True Financial Thriller* (Hoboken, NJ: Wiley, 2010), 179.

Markopolos, Harry, Frank Casey, Neil Chelo, Gaytri Kachroo, and Michael Ocrant. *No One Would Listen: A True Financial Thriller*. Hoboken, NJ: Wiley, 2010.

11. Corporate or Group Author   Use the corporation or group as the author; it may also be the publisher.

11. Human Rights Watch, *World Report of 2015: Events of 2014* (New York: Seven Stories Press, 2015), 11.

Human Rights Watch. *World Report of 2015: Events of 2014*. New York: Seven Stories Press, 2015.

12. Unknown Author   When no author is listed on the title or copyright page, begin the entry with the title of the work. In the bibliography, alphabetize the entry by the first word other than *A*, *An*, or *The*.

12. *Letting Ana Go* (New York: Simon Pulse, 2013), 118–20.

Letting Ana Go. New York: Simon Pulse, 2013.

13. Translated Book   List the author first and the translator after the title. Use the abbreviation "trans." in a note, but spell out "Translated by" in the bibliography.

13. Elena Ferrante, *The Story of the Lost Child*, trans. Ann Goldstein (New York: Europa Editions, 2015), 34.

Ferrante, Elena. *The Story of the Lost Child*. Translated by Ann Goldstein. New York: Europa Editions, 2015.

14. Edition Other Than the First   Give the edition information following the title.

> 14. Alan Brinkley, *The Unfinished Nation: A Concise History of the American People*, 6th ed. (New York: McGraw-Hill, 2010), 627.

> Brinkley, Alan. *The Unfinished Nation: A Concise History of the American People.* 6th ed. New York: McGraw-Hill, 2010.

15. Untitled Volume in a Multivolume Work   In the notes, give the volume number and page number, separated by a colon, for the specific location of the information referred to in your text. In the bibliography, if you have used all the volumes, give the total number of volumes after the title, using the abbreviation "vols." ("2 vols." or "4 vols."). If you have used one volume, give the abbreviation "Vol." and the volume number after the title.

> 15. Fang Hanqi, ed., *A History of Journalism in China* (Singapore: Silkroad Press, 2013), 7: 243–49.

> Hanqi, Fang, ed. *A History of Journalism in China.* Vol 7. Singapore: Silkroad Press, 2013.

16. Titled Volume in a Multivolume Work   Give the title of the volume to which you refer, followed by the volume number and the general title for the entire work.

> 16. Rick Atkinson, *The Guns at Last Light: The War in Western Europe, 1944–1945*, vol. 3 of *The Liberation Trilogy* (New York: Henry Holt, 2013), 345–49.

> Atkinson, Rick. *The Guns at Last Light: The War in Western Europe, 1944–1945.* Vol. 3 of *The Liberation Trilogy.* New York: Henry Holt, 2013.

17. Book in a Series   The series name follows the title and is capitalized as a title but is not italicized. If the series numbers its volumes, include that information as well.

> 17. James Mann, *George W. Bush*, American Presidents Series 43 (New York: Times Books/Henry Holt, 2015), 8.

> Mann, James. *George W. Bush.* American Presidents Series 43. New York: Times Books/Henry Holt, 2015.

18. Republished Book   Place the original publication date before the publication information for the reprint.

18. James, King of England, *The Political Works of James I*, ed. Charles Howard McIlwain (1918; repr., Whitefish, MT: Kessinger, 2010), 74.

James, King of England. *The Political Works of James I*. Edited by Charles Howard McIlwain. 1918. Reprint, Whitefish, MT: Kessinger, 2010.

19. Author with an Editor   List the author at the beginning of the citation and add the editor's name after the title. In notes, use the abbreviation "ed." before the editor's name. In the bibliography, include the phrase "Edited by" before the editor's name.

19. Frederick Douglass, *Narrative of the Life of Frederick Douglass, an American Slave*, ed. Ira Dworkin (New York: Penguin Books, 2014), 114.

Douglass, Frederick. *Narrative of the Life of Frederick Douglass, an American Slave*. Edited by Ira Dworkin. New York: Penguin Books, 2014.

20. Anthology or Collection with an Editor   To cite an entire anthology or collection of articles, give the editor(s) before the title of the collection, adding a comma and the abbreviation "ed." or "eds."

20. Ben Marcus, ed., *New American Stories* (New York: Vintage Books, 2015).

Marcus, Ben, ed. *New American Stories*. New York: Vintage Books, 2015.

21. Foreword, Introduction, Preface, or Afterword   Give the name of the writer of the foreword, introduction, preface, or afterword followed by the appropriate phrase ("introduction to," "preface to," and so on) before the title of the book. If the writer of the introduction or other part differs from the writer of the book, after the title insert the word "by" and the author's name.

21. Martin Stannard, preface to *Muriel Spark: The Biography* (New York: Norton, 2010), xv–xxvi.

Stannard, Martin. Preface to *Muriel Spark: The Biography*, xv–xxvi. New York: Norton, 2010.

22. Chapter in a Book or Selection in an Anthology   Give the author and title (in quotation marks) for the chapter or selection. Then give the title, editor (if any), and publication data for the book or anthology. In the bibliography, give the inclusive page numbers before the publication data.

22. Saïd Sayrafiezadeh, "Paranoia," in *New American Stories*, ed. Ben Marcus (New York: Vintage Books, 2015), 3–29.

Sayrafiezadeh, Saïd. "Paranoia." In *New American Stories*, edited by Ben Marcus, 3–29. New York: Vintage Books, 2015.

23. Published Proceedings of a Conference Cite as for an anthology or collection with an editor (see also entry 20 on p. 393).

23. Derek McAuley and Simon Peyton-Jones, *Proceedings of the 2010 ACM-BCS Visions of Computer Science Conference* (Swindon, UK: British Informatics Society, 2010).

McAuley, Derek, and Simon Peyton-Jones. *Proceedings of the 2010 ACM-BCS Visions of Computer Science Conference*. Swindon, UK: British Informatics Society, 2010.

24. Paper Published in the Proceedings of a Conference Cite as a chapter in an edited book (see also entry 22 on p. 393).

24. Dale Miller, "Finding Unity in Computational Logic," in *Proceedings of the 2010 ACM-BCS Visions of Computer Science Conference* (Swindon, UK: British Informatics Society, 2010), 2.

Miller, Dale. "Finding Unity in Computational Logic." In *Proceedings of the 2010 ACM-BCS Visions of Computer Science Conference*, 1–13. Swindon, UK: British Informatics Society, 2010.

25. Sacred Text Cite sacred texts only within the text of your document. A note should include the book, chapter, and verse, but not a page number.

25. Deut. 5:1–21 (New Revised Standard Version).

26. Published Dissertation or Thesis Give the author and title, the phrase "PhD diss." or "master's thesis," followed by information about the institution that granted the degree and the year. Include the publication number from ProQuest if appropriate.

26. Anthony Colello, *Affirmative Action Bans and Minority Employment: Washington State's Initiative 200* (PhD diss., Georgetown University, 2011), 41–2, ProQuest (AAT 1491319).

Colello, Anthony. *Affirmative Action Bans and Minority Employment: Washington State's Initiative 200*. PhD diss., Georgetown University, 2011. ProQuest (ATT 1491319).

27. Unpublished Dissertation or Thesis Give the author and title, in quotation marks. Then include the phrase "PhD diss." or "master's thesis," information about the institution that granted the degree, and the year.

27. Joshua Glenn Iddings, "Writing at One Appalachian High School" (PhD diss., Purdue University, 2013), 96.

Iddings, Joshua Glenn. "Writing at One Appalachian High School." PhD diss., Purdue University, 2013.

28. Abstract of a Dissertation or Thesis   Provide information as you would for an article in a journal (see also entry 29 below). Add information about Dissertation Abstracts International.

28. Yi Mou, "Social Media and Risk Communication: The Role of Social Networking Sites in Food-Safety Communication" (PhD Diss., University of Connecticut, 2012), abstract, *Dissertation Abstracts International 74* (2013).

Mou, Yi. "Social Media and Risk Communication: The Role of Social Networking Sites in Food-Safety Communication." PhD Diss., University of Connecticut, 2012. Abstract, *Dissertation Abstracts International 74* (2013).

Sources in Journals, Magazines, and Newspapers

29. Article in a Journal   After the journal title, include the volume number, a comma, and the issue number after the abbreviation "no." (Note that volume and issue information is not italicized.) Then give the year in parentheses, followed by a colon. In the note, give the specific page number to which you are referring; in the bibliography, give inclusive page numbers of the entire article.

29. Kate McCoy, "Manifesting Destiny: A Land Education Analysis of Settler Colonialism in Jamestown, Virginia, USA," *Environmental Education Research 20*, no. 1 (2014): 86.

McCoy, Kate. "Manifesting Destiny: A Land Education Analysis of Settler Colonialism in Jamestown, Virginia, USA." *Environmental Education Research 20*, no. 1 (2014): 82–97.

If the article is obtained from a database, follow the publication information with the name of the database, any number assigned to the source, and the DOI. If a DOI is not available, provide a stable URL.

30. Alessandro Pes, "Becoming Imperialist: Italian Colonies in Fascist Textbooks for Primary Schools," *Journal of Modern Italian Studies 18*, no. 5 (2013): 609–11, Academic Search Premier (92017350), doi:10.1080/1354571X.2013 .839519.

Pes, Alessandro. "Becoming Imperialist: Italian Colonies in Fascist Textbooks for Primary Schools." *Journal of Modern Italian Studies 18*, no. 5 (2013): 599–614. Academic Search Premier (92017350), doi:10.1080/1354571X.2013.839519.

If the article is obtained from the Web, provide the DOI or, if a DOI is not available, the URL.

31. Gary Fields, "Palestinian Landscape in a 'Not-Too-Distant Mirror,'" *Journal of Historical Sociology 23*, no. 2 (June 2010), doi: 10.1111/j.1467-6443 .2010.01373.x.

Fields, Gary. "Palestinian Landscape in a 'Not-Too-Distant Mirror.'" *Journal of Historical Sociology 23*, no. 2 (June 2010). doi:10.1111/j.1467-6443.2010.01373.x.

TUTORIAL

How do I cite articles from periodicals using Chicago *style?*

Periodicals include journals, magazines, and newspapers. This tutorial gives an example of a *Chicago*-style footnote or endnote for a print magazine article. (An example of the bibliography entry for this source is at the bottom of the page.) Models for citing articles from journals and newspapers are on pp. 395–99. If you need to cite a periodical article you accessed electronically, follow the guidelines below and see p. 397.

Note

2. Jessica Bulman-Pozen, "Partisan Federalism," *Harvard Law Review*,

127, no. 4, 2014, 1084.

A **The author.** In the note, give the first name first. Follow the last name with a comma. Separate the names of multiple authors with commas; use the word "and" before the final author's name.

B **The article title.** Give the full title; include the subtitle (if any), preceded by a colon. Put the article title and subtitle in quotation marks, capitalizing all major words.

C **The periodical title.** Italicize the periodical title, and capitalize all major words.

D **Publication information and date.** For journal articles, include the volume and issue number followed by the year. For monthly magazines, give the month and year. For weekly magazines, include the day of publication (September 6, 2010). Do not abbreviate the month. Use a comma after the year.

E **Specific page number(s).** Give the specific page or pages on which you found the information, unless you are referring to the article as a whole. For numbers 100 and above, give only the last two digits and any other preceding digits if different from the first number (22–24, 409–10, 1437–45, 599–601).

Bibliography Entry

In the bibliography, give the author's last name first, separate the elements by periods, and give inclusive pages for the entire article.

Bulman-Pozen, Jessica. "Partisan Federalism." *Harvard Law Review*, 127, no. 4, 2014, 1078–146.

How do I cite articles from databases using Chicago *style?*

Libraries subscribe to services such as LexisNexis, ProQuest, InfoTrac, and EBSCOhost that provide access to databases of digital texts. The databases provide publication information, abstracts, and the complete text of documents in a specific subject area, discipline, or profession. (See also Chapter 10.)

This tutorial gives an example of a *Chicago*-style footnote or endnote for a journal article accessed via a database. (An example of the bibliography entry for this source is at the bottom of the page.) To cite magazine and newspaper articles from databases, see also pp. 395–99.

Note

3. Aspasia Stephanou, "A 'Ghastly Operation': Transfusing Blood, Science and the Supernatural in Vampire Texts," *Gothic Studies* 15, no. 2 (November 2013): 59, EBSCOhost (93303198), doi:10.7227/GS.15.2.4.

A **The author.** In the note, give the first name first. Follow the last name with a comma. Separate the names of multiple authors with commas; use the word "and" before the final author's name.

B **The article title.** Give the full title; include the subtitle (if any), preceded by a colon. Put the article title and subtitle in quotes, capitalizing all major words.

C **The journal title.** Italicize the journal title, and capitalize all major words.

D **The publication information.** Insert the volume number followed by a comma, and then give the abbreviation "no." and the issue number. Include the year (and month or season, if given) in parentheses followed by a colon and the specific page number(s) of the reference. (In the bibliography, give inclusive page numbers.) End with a comma.

E **The database information and DOI number.** Give the name of the database, followed by the database's identification number for the article in parentheses. Then include a comma and the DOI number, if one is available.

F **The access date (not shown).** For articles that do not include a publication date, include the word "accessed" and the date of access after the publication information.

Bibliography Entry

Stephanou, Aspasia. "A 'Ghastly Operation': Transfusing Blood, Science and the Supernatural in Vampire Texts." *Gothic Studies*, 15 no. 2 (November 2013): 53-65. EBSCOhost (93303198), doi:10.7227/GS.15.2.4.

30. Article in a Monthly Magazine Magazines are cited by their dates rather than by volume and issue.

30. Peter Huber, "Better Medicine," *Reason*, March 2014, 25.

Huber, Peter. "Better Medicine." *Reason*. March 2014, 22–30.

If the article is obtained from the Web, provide the DOI or, if a DOI is not available, the URL.

31. Jacob Seigel, "The History and Logic of Military Ultimatums, from Suez to Crimea," *The Daily Beast*, March 3, 2014, http://www.thedailybeast.com /articles/2014/03/03/the-history-and-logic-of-military-ultimatums-from-suez-to -crimea.html.

Seigel, Jacob. "The History and Logic of Military Ultimatums, from Suez to Crimea." *The Daily Beast*, March 3, 2014. http://www.thedailybeast.com/articles/2014/03/03 /the-history-and-logic-of-military-ultimatums-from-suez-to-crimea.html.

31. Article in a Weekly Magazine Cite like a monthly magazine, but provide the day of publication.

31. Marty Makary, "The Cost of Chasing Cancer," *Time*, March 10, 2014, 24.

Makary, Marty. "The Cost of Chasing Cancer." *Time*, March 10, 2014, 24.

32. Article in a Newspaper If the name of the newspaper does not include the city, insert the city before the name (and italicize it). If an American city is not well known, name the state as well (in parentheses, abbreviated). Identify newspapers from other countries with the city in parentheses (not italicized) after the name of the newspaper.

Eugene (OR) Register-Guard

Sunday Times (London)

Page numbers may be omitted, since separate editions of the same newspaper may place articles differently. If a paper comes out in more than one edition, identify the edition after the date.

32. Otis Taylor Jr., "Tax Proposals Hard for Soda Fans to Swallow," *San Francisco Chronicle*, October 13, 2016, Bay Area edition.

Taylor, Otis, Jr. "Tax Proposals Hard for Soda Fans to Swallow." *San Francisco Chronicle*, October 13, 2016, Bay Area edition.

33. Unsigned Article in a Newspaper or Magazine If no author is given, begin the note with the title of the article; begin the bibliography entry with the title of the periodical.

33. "Ayes Straight Ahead," *Boston Globe*, October 14, 2016.

Boston Globe. "Ayes Straight Ahead." October 14, 2016.

34. Letter to the Editor   Treat as a newspaper article. If no title is provided, place "Letter to the editor" in the title position.

34. James Randi, letter to the editor, *Smithsonian*, October 2016.

Randi, James. Letter to the editor. *Smithsonian*, October 2016.

35. Review   Give the author of the review, the review title, if any, and then the words "review of" followed by the title and author of the work reviewed and the author or editor (for books) or director or performer (for movies, plays, and similar productions).

35. Stephen Holden, "Students Caught in the School Squeeze," review of *Waiting for Superman*, directed by Davis Guggenheim, *New York Times*, September 23, 2010.

Holden, Stephen. "Students Caught in the School Squeeze." Review of *Waiting for Superman*, directed by Davis Guggenheim. *New York Times*, September 23, 2010.

Reference Works

36. Entry in Encyclopedia, Dictionary, Thesaurus, Handbook, or Almanac   In notes, provide the title of the work (italicized), the edition, the abbreviation "s.v." (for *sub verbo*, or "under the word"), and the title of the entry.

36. *Encyclopaedia Britannica*, 15th ed., s.v. "Lee, Robert E."

Chicago does not recommend including reference works such as encyclopedias or dictionaries in the bibliography.

37. Government Publication   In general, give the issuing body, then the title and any other information (such as report numbers) that would help your readers locate the source. Follow with the publication data and the page numbers if relevant. You may abbreviate "Government Printing Office" as GPO.

37. U.S. Senate, Special Committee on Aging, *Social Security: Improvements to Claims Process Could Help People Make Better Informed Decisions about Retirement Benefits* (Washington, DC: GPO, 2016), 7.

U.S. Senate. Special Committee on Aging. *Social Security: Improvements to Claims Process Could Help People Make Better Informed Decisions about Retirement Benefits*. Washington, DC: GPO, 2016.

38. Pamphlet, Report, or Brochure   Cite it as you would a book (see p. 390).

38. *Facts: Scripps Institution of Oceanography* (San Diego: University of California, 2012).

Facts: Scripps Institution of Oceanography. San Diego: University of California, 2012.

Field Sources

39. Personal Interview   Give the location and date in a note. Do not include unpublished interviews in the bibliography.

> 39. Rachel Stein, interview by author, Pittsburgh, June 2, 2017.

40. Letter or Other Personal Communication   Do not include personal communications such as letters or phone calls in the bibliography. In a note, give the name of the person with whom you communicated, the form of communication, and the date.

> 40. Meghan McKennan, conversation with author, March 5, 2017.

> 41. Sangita Thakore, letter to author, November 12, 2017.

41. Survey   *Chicago* does not specify how to cite unpublished survey results. Cite them in your text as you would a personal communication (see entry 40).

42. Observation Notes   *Chicago* does not specify how to cite observation notes. Cite them in your text as you would a personal communication (see entry 40).

43. Lecture or Public Address   Provide the title, the nature of the speech (such as lecture or keynote address), the name of the organization sponsoring the meeting or lecture, and the location and date it was given.

> 43. Anna Deavere Smith, "On the Road: A Search for American Character" (lecture, John F. Kennedy Center for the Performing Arts, Washington, DC, April 6, 2015).

Smith, Anna Deavere. "On the Road: A Search for American Character." Lecture presented at John F. Kennedy Center for the Performing Arts, Washington, DC, April 6, 2015.

Media Sources

44. Film or Video   Provide the title first, the name of the director, the year it was filmed, the company, the year it was released, and the medium (film, videocassette, DVD).

> 44. *Michael Jackson's This Is It*, directed by Kenny Ortega (2009; Culver City, CA: Sony Pictures, 2010), DVD.

Michael Jackson's This Is It. Directed by Kenny Ortega. 2009; Culver City, CA: Sony Pictures, 2010. DVD.

For videos found on the Web, provide the sponsoring organization and include the words "video file" after the publication information. Provide the DOI or, if a DOI is not available, the URL. If there is no author's name, list the creator's screen name.

45. *How to Make a Traditional Origami Crane,* created by GeckoGeekFr (YouTube: January 6, 2010), Video file, http://www.youtube.com/watch?v=jUZaOWibCcs.

How to Make a Traditional Origami Crane. GeckoGeekFr. YouTube. January 6, 2010. Video file. http://www.youtube.com/watch?v=jUZaOWibCcs.

45. Television or Radio Program   *Chicago* does not specify how to cite a television or radio program. Cite as you would a video recording, identifying the medium as "television program," "television broadcast," "radio program," or "radio broadcast."

46. Sound Recording, Audio Clip, or Podcast   Give the composer and title of the recording, the performers and conductor, the label, the identifying number, and the format.

46. Pyotr Ilyich Tchaikovsky, *Symphony No. 5, Romeo and Juliet Fantasy Overture,* Royal Philharmonic Orchestra, conducted by Daniele Gatti, Harmonia Mundi, MU907381, compact disc.

Tchaikovsky, Pyotr Ilyich. *Symphony No. 5, Romeo and Juliet Fantasy Overture.* Royal Philharmonic Orchestra, conducted by Daniele Gatti. Harmonia Mundi, MU907381, compact disc.

For audio clips or podcasts accessed on the Web, add the DOI or URL after the publication information.

47. Cheryl Jones-Walker, *Learning and Becoming: The Construction of Identity in Urban Classrooms,* Swarthmore College, May 21, 2010, Audio podcast, http://media.swarthmore.edu/faculty_lectures/?p=182.

Jones-Walker, Cheryl. *Learning and Becoming: The Construction of Identity in Urban Classrooms.* Swarthmore College. May 21, 2010. Audio podcast. http://media.swarthmore.edu/faculty_lectures/?p=182.

Other Digital Sources

All digital sources should include either a publication date, a revision or "last modified" date, or an access date. After the date, include a DOI or, if the source does not have a DOI, a stable URL.

47. Nonperiodical Website

47. Abby Mendelson, "Roberto Clemente: A Form of Punishment," Pittsburgh Pirates, MLB.com, May 24, 2013, http://mlb.mlb.com/pit/history/pit_clemente.jsp.

Mendelson, Abby. "Roberto Clemente: A Form of Punishment." Pittsburgh Pirates. MLB.com. May 24, 2013. http://mlb.mlb.com/pit/history/pit_clemente.jsp.

48. Article Posted on a Wiki   Cite online postings to Wikis in the text but not in the bibliography.

48. "Native Americans," *Davis Wiki*, accessed March 4, 2014, http://daviswiki .org/Native_Americans.

49. Blog   Put the word "blog" in parentheses following the name of the blog, if it is not already part of the name.

49. Donna Haisty Winchell, "In Arizona, Is It Ethics or Economics?" *Argument and the Headlines* (blog), *Bits: Ideas for Teaching Composition*, March 3, 2014, http://bedfordbits.colostate.edu/index.php/2014/03/03/in-arizona-is-it-ethics-or -economics/.

Winchell, Donna Haisty. "In Arizona, Is It Ethics or Economics?" *Argument and the Headlines* (blog). *Bits: Ideas for Teaching Composition*, March 3, 2014. http:// bedfordbits.colostate.edu/index.php/2014/03/03/in-arizona-is-it-ethics-or -economics/.

50. E-mail Message   *Chicago* recommends that personal communication, including e-mail, not be included in the bibliography, although it can be cited in your text. Note that the *Chicago Manual* prefers the hyphenated version of the word "e-mail."

50. Brysa H. Levy, e-mail message to author, January 4, 2014.

51. Online Posting to a Discussion Group   Like e-mail, online postings are considered personal communication and are therefore listed in the text only, not in the bibliography. Include a URL for archived postings.

51. Robin Griffith to *Developing Digital Literacies* NCTE discussion group, October 23, 2015, http://ncte.connectedcommunity.org/community-home/digest -viewer/viewthread GroupID=1693&MID=24520&tab=digestviewer&CommunityKey =628d2ad6-8277-4042-a376-2b370ddceabf.

V Documenting Sources

TUTORIAL

How do I cite works from websites using Chicago *style?*

You will likely need to search the website to find some of the citation information you need. For some sites, all of the details may not be available; find as many as you can. Remember that the citation you provide should allow readers to retrace your steps electronically to locate the sources. Consult pp. 401–2 for additional models for citing Web sources.

Note

B

4. "Public Divided Over Increased Deportation of Unauthorized Immigrants,"

C   **D**

Pew Research Center for the People & the Press, Pew Research Center,

E   **F**

February 27, 2014, http://www.people-press.org/2014/02/27/public-divided

-over-increased-deportation-of-unauthorized-immigrants/.

A **The author (not shown).** In the note, give the first name first. Follow the last name with a comma. Separate the names of multiple authors with commas; use the word "and" before the final author's name. If no specific author is named, as in this case, begin with the title of the work.

B **The title of the work.** Give the full title; include the subtitle (if any), preceded by a colon. Put the article title and subtitle in quotation marks, capitalizing all major words.

C **The name of the website.** Do not italicize the name of the website unless it is the name of a book or periodical.

D **The name of the sponsoring organization.** If the sponsor's name is not visible on the document page, look at the bottom of the site's home page.

E **Date of publication or last modification or access.** If there is no date of publication, include the date the page was last modified or the date on which you accessed the page.

F **The URL.** Give the URL in full; do not use underlining or angle brackets, and be sure not to introduce any new hyphens or slashes. End with a period.

Bibliography Entry

"Public Divided Over Increased Deportation of Unauthorized Immigrants."
    Pew Research Center for the People & the Press. Pew Research Center.
    February 27, 2014. http://www.people-press.org/2014/02/27/public
    -divided-over-increased-deportation-of-unauthorized-immigrants/.

Chicago-Style Research Essay

The Costs of Outsourcing War:
Private Military Corporations in Iraq and Afghanistan — Title of essay

Nicholas Brothers — Writer's name

ENG 108-11
Professor Dawn Terrick
October 20, 2011

Title of course,
instructor's
name, and date

The Costs of Outsourcing War:

Private Military Corporations in Iraq and Afghanistan

> Title of essay repeated

The United States is considered the preeminent military power of the world. Yet, it is also a military force that today cannot get to the battlefield, feed and house its soldiers, or even protect its bases without the support of a network of nonstate actors. These organizations are sometimes listed on stock exchanges worldwide; they have glossy, professional websites and legions of press agents and lobbyists. They are private military corporations (PMCs). Their duties range from cooking and cleaning to planning and even carrying out covert operations to capture Osama bin Laden. But military privatization comes at a severe price — not just in terms of dollars, but also in terms of national security, democratic ideals, and human lives. By relying heavily on PMCs to carry out military operations, the U.S. Department of Defense is undermining its own counterinsurgency efforts in Iraq and Afghanistan.

> Thesis states Nicholas's main point.

Our country's reliance on private military corporations did not happen overnight, and although the corporatization of PMCs is relatively new, the idea of privatization is not. From the time of Alexander the Great to the Napoleonic era, private soldiers made up the bulk of military forces. Citizen armies emerged with the invention of cheap, easy-to-use muskets in the early 19th century. Yet as recently as the Cold War, U.S. armed forces were traditionally organized, with conventional army, naval, and air units in combat against similar Soviet units. The idea, of course, was for the military to be self-sufficient. However, as P. W. Singer explains in his book *Corporate Warriors: The Rise of the Privatized Military Industry*, when the Cold War ended in 1991, the Department of Defense began closing bases and dissolving or combining units, setting the stage for the large-scale outsourcing of military operations.[1] Jonathan Euchner, professor of political science at Missouri Western State University, explained that the shift to PMCs must be seen in the context of the overall privatization movement within the U.S. government that began in 1978 under President Jimmy Carter and gained momentum during the 1980s and 1990s.[2] While the role of PMCs remained modest throughout the 1990s, new military engagements after 9/11 provided new opportunities for PMCs. As detailed by investigative journalist Jeremy Scahill in his book *Blackwater: The Rise of the World's Most Powerful Mercenary Army*, the War on Terror as prosecuted by the Bush administration accelerated the privatization of military functions. The new secretary of defense Donald Rumsfeld would codify this concept, which became known as the Rumsfeld Doctrine.[3] In this

> Interviewee tag indicates the use of field research.

> The name of the book identifies the source of the summarized information.

> Summarized material

Brothers 3

doctrine, a highly mobile infantry force supported by airstrikes and by contractors would chase Osama bin Laden and al Qaeda in retaliation for the terrorist attacks on the World Trade Center and the Pentagon. The demand for contractors skyrocketed after the invasion of Iraq, with an overextended military needing more and more support as the repeated deployments dragged on for years. Now, the United States is in the final stages of its involvement in one foreign conflict and intractably embroiled in another. The combat mission in Iraq officially ended on August 31, 2010, but, with an insurgency that's growing stronger rather than weaker in Afghanistan, the planned 2011 withdrawal from that theater of war will likely be scaled back.[4]

> First two paragraphs offer background information and history to orient readers.

Today, companies like DynCorp and Blackwater (now Xe Services) are some of the biggest, most diversified PMCs in a crowded market. In a 2007 online chat with the *Washington Post*, Singer, director of the 21st Century Defense Initiative of the Brookings Institution, asserted that at the time there were about 170 firms doing business in Iraq alone.[5] A July 2010 analysis by the Congressional Research Service reported that "contractors make up 54% of the workforce in Iraq and Afghanistan," meaning that contractors slightly outnumbered U.S. soldiers deployed to those countries. More than 13,000 of these contractors are armed.[6] With so many firms and their contractors in play, the dollar amounts involved are unsurprisingly high. The Congressional Budget Office estimated that the Department of Defense spent $76 billion on contractors in Iraq between 2003 and 2007.[7] The staggering cost raises an important question in the mind of any taxpayer: What are we getting for that money?

> Nicholas introduces a government document as the source of the quoted information.

> A colon (:) is not used when the quoted text is part of the sentence.

> A partial quotation is integrated effectively into the sentence.

> Nicholas poses a question that he will answer in his essay.

As Dr. Euchner pointed out, the civilian and military leadership of the United States is attracted to contractors because they offer streamlined services, with supposedly less bureaucracy and fewer regulations. As Erik Prince, the cofounder and owner of Blackwater/Xe Services, put it, "Our corporate goal is to do for the national security apparatus what FedEx did to the postal service."[8] However, critics of PMCs would say that we're buying the services of mercenaries, since both contractors and mercenaries are essentially hired guns. Throughout his book, Scahill provocatively uses "private military corporation" and "mercenary" as interchangeable terms, underscoring their similarities but failing to provide definitions of either. Yet a look at definitions in Singer's *Corporate Warriors* reveals that PMCs and traditional mercenaries differ in several key ways. Perhaps the most important difference is that a private military corporation is just that: a legal corporate entity[9] (as opposed to the illegal adventurer or ragtag squad evoked by the word "mercenary"). Another significant

> Speaker tag gives us context for the quotation.

> Nicholas points out a disagreement between two of his sources.

distinction is that PMCs offer a wide range of services — "training, logistics, support, operational support, post-conflict resolution," according to the head of the PMC Sandline[10] — while mercenaries can rarely do more than engage in combat. However, while PMCs, unlike most mercenaries, are legal, corporate, and diversified in their capabilities, several high-profile abuse cases reveal that it is no wiser to rely on PMCs than on the mercenaries of old.

> Writer's name is followed by the page number.

Numerous examples of abuses, negligence, and outright crimes have taken place since the post-9/11 expansion of the private military industry, and only a handful can be recounted here: A 2002 *Salon* feature details the experiences of the whistleblowers who exposed the sex trafficking that DynCorp International employees, under contract to service helicopters during peacekeeping operations, engaged in while stationed in Bosnia.[11] Scahill writes of the largely underreported involvement of contractors from the San Diego–based Titan Corporation and the Virginia-based CACI in the now infamous torture of Iraqi detainees at the Abu Ghraib prison compound in 2004.[12] And in what has become known as the Nisour Square Massacre, Blackwater employees killed 17 Iraqi civilians at a busy intersection in Baghdad.[13] These are, of course, only a small sampling of contractor abuses, but they are clearly criminal actions — incidents that can't be explained away as an errant bullet or malfunctioning "smart" bomb.

> The name of the website is used to identify the source.

It might be argued that these abuses are the actions of the individuals hired by a corporation, not part of corporate policy. And it might be further argued that in some of these cases, regular U.S. troops can and have committed similar crimes (and in the case of Abu Ghraib, were participating right along with the contractors). But a major difference between a contractor and a U.S. soldier is accountability. While there might exist the same opportunity to commit crimes between the private and public sectors, there are clear consequences in place for regular troops, who are subject to the Uniform Code of Military Justice (UCMJ). As of October 2010, 34 U.S. Army soldiers had been court-martialed on charges of murder or manslaughter of civilians in conflict zones in Iraq and Afghanistan, and 22 of those soldiers were convicted.[14] In contrast, it was only in 2006 that the UCMJ was amended so that contractors could be charged with criminal actions under the court-martial system.[15] Unlike regular troops, contractors are backed by strong money: Lobbying groups fight hard and spend millions to make sure the corporations are not held accountable.[16] Although charges were brought against five Blackwater men for the 2007 Nisour Square Massacre, the case

Brothers 5

was dismissed when the judge ruled that the prosecutors could not use statements that the accused had given to State Department investigators on the condition that the information could not be applied as evidence. As reporter James Risen explains in a recent *New York Times* article, "The Blackwater personnel were given a form of immunity from prosecution by the people they were working for and helping to protect."[17] Though the State Department has appealed the Nisour Square case, there have yet to be serious legal consequences for these and other contractors who commit crimes.

The atmosphere of lawlessness inherent in battle zones is compounded by the illegal acts of some of these contractors, which, in a low-intensity conflict, may turn citizens into insurgents. The Army Field Manual states that "people who have been maltreated or have had close friends or relatives killed . . . may strike back at their attackers. Security force abuses . . . can be major escalating factors for insurgencies."[18] And, as the Congressional Research Service report points out, Iraqi and Afghan civilians don't always know the difference between a U.S. soldier and a contractor, meaning that, in the minds of the people, the actions of contractors directly reflect on the U.S. military.[19] However, despite the people's inability to tell them apart, contractors and U.S. soldiers have significantly different motivations. By definition, those in the military are serving their commander-in-chief while those hired as contractors are serving a for-profit company. In regards to PMCs' bottom lines, it would actually be advantageous to shoot first and ask questions later, engendering more fear and insecurity and therefore the need for more contracted security guards. This positive feedback loop should not be considered as some elaborate conspiracy; the situation is merely part of the culture and nature of profit-motivated actors. It's the reason why, until the last couple of decades, defense operations have overwhelmingly been left up to the public, not the private, sector: Ultimately, the motivation of profit is not necessarily in line with the motivation of national security.

Given the potential costs in justice and national security, why hire contractors at all? Ironically, perhaps the most often cited reason for using private contractors is that using these corporations saves the taxpayer money since the government can hire them on an as-need basis and does not have to pay for contractors' training, health care, or pensions.[20] Professor Allison Stanger of Middlebury College challenges this notion in her 2009 book *One Nation under Contract: The Outsourcing of American Power and the Future of Foreign Policy* when she points out that nearly all private contractors

Tag indicates the source of the paraphrased information.

Paraphrased information

Source of paraphrased information is provided in a note.

Nicholas returns to his original question and asks a more in-depth one.

previously served in the military, meaning that many of them are receiving pension payments anyway. Stanger writes that "the federal government is effectively paying for the training and retirement of the contractors it hires, all appearances to the contrary, as well as paying double or triple the daily rate for their services."[21] Therefore the Department of Defense would actually save taxpayers money by reversing the trend of privatization.

However, reducing the role of PMCs is very difficult because the more money the U.S. government spends hiring these firms, the more these firms can afford to offer in salary, and the more soldiers aspire to leave the military to work for private companies.[22] A brain drain occurs, sapping the strategic and tactical knowledge of the military, thus creating an increased need for PMCs. Lt. Col. Michael Brothers, who enlisted in 1981, described this process as one that has been emotional for many in the armed forces as men and women in uniform saw their chosen specialties phased out or privatized out from under them.[23] Essentially, PMCs have created a void, filled it, and re-created the void so they can refill it, ad infinitum. This makes it increasingly difficult to reverse the current state of overreliance on PMCs since, according to the Congressional Research Service report, "many analysts now believe that DOD [the Department of Defense] is unable to successfully execute large missions without contractor support."[24] The vicious cycle of paying for help and then becoming more helpless makes it imperative that the United States ends its dependence on PMCs as soon as possible.

Brackets clarify the abbreviation used in the original quotation.

U.S. citizens should better understand how our military operations are carried out overseas, since the wars in Iraq and Afghanistan affect our security, our taxes, and our consciences as Americans. But we in the polity have not demanded that contractors paid by the government for military services be held accountable for their actions, and neither have we demanded that our leaders recognize and address the growing threat to national security PMCs represent. A recent bill called the Stop Outsourcing Security Act, submitted to both houses of Congress by Representative Jan Schakowsky (D-Ill.) in the House and Senator Bernie Sanders (I-Ver.), offers one potential route to intervention. The act would "prohibit the use of private contractors for military, security, law enforcement, intelligence, and armed rescue functions unless the President tells Congress why the military is unable to perform those functions."[25] The passage of this act could be the first step in the process of phasing out the use of private contractors and returning military operations to the public sector. On her website, Schakowsky urges Americans to contact their representatives to cosponsor the legislation and become citizen cosponsors of the Stop Outsourcing Security Act themselves. In the end, we as voters and taxpayers must ask ourselves, who do we want to carry out U.S. defense missions abroad: those accountable to the U.S. military, or those beholden to private corporations? Given the costs in justice and in dollars, it's clear that the U.S. military has come to overrely on PMCs to a point that is dangerous to national security and national interests. This reliance must be reduced, perhaps excised entirely.

Nicholas concludes with a strong, clear statement of his position.

Brothers 8

Notes

List of notes on a separate page, heading centered

Entries listed in order of appearance in the essay

1. P. W. Singer, *Corporate Warriors: The Rise of the Privatized Military Industry* (Ithaca: Cornell University Press, 2003), 15–16.

Field research

2. Jonathan Euchner, personal interview, September 25, 2010.

Book with one author

3. Jeremy Scahill, *Blackwater: The Rise of the World's Most Powerful Mercenary Army*, 2nd ed. (New York: Nation Books, 2007), 49–51.

4. C. J. Chivers et al., with contributions from Jacob Harris and Alan McLean, "View Is Bleaker Than Official Portrayal of War in Afghanistan," *New York Times*, July 25, 2010, http://www.nytimes.com; Eric Schmitt, Helene Cooper, and David E. Sanger, "U.S. Military Seeks Slower Pace to Wrap Up Afghan Role," *New York Times*, August 11, 2010, http://www.nytimes.com.

Semicolon indicates that note 4 includes two distinct sources

5. P. W. Singer, "Break the Blackwater Habit: We Can't Fight the War without the Company — But We Won't Win with It on Our Payroll," *Washington Post*, October 8, 2007, http://www.washingtonpost.com.

Government report

6. Moshe Schwartz, *Department of Defense Contractors in Iraq and Afghanistan: Background and Analysis*, Congressional Research Service, July 2, 2010, 18.

7. Ibid., 2.

Indicates source of material is the same as that for the previous note, but on a different page

A source quoted within another source

8. Erik Prince speaking at West 2006 conference, January 11, 2006, quoted in Scahill, *Blackwater*, xix.

9. Singer, *Corporate Warriors*, 46.

Abbreviated reference to source identified in note 1

10. Andrew Gilligan, "Inside Lt. Col. Spicer's New Model Army," *Sunday Telegraph*, November 24, 1998, quoted in Singer, *Corporate Warriors*, 46.

Article from an online magazine

11. Robert Capps, "Outside the Law," *Salon*, June 26, 2002, http://www.salon.com.

12. Scahill, *Blackwater*, 221.

13. Charlie Savage, "Judge Drops Charges from Blackwater Deaths in Iraq," *New York Times*, December 31, 2009, http://www.nytimes.com.

14. Charlie Savage, "Case of Accused Soldiers May Be Worst of 2 Wars," *New York Times*, October 3, 2010, http://www.nytimes.com.

15. P. W. Singer, "The Law Catches Up to Private Militaries, Embeds," Brookings Institution, August 25, 2010, http://www.brookings.edu.

16. Barry Yeoman, "Soldiers of Good Fortune," *Mother Jones*, May 2003, http://www.motherjones.com/politics.

17. James Risen, "Efforts to Prosecute Blackwater Are Collapsing," *New York Times*, October 20, 2010, http://www.nytimes.com.

Article in a daily newspaper

V Documenting Sources

18. Department of Defense, *Counterinsurgency*, FM 3-24, December 2006, quoted in Schwartz, *Department of Defense*, 16.

19. Schwartz, *Department of Defense*, 16.

20. David Isenberg, "Contractors and Cost Effectiveness," CATO Institute, December 23, 2009, http://www.cato.org.

21. Allison Stanger, *One Nation under Contract: The Outsourcing of American Power and the Future of Foreign Policy* (New Haven, CT: Yale University Press, 2009), 96–97, quoted in Isenberg, "Contractors and Cost Effectiveness."

22. Robert Young Pelton, *Licensed to Kill: Hired Guns in the War on Terror* (New York: Three Rivers Press, 2007), 58, quoted in Scahill, *Blackwater*, 221.

23. Michael Brothers, phone interview, September 20, 2010.

24. Schwartz, *Department of Defense*, 1.

Nonperiodical website ——— 25. Jan Schakowsky, "Contracting," Congresswoman Jan Schakowsky, last modified October 11, 2010, http://schakowsky.house .gov.

Brothers 10

Bibliography

Capps, Robert. "Outside the Law." *Salon*, June 26, 2002. http://www
.salon.com.

Chivers, C. J., et al., with contributions from Jacob Harris and
Alan McLean. "View Is Bleaker Than Official Portrayal of War
in Afghanistan." *New York Times*, July 25, 2010. http://www
.nytimes.com.

Hemingway, Mark. "Blackwater's Legal Netherworld." *National Review
Online*, September 26, 2007. http://www.nationalreview.com.

Isenberg, David. "Contractors and Cost Effectiveness." CATO Institute.
December 23, 2009. http://www.cato.org.

Pelton, Robert Young. *Licensed to Kill: Hired Guns in the War on
Terror*. New York: Three Rivers Press, 2007. Quoted in Scahill,
Blackwater, 221.

Risen, James. "Efforts to Prosecute Blackwater Are Collapsing." *New
York Times*, October 20, 2010. http://www.nytimes.com.

Savage, Charlie. "Case of Accused Soldiers May Be Worst of 2 Wars."
New York Times, October 3, 2010. http://www.nytimes.com.

——. "Judge Drops Charges from Blackwater Deaths in Iraq." *New
York Times*, December 31, 2009. http://www.nytimes.com.

Scahill, Jeremy. *Blackwater: The Rise of the World's Most Powerful
Mercenary Army*. 2nd ed. New York: Nation Books, 2007.

Schakowsky, Jan. "Contracting." Congresswoman Jan Schakowsky. Last
modified October 11, 2010. http://schakowsky.house.gov.

Schmitt, Eric, Helene Cooper, and David E. Sanger. "U.S. Military Seeks
Slower Pace to Wrap Up Afghan Role." *New York Times*, August
11, 2010. http://www.nytimes.com.

Schwartz, Moshe. *Department of Defense Contractors in Iraq and
Afghanistan: Background and Analysis*. Congressional Research
Service, July 2, 2010.

Singer, P. W. "Break the Blackwater Habit: We Can't Fight the War
without the Company — But We Won't Win with It on Our
Payroll." *Washington Post*, October 8, 2007. http://www
.washingtonpost.com.

——. *Corporate Warriors: The Rise of the Privatized Military Industry*.
Ithaca, NY: Cornell University Press, 2003.

——. "The Law Catches Up to Private Militaries, Embeds." Brookings
Institution. August 25, 2010. http://www.brookings.edu.

Stanger, Allison. *One Nation under Contract: The Outsourcing of
American Power and the Future of Foreign Policy*. New Haven, CT:
Yale University Press, 2009. Quoted in Isenberg, "Contractors
and Cost Effectiveness."

Yeoman, Barry. "Soldiers of Good Fortune." *Mother Jones*, May 2003.
http://www.motherjones.com/politics.

Entries listed
alphabetically by
author

Article from an
online magazine

Article in a daily
newspaper

Book with one
author

Nonperiodical
website

Government
report

Dashes indicate
that these
sources are also
by Singer

V Documenting Sources

23

Using CSE Style

 Key Questions

23a. How do I cite sources within the text of my document? 416

23b. How do I prepare the reference list? 416

CSE stands for the Council of Science Editors. In this book, CSE style is based on the eighth edition of *Scientific Style and Format: The CSE Manual for Authors, Editors, and Publishers.*

CSE style, used primarily in the physical sciences, life sciences, and mathematics, recommends two systems:

- a citation-sequence system, which lists sources in the reference list according to the order in which they appear in the document
- a name-year system, which is similar to the author-date system used by the APA (see Chapter 21)

This chapter describes and provides models for the citation-sequence system. For more information on CSE style, visit the Council of Science Editors website at **councilscienceeditors.org**.

To see Joshua Woelfle's research essay formatted in CSE style, turn to p. 428.

CITATION TUTORIALS FOR REFERENCE CITED ENTRIES

CITATIONS WITHIN YOUR TEXT

ENTRIES IN YOUR REFERENCE LIST

23a

How do I cite sources within the text of my document?

The CSE citation-sequence system uses sequential numbers to refer to sources within a document. These numbers, in turn, correspond to numbered entries in the reference list. This approach to citing sources reduces distraction to the reader and saves space within a document.

1. Format and Placement of the Note   Sources are cited using superscript numbers or numbers placed in parentheses. Superscript numbers should be formatted in a font one or two points smaller than the body text:

> The anomalies in the data[3] call the study's methods into question.

> The anomalies in the data (3) call the study's methods into question.

2. Citing a Previously Mentioned Source   Use the first number assigned to a source when citing the source for the second time. In the following examples, the author is referring to sources earlier numbered 3, 9, and 22:

> The outlying data points[3,9,22] seem to suggest a bias in the methodology.

> The outlying data points (3,9,22) seem to suggest a bias in the methodology.

3. Citing a Source within a Source   When referring to a source cited in another source, use the phrase "cited in":

> The results[12(cited in 8)] collected in the first month of the study . . .

> The results (12 cited in 8) collected in the first month of the study . . .

23b

How do I prepare the reference list?

CSE style specifies that you should create a list of works that are cited in your document or that contributed to your thinking about the document. Sources cited should be identified in a section titled "References," while sources that contributed to your thinking should be given in a section titled "Additional References."

There are two exceptions: personal communication and oral presentations.

Personal communication, such as correspondence and interviews, is cited only in the text of your document, using the term "unreferenced" to indicate that it is not found in the reference list:

> . . . this disease has proven to be resistant to antibiotics under specific conditions (2014 letter from Meissner to me; unreferenced, see "Notes").

Typically, information about personal communication is placed in a "Notes" or "Acknowledgments" section. Similarly, oral presentations at conferences that are not available in any form (such as microform, reference database, conference proceedings, or online) should be cited in the text of your document but not included in your reference list.

The *CSE Manual* does not specify the location of the reference list, deferring instead to the formatting guidelines of individual journals in the sciences. In general, however, the reference list appears at the end of print documents and linear documents that are distributed electronically (such as word processing files or newsgroup posts). In the case of longer documents or documents in which sections of a book (such as chapters) are intended to stand on their own, the reference list might appear at the end of each section or chapter. In digital documents that use links, such as websites, the reference list often is a separate page to which other pages are linked.

To see an example of a CSE-style reference list, turn to p. 433.

Books, Conference Proceedings, and Dissertations

4. One Author Give the author's last name and first initial with no comma. Next, include the title, capitalizing only the first word and proper nouns, followed by publication information. Include the state abbreviation in parentheses after the city. If the book was obtained on the Web, provide the URL. If a DOI (digital object identifier, a unique number assigned to specific content) is provided, include it.

4. Leonard C. The meat racket: the secret takeover of America's food business. New York (NY): Simon & Schuster; 2014.

5. Coyer, M. Literature and medicine in the nineteenth-century periodical press. Edinburgh (GB): Edinburgh University Press; 2017 [cited 2017 May 7]. https://www.ncbi.nlm.nih.gov/books/NBK402314/.

5. Two or More Authors List the authors in the order in which they appear on the title page, each of them last name first. (If there are more than ten authors, list the first ten followed by a comma and "et al.") Note that periods are not used after initials. Separate authors with commas. When using CSE style, abbreviate "United Kingdom" as "GB."

5. Willis KJ, McElwain JC. The evolution of plants. 2nd ed. Oxford (GB): Oxford University Press; 2014.

6. Corporate or Group Author Identify the organization as the author.

6. National Geographic. The national parks: an illustrated history. Washington (DC). National Geographic Society; 2015.

TUTORIAL

How do I cite books using CSE style?

PUBLISHING
AND THE
ADVANCEMENT OF
SCIENCE

*From Selfish Genes to
Galileo's Finger*

MICHAEL RODGERS

Imperial College Press

When citing a book, use the information from the title page and the copyright page (on the back side of the title page), not from the cover or a library catalog. This tutorial gives an example of a citation using the CSE citation-sequence system. Consult pp. 417–21 for additional models for citing books.

A **B**

1. Rodgers M. Publishing and the advancement of science: from selfish genes

C **D** **E** **F**

to Galileo's finger. London (GB): Imperial College Press; 2014. 178 p.

A **The author.** Give the last name first, followed by initials for first and middle names. Separate the last name and initials with only a space, not a comma. Do not separate initials. Separate the names of multiple authors with commas (Cobb C, Fetterolf ML). End with a period.

B **The title.** Give the full title; include the subtitle (if any), preceded by a colon. Capitalize only the first word of the title and proper nouns. Do not underline or italicize the title or subtitle. End with a period.

C **The city of publication.** If more than one city is given, use the first one listed. Include the state abbreviation in parentheses after the city. Insert a colon.

D **The publisher.** Give the publisher's name, omitting *The* at the beginning. Insert a semicolon.

E **The date of publication.** Use the publication date if one is given; otherwise use the copyright date. If a month of publication is given, use that as well (2013 Aug).

F **The number of pages (optional).** If desired, give the total number of pages contained in the book, followed by the letter "p" and a period. (This information is optional according to the *CSE Manual*; check with your instructor to find out if you should include it.)

7. Unknown Author   Begin with the title.

7. Images of Canterbury. Derby (GB): DB Publishing; 2015. 179 p.

8. Translated Book   Identify the translator after the title, giving last name first.

8. Villani C. Birth of a theorum: a mathematical adventure. DeBevoise M, translator. New York (NY): Farrar, Straus and Giroux; 2015.

9. Book in an Edition Other Than the First   Note the edition (for instance, "2nd ed." or "New rev. ed.") after the title and with a separating period.

9. Roberts N. The holocene: an environmental history. 3rd ed. Oxford (GB): Wiley-Blackwell; 2014.

10. Multivolume Work   Include the total number of volumes if you are making a reference to all volumes in the work, or "Vol." followed by the specific volume number followed by the title of that volume (if that volume is separately titled).

10. Serway RA, Jewett JW. Physics for scientists and engineers. Vol. 5. 9th ed. Pacific Grove (CA): Brooks-Cole; 2013.

11. Authored Book with an Editor   Identify the editor(s) before the publication information.

11. Einstein A. The cosmic view of Albert Einstein: writings on art, science, and peace. Martin W, Ott M, editors. New York (NY): Sterling Publishing; 2013.

12. Book in a Series

12. Rosenberg A, Arp B, editors. Philosophy of biology: an anthology. Chichester (GB): Wiley-Blackwell; 2010. (Blackwell philosophy anthologies; 32).

13. Anthology or Collection with an Editor   To cite an anthology of essays or a collection of articles, treat the editor's name as you would an author's name but identify with the word "editor."

13. Carlson BM, editor. Stem cell anthology. London (GB): Academic Press; 2010.

14. Chapter in an Edited Book or a Work in an Anthology   List the author and title of the section; then include the word "In" followed by a colon, the editor's name (last name first followed by initials) and the word "editor." Include the book title, place, and publisher, and note the inclusive pages of the section. Note that page range numbers are given in full.

14. Hawks J. Human evolution. In: Losos JB, editor. The Princeton guide to evolution. Princeton (NJ): Princeton University Press; 2017. p. 183–188.

15. Foreword, Introduction, Preface, or Afterword of a Book   If the part is written by someone other than the author of the book, treat it as you would a chapter in an edited book (see entry 14), identifying the author or editor of the book before the book title.

15. Groopman J. Introduction. In: Cohen J, editor. The best of the best
    American science writing: ten years of the series. New York (NY): Ecco; 2010;
    p. ix–xv.

16. Chapter of a Book   If you wish to refer to a chapter of a book, identify the chapter of the book after the publication information. End with the inclusive pages of the chapter.

16. Cantu R, Hyman M. Concussions and our kids: America's leading expert on
    how to protect young athletes and keep sports safe. Boston (MA): Houghton
    Mifflin Harcourt; 2013. Chapter 9, After concussions; p. 127–142.

17. Published Proceedings of a Conference   List the editors of the proceedings as authors or, if there are no editors, begin with the name and year of the conference. Then give the title of the publication; the date of the conference; the place of the conference; and the place of publication, publisher, and date.

17. Platts H, Barron C, Lundock J, Pearce J, Yoo J, editors. TRAC 2013.
    Proceedings of the 23rd Annual Theoretical Roman Archaeology Conference;
    2013; London. Oxford (GB): Oxbow Books; c2014; 160 p.

18. Paper Published in the Proceedings of a Conference   Format the citation as you would a chapter in an edited book.

18. Paten B, Diekhans M, Earl D, St. John J, Ma J, Suh BB, Haussler D. Cactus
    graphs for genome comparisons. In: Berger B, editor. RECOMB 2010. Research
    in computational molecular biology, 14th annual international conference
    proceedings; 2010 Apr 25–28; Lisbon, Portugal. Berlin (DE): Springer-Verlag;
    c2010; p. 410–425.

19. Published Dissertation or Thesis   Use the general format for a book, adding the word "dissertation" or "thesis" in square brackets after the title. Treat the institution granting the degree as the publisher. If the place is not listed on the dissertation but can be inferred, use brackets around the place as shown here. If the dissertation was obtained on the Web, provide the URL. If a DOI (digital object identifier, a unique number assigned to specific content) is provided, include it.

19. Prescott JW. Computer-assisted discovery and characterization of imaging
    biomarkers for disease diagnosis and treatment planning [dissertation].
    [Columbus (OH)]: Ohio State University; 2010; 191 p.

20. Yang H. Topics in gravitational-wave science: macroscopic quantum mechanics and black hole physics [dissertation]. Pasadena (CA): California Institute of Technology; 2013; 339 p. ProQuest Dissertations and Theses. Ann Arbor (MI): ProQuest; c2013. http://search.proquest.com.ezp-prod1.hul.harvard .edu/docview/1496774506?accountid=11311.

20. Unpublished Dissertation or Thesis Use the general format for a book, adding the word "dissertation" or "thesis" in square brackets as a final element of the title. Treat the institution granting the degree as the publisher.

20. Wagner KP. A generalized acceptance urn model [dissertation]. Tampa (FL): University of South Florida; 2010.

Sources in Journals, Magazines, and Newspapers

21. Article in a Journal Abbreviate and capitalize all of the major words in a journal's title; omit articles, conjunctions, and prepositions. The *CSE Manual* includes specific guidelines for citing journal titles. A semicolon separates the year and volume number. If there is an issue number, include it in parentheses, followed by a colon and the page numbers. There are no spaces between the year, volume number, and page numbers.

21. Gauthier S, Leuzy A, Racine E, Rosa-Neto P. Diagnosis and management of Alzheimer's disease: past, present and future ethical issues. Prog Neurobiol. 2013;110:102–113.

If the article was obtained through a database, give the name of the database, the location and parent company of the database, the date of access, the full URL for the article, and the DOI (digital object identifier, a unique number assigned to specific content) if one is provided.

22. Chen M, Schlief M, Willows RD, Cai Z-L, Neilan BA, Scheer H. A red-shifted chlorophyll. Science. 2010 Sep 10 [accessed 2014 Feb 1]:1318–1319. Expanded Academic ASAP. Farmington Hills (MI): Thomson Gale; c2010. http://web4.infotrac.galegroup.com. doi:10.1126/science.1191127.

If the article was obtained on the Web, provide the access date and the URL. If a DOI is provided, include it.

23. Pitaval A, Tseng Q, Bornens M, Thery M. Cell shape and contractility regulate ciliogenesis in cell cycle — arrested cells. J Cell Biol. 2010 [accessed 2013 Aug 23];191(2):303–312. http://jcb.rupress.org/content/191/2/303 .full?sid=d8f7c638-68dc-4082-99a8-ca19a37d72fe. doi:10.1083/ jcb.201004003.

TUTORIAL

How do I cite articles from periodicals using CSE style?

Periodicals include journals, magazines, and newspapers. This tutorial gives an example of a citation for a print magazine article. Models for citing articles from journals and newspapers are on pp. 421–24. If you need to cite a periodical article you accessed electronically, follow the guidelines below and see p. 423.

A **B**

2. Durnford AJ, Harrisson SE, Eynon CA. Kitesports: a new source of major

C **D** **E** **F**

trauma? Report of four cases and literature review. Trauma. 2014;16(1):23–26.

A **The author.** Give the last name first, followed by initials for first and middle names. Separate the last name and initials with only a space, not a comma. Do not separate initials. Separate the names of multiple authors with commas (Cobb C, Fetterolf ML). End with a period.

B **The article title.** Give the full title; include the subtitle (if any), preceded by a colon. Capitalize only the first word of the title and proper nouns. Do not underline or italicize the title or subtitle. End with a period.

C **The periodical title.** Do not underline or italicize the periodical title; abbreviate and capitalize all major words. Omit articles, conjunctions, and prepositions. The *CSE Manual* includes guidelines for abbreviating journal titles. Do not abbreviate one-word titles or one-syllable words in a journal title. End with a period.

D **The date of publication.** For journal articles, include the year followed by a semicolon. For magazines and newspapers, include the abbreviated month and, if available, the day (2014 Apr 13), followed by a colon.

E **Volume and issue number.** For journal articles, include the volume number followed by the issue number in parentheses, if available, and a colon.

F **Inclusive page number(s).** Give the page numbers on which the article appears; list the numbers in full (154–177; 1187–1188). Do not add a space between the colon and the page numbers. End with a period.

How do I cite articles from databases using CSE style?

Libraries subscribe to services such as Lexis-Nexis, ProQuest, InfoTrac, and EBSCOhost that provide access to databases of digital texts. The databases provide publication information, abstracts, and the complete text of documents in a specific subject area, discipline, or profession. (See also Chapter 10.) This tutorial gives an example of a reference in CSE citation-sequence style.

3. Galindo-Cardona A, Acevedo-Gonzalez JP, Rivera-Marchand B, Giray T.

Genetic structure of the gentle Africanized honey bee population (gAHB) in Puerto Rico. BMC Genetics. 2013 [accessed 2014 Jun 9];14(1):1–11. Academic Search Premier. Ipswich (MA): EBSCO; c2013. http://search.ebscohost.com. doi:10.1186/1471-2156-14-65.

A **The author.** Give the last name first, followed by initials for first and middle names. Separate the last name and initials with only a space, not a comma. Do not separate initials. Separate the names of multiple authors with commas (Cobb C, Fetterolf ML). End with a period.

B **The article title.** Give the full title; include the subtitle (if any), preceded by a colon. Capitalize only the first word of the title and proper nouns. Do not underline or italicize the title or subtitle. End with a period.

C **The periodical title.** Do not underline or italicize the periodical title; abbreviate and capitalize all major words. Omit articles, conjunctions, and prepositions. The *CSE Manual* includes guidelines for abbreviating journal titles. Do not abbreviate one-word titles or one-syllable words in a journal title. End with a period.

D **The date of publication.** For journal articles, include the year followed by a semicolon. For magazines and newspapers, include the month and, if available, the day, followed by a colon and a date of access in brackets.

E **Volume and issue number.** For journal articles, include the volume number followed by the issue number in parentheses, if available, and a colon.

F **Inclusive page number(s).** Give the page numbers on which the article appears; list the numbers in full (154–177; 1187–1188). Do not add a space between the colon and the page numbers. End with a period.

G **Database, URL, and DOI.** Give the name of the database followed by a period. Then list the location and parent company of the database. Provide the full URL for the article, even if accessed via a database. Follow with a period. Then give the DOI number if one is provided, ending with a period.

22. Article in a Magazine   Magazines are not identified by volume. Give only the date (year, month, day for weekly magazines; year and month for monthly magazines). Abbreviate all months to their first three letters.

22. Romero J. Marsquakes could support life deep within the red planet. Sci News. 2016 Sep 28:34–36.

23. Article in a Newspaper   Treat newspaper articles as you would magazine articles, identifying their pages by section, page, and column on which they begin (in parentheses). If the article was obtained from the Web, provide the access date and the URL.

23. Jalonick MC. Suit says toys in Happy Meals break the law. Boston Globe. 2010 Jun 23;Sect. B:11 (col. 1).

24. Kolata G. Stem cell biology and its complications. New York Times. 2010 Aug 24 [accessed 2010 Dec 15]. http://www.nytimes.com/2010/08/25/health/ research/25cell.html.

24. Unsigned Article in a Newspaper   Begin the entry with the title of the article. "Anonymous" is not permitted in CSE style.

24. A mouse to save your wrist and hand. Boston Globe. 2010 Nov 29;Sect. B:8 (col. 3).

Reference Works

25. Encyclopedia, Dictionary, Thesaurus, Handbook, or Almanac   Begin with the title of the reference work and information about the edition. Identify the editor, if listed. Provide the publisher and publication date.

25. Encyclopedia of global warming. Dutch SI, editor. Pasadena (CA): Salem Press; 2010.

26. Map or Chart   Use the name of the area in place of an author. Follow with the title, type of map in brackets (such as "physical map" or "demographic map"), the place of publication and publisher, and a description of the map. If the map is part of a larger document, such as an atlas, provide publication information for the document and the page number(s) of the map.

26. Netherlands. Independent Dutch breweries [demographic map]. In: The world atlas of beer. London (GB): Octopus Publishing Group; 2012. p. 137. Color.

27. Pamphlet   Format entries as you would for a book (see also entry 4 on p. 417).

27. National Alliance on Mental Illness. Depression. Arlington (VA): NAMI, the National Alliance on Mental Illness; 2012.

Media Sources

28. Film or Video   Give the title, then the type of medium identified in square brackets, followed by individuals listed as authors, editors, performers, conductors, and so on. Identify the producer if different from the publisher. Provide publication information, including a physical description of the medium.

28. Great migrations [DVD]. Hamlin D, Serwa C, producers. Washington (DC):
    National Geographic; 2010. 3 DVDs: 200 min.

29. Television or Radio Program   CSE style does not provide guidance on citing television or radio programs. Cite the title of the program, with the medium designator in brackets, followed by information about the series (if any), including individuals such as the producer, writer, director, and the place and date of broadcast at the end.

29. Iceman reborn [television program]. Apsell PS, senior executive producer.
    Nova. New York (NY): Thirteen/WNET; 2016 Feb 17.

30. Sound Recording   Cite as you would a film or video recording.

30. Howler monkeys: singing into the night [sound recording]. Carroll B, sound
    recordist. Keene (NH): Belize Bruce; 2013.

Field Sources

31. Personal Interview   Treat unpublished interviews as personal communication (see p. 416). Cite them in the text only; do not cite them in the reference list.

32. Personal Letter   Cite personal letters as personal communication (see p. 416). Cite them in the text only; do not cite them in the reference list.

33. Lecture or Public Address   Like an unpublished paper presented at a meeting, lectures or public addresses are treated as personal communication and are cited only in the text (see p. 416).

Other Digital Sources

34. Website

34. US Geological Survey. Washington (DC): US Department of the Interior;
    [updated 2010 Sep 28; accessed 2010 Dec 16]. http://www.usgs.gov.

35. Document on a Website

35. Strauss G. National Geographic Daily News. Washington (DC): National
    Geographic Society. Enlisting an army to save a forest. 2016 Oct 5
    [accessed 2017 Jan 7]. http://news.nationalgeographic.com/2016/10/
    erika-cuellar-explorer-moments-rain-forest-South-America/.

TUTORIAL

How do I cite works from websites using CSE style?

You will likely need to search the website to find some of the citation information you need. For some sites, all of the details may not be available; find as many as you can. Remember that the citation you provide should allow readers to retrace your steps electronically to locate the sources. Consult pp. 425–27 for additional models for citing Web sources. [NASA.]

A   **B**
4. National Aeronautics and Space Administration. Raisin' mountains on Saturn's

C
moon Titan. Pasadena (CA): National Aeronautics and Space Administration;

D   **E**
2010 Aug 12 [accessed 2011 Feb 3]. http://www.nasa.gov/mission_pages/

cassini/whycassini/cassini20100812.html.

A **The author.** Give the name of the organization or individual author, last name first followed by initials for first and middle names. Separate the last name and initials with only a space, not a comma; separate the names of multiple authors with commas (Cobb C, Fetterolf ML). End with a period.

B **The document title.** Give the full title; include the subtitle (if any), preceded by a colon. Capitalize only the first word of the title and proper nouns. Do not underline or italicize the title or subtitle. End with a period.

C **Publisher information.** Give the place of publication followed by a colon, then the publisher or sponsoring organization followed by a semicolon.

D **Publication date and date of access.** Give the date of publication or the copyright date on the website; if available, include the date of modification or update in brackets. Then give the date of access in brackets. End with a period.

E **The URL.** Give the URL, followed by a period.

36. E-mail Message   E-mail messages are considered personal communication (see p. 416). Cite them in the text only; do not cite them in the reference list.

37. E-mail Discussion List Message

37. Williams JB. Re: Tomato seed question. In: BIONET. [London (GB); Medical Research Council]; 2010 Nov 1, 7:57 am [accessed 2010 Nov 15]. http://www.bio.net/bionet/mm/plantbio/2010-November/027780.html.

38. Article Posted on a Wiki

38. Epidemic and pandemic spread. In: Influenza [updated 2014 Mar 1; accessed 2014 Mar 25]. http://en.wikipedia.org/wiki/Influenza#Epidemic_and _pandemic_spread.

39. Entry or Comment on a Blog

39. Reynolds G. Phys Ed: Brains and Brawn. In: Well. 2011 Jan 19 [accessed 2011 Jan 22]. http://well.blogs.nytimes.com/2011/01/19/phys-ed-brains-and -brawn.

CSE Citation-Sequence Style Research Essay

Unnumbered title page includes a descriptive title with all major words capitalized, the student's name, the course name, and the date. All information is centered on the page.

Promising Advancements in Modern Cancer Treatment

Joshua Woelfle

Biology 597
Professor Diaz
May 3, 2014

Page numbering
begins on first
page of paper
body. A short
title is included
before the page
number.

Promising Advancements 1

Chemotherapy is just medieval. It's such a blunt instrument.

We're going to look back on it like we do the dark ages.

— Dr. Eric Topol (Unreferenced, see "Notes")

A source not
included in the
reference list

Cancer afflicts over a million Americans every year and proves
fatal to nearly half of those afflicted. (1) Over the years, scientists
have made great strides in understanding the disease, but cancer's
widely varied and adaptive nature has made finding a cure nearly
impossible. Fortunately, scientists have achieved greater success in
controlling cancer, and several promising advancements may soon
overtake the traditional treatment options of chemotherapy and
radiation. Two of these advancements, anticancer drugs targeting
out-of-control cell-growth signaling enzymes and multi-drug
resistance (MDR) proteins, may soon relegate the traditional
options of chemotherapy and radiation — along with their extremely
detrimental side effects — to the past.

Source
references
are shown in
parentheses.

Since the 1940s, nonsurgical cancer treatment has consisted
almost exclusively of chemotherapy and radiation. These treatments
function by destroying rapidly proliferating cells throughout the body
and are detrimental to cancer because, by its very definition, cancer
is a mass of rapidly dividing invasive cells. Unfortunately, there are
a number of other cell types within the body that also divide rapidly,
such as hair, skin, and epithelial cells, all of which suffer the same
fate as cancer cells when these treatments are used. Additionally,
chemotherapy causes a vast array of harmful side effects, including
immunosuppression, fatigue and nausea, neurological disorders, and
organ damage (2) which, even if the cancer is contained, may
negatively affect the patient's quality of life.

Body of paper is
double-spaced,
with one-
inch margins
on all sides.
Paragraphs are
indented one-
half inch.

Despite these harmful side effects, chemotherapeutic drugs would
be a viable option if they were effective at completely removing cancer
from the body. However, the 1997 discovery of cancer stem cells
(3) proved that this is not the case. Cancer stem cells behave in much
the same way as other stem cells, with the ability to differentiate into
various tumor cells as required. This allows cancer stem cells to adapt
as necessary based on environmental conditions, and often overcome
adverse effects caused by treatment. More detrimentally, cancer stem
cells propagate slowly, so they are not targeted by chemotherapy or
radiation. Thus, there is always the possibility of relapse for patients
who have "successfully" undergone chemotherapy.

Fortunately, alternate options are becoming available that seem
to be more effective than traditional treatments at removing cancer,

while simultaneously eliminating many of the harsh side effects. At the forefront of these new treatment options are designer drugs targeting enzyme proteins whose overactivity have been shown to cause cancer. To understand anti-enzyme drug therapy, we must first understand the structure and function of these pro-cancer enzymes. Cancer develops primarily through genetic mutations that alter the body's cellular equilibrium and allow cells to proliferate and migrate without restriction. These requirements, dubbed the "hallmarks of cancer," (4) are required for the successful development of the disease. Specifically, for cancer to arise, it must: secure blood supply for growing cells via angiogenesis, allow for unlimited and unrestricted division by manipulating the cell cycle and telomeres, overcome growth restrictions, prevent cell suicide, and invade surrounding tissue or colonize new sites in the body. These changes require multiple genetic mutations and are regulated by a wide variety of enzymes, many of which are specifically altered in cancer. These specific alterations are the backbone of enzyme-directed cancer treatment research.

Enzyme therapy works by targeting and restricting the cancer-specific enzymes required to sustain cancer's development and longevity. By disabling the mutated enzymes that make the hallmarks of cancer possible, the disease is prevented from further development, as opposed to chemotherapy, which merely destroys already-established cancer cells. Scientists are researching several different enzymes for this therapy. One of these is heparanase, an enzyme that stimulates cell migration. (5) Scientists are also experimenting with a variety of tyrosine kinases that, when mutated, allow unrestricted growth in cancer cells. Of particular note is the recently released drug Gleevec, which targets tyrosine kinase BCR-Abl and is showing positive results in treating leukemia with minimal adverse effects. (6) The success of Gleevec is demonstrative of the power of enzyme inhibitor-based cancer treatment, and many researchers believe the combined power of several enzyme restriction drugs is the next step in cancer treatment. These drugs have the ability to fully restrict tumor growth while allowing patients to maintain a quality of life that is much higher than that of patients undergoing traditional cancer treatments.

Unfortunately, cancer is doing its part to counteract these advances in treatment. Most notably, cancer has begun utilizing the body's own defenses to form resistances to cancer treatment drugs, including enzyme inhibitors. These adaptations, dubbed "multi-drug resistance" cancers, or MDR, can arise through several different mechanisms, each requiring different treatment. The most common and widely understood of these mechanisms is the manipulation of p-glycoprotein (PGP) by cancer cells. Ironically, the body uses PGP as a means of toxin defense. PGP is most commonly expressed to protect highly susceptible areas of the body, such as the blood-brain barrier and the testes, and it functions by capturing and expelling toxins from these areas. Some forms of cancer have adapted to express high levels of PGP, which recognizes cancer-targeting drugs (both chemotherapeutic and enzyme inhibitor) as foreign and expels them from the cancer cell, preventing effective treatment. While this adaptation may seem scary enough already, it is compounded by the fact that cancer has also been shown to increase expression of PGP after the initial round of drugs. (7) So even if there was some initial success, the drug's performance will continually decrease in MDR cancers. While PGP-mediated drug resistance is the most common form of MDR, it is also the most treatable resistance and can be combated through the use of PGP inhibitors. These inhibitors function precisely as their name implies: by inhibiting the function of PGP throughout the body, thereby preventing cancer cells from expunging drugs and making them susceptible to the same treatments as typical cancers. Previously, researchers criticized this method of overcoming MDR cancer, and rightly so, because delivery of inhibitors was systemic, resulting in crippled toxin defense systems throughout the body. However, recent research suggests that PGP inhibitors can be altered for both direct delivery to cancerous cells and increased cancer cell specificity. (8) When these alterations are perfected, PGP-mediated MDR will become a negligible issue in cancer treatment since it can be countered with no foreseeable side effects.

Aside from PGP-assisted resistance, the most prevalent forms of multi-drug resistance are those mediated by tumor-suppressor and oncogenic mutations. These resistances commonly operate via the same principles as PGP, by expelling cytotoxic drugs from the cancerous cell before they can cause harm. However, they are the result of mutations in a variety of different genes, which makes treatment of these various MDR mutations very difficult. So while research is being conducted on developing drugs to inhibit the protein responsible for some of the more prevalent of these mutations (namely, those involving the MRP gene), the most promising option is also the most simplistic: rather than disable resistances, bypass them. Several methods are currently undergoing testing that utilize this simple concept to combat MDR cancer in vastly different ways. The first, which is being tested by various pharmaceutical companies, involves overloading tumor cells with anticancer (cytotoxic) drugs that are rapidly absorbed and fast acting. This process allows the drugs to act before the cancer cell can expunge a substantial amount, effectively negating the resistance mechanisms of the cell. While this method does serve to counter MDR mechanisms, its shortcomings are the same as those of traditional cancer treatment options: the possible side effects are very detrimental. Because this method most often utilizes typical cytotoxic drugs (and at a higher dosage), the patient is exposed to the negative effects of whichever drug is being administered. Therefore, this method will remain only situationally viable until researchers can develop a sufficiently fast-acting and rapidly absorbed drug that does not pose the risks of currently available compounds.

In contrast to the above method, which utilizes traditional drugs in nontraditional doses to bypass resistance, research being led by Victor Keute and Thomas Efferth aims to use nontraditional compounds that actively bypass cancer cell resistance, rather than just overloading it. Keute and Efferth are examining the active compounds in African medicinal plants for cytotoxic effects. They have identified at least four different compounds in the benzophenone family that exhibit cytotoxic properties and, surprisingly, these compounds seem able to destroy drug-resistant cancer cells just as easily as they can destroy nonresistant cells. (9) This research is still in its infancy, so while thorough clinical trials to examine the viability and potential side effects of these compounds have not yet been conducted, the outlook of this research is very promising.

Many billions of dollars are spent annually on cancer research. Even so, chemotherapy and radiation have remained the dominant treatment options for more than six decades, in spite of their often severe side effects. These outdated methods have done their part to lower the mortality rate of cancer patients, but at an often substantial cost to their quality of life. Fortunately, recently developed enzyme inhibitor-based drugs, which show great promise in combating the disease with much less substantial side effects, seem poised to replace chemotherapy as the preferred cancer treatment option. Additionally, researchers are in the process of developing several different methods to combat multi-drug resistance in cancer to deal with this ever-increasing complication. If proven successful, these combined options could revolutionize the world of cancer treatment, providing hope to the millions afflicted and bringing us one step closer to removing cancer from the list of most fatal diseases worldwide.

The reference list is titled "References" and begins on a new page.

The reference list is not alphabetical. Sources are numbered and listed in the order in which they appear in the document.

Promising Advancements 5

References

1. National Cancer Institute. SEER stat fact sheets: all sites. Bethesda (MD): National Cancer Institute; 2013 [accessed 2014 Jan 9]. http://seer.cancer.gov/statfacts/html/all.html.

2. Stanford Medicine Cancer Institute. Chemotherapy drugs and side effects. Stanford (CA): Stanford Medicine; 2014 [accessed 2014 Jan 21]. http://cancer.stanford.edu/information/cancerTreatment/methods/chemotherapy.html.

3. Bonnet D, Dick JE. Human acute myeloid leukemia is organized as a hierarchy that originates from a primitive hematopoietic cell. Nat Med. 1997;3(7):730–737.

4. Hanahan D, Weinberg RA. Hallmarks of cancer: the next generation. Cell. 2011;144(5):646–674.

5. Seppa N. Keeping cells under control: enzyme suppression inhibits cancer spread. Sci News. 2004 Aug 28:134.

6. Pray L. Gleevec: the breakthrough in cancer treatment. Nat Ed. 2008;1(1):37. http://www.nature.com/scitable/topicpage/gleevec-the-breakthrough-in-cancer-treatment-565.

7. Ichihashi N, Kitajima Y. Chemotherapy induces or increases expression of multidrug resistance-associated protein in malignant melanoma cells. Br J Dermatol. 2001 Apr [accessed 2014 Jan 8]; 144(4):745–750. PubMed. Bethesda (MD): Natl Cent for Biotechnol Inf; c2001. http://www.ncbi.nlm.nih.gov/pubmed/11298532.

8. Kanghui Y, Jifeng W, Xun L. Recent advances in research on P-glycoprotein inhibitors. BioSci Trends. 2008 [accessed 2014 8 Jan];2(4):137–146. http://www.biosciencetrends.com/action/downloaddoc.php?docid=141.

9. Gutierrez D. African medicinal plants may stop tumor growth from multi-drug resistant cancers: research. Nat News. 2013 Jun 26 [accessed 2014 Jan 9]. http://www.naturalnews.com/040947_cancer_treatment_african_plants_medicinal_herbs.html.

Additional References

DeVita VT Jr, Chu E. A history of cancer chemotherapy. Cancer Res. 2008;68(21):8643–8653. PubMed. Bethesda (MD): Natl Cent for Biotechnol Inf; c2008. http://www.ncbi.nlm.nih.gov/pubmed/18974103.

Mukherjee S. The emperor of all maladies: a biography of cancer. 2010. New York (NY): Scribner; 2010.

Persidis A. Cancer multidrug resistance. Nat Biotech. 1999;17:94–95. http://www.nature.com/nbt/journal/v18/n10s/full/nbt1000_IT18.html.

Titles of books and periodicals are neither underlined nor italicized. All major words in the titles of periodicals are capitalized. For all other sources, only initial words of the main title and proper nouns and adjectives are capitalized.

The student included a list of additional resources, in alphabetical order, that were consulted but not cited in the paper.

V Documenting Sources

Promising Advancements 6

Szakacs G, Paterson JK, Ludwig JA, Booth-Genthe C, Gottesman MM.
   Targeting multidrug resistance in cancer. Nat Rev Drug Discov.
   2006;5(3):219–234.
Thomas H, Coley H. Overcoming multidrug resistance in cancer: an update
   on the clinical strategy of inhibiting P-glycoprotein. Cancer Control.
   2003;10(2):159–165.

Notes include unreferenced sources, such as the quote shown here. ———————————— Notes

Topol E. Quote taken from a 2013 genetics symposium in San Diego.

Index

Your Research Questions — Answered!

We surveyed students, instructors, and academic librarians about your most frequently asked research-related questions. Here are the top twenty FAQs and where you can find answers to them in the book:

1. How do I cite sources within the text of my document? See pp. 322, 328, 357, 387, 416

2. How do I prepare a list of works cited/reference list? See pp. 331, 360, 388, 416

3. How can I develop my thesis statement? See p. 195

4. How do I integrate sources? See p. 251

5. How do I develop and refine my research question? See p. 41

6. How can I focus my topic? See p. 35

7. How should I organize my information and ideas? See p. 121

8. How can I support my argument? See p. 205

9. How do I read sources critically? See p. 61

10. What should I pay attention to as I read? See p. 66

11. How can I explore my topic? See p. 28

12. How do I evaluate a source? See p. 76

13. How many times should I read a source? See p. 58

14. How can I use my conclusion to frame my issue? See p. 243

15. How can I use my introduction to frame my issue? See p. 239

16. How can I approach an assignment? See p. 15

17. How can I search for sources with digital tools? See p. 155

18. How should I revise my document? See p. 292

19. How should I edit my document? See p. 297

20. How do I create a working bibliography? See p. 102